PULL-UPS IN PARADISE

I0141190

GREG AMUNDSON

PULL-UPS IN PARADISE

Copyright © 2020 Greg Amundson

ISBN 978-0-578-81301-1

By Greg Amundson

3703 Portola Drive, Santa Cruz, CA 95060

www.GregoryAmundson.com

Edited by Cindy Bond

Layout and Design by Katie Sanchez

Artwork by Karl Eagleman

Published by:

Eagle Rise Publishing, Virginia Beach, VA.

EagleRisePublishing.com

Printed and bound in the USA and UK on acid-free paper.

Additional books can be purchased through Amazon.

PRAISE FOR THE WORK OF GREG AMUNDSON

"Greg Amundson is a true warrior leader and monk. His deep commitment to his faith, and ability to communicate that faith through his passion for the warrior mindset, is unparalleled. *The Good Soldier* is another lighted path that Greg has provided for those searching for Truth."

— *Mark Divine*, U.S. Navy SEAL (Retired) *New York Times* bestselling author of
The Way of the SEAL, Unbeatable Mind and *Staring Down the Wolf*

"Greg's ability to transcend boundaries and speak to the essence of spirituality is profound and encouraging."

— *Scott McEwen*, #1 *New York Times* bestselling co-author of *American Sniper*;
national bestselling *Sniper Elite* series, and the new *Camp Valor* series of novels

"I often tell people at my seminars, 'We don't need more Buddhists in the world, we need more Buddhas. We don't need more Christians, we need more Christ-like beings.' And such is the case with my amazing, breathing brother Greg Amundson. He's not one of those wishy-washy, praise the Lord, in-your-face, superficial Christians: He is a former SWAT Operator, DEA Special Agent, U.S. Army Captain, and CrossFit athlete and coach. He is a spiritual warrior, and he carries God in his heart. Greg's sermons, lectures and books teach the principles of spiritual development that can change your life."

— *Dan Brulé*, world renowned lecturer and international
bestselling author of *Just Breathe*

"Greg Amundson is the epitome of a modern day warrior. He leads in all aspects of his life: as a warrior, as a Christian, and as a fitness expert. He writes with magical simplicity, yet is rigorous in his research and reasoning. As a leadership and motivation coach, when I need my own motivation I look to Greg Amundson. His track record of proving the validity of his message in his own life, and the lives that his message touches, is astounding."

— *Jason Redman*, Navy SEAL (Retired) and *New York Times* bestselling author
of *The Trident: the Forging and Reforging of a Navy SEAL Leader*

"Greg Amundson is one of the most prolific author's and speakers of our time, and his work will profoundly bless your life."

— **Dr. Gabrielle Lyon**, DO, Special Operations, Task Force Dagger

"Greg Amundson's new book *The Good Soldier* contains a visionary message on leadership, self-mastery, and walking the path of a modern day warrior. This is a profound and encouraging read that has reinvigorated my desire to be of service to others. Hooyah!"

— **Joe De Sena**, Spartan Founder & CEO and #1 *New York Times* bestselling author of *Spartan Up!*

"Greg Amundson has the ability to weave the warrior mindset and biblical message in a way that cuts to my heart. His sermons and books encourage me to put God first, strive for self-mastery, and be of greater service to others."

— **Jay Dobyns**, ATF Special Agent (Retired) *New York Times* bestselling author of *No Angel* and *Catching Hell*

"Few claim Jesus Christ as their Lord and Savior with as much enthusiasm, or as eloquently and boldly, as Greg does in his new book, *Pull-ups in Paradise*. Greg's insightful and scholarly presentation of 'The Word' establishes him as a creditable defender of the Christian faith. Greg understands the connection between Mind, Body and Spirit, and how their integration impacts our ability to follow Jesus Christ, and he leads us on that journey with passion and purpose."

— **Dr. Ron Gellis**, PHD, Clinical, Forensic and Sports Neuropsychologist, and CEO of Integrated Recovery Foundation

"In the early days of CrossFit, Greg and I became 'famous' for the battles between us, as we demonstrated intensity in the classic CrossFit workouts. These battles with Greg never felt like we were pitted against each other, but instead, we had a feeling of being with each other. Greg's new book, *Pull-ups in Paradise*, will help show you that with Jesus, you can also be with those you coach, live with, and love, even through the most intense times life throws at you, and especially when the world is telling you it's all about you."

— **Josh Everett**, CrossFit Level I Seminar Staff and Strength and Conditioning Coach to Collegiate Athletics and the DOD

ALSO BY GREG AMUNDSON

PUBLISHED BOOKS

Your Wife is NOT Your Sister
Robertson Publishing – 2012

Firebreather Fitness
(with TJ Murphy) Velo Press – 2016

The Warrior and The Monk
Robertson Publishing – 2018

Above All Else – A Year of Increasing Wisdom, Stature, and Favor
Eagle Rise Publishing – 2018

Victory! – A Practical Guide to Forging Eternal Fitness
Eagle Rise Publishing – 2019

The Good Soldier
Eagle Rise Publishing – 2019

Knowledge of the Most High
Eagle Rise Publishing – 2020

Strength to Love
Eagle Rise Publishing – 2020

CROSSFIT® JOURNAL ARTICLES

A Chink in My Armor
Coaching the Mental Side of CrossFit
CrossFit HQ – 2851 Research Park Drive, Santa Cruz, CA.
Diet Secrets of the Tupperware Man Vol. I
Diet Secrets of the Tupperware Man Vol. II
Forging Elite Leadership
Good Housekeeping Matters
How to Grow a Successful Garage Gym
Training Two Miles to Run 100

ACKNOWLEDGMENTS

First and foremost, I am exceedingly grateful for the everlasting love and embrace of God and His Son, Jesus Christ. For my beloved parents, Raymond and Julianne Amundson, who encouraged me from a young age to develop my mind, body, and spirit in such a manner that I could be of greater service to others. A great deal of appreciation is extended to Brooklyn Taylor and Katie Sanchez for their brilliant layout and design contributions to this book. I am indebted to the great pastoral mentors and educators whose leadership has deeply influenced my understanding of doctrine and theology: Mark Divine, Dan Brulé, Ken Gray (in memoriam), Chaplain Richard Johnson, Pastor Dave Hicks, Dr. Deepak Chopra, Raja John Bright, Dr. Gary Tuck, Dr. Gerry Breshears, Dr. Reid Kisling, Dr. Steve Korch, Dr. Adam Nigh, Pastor René Schlaepfer, Pastor Max Lucado, Bishop Robert Barron, and Dr. Charles Stanley. Finally, to the students and exemplary teaching staff at Western Seminary, may you continue to experience "Gospel Centered Transformation" in every area of your life.

DEDICATION

"Children, obey your parents in everything,
for this pleases the Lord."

— Colossians 3:20

This book is dedicated in loving memory
to my mom and dad, who provided me with the greatest
example of a "Heart like Christ" I have ever known.

"God is more worthy of your pursuit, attention, and love than
all the other passions of the world combined."

— Dr. Raymond Amundson

"God is entirely devoted to your personal advancement."

— Julianne Amundson

TABLE OF CONTENTS

INTRODUCTION

INTRODUCTION

IN DECEMBER 2001, SHORTLY AFTER my first week of CrossFit® training, I asked Coach Glassman, the founder of CrossFit, how to explain to my friends and family the magic of what was taking place within the gym. Coach looked at me and enthusiastically exclaimed, "It's easy, kid! CrossFit is what CrossFit does."

After nearly 20 of service within the CrossFit community, I think I am finally starting to understand the greater implications of the principle involved: in the *physical realm*, rather than a speculative approach to defining CrossFit, the program can be understood in a practical, observable, and objective manner. By looking closely at the methodology of CrossFit, and its inherent focus on constantly varied functional movement performed at high intensity, we can develop a sound grasp of the beauty and magnitude of the program.

However, we must not stop there. Our community is primed to forge more than just physical adaptation—we must challenge any preconceived notion that CrossFit is limited to the objective realm of our senses. It is high time that our community started to focus on the *spiritual realm*.

You see, my friends, if we restrict our definition of CrossFit to the physical expression of the program, we become subject to the longstanding admonishment that "people look at the outward appearance, but God looks at the heart" (1 Samuel 16:7). Nearly a lifetime of athletic training has led me to understand that what happens within our minds and hearts is truly the greatest expression of our ability to meet the goal of the CrossFit program: *to increase in work capacity across broad time and modal domains.* However, unlike the physical skills we learn and practice within the gym, the Bible teaches that there are some things we cannot do on our own. In the gym, we need a spotter—in life, we need a Savior.

By way of illustration, consider the attendees at the Level I Course: They are taught that the key to increasing in work capacity (i.e., going faster in "Fran") is adhering to the athletic principle of moving large loads, long distances, very quickly! And how is this achieved? The disciplined athlete learns they must follow one of the universal principles of functional movement:

they are instructed to accelerate the object through a relay of contractions from *core to extremity*. This powerful and controlled series of contractions allows the athlete to produce power—and power is defined as intensity—and intensity is the *independent variable most commonly associated with maximizing the rate of return on favorable adaptation.*

And herein we arrive at the cornerstone of the biblical solution to every problem that we will ever face. We must focus on the *spiritual equivalent* of the *physical independent variable,* which is our *True Core:* reconciliation with God through a saving relationship with Jesus Christ. When we "seek first the Kingdom of God," we allow for God's grace to positively and constructively influence all of the extremities of our life (Matthew 6:33). This means that when God is in first place (*our Core*), then all the other pieces of our life fit perfectly into place (*the extremity*). In the words of C. S. Lewis, "When we look for Christ we will find Him, and with Him everything else thrown in."[1]

The bottom-line Scantron-test truth is this: God is the independent variable of our life. By grace through faith in Christ, the believer is reconciled with God, indwelt by the Holy Spirit, and equipped to maximize their life in a supernatural way (Ephesians 2:8–9; Acts 1:8, 2:4–39).

BRINGING CHURCH INTO THE GYM

MY HEART IS DEEPLY INVESTED in the CrossFit community. Echoing the famous closing remarks of the Level I Course, for 20 years I've been, "knocking on my neighbor's door and teaching them how to squat." From Norway to Kenya, I have traveled the world educating and inspiring thousands of people about the methodology that makes them better versions of themselves. Time and time again, I find myself utterly amazed by the realization that the greatest adaptation to the tangible training space in the gym is ultimately the intangible training space between our ears.

---

[1] C. S. Lewis, *Mere Christianity* (New York, NY: Collier Books, 1963), p. 175.

I love the methodology of CrossFit and everything that the community stands for. However, I also fear that for many people—myself included—CrossFit can become a form of idolatry. Biblically speaking, "idol worship" means to put something other than God into the rightful place reserved for God alone. If God is that to which we give all of our time, energy, thought, and attention, then many of us are clearly engaged in worshipping things that are the idol of our own creation. When idolatry happens in any degree, our entire world begins to revolve around what we worship. Speaking from experience, this inherently sinful act of disobedience to God can creep into our life in unexpected and ensnaring ways.

That being said, God has an amazing way of putting Christian leaders in the right place at the right time, to help change the course of history. I believe that CrossFit athletes can be a catalyst for the Gospel message right between the four walls of their CrossFit Box—and it's my prayer that this book can help you accomplish that awesome mission. In other words, I hope this book will motivate you to proclaim the Gospel right in your own backyard.

During a CrossFit Certification Course in Seattle in 2004, I was privy to the firsthand utterance of this nearly proverbial statement: "The greatest adaptation to CrossFit takes place between the ears." In the twinkling of an eye came the remarkable insight that rather than focusing on the objective physical benefits of the program, I should turn my attention inward to the more subjective and intangible effects of CrossFit upon my mind. This realization led me to develop the "CrossFit Goal Setting and Positive Self-Talk Course" and the subsequent teaching of thousands of athletes about the power of their mind.[2] However, it wasn't until the start of my biblical and theological studies at Western Seminary in September 2017 that God helped me see that the final frontier for CrossFit would not be physical or even mental—it was going to be spiritual. In this sense, the CrossFit community is a "micro-nation" to which Christian leaders have been commissioned to make disciples and share the good news of Jesus Christ (see Matthew 28:19–20).

---

[2] For further information on CrossFit Goal Setting and Positive Self-Talk, I recommend the CrossFit YouTube documentary on the course in addition to the CrossFit journal article "Forging Elite Leadership."

Reasoning from this fact, the question then becomes this: How do we bring faith into the gym? I have found that when preaching to the micro-nation inside the gym, it is imperative that Christian leaders are able to relate the Gospel within the context and framework of the CrossFit culture. As a first step, we need to ground ourselves in a solid understanding of the Bible and systematic theology. Biblical revelation treats God's attributes and qualities not in a speculative way, but rather in an objective and practical manner.[3] There is a vital connection between the God of the Holy Bible and the way we are called to relate to Him. Furthermore, there is a direct relationship between who God is, what God does as revealed within His Word, and what God perfectly demonstrates in the life of His Son, Jesus Christ. In the life of Jesus, we see that the attributes and qualities of God that are revealed by what Jesus said and did are the supreme representation of what God does, and are therefore both quantitative and qualitative evidence of who He is (Hebrews 1:1–3).

The Bible teaches that God's actions are not random, spontaneous, or erratic. Rather, they are outflows of His nature and essential Being. Therefore, by increasing our knowledge about God, we can correctly relate to God by aligning our thoughts and actions in accordance with what Scripture says that God is like. Additionally, we can best equip ourselves to confidently and competently teach others about the God we have come to know, to trust, and most importantly, to "love with all our heart, all our mind, and all our soul" (Matthew 22:37).

When we fully understand who God is, we will see Him, relate to Him, and love Him as the One True God, the God of Heaven and Earth. We will make Him our Lord and Savior, the one whom we aim to please, and whose will we are desirous of fulfilling during our lifetime. Increasing knowledge of God will encourage us to fashion ourselves and others after the Prophet Samuel, whose response when the Lord called him was, "Speak LORD, for your servant is listening" (1 Samuel 3:10). Samuel did not capitalize on this opportunity to pour out his needs to the Lord by saying, "Listen, LORD, your servant speaks."

---

[3] Millard Erickson, *Christian Theology* (Grand Rapids, MI: Baker Academic, 2013), p. 720. The chapter in *Christian Theology* on *The Goodness of God* was instrumental in helping me frame and conceptualize the ideas in the introduction of this book.

When we adopt this inverted theology and approach to our relationship to God, we in effect presume to know what is best for our lives and sinfully construct a god onto ourselves. But we must remember, as the Bible so emphatically seeks to teach, that it was God who created us, as opposed to the idolatrous design of a god created after our own fashion and needs.[4]

God created us in His image, and He therefore knows what is best for us in the long run. We will stand before God in the final judgment, not God before us (Romans 14:11). As we increase in the wisdom, knowledge, and revelation of what God does and who He is, we will join with Jesus in proclaiming, "Holy is your name. Your kingdom come, your will be done, on earth as it is in heaven" (Matthew 6:10). I pray that the theology and doctrine contained in this book will educate and inspire you to share your love for God with others, and that together we would forge a Christian community in the CrossFit culture by bringing the *Gospel into the gym.*

Three, two, one, go!

Greg Amundson
SANTA CRUZ, CA 2020

---

[4] William Barclay, *The Acts of the Apostles New Daily Study Guide* (Louisville, KY: Westminster John Knox Press, 1953), p. 155.

A NOTE TO GYM OWNERS

HOW TO USE THIS BOOK

MY DRUG ENFORCEMENT ADMINISTRATION (DEA) chief firearms instructor once told me that, "slow is smooth, smooth is fast." In this sense, for the past nine years I've been slowly and smoothly bringing the Gospel into my gym at CrossFit Amundson in Santa Cruz, California. I use the whiteboard as a pulpit from which I brief athletes on the physical WOD (workout of the day) in addition to the spiritual WOD (Word of the day). Seemingly overnight, what started as a short Gospel message around the whiteboard moments before a workout has transformed into a weekly Church service inside the gym complete with worship music, prayer, fellowship, and an exegetical teaching from Holy Scripture. During the COVID-related closure of gyms, our ministry adapted, took to Zoom®, and was immediately blessed by increasing attendance from our hometown athletes in addition to new attendees from around the world.

Reflecting on the ministry experiences of the past nine years, in addition to my biblical and theological studies at Western Seminary, I felt strongly that a tipping point of theory and practical application had been reached. I had seen firsthand the transformational power of the Gospel, both in my own life and within the lives of the thousands of athletes who had crossed the threshold into my gym. I had the overwhelming conviction in my heart that 20 years ago God had strategically placed me at the inception of the CrossFit program for the very purpose of being a catalyst for the proclamation of the Gospel within the fitness community. In other words (and respectfully adapting the slogan of the U.S. Army Chaplain Center and School), I felt a calling to bring CrossFit athletes to God, and to bring God to CrossFit athletes.

With all humility and sincerity, I've learned a few things about bringing faith into the gym. One of the most remarkable insights that I hope to impress upon you is the incredible influence that a Christian coach can have upon athletes searching for more meaning, purpose, and passion in life (and that's pretty much everyone). I make this bold proposition with confidence because I believe that the bridge between teaching the principles of athleticism and teaching the tenants of systematic theology is shorter than one might initially think. For example, in the context of CrossFit, coaches (I use this term broadly) are ready and well prepared to answer questions that athletes have about their health and fitness.

The bond and sense of trust established between the coach and athlete as a result of the athlete's increasing physical capacity quickly becomes the foundation for teaching on matters of ethics, universal law, morality, character, and justice. These principles of humanity are now just a short box-jump away from sharing the Gospel and the full revelation of Holy Scripture.

Because of the significant influence that Box owners have upon athletes seeking answers to questions about God and religion, it is imperative that Christian leaders have a sound understanding of the Bible, doctrine, and theology. This being the case, the setting and framework for this book includes a dialogue between the character "Fran" and the owner of her Box, a Seminary-trained CrossFit Coach (i.e., Pastor), all of which takes place around a whiteboard. The coach helps guide Fran through the tough questions of the Christian faith by using illustrations, context, and examples that she can relate to and understand. The great majority of the significant topics of Christianity are explored and treated throughout this book in a logical and progressive manner. The book is designed and formatted in such a way that you can choose to read the content from beginning to end, or engage in topics at specific points that might be pressing in your walk with the Lord or of benefit to the athletes whom you shepherd. The book culminates with a seamless transition from theory to application by equipping the reader with 12 Bible lessons that can be immediately shared within the gym.

The doctrine and theology that I teach within the following pages have been significantly shaped by my graduate studies at Western Seminary and the contributions of scholars Millard Erickson, John Frame, C. S. Lewis, and A.W. Tozer.

Last but certainly not least, I encourage you to read this book in one hand and your Bible in the other.

PART ONE

SHADOW OF THE ALMIGHTY

CHAPTER ONE

REVELATION OF HOLY SCRIPTURE

CHAPTER SUMMARY:

THEOLOGY IS A DISCIPLINE of study that seeks to understand the God specifically revealed within the Holy Bible and to provide a Christian understanding of reality. Theology has the practical benefit of helping shape the way people view the world, make decisions, and relate to themselves, to other people, and most importantly, to God. The study of God is possible in two ways: general revelation and special revelation. General revelation is found in nature, history, and humanity; special revelation is only possible through the study and proclamation of Holy Scripture.

If theology is the study of God, and God is beyond our comprehension, Fran is confused about how theology is even possible in the first place. Where do we begin?

THE STUDY OF GOD is a wonderful and life-changing endeavor. It is life changing in the sense that one cannot help but be shaped by the object of our study, concentration, and focus.[5] Because God is the object of our study, as we draw near to God, God simultaneously draws near to us (James 4:8). Fran, your concern that God is beyond our comprehension was also a concern of the Apostle Paul, who argued that without the illuminating power of the Holy Spirit, a correct understanding of God could not be achieved (1 Corinthians 2:14–15). Thankfully, as believers in Jesus Christ, the indwelling power of the Holy Spirit explains spiritual realities to us through Spirit-taught words (1 Corinthians 2:13). In other words, as believers in Jesus, we "have the mind of Christ" (1 Corinthians 2:16) and can therefore come to know God.

God is a compassionate and merciful God, and He accommodates the limitations of human understanding by a process we define as "revelation." In the general sense of the term, this means that God has communicated and displayed Himself to all persons at all times and places through nature (Psalm 19:1–3), history (Acts 17:26), and mankind (Romans 2:11–16).[6]

However, the superior way that God reveals Himself, and the means by which we can best know Him, is referred to as "special revelation." This is what makes the study of God so wonderful! The means of God's special revelation were accomplished by His manifestation through historical events (Deuteronomy 26: 5–9; Acts 13:16–41); His divine speech (2 Timothy 3:16–17; 2 Peter 1:20–21); and, most importantly, through the incarnation of His Word in the person of Jesus Christ (Colossians 1:15–19; Hebrews 1:2–3).

Because Jesus Christ is the exact representation of God's being (Hebrews 1:3), by studying the Bible we can both read *about God*, and through Jesus, come to experience a loving and saving relationship *with God*.

---

[5] The Christian mystic A. W. Tozer wrote, "What comes into our minds when we think about God is the most important thing about us. We tend by a secret law of the soul to move toward our mental image of God." *Knowledge of the Holy* (New York, NY: Harper Collins, 1961), p. 1.

[6] Millard Erickson, *Christian Theology* (Grand Rapids, MI: Baker Academic, 2013), p. 122.

Fran wants your advice on how to handle the wide range of theological views within her gym. How can she maintain her convictions while interacting with people of other religions and worldviews?

THE BIBLE MAKES A STRONG case for unity in the Church (Ephesians 4:11–13). Rather than division among believers, the Apostle Paul encouraged Christians to be "perfectly united in mind and thought" (1 Corinthians 1:10). Paul further warned the Church about "foolish controversies" that are completely "unprofitable and useless" (Titus 3:9). On the other hand, Paul also seemed to foresee that divisive people were unavoidable, and therefore provided guidance on how to handle these sensitive matters (Titus 3:10). The Bible clearly calls believers to strict adherence to sound doctrine and obedience to God's Word (2 Timothy 3:16–17). Therefore, there can arise a sense of "tension" between maintaining harmony and unity in the Church and unequivocal devotion to the inspired Word of God (2 Peter 1:20–21) and commands of Jesus Christ (John 14:15). What is one to do?

For these reasons, some theologians have made a case for what is known as "levels of essentiality."[7] These levels allow someone to determine if the matter at hand is essential to sound biblical doctrine or merely a matter of insignificant controversy. The four levels are die for, divide for, debate for, and decide for. The most significant is what is called "die for." To deny these areas of doctrine would be equated with knowingly disobeying Jesus Christ. The second area, "divide for," means a disagreement of doctrine that would require a Church division. It does not mean, however, that one particular group are no longer Christian. The third area, "debate for," means that Church leaders may enter into theological debate over the issues at hand. It is important in these debates to focus on the essentials of the Christian faith and not be sidetracked by irrelevant issues (Acts 15:13–21). Finally, there is the matter of "decide for," which is not a matter of division, but rather lends itself to the diversity of the Church.

---

[7] The "levels of essentiality" were brought to my attention in a lecture at Western Seminary by Dr. Adam Nigh in addition to the work of Dr. Gerry Breshears.

In all matters of determining essentiality, it is important to heed the words of the Apostle Paul and "make every effort to do what leads to peace and mutual edification" (Romans 14:19). The four levels of essentiality will provide ministry leaders with a framework for determining the category in which to place a particular matter of contention or disagreement within the box.

Fran would like to understand Thomas Aquinas's cosmological argument for God's existence from motion. She thinks it might help convince her atheist friend to become a Christian. Explain the argument for her and whether you think she should use it to teach her friend about God.

———————————

THOMAS AQUINAS'S COSMOLOGICAL ARGUMENT for the existence of God could be summarized by the idea that everything is dependent upon something else for its existence. Aquinas further maintained that the existence of God could be proven by pure reason and without drawing on biblical revelation. Aquinas held that God could be proven through the process of observing movement. Everything in movement was put into motion, or caused to be moved, by another object. Yet, if this logic were to be perpetually reverse engineered, then there must come a point of a single "uncaused cause" or "unmoved mover." Thus, according to Aquinas, the great "uncaused cause" was God. The fundamental problem with this approach, especially if it is used for the purpose of evangelism, is that without special revelation, we learn nothing about the nature of the god described by Aquinas. In other words, further proof is still necessary in order to demonstrate that the god whose existence seems to be proven by Aquinas's cosmological argument is the same God of the Bible.[8]

Fran, for this reason, I recommend that you share with your atheist friend the God who has revealed Himself in the Bible and in the life of Jesus Christ. Our starting point for sharing our faith should always be along the lines of explaining our belief in one Triune God who is loving and all powerful; has graciously revealed Himself in nature, history, and mankind; and has specially revealed Himself in the Bible and life of Jesus.

---

[8] Erickson, p. 19.

Perhaps the best paraphrased Scripture to share with your atheist friend to explain this incredible truth is that "in the past, God spoke through the prophets, but in these last days he has spoken to us by his Son, who is the radiance of God's glory and the exact representation of his being" (Hebrews 1:1–3). This verse can inspire your friend to enter into a relationship with Jesus and to realize that "in Jesus is life, and that life is the light of all mankind" (John. 1:4).

What does it mean to speak of an "onto-relation" between Christ and God the Father? Why is this important for the doctrine of revelation?

ONE OF THE BEST WAYS to understand and appreciate the "onto-relation" between Christ and God the Father is from the perspective of a remarkable verse from Hebrews: "The Son is the radiance of God's glory and the exact representation of his being" (Hebrews 1:3a). Unpacking this verse leads to the realization that Jesus Christ, although fully a human being during His time on Earth, was simultaneously also fully God; or, to use the words of the Apostle Paul, "For in Jesus Christ all the fullness of the Deity lives in bodily form" (Colossians 2:9) and "God [the Father] was pleased to have all his fullness dwell in him" (Colossians 1:19). In other words, in the incarnation of Jesus Christ, everything that Jesus subsequently said and did was a special revelation of God the Father.[9]

It is important to note that the author of Hebrews described Jesus as the "radiance of God's glory" and the exact "representation" of God's being. The words "radiance" and "representation" could be explained in the context of the Sun. We are able to enjoy the radiance of the Sun's rays—they warm us and sustain life on Earth. However, we certainly understand there is a distinction between the Sun itself and the rays of the Sun that ultimately reach Earth. Similarly, because God is Spirit (John 4:4) and therefore nobody can actually "see" the Father (John 1:18; 6:46), we can nevertheless "see" the exact representation of the Father in the person of Jesus Christ. In other words, "the pinnacle of God's acts is to be found in the life of Jesus."[10]

[9] Erickson, p. 156.

[10] Erickson, p. 157.

In this sense, the words of Jesus, in addition to His actions, behaviors, and character, were such a perfect representation of God the Father Himself, that Jesus could say: "Anyone who has seen me has seen the Father" (John 14:9).

The "onto-relation" between Christ and God the Father serves our doctrine of revelation by opening our mind and heart to the realization that although no one has ever seen God (John 1:18a), we can still enter into a personal and loving relationship with Jesus, who "is himself God and is in closest relationship with the Father" (John 1:18b).

Fran wants you to explain the four aspects of Christ's preparation of His apostles to extend His own preaching and teaching.

———————————

A WONDERFUL ENTRY POINT into the four aspects of Christ's preparation for His apostles to extend His own teaching is the "Great Commission" of Matthew 28:18–20. In these verses, we are able to understand four distinct expectations that Jesus had for His apostles and for all future generations of believers. The first aspect of Christ's preparation was to "go and make disciples" (Matthew 28:18). This command was based on the fact that "all authority in heaven and on earth had been given to Jesus" (Matthew 28:18). This does not mean that what Jesus said and did during His time on Earth would be anything less authoritative than what He would do or say in the resurrection. Rather, it means that unlike the limited sphere of His influence during His incarnated time on Earth, He would now enjoy universal authority, domain and rule "over heaven and earth." The disciple-making process must therefore involve bringing people into relationship with the Trinity of the Father, Son, and Holy Spirit, as Jesus Himself commands.

Secondly, Jesus calls His apostles to "baptize" people. Here, Jesus distinctly includes the Trinity as the means by which believers are to be brought into a proper relationship with God. Third, Jesus calls His apostles to "teach" other believers everything that they had learned from Him. The expectation that Jesus has for His teaching is that it would continue "to the very end of the age."

In other words, there will never be a time when the teaching of Jesus is outdated. Finally, there is a call to not just "learning" about what Jesus taught, but to "obeying" what they have heard. In this sense, a believer may be recognized not just by what they say, but also by what they do.

Fran wants to know if the Bible is factual and accurate. For example, Judges 3:31 tells us that Shamgar killed 600 Philistines with an ox goad. Let's say that you and Fran went back in a time machine and discovered that there were actually 593 Philistines killed. Is that an error in Scripture? Why or why not?

WHEN READING THE BIBLE, in particular sections of the Bible dealing *with what appear to be* very specific numbers, it is important to understand the cultural setting of the biblical author at the time these statements were recorded.[11] Although in our current cultural setting, there is an inherent expectation that a television news reporter would be specific with regards to the number of people killed or injured in a scene of violence, the standards of exactness were not the same at the time that the books of the Bible were recorded. This in no way means that what the biblical author recorded was not true. Rather, we mean that what the biblical author recorded is fully true in the context of the culture of its time.[12]

What is perhaps most important to remember is that the biblical author, inspired and "carried along" by the power of the Holy Spirit (1 Peter 20–21), recorded certain events in accordance with God's specific purposes. Therefore, the exactness of any particular report is far less important than the message that God was attempting to convey through the author.

Taking into account the battle recorded in Judges 3:31: if we were to discover that Shamgar *only killed 593* Philistines, as opposed to the 600 recorded in Scripture, we would not deduce that there was an error in the Bible. Rather, the purpose of the author was to demonstrate the fact that a *large number of Philistines* were killed by a single person, which, given the modern sophistications in offensive military technology, is extraordinary and could only be accomplished with God!

---

[11] Erickson, p. 203.
[12] Erickson, p. 203.

Fran wants to understand what it means to say that the Bible has "authority" over someone's life.

IN UNDERSTANDING THE AUTHORITY of the Bible, in addition to it being the *final authority* (referred to in Latin as *Sola Scriptura*), it is helpful to investigate two other ways of qualifying what is meant by the word *authority*. First of all, we should begin with a general sense of what we mean by the *authority of the Bible*. If we were to "reverse engineer" the words contained within the Bible, we would discover that they are "God-breathed" (1 Timothy 3:16) and are therefore from God Himself. In other words, God the Father and Jesus Christ (Matthew 28:18–20) give the Bible its authority. Therefore, the authority of the Bible, coming directly from God, has the supreme right to command proper belief (1 Timothy 4:16) and action (Titus 1:6–9).[13]

In addition to understanding the Bible as the *final authority,* we may also understand the Bible as being the *sole authority* (referred to in Latin as *Solo Scriptura*). This view would include the work of the Holy Spirit in giving the Bible authority, which illuminates and brings about the comprehension of the biblical text. The Apostle Paul argued that people without the Spirit would not be able to understand the Word of God (1 Corinthians 2:14).

The final view of the authority of the Bible is that it *is an authority*. This view would perhaps include the authority of other non-Christian sacred texts in addition to emphasizing human reason as a means of establishing the Bible's meaning, authority, and divine origin.[14] One way of understanding the difference between the Bible being the *sole authority* and *an authority* is in the context of objective and subjective components of authority. The objective view holds that the Bible automatically brings people into contact with God. On the other hand, the more subjective view holds that the Holy Spirit is the chief authority for the Christian.[15] For our purposes, it is best to understand that a combination of both views is important.

---

[13] Erickson, p. 212.

[14] Erickson, p. 216.

[15] Erickson, p. 216.

The written Word of God, when read by a believer and understood through the illuminating and indwelling power of the Holy Spirit, enables them to take on the "mind of Christ" (1 Corinthians 2:16) and come to love and appreciate the Bible as the authoritative Word of God.

CHAPTER TWO

KNOWLEDGE OF THE MOST HIGH

CHAPTER SUMMARY:

THE HOLY SCRIPTURES REVEAL that God is personal, all-powerful, eternal, and present everywhere (and at all times!) within His creation. God is also permanently unchanging in His greatness and perfection. Although God is both active and present within His creation, He is also superior to and entirely independent of anything that He has created. As we will discover in this chapter, there is no tension between God's love and His justice. Finally, the Scriptures systematically reveal that God is One and Three Persons (the Trinity) at the same time. Christianity is the only major world religion that makes this astounding claim about God.

Fran wants to know why everyone refers to God in the masculine. After all, if God is spirit and not a physical creature, why do people mostly speak of Him as male? Is it appropriate to see the feminine in God or to call God "she"?

———————————

IN ORDER TO ANSWER this question, we have to "begin at the beginning," with one of the most important revelations about God found within the Bible: "God is spirit, and his worshippers must worship in the Spirit and in truth" (John 4:22). These words are very important, for although on one hand Jesus said, "God is spirit," on the other hand, Jesus referred to God in the masculine sense when He said, *"his* worshipers must worship *him."* In other words, we can affirm from this Scripture that you are correct in understanding that God is Spirit. But the question still remains as to why we speak of God in the masculine sense. I want to help unpack this for you in two ways.

First, we have to understand that the God of the Bible is a relational God. God is intimately concerned with shaping and directing the lives of His worshipers. God has all the capacities that we normally associate with personality: knowing, feeling, willing, and acting.[16] What is key to the nature of God's relationship to His worshipers is that He wants to *Father* us. This was at the heart of Jesus's teaching, and the very first words of the prayer that Jesus taught His disciples (Matthew 6:9). What we know about God the Father is that He is a loving and good Father who can be approached by His children (Psalm 65:4; Jeremiah 29:13; Romans 5:1–2; Matthew 6:25–33).

Second, in the life and person of Jesus Christ, we have the most perfect image of God Himself (Hebrews 1:3; Colossians 2:9). The author of Hebrews described Jesus as the "exact representation of His being." The Greek word *charaktēr,* which the author used for "representation," literally translates as "from the same as." To reverse engineer the *Father begetting the Son,* we can deduce that if Jesus is "from the same as" God the Father, then the best understanding of God revealed by Jesus is in the masculine sense.

---

[16] Erickson, p. 241.

I should point out to you, Fran, that there are a few places in the Bible that speak of God using a feminine metaphor. For example, God is described as "crying out in labor" as He came to the aid of Israel (Isaiah 42:14). Nevertheless, in the historical and cultural time of the Bible, it was not necessarily uncommon for a mothering metaphor to be used in reference to males. A wonderful example of this is arguably one of the greatest male figures of the Bible, none other than King David, who is described as "fierce as a wild bear robbed of *her cubs*" (2 Samuel 17:8). Therefore, although there are cases in the Bible in which a feminine and mothering metaphor is used about God (or in the case of David, about men in general), they should still be interpreted in the context of understanding a relational aspect of God in which He is most clearly portrayed as masculine.

God's love and His wrath seem contradictory to Fran and hard for her to understand. Fran wants to know how she can relate to them without God appearing to be mean or sentimental.

FRAN, AT FIRST GLANCE, it would indeed seem that God's love and His wrath contradict each other. However, let me help you understand that God's love and wrath are in fact two sides of the same coin. Establishing God's love is the "top side" of the coin. We learn in the Bible that "God is love" (1 John 4:8) and that He is "the God of love and peace" (2 Corinthians 13:11). Furthermore, God describes Himself as "slow to anger, abounding in love and faithfulness" (Exodus 34:6). What, then, could lead such a loving God to wrath? Again we turn to the metaphor of the two-sided coin, which is nevertheless *still the same coin.* In other words, because we know that God is an integrated being and His divine attributes are harmonious, we must understand *love* and *wrath* in light of each other.[17]

In God's self-disclosure to Moses, He revealed that He was a God of both *love* and *justice.* Although God "maintains love to thousands," He will "not leave the guilty unpunished" (Exodus 34:7). We learn in the Bible that there will be a penalty for sin (Romans 6:23). However, we also discover in

---

[17] Erickson, p. 267.

the Bible that God rewards those who seek after Him and are obedient to His commands (Deuteronomy 28:1–2). We can deduce therefore that God is a God of fairness and justice. He rewards and He punishes in accordance with His perfect justice. Although there seems to be tension between this love and wrath (or justice), there is in fact only tension if the two *are independent of each other.* In other words, love cannot be understood unless seen as including justice, and justice without love lacks mercy. However, when wrath and love are evenly and justly distributed, God perfectly demonstrates His concern for the welfare of all humanity.[18]

Fran, it is important to understand the worldview of the biblical author at the time that the Bible was written. Very often, the biblical author was attempting to differentiate between the One True God of the Bible and other gods that were worshipped within the cultures and people groups of the time. With other gods, it was impossible to tell what they would be feeling on any given day: love one day, wrath the next. However, with the God of the Bible, His love and wrath mutually abide together, and are collectively and cohesively part of His integrated nature.

Additionally, God's love provides context for His wrath, and vice versa. For example, consider a human father who stood idle while their son or daughter experienced suffering at the hand of evil. In this illustration, the father's love for their child would compel them to confront the evil that had befallen their child.[19] Relating the illustration to the God of the Bible, how much more likely will He be to confront any evil that befalls His beloved children? Therefore, we discover that God's wrath, justice, and anger all arise out of and *from His love* (Romans 12:9).[20] Fran, in other words, this is good news for you and me! We learn from the Bible that through His justice, anger, and even wrath, God truly and perfectly loves.

---

[18] Erickson, p. 268.

[19] A similar illustration was portrayed in Michael Reeves's book *Delighting in the Trinity,* p. 118.

[20] Reeves, p. 119.

Fran wants to know how the concept of God's omnipresence relates to the biblical concept of temple, especially as it culminates in the Church as the temple of the Holy Spirit. What meaning or value can there be in speaking of God being present in His temple or Church if He is present literally everywhere and always?

———————————

THIS IS A GREAT QUESTION that sooner or later crosses the mind of every spiritual seeker. The word *omnipresence* means that God is everywhere simultaneously (Jeremiah 23:24; Psalm 139:7–10).[21] Theologians commonly refer to this attribute of God as an *incommunicable attribute*, which simply means there is no counterpart found in humans.[22] For example, even with the most high-speed supersonic jet, no human could ever be *everywhere at the exact same time.* However, God can!

The question, therefore, that should be on our mind and heart is this: If God is *everywhere at the same time,* but I am *only here and now,* how can I relate to God? I believe that this is the reason that the biblical concept of the temple and Church is so important. Although God is omnipresent, He graciously accommodates humanity by making Himself present and available in a particular geo coordinate (for example, the Church or temple) in which we can essentially "find Him" and experience His presence (1 Kings 8:10-11; 12–66).

In the Old Testament, the temple was instrumental to the relationship between God and His worshippers. In fact, in the Bible, God would often reveal His anger, frustration, and displeasure when His temple was neglected (Haggai 1:3–6). In this sense, in the Old Testament, the temple was important to God and important to His people. In other words, Fran, we need the temple, and the temple needs us!

Now, Fran, here is where things get really exciting. The Apostle Paul takes the historical significance of the temple to astonishing new heights. Paul explains that *you and I are temples for God's Spirit* (1 Corinthians 6:19). I believe two significant conclusions can be drawn from this: The first is that

---

[21] Erickson, p. 237.

[22] Erickson, p. 237.

each individual believer who puts their faith in Jesus Christ becomes a temple for God's presence (Acts 2:28). Rather than having to go to a specific place or locality to worship God, we can now experience God's presence at any time, and in any place (1 John 14:6). The second conclusion is that the presence of the *temple within us* now compels the individual believer to gather with other believers to form the *body of the Church*. In fact, it could even be implied that this was the hope and expectation of Jesus when he said, "When two or more gather in my name, I am there among them" (Matthew 18:20).

Fran wants to know if it is possible to speak of God as changing His mind.

FRAN, THE BIBLE MAKES a strong argument that God is unchanging (Psalm 102:26–27). In fact, God goes so far as to say of Himself: "I the LORD do not change" (Malachi 3:6). Unlike we humans, who tend to change our *thinking* from moment to moment, even the very *thoughts* of God are permanent (Psalm 33:11). James uses the beautiful illustration of "shifting shadows" (James 1:17) to contrast the fragility, uncertainty, and impermanence of humanity with the permanence of God.

The very idea of "God changing" challenges our theology in several ways. If God "changed," then every attribute and quality of God would also be subject to change. In other words, our understanding of God would be in grave jeopardy. For example, God could simply be a God of holiness on one day, and a God of evil on another. In many respects, the fact that we know God is unchanging is foundational to how we imagine and understand Him. The Bible teaches that God does not change His mind, plans, or actions, nor do His attributes or qualities either increase or decrease. God remains the same and unchanged regardless of what occurs (Numbers 23:19; 1 Samuel 15:27–30).[23]

Fran, although I've made a strong case here for the fact that God does not change His mind, let me draw your attention to a few parts of the Bible where it seems like He does! For example, in the book of Jonah, God said that He was going to destroy the people of Nineveh (Jonah 1:2, 3:4). However,

---

[23] Erickson, p. 249.

after the people repented, "God saw what they did and how they turned from their evil ways, he relented and did not bring on them the destruction he had threatened" (Jonah 3:10). We may interpret from these verses something very important. First of all, because we know that God's wisdom and knowledge are infinite, we may conclude that God knew that the people of Nineveh would repent. Therefore, from the *human perspective*, God changes His mind. But from *God's perspective,* He did what He intended to do all along.

Second, it is important to note that when God seems to change His mind, the context is God withholding punishment or death (2 Kings 20:1–6). For example, notice in the instance of Nineveh that God did not bring on the people the punishment that He had *threatened.* In other words, we may conclude that the *threat* was part of God's sovereign means by which He meant to influence a change in their behavior. In this sense, God did not change His mind, the people of Nineveh did! Perhaps the best illustration of this principle is when God explained to the prophet Jeremiah, "If a nation I warned repents of its evil, then I will relent and not inflict on it the disaster I had planned" (Jeremiah 18:7–8).

Fran wants to understand the implications of divine transcendence. What does it mean to speak of God as both *immanent* and *transcendent*?

FRAN, ONE OF THE ways that theologians discuss God's being is to think in terms of God's nearness and distance, which is referred to as His *immanence* and *transcendence*. I want to help you understand the implications of God's transcendence. This is very important because the very concept of God's transcendence teaches that God is separate from and independent of His creation.[24] For example, the Prophet Isaiah wrote that God's ways are *higher* than our ways, and God's thoughts are *higher* than our thoughts (Isaiah 55:8–9). This would seem to suggest that God is above and beyond our sense of time, space, reality, and even thinking. However, although God is supremely *above us*, God is also intimately *involved within His creation*, which theologians have described as God's immanence. For example, on one

---

[24] Erickson, p. 282.

hand, Isaiah wrote that God is "seated on a throne, high and exalted" (Isaiah 6:1), which would suggest God's transcendence; yet on the other hand, Isaiah declares that "the whole earth is full of His glory" (Isaiah 6:5), which would suggest God's immanence. This marvelous contrast between God's ability to be high above us, yet also simultaneously involved within His creation, is one of the great mysteries of the Christian faith.

The idea that God is a Being that is independent and high above the universe is found throughout the Bible (Psalm 113:5–6; John 8:23).[25] Therefore, the theological task before us is to determine which expression of God's transcendence is most helpful to conceptualize this truth and communicate it to others.[26]

Some great theological thinkers have based their understanding of transcendence from the perspective of eschatology. This means that God does not only reveal Himself through the historical accounts of the Bible, nor is God limited to residing within our understanding of "present time" occurrences.[27] Rather, the eschatological model of transcendence suggests that God resides and functions from a future reality "that we have not yet been."[28]

Fran, consider the following illustration to help make sense of this concept. We tend to think of movement in the context of going from "Point A" to "Point B." However, the eschatological view of transcendence would shift the metaphor from "A to B" to a change of state. In other words, rather than moving from where you are now ("Point A") to where God is ("Point B"), you move from where you are in the sense of "Now" to where you will be "Then." Or, expressed in another way, you move from "Present" to "Future." One particular account from Jesus's ministry to help explain this concept is when Jesus foretold His return "in the clouds with great power and glory" (Mark 13:26). In this case, Jesus is not describing His impending transcendence to a particular location (such as "Point B"), but rather to a future reality in which He would reside "ahead of us" and, at a future time, we would meet with Him again.

---

[25] Erickson, p. 283.

[26] Erickson, p. 283.

[27] Erickson, p. 287.

[28] Erickson, p. 287.

Fran wants your help in understanding why the Trinity is important for a proper construct of creation. She also wants to know what God was doing before the beginning of the world.

FRAN, UNDERSTANDING THE TRINITY is absolutely paramount to our correct understanding of God, His purposes in creation, and what He was doing *before creation began.* Consider this: in just the first few lines of the Bible, we are introduced to the fact that "In the beginning God created" (Genesis 1:1). What logical conclusion can we draw from this single verse? That the God of the Bible is the Creator—He is the Supreme Being who created everything out of "no thing" (Hebrews 11:3; John 1:1–3). And because God is the Creator, the next logical conclusion we could infer about God is that He wants to *rule His creation.* And if we stop here, then what we have is a God who is *mainly* a Creator-Ruler.

However, and Fran, this is the critical point, if we stop with the idea that God is the Creator Ruler, then we could be mistakenly led to believe that God needs to *rule over creation* in *order to be who He is.*[29] And if we were content to believe this false concept of God, we would miss all the beauty of the Triune God that reveals Himself within the totality of the biblical message.

Therefore, we are compelled to move beyond the idea that God is only a Creator, or only a Ruler, into the magnificent realization that at the most fundamental level, God is *relational.* And in what capacity does God relate to His creation?

To answer this question, we look to Jesus Christ, who is Himself the perfect representation and image of God (Hebrews 1:3). When we start with the fact that Jesus is the Son of God (Hebrews 1:5; Psalm 2:7; Luke 1:35), then by causation of Christ's life on Earth, we know that he has a Father (John 8:42). In other words, "just the fact that Jesus is 'the Son' really says it all. Being a Son means he has a Father."[30] Furthermore, by Jesus's own testimony, we know that even before the world was created, God the Father and Jesus were together (John 1:1–2, 8:58, 10:30, 17:24). That is why Jesus said, "Father, you loved me even before the creation of the world" (John 17:24). The conclusion

---

[29] Reeves, p. 19.

[30] Reeves, p. 19.

we draw from this paints a far superior picture than simply limiting God to a Creator or Ruler. We discover that before God created the world as we know it, God the Father was loving His Son.[31]

You see, Fran, the Trinity helps shape within our minds and hearts the essence of God's most foundational quality: The fact that He is a Father. When we begin with this, then everything else that He does flows from and is in alignment with His fatherly intentions. In other words, God continues to Rule, and He continues to Create and sustain life, and He even disciplines, but He does all these things in a fatherly way (Hebrews 12:7; Psalm 103:3; Isaiah 63:16). And through faith in Jesus, we become the adopted sons and daughters of God (Galatians 3:26; Ephesians 1:5). This means that God relates to us as His children, and we relate to God as our Father (Matthew 6:9). And this is good news indeed!

Fran wants to know why understanding the Trinity is important for a proper concept of salvation.

FRAN, I WANT TO share with you a concept that has helped me immensely in shaping my understanding of the importance of the Trinity in relation to salvation. I often reflect on the implications of the fact that I am made in the image of God (Genesis 1:26–27). If I am made in God's image, then I should be able to detect a reflection of God's attributes within myself. The Trinity reveals that God is a *Fatherly* and *relational* God who loved His son Jesus Christ even before the world began (John 17:24). Based on this understanding of the relationship between the Father and Jesus in eternity, it becomes entirely characteristic of God to turn and create others for the purpose of loving them, and also relating to them as Father.[32] In this sense, Jesus was the blueprint for all of creation.[33] God the Father was so delighted with Jesus that His love for Jesus overflowed. And what was the result of this overflowing love? According to the Apostle Paul, Jesus would ultimately become the firstborn over many sons (Romans 8:29).

---

[31] Reeves, p. 21.

[32] Reeves, p. 43.

[33] Reeves, p. 43.

Jesus taught that the first and greatest commandment was to love God with all your heart, soul, and mind, and the second was to love your neighbor as yourself (Matthew 22:36–39). Reflecting on the fact that we are made in the image of God, we see the fundamental principle that Jesus was teaching. Because God relates to His creation as a loving Father, and we are made in His image, as image bearers of God we should therefore love God and each other. Fran, this is what I meant when I said that I should be a *reflection* of God's attributes. I should try to love God and others as God loves me.

So, Fran, here is a preliminary question that will ultimately take us to the importance of the Trinity in relation to salvation: If we were made to reflect God and to be His image bearers, what went wrong? In Genesis we find our answer. Rather than loving God, Adam and Eve turned their love from God onto themselves. In other words, rather than loving God as Jesus commands, they "became lovers of pleasure rather than lovers of God (2 Timothy 3:4). Eve noticed the tree on the fruit was *pleasing* to look at and *desirable* for gaining wisdom *for herself* (Genesis 3:6). In other words, the love that Eve should have focused on God became twisted, perverted, and misdirected: it was focused on herself.[34]

And, Fran, here is where we see the astonishing love that the Father has for His creation, and how God can ultimately work out everything into a pattern for good (Romans 8:28). It was Adam and Eve's sin, and mankind's subsequent fallen state, that reveals the depths of God's love. God so deeply loved mankind that He sent Jesus to rescue us (John 15:16). In other words, it's not that mankind is trying to make our way back to God. To use the words of the Apostle John, "This is love: not that we loved God, but that He loved us and sent His Son as an atoning sacrifice for our sins" (1 John 4:8–10).

You see, Fran, in Jesus we observe the most perfect image of the Triune God (Hebrews 1:3; Colossians 1:19, 2:9; cf. John 20:31). In Jesus we see that God is Father, Son, and Spirit: Jesus is begotten by the Father and anointed by the Spirit (John 20:31).[35] Jesus then willingly lays down His life for us (John 10:18, 15:13) in order to reconcile God's creation onto Himself (2 Corinthians 5:18).

---

[34] The concept of *turned love* was identified in Reeves, p. 65.

[35] Reeves, p. 80.

When you place your faith in Jesus you receive eternal salvation (Acts 16:30–31). That is why the Apostle Paul could confidently write to the Church in Rome: "When you confess with your mouth 'Jesus is Lord,' and believe in your heart that God raised him from the dead, then you will be saved" (Romans 10:9). This means that not only did the Father send the Son to take our sin, and thereby take our status as condemned sinners by grace; the Father has also given us the status the Son has by nature, a child of God. Salvation, then, isn't just getting us off the hook for our sin and putting us back into relation with God; it brings us into a new relation to God, one within the Trinity, that even pre-fallen Adam and Eve did not have by nature but could only be given by grace. And that is good news indeed!

CHAPTER THREE
CREATION, ELECTION, AND PROVIDENCE

CHAPTER SUMMARY:

THE BIBLE REVEALS THAT God has a definite plan for history. Calvinists believe that God's plan is prior to human decision and action, while Arminians tend to place more emphasis on human freedom. Although strong arguments are made on both sides, we will argue that the plan of God is unconditional rather than conditional or dependent on human decision and action. Christians can have confidence in the greatness of God's plan in the created universe and everything that is within it. In addition, Christians can maintain confidence that God is still actively at work within His creation in preserving it and guiding it toward His intended purpose.

Words like "election" and "predestination" make Fran uncomfortable, and she wants to know if they are even biblical. How can you help guide her toward a biblical foundation on the topic?

FRAN, BEFORE SPECIFICALLY ADDRESSING your question regarding the biblical foundation for "election" and "predestination," I want to elevate your perspective to provide greater context and clarity for your concerns. In other words, questions of predestination are the narrower form of the broader question that asks: Does God have a plan that includes everything that occurs and is He now bringing that plan into effect?[36]

The answer to this question is a resounding *Yes!* In fact, this is exactly what Peter explained to the Israelite crowd in regard to Jesus Christ, who as part of God's *deliberate plan and foreknowledge,* was put to death on the cross (Acts 2:22–23). Keep in mind, however, that if we were to stop here with Jesus's death, we would certainly have reason to be uncomfortable with any notion of predestination. After all, what kind of God would predestine His own Son to be put to death? However, from the higher perspective, we discover that God's predestined reason fit within the totality of His perfect plan as explained by the Apostle John: "For God so loved the world that He sent His only Son, that whoever believes in him shall not perish but have eternal life" (John 3:16).

Therefore, what is most important to understand in regard to your question is the theme and context in which the words "election" and "predestination" should be applied. The biblical authors, in particular the Apostle Paul, firmly held that everything that comes to pass is part of God's plan and is in the best interest of His children (Ephesians 1:11–12). This means that rather than being *concerned* regarding election and predestination, you should instead *rejoice* knowing that God is working for the good of those who love Him (Romans 8:28). So, you see, Fran, the fruit of your question will be discovered when you ask, "What am I *predestined for?*" When you ask *this question,* the answer is astounding! You are predestined to be conformed to the image of Jesus Christ himself (Romans 8:29). In other words, God has indeed chosen you in Christ and *predestined you* "in accordance with His pleasure and will—to the praise of His glorious grace" (Ephesians 1:5–6).

[36] Millard Erickson, *Christian Theology* (Grand Rapids, MI: Baker Academic, 2013), p. 322.

Finally, Fran, it is important to understand the greater implications of terms like predestination and election, which is that these concepts are intimately woven into the very fabric of God's nature. In addition, they are inseparable from doctrines of God, including His omnipotence and omnipresence. In fact, for the Old Testament biblical authors, it was practically inconceivable for anything to occur *without God's predestination*. For example, in the Hebrew mind, the expression "it rained" would be seemingly impossible to comprehend. This was because for the Hebrews, rain could only happen if God *sent the rain*.[37] This is why the Prophet Isaiah could write something as astounding as, "God makes known the end from the beginning, from ancient times, what is still to come" (Isaiah 46:10). The image of God as the omnipotent creator and sustainer of all things, combined with His personal and loving nature, demonstrates that He is not an abstract force in opposition to His creation. Rather, God is our loving Father who deeply cares about each and every one of His children (John 4:11).

Fran is really interested in the concept of human freedom and God's will. She wants you to summarize the difference between hard determinist, libertarian, and compatibilist theories of human freedom.

FRAN, CONTINUING THE LINE of thought from your question on election and predestination, we now turn our attention to the matter of human freedom. In other words, if God has *predestined* us for something, where is there room for individual decision making and human autonomy? There are three general approaches to human freedom that I would like to summarize for you. Let's begin with the idea of *compatibilistic freedom*, which will be a good pathway into the *libertarian* view of freedom.

Fran, when I was in the U.S. Army, my commanding officer was a very intimidating person. However, in addition to his frightening presence and the fact that by the sheer nature of his rank he could *command me to do something*, he had an uncanny ability to compel my obedience according to the desires of

---

[37] Erickson, p. 320.

my own free will. It was a combination of his command presence, credibility, knowledge, persuasion, and overall charisma that seemed to influence my thinking in such a fashion that I *intrinsically wanted to do what he said.* Now, Fran, think of God as the elevated and superior Commanding Officer. In this sense, God is the Divine Person of unlimited charisma.[38] The compatibilist view of human freedom holds that God's will is so attractive that human beings willfully and joyfully obey.[39]

On the other hand, the *libertarian* view of human freedom (also referred to as *incompatibilistic freedom)* would contend that humans always have independence of will and power to act or refrain from acting in a particular way. For example, consider the case of Jonah: Although God told Jonah to "Go to the great city of Nineveh and preach against it" (Jonah 1:2), we discover that "Jonah ran away from the LORD and headed for Tarshish instead" (Johan 1:3). At this point in the story, the Bible seems to suggest that even a great prophet like Jonah who loved God had autonomy and the ability to act in opposition to His will. However, as the story continues, we discover something remarkable. Everything other than Jonah was in submission to God's will! Even the wind and the sea obeyed God (Jonah 1:4). In this sense, God made the conditions surrounding Jonah so compelling that ultimately Jonah "obeyed the word of the LORD and went to Nineveh" (Jonah 3:3).

Fran, here is an analogy that might help you make sense of the *libertarian* view of human will as truly "free," while at the same time only possible in cooperation with the Sovereign Will of God. Imagine an ocean liner full of passengers that departs from England with a destination of New York. On board this mighty vessel, the passengers are free to exercise the independence of their will. However, while they are exercising free will, the ocean liner is steadily bound for its predetermined final destination of New York. In this sense, God is the ocean liner, and humanity is bound up within His Will as He progresses history in the direction He has predetermined.[40]

Finally, there is the hard determinist view of human freedom. This view asserts that God's plans and will come first, and that human decision making

---

[38] Erickson, p. 331.

[39] Erickson, p. 331.

[40] A similar illustration and analogy was identified in C. S. Lewis's book *Mere Christianity.*

and actions are the consequence.[41] In this view, God is not dependent upon what humans do or do not do in the accomplishment of His will. One of my favorite biblical accounts of this view of human freedom is found in the Old Testament book of Esther. In attempting to convince his daughter Esther to report to King Xerxes the plot against the Jews, Mordecai said, "If you remain silent at this time, relief and deliverance for the Jews will arise from another place—and who knows but that you have come to your royal position for such a time as this?" (Esther 4:14) This account would seem to suggest that independent of Esther's choice, God's sovereign will and predetermined course of action would ultimately be fulfilled. When Esther was confronted with the reality of the situation, she acted in accordance with God's will and therefore His *predestined course of action*; Esther decided to speak to the King in defense of the Jewish people, and, as a result, God's will was fulfilled.

Fran wants to know what it means to speak of creation *ex nihilo*. What false conceptions of creation is it meant to guard against? What is its relation to Christology?

FRAN, IN THE SIMPLEST of terms, to speak of creation *ex nihilo* means that God created *everything out of nothing (without any preexisting materials)*. Or, put another way, God created *every-thing* out of *no-thing*. A more precise definition would state that God created the entire universe and everything in it independent of preexisting materials (Genesis 1:1; John 1:1-3). This also implies that God created without compulsion or necessity and entirely of His own free will. God is therefore the supreme reality, and everything that exists within His creation is ultimately for His purpose and glory (Psalm 19:1; Colossians 1:16). The progression of this understanding should now point to the self-evident fact that God Himself is neither begotten nor made (Psalm 100:3).

Now, Fran, to speak of creation *ex nihilo* and the fact that God is neither begotten nor made becomes absolutely essential to our understanding of Christology and the deity of Jesus Christ (Colossians 2:9). The Christian believes that humanity was created by God and is therefore separate from

---

[41] Erickson, p. 326.

Him (Genesis 1:26). On the other hand, Jesus Christ was *not made by God nor is Jesus separate from Him*. Rather, Jesus is *begotten of the Father*. This means that Jesus was with God eternally even *before the creation of the world* (John 1:1–3). In the words of the Apostle Paul, Jesus "is the image of the invisible God" and "was before all things" (Colossians 1:15–17). Furthermore, according to the author of the letter to the Hebrews, Jesus is "the radiance of God's glory and the exact representation of His being" (Hebrews 1:3). In other words, Fran, rather than falsely believing that Jesus was created by God, the Christian holds that *Jesus is God!*

Fran, in addition to understanding the positive application of the concept of creation *ex nihilo*, it is also important to understand what false and negative conceptions of creation it is meant to guard against. Remember that *ex nihilo* means that God created the entire universe out of no preexisting materials. The implication is therefore that God did not use something, fashion something, or adapt something that already existed independently of Him. This is critical to the Christian understanding of creation, and protects from the false dualistic belief that something could have potentially existed before God, or exclusive and independent of His will and design.

The idea that something existed before or alongside God would threaten the idea of God's infinitude, for it would suggest that something other than the eternal God had already existed apart from His creation. In addition, it protects against the idea that the "nothing" that God created was some type of "substance" or "invisible matter" that already existed. In other words, to think of "nothing," we are in fact describing "the absence of reality."[42] Perhaps the best description of *ex nihilo* comes from the Apostle John, who wrote that, "Through him all things were made; without him nothing was made that has been made" (John 1:3).

Finally, *ex nihilo* guards against the emanation view of creation, which suggests that humanity is an outflow from God's nature and therefore a part of Him. The danger of this view is that creation (and in particular humanity) can be seen as still divine, which leads to pantheism.[43] In other words, pantheism would suggest that "creation is a change of status, rather than a beginning of

---

[42] Erickson, p. 342.

[43] Erickson, p. 348.

a being."[44] The Christian view of creation *ex nihilo* rejects this outright and insists that humanity and all of creation are dependent on God their Creator.

Fran wants to you to explain what *dualism* is. Why is it contrary to a properly held Christian understanding of creation? What are some practical examples of it, and why are they damaging?

FRAN, CONTINUING OUR DISCUSSION of creation *ex nihilo,* I now want to equip you to understand one of the most challenging questions that Christians face: If God created the Universe *ex nihilo,* and there is evil in the Universe that God created, wouldn't that mean that God created evil? First, let's begin by considering the implications of this question. If the universe contained evil as perceived by humanity, it would imply that the evil we perceive is judged by a standard we also perceive as right and good. And rightly so, because the Christian believes that the universe created by God is not just good, but very good (Genesis 1:31)! Although there is evil in the world, the Christian view is that this is a good world that has gone wrong but still retains the biblical record of its goodness, or, as C. S. Lewis said, "the memory" of the good world that God created.[45]

On the other hand, dualism holds that there are two independent powers at the back of everything, and that one of the powers is good and the other power is evil. In this sense, dualism would contend that the universe is a battlefield engaged in an endless war. The two opposing forces of "good" and "evil" are both in themselves eternal realities that are in opposition to each other.[46]

Needless to say, dualism is a direct challenge to the Christian doctrine of creation, which holds that there is no ultimate reality other than God. To say that there are two eternal realities would undermine our belief that God created the universe out of "no-thing" and that God is the independent, Supreme, and only infinite reality that there is. For dualism to have any standing, the Christian would be forced to concede that God must have brought the universe into existence through the use of some preexisting material. This was a view

---

[44] Erickson, p. 348.

[45] Lewis, p. 33.

[46] Erickson, p. 346.

prominent in early Greek thought that taught a particular type of matter–form dualism. This type of dualism held that creation consisted in a force (either someone or something) bringing together the "form" or "idea" of something out of the "matter" that was unformed or unstructured.

However, for the Christian, this view will not suffice. God did not "form together" matter that was preexistent. Rather, God created both the form and the matter *ex nihilo*. The Bible is very clear on this, teaching that everything came from God and that at the time of creation, God declared that it was good (Genesis 1:10, 12, 18, 21, 25). Then, at the completion of the totality of creation, God declared that everything "was very good" (Genesis 1:31). As distinct from dualism, which could contend that part of the "matter" from which God created was originally evil in nature, the Christian holds that there was nothing evil within God's creation in the first place.[47]

Fran has a lot of friends in the gym who argue for the "big bang" theory of creation. She asks you to explain the different theological theories about how the creation account of the Bible can be reconciled with the geological record.

———————

FRAN, THE BIBLE STATES that in addition to creating the universe *ex nihilo,* God did all His creative work in six days (Genesis 1:31). According to the Hebrew term *yom,* it had long been presumed that each "day of God's work" was equal to a 24-hour period. Starting with this foundational application and understanding of the term *yom,* Archbishop James Ussher used biblical genealogies to arrive at a date of 4004 BC for the creation of the earth.

This would mean that creation is no more than approximately 6,000 years old.[48] This conclusion held merit until the development of modern geology, which started to create tension between science and theology in regard to the age of creation.

Therefore, a question that both science and theology now contemplate has arisen directly from the biblical record of God's creative work. One approach to investigating the age and nature of the earth outside the realm of the Bible has been to study the age of the earth through analyzing radioactive materials.

[47] Erickson, p. 346.
[48] Erickson, p. 350.

From these tests, there is a consensus among most scientists that the earth is approximately 5 or 6 billion years old.[49] How then can we reconcile the scientific and biblical account of the earth's age? Six different approaches have been put forth that we will now explore.

The first is the "gap theory," which holds that there was an original creation of the earth billions of years ago (the creation described in Genesis 1:1). However, something happened that resulted in the original creation of Genesis 1:1, subsequently becoming empty and void, as described in Genesis 1:2. Following the void, God re-created the earth a few thousand years ago, populating it with all the species the world now contains. The scientific age of the earth and fossil records showing creation over a longer period are to be attributed to the first creation.

The second theory, the "flood theory," views the earth as only a few thousand years old. At the time of Noah, the earth was covered by a flood that resulted in waves with a force of 1,000 miles an hour. The force of the waves deposited and solidified rock under such tremendous pressure that the several billion years that geologists say would ordinarily be required to create the earth was instead accomplished in a much shorter period of time.[50]

The third theory is the "ideal time" theory. This is a novel proposition that reverse engineers the "age" of Adam at the time of his creation. The theory suggests that when Adam was created (distinctly different from being born) he was the ideal age that God intended him to be. Starting with this basic and seemingly self-evident proposition, the theory then extends or "reverse engineers" this principle by arguing that each part of creation was likewise developed at an "ideal age."

The fourth theory, the "age-day theory," takes a closer and more systematic view of the Hebrew word *yom*. Although this word frequently did in fact refer to a 24-hour period, it was not strictly limited to that definition. In this sense, *yom* could also refer to an "epoch," or much longer period. In other words, the age-day theory holds that God created the universe in a series of acts over long periods of time.[51]

---

[49] Erickson, p. 350.

[50] Erickson, p. 351.

[51] Erickson, p. 351.

The "pictorial-day" theory (also called the literary framework) holds that the days of creation should be understood as more a matter of logical structuring than strictly a chronological ordering. In other words, the biblical author arranged the material in a grouping that took the form of six periods.[52]

The final theory, the "revelatory-day" theory, seems to suggest that the "story of creation" was revealed to the author on six different days. However, the days of revelation to the author do not necessarily limit creation to being made within six days. This theory holds that although the actual creation of the universe may have taken much longer, the revelation of that creation to the biblical author took place in six twenty-four hour periods of time.[53]

Although all these theories have points of strength in their favor, they also all have their difficulties. Fran, I am currently rather fascinated by the ideal-time theory. Although the biblical record does not prohibit the idea that Adam could have been an infant at birth, it seems to suggest that Adam was already an adult at the "ideal-age" God intended him to be. For example, at the time of Adam's creation, he was of the "ideal-age" that included a level of development and maturity necessary to be assigned the duty of caring for and working in the garden (Genesis 2:15). In addition, Adam was of sufficient maturity and "ideal-age" to have the awesome responsibility of naming the wild animals (Genesis 2:19–20).

Similar to the "ideal-age" of Adam at the time of his creation, when Eve was created, she was brought forth at the ideal age for her life. In addition, she was also the "ideal-age" to be a compatible and suitable partner to Adam. Thus, the two human beings first created by God were brought forth into the created order at their ideal-age time. If this were the case, it becomes foreseeable that God could have extended this "ideal-age" quality of His design to the rest of creation.

---

[52] Erickson, p. 351.
[53] Erickson, p. 351.

Fran is having a hard time understanding how evil can exist in the world that God created. She wants you to help her make sense of it all.

————————————

FRAN, ONE OF THE more complex and challenging questions of theology is making sense of the inherent problem of evil in the world. It is challenging because evil would seem to undermine already established doctrines of God, mainly His omnipotence and His goodness. For if God is the omnipotent creator and sustainer of all things, then by extension of this very attribute, wouldn't God be responsible for sustaining and upholding evil? And how can we harmonize the doctrine of God's goodness alongside the evil so evident on the front page of every major newspaper, in addition to our social media feeds?

These problems are also complex, for even narrative accounts from the Bible would seem to suggest that God's wrath is in itself evil (Numbers 11:33). In other words, would not some of the actions of God, if performed by a being other than God, be likewise judged as evil? This type of evil is often referred to as *moral evil* and involves the choice processes of individual free moral agents. Moral evil would account for war, rampage shootings, abuse, and a whole host of additional crimes. On the other hand, there is what we could refer to as "natural evil," which is not the result of human action, but rather an aspect of nature that seems to be in direct opposition to the basic tenet of general human welfare. This type of evil is commonly referred to in the media as "natural disasters" that seem to be inseparable from God's creation: Earthquake, fires, and massive storms are at the top of the list. Are not these acts of nature an extension of God's creation and therefore attributable to Him as the solely responsible party for catastrophic human death and injury?[54]

David Hume, the author of the book *Dialogues Concerning Natural Religion,* contended that if God is willing to prevent evil, but simply not able to, then He is by implication not an omnipotent God. On the other hand, if He is able, and therefore truly omnipotent, but not willing to confront evil, then He is malevolent. And for the Christian who holds that God is both omnipotent and good, how can the persistence of evil be rectified?[55]

---

[54] The distinction between natural and moral evil was identified in *Christian Theology*, p. 385.
[55] Erickson, p. 384.

These are indeed challenging questions that have been the subject of debate among our world's most esteemed theologians. Fran, believe me when I say that just like you, I am often at a loss for words in explaining evil, especially considering my encounter with it on a fairly regular basis in my law enforcement profession. However, in the micro-context of law enforcement, I have noticed a theme: in the long run, what victims of crime often perceive as an unexplainable and unjustifiable evil is somehow fashioned into conditions for their betterment. When we apply this insight from the micro-context to the biblical account, we see a very similar pattern. Perhaps this was best expressed in the account of Joshua, who, after having been sold into slavery by his brothers, was able to say, "You intended to harm me, but God intended it for good" (Genesis 50:20).

On the surface, this verse seems to be self-contradicting. How can something be intended for harm and at the same time also intended for good? An illustration from my law enforcement career might be of assistance: officers are taught self-defense techniques that often involve martial arts movements intended to redirect an assailant's attack. Here is the series of events that unfolds: the assailant intends to strike the officer, but the officer redirects their assault and uses the assailant's force to ultimately off-balance them and then apprehend them. The assailant's apprehension prevents any further harm to himself, the officer, or the public. In this sense, what the assailant intended for harm was ultimately used for good! Now, if we were to extend this illustration and make God the "master martial artist," then He becomes the One capable of redirecting everything we perceive as evil (both natural and moral evil) in such a way that it becomes the very means of doing good.[56]

Ultimately, the Christian holds that in the long run, God is working out everything in a pattern for good for those that love Him (Romans 8:28). In this sense, although humans have free will, and may use that will in a fashion that is against God's intention for creation, God can still work every "present suffering" into a "glory that will be revealed to us" (Romans 8:18). Fran, here is an analogy that might help you make sense of this concept. Imagine an ocean liner full of passengers that departs from England with a destination of New York. On board this mighty vessel, the passengers are free to exercise the

---

[56] Erickson, p. 374.

independence of their will. This use of free will may be in conformity to God's intention for creation or in opposition to it. However, while the passengers are exercising their free will, the ocean liner is steadily bound for its predetermined final destination. In this sense, God is the ocean liner and humanity is bound up within His Will as He progresses history in the direction He has predetermined.[57] Our "New York" final destination is an "eternal glory" that will far outweigh any suffering we experience in the world (2 Corinthians 4:17)!

Fran wants to know about the recent development of demythologization in the context of angels and demons in the Bible.

FRAN, THE NEW TESTAMENT scholar Rudolf Bultmann created some waves in the theological community when he proposed that much of the New Testament was written under a unique mythological worldview. Bultmann argued that the original biblical writers believed that reality was structured on a three-level or three-tiered worldview, which included the upper level of heaven; the middle level of earth; and the level beneath the world, which was hell. Within each of these distinct "levels" or "tiers" were specific beings that resided within their realms. God and the angels presided in the upper level, human beings in the middle, and demons and the devil in the bottom. The middle level, where humans presided, was greatly impacted and human actions were often the direct result of angelic and demonic beings' intervention.[58]

Bultmann theorized that to the biblical authors, human sickness was the cause of demonic possession and a return to wellness was the result of casting the demon out of the individual. Bultmann argued that the biblical authors were writing to an audience that shared this understanding of reality. However, the modern Christian is no longer bound by the same understanding of reality. Bultmann therefore concluded that when the Christian reads the Bible today, they should not necessarily and outrightly discard the myths of demon possession and angelic intervention. Rather, the Christian today simply

---

[57] A similar illustration and analogy was identified in C. S. Lewis's book *Mere Christianity.*
[58] Erickson, p. 69.

needs to reinterpret them and find meaning and application within a more culturally appropriate and modern understanding.[59]

In the context of angels, Bultmann contended that there was nothing special or unique (and therefore Divinely revelatory) about their prominence in Scripture. Bultmann explained that the New Testament authors were simply reflecting the popularly held ideas and beliefs of their day, which we can now understand to be a myth. In this sense, Bultmann created what could be described as a finely tuned hermeneutic in which the modern Bible reader reinterprets all accounts of the supernatural presence of an angel or demon as merely a myth.

For our purposes of reading the Bible today, I think it is best to apply the more universal hermeneutic of understanding angels and demons within the context intended by the original authors. They felt strongly that angels were present within the world and were oftentimes sent by God to "serve those who will inherit salvation" (Hebrews 1:14). In addition to angels serving mankind, the Apostle Paul felt certain that our struggle is not against "flesh and blood" but rather against "spiritual forces of evil in the heavenly realms" (Ephesians 6:12).

Furthermore, and perhaps most importantly, we should take special note that Jesus specifically chose to heal people by casting out demons but did not necessarily attribute all illness to demonic activity (Luke 13:32). In those cases where Jesus determined the cause of the illness to be demonic possession, He cast the demon out and returned the person to health (Matthew 17:15–18). However, in other instances of addressing the same type of illness, Jesus did not make any mention of demons (Matthew 4:24). Therefore, we could conclude that the biblical authors, and in particular Jesus, were specific and intentional in their reference to the work of demons. In this sense, it is best to read the Bible with the same perspective and understanding of angelic and demonic activity that the original authors and audience held.

---

[59] Erickson, p. 69.

PART TWO

THE HOLY ONE OF GOD

CHAPTER FOUR

HUMANITY AND SIN

CHAPTER SUMMARY:

THE CHRISTIAN VIEW OF HUMANITY is that a human being is a creature made in the image of a loving God. This means that human beings have no independent existence outside of God. In other words, human beings "came into being" because God willed that they should exist and independently acted to bring them to life. Without God, human beings would not be alive, and everything that humans have derives from God. Furthermore, the image of God in a human being is essential to understanding what makes us human. Sin within the human race is any evil action or motive that is in opposition to God. The Bible plainly teaches that sin is a failure to let God be God, or to place something or someone other than God in the place of God's supremacy.

Fran wants to know about the different theories of humanity and human origin.

———————————

FRAN, UNDERSTANDING THE ORIGINS of mankind and the doctrine of humanity is foundational to understanding the nature of God and the totality of His creation. In fact, because mankind is made in the image and likeness of God (Genesis 1:26–27), we are in a unique and privileged position to learn something about God as we simultaneously learn something about ourselves. I want to share with you five different theories for our human origins in addition to the specific model that I think is most compelling to teach within the gym. Before we begin, consider for a moment the greater implications of the word *origin* as opposed to *beginning*. The word *origin* implies far more than simply the *beginning* of someone's life. *Origin* carries the more significant and soul-shaping connotation of the *purpose of each individual's existence.*[60] In other words, theology is far more concerned with *what purpose* lies behind each individual's presence on earth, rather than only narrowly focusing *on how* humans came to be here (Psalm 8:4–6). The Bible teaches that the "big picture" of humanity's origin is that a loving, wise, and all-powerful God created the human race to love Him and enjoy a relationship with Him (John 6:40, 15:5; 1 John 3:1).

The first view of human origins is called *naturalistic evolution* and deals primarily with understanding the human species apart from a supernatural explanation.[61] According to this view, all that was needed for the existence of the human race is atoms in motion. These atoms in motion, in addition to a combination of time and chance, were sufficient to fashion what we currently see in the human race. Needless to say, if we are to take seriously the Word of God in the creation account of Genesis (Genesis 1:26–27; 2:7; cf. 1 Corinthians 11:7; James 3:9), then we immediately see this view of humanity is in direct opposition to God's direct and personal involvement in the creation of humans.

———————————

[60] Millard Erickson, *Christian Theology* (Grand Rapids, MI: Baker Academic, 2013), p. 439.
[61] Erickson, p.h 443.

The second theory of human origins is called *fiat creationism* and holds that in one direct act, God brought into being virtually instantaneously everything that exists.[62] This view implies two unique features. The first is the relative immediacy and "newness" of what occurred in creation. The other feature of this view is God's direct and divine work in the creation of everything within the universe. Rather than employing previously existing material, God created everything as a "fresh start." When God created humanity, He did so in an entirely unique and direct way. Furthermore, and along the same lines of the "fresh start" concept, new species (to include the human race) did not arise as modifications or alterations of an existing species, but were also "fresh starts."[63]

The third theory of human origins is called *deistic evolution* and holds that God began the process of evolution and, in a modern sense of the word, "programmed" the laws of creation that subsequently resulted in producing everything that currently exists. Another way of understanding this theory is that God, in His role of the "master programmer," designed the universe with everything needed for continued and perpetual development and then withdrew from active involvement.[64] From a theological perspective rooted in the Bible, it is important to note that *deistic evolution* holds that with the exception of the very beginning of matter, there is no direct activity of a personal and loving God during the ongoing creative process.[65]

The fourth theory of human origins is called *theistic evolution* and holds that in addition to God's bringing the first humans to life (similar to what *deistic evolution* holds), He continued to work internally and directly with His creation for His purposes and goals. This view holds that God also works supernaturally within His creation, but when He does, God utilizes already existing materials. For example, *theistic evolution* would teach that although God created the first human, He did so by using an existing creature.[66]

---

[62] Erickson, p. 444.

[63] Erickson, p. 444.

[64] Erickson, p. 445.

[65] Erickson, p. 445.

[66] Erickson, p. 446.

God created a human soul and "infused it into one of the higher primates."[67] In the process, God transformed this former creature into the first human. In this sense, while God did in fact create the spiritual nature of Adam, Adam's physical nature was the process and product of evolution. Needless to say, there is no difficulty reconciling this view with the scientific data.

The final theory of the origins of humanity is referred to as *progressive creationism*. This view sees the creative work of God as a combination of *de novo* (created afresh) and possessive operation.[68] In the context of *de novo* acts of creation, God did not simply make use of previously existing forms of life. Rather, as in the case of mankind, God brought to life an entirely new creature. This means that God specifically created Adam's *physical and spiritual* nature. Yet on the other hand, between God's acts of *de novo* creation, progressive creationism gives room to the idea that various species of God's first creation developed through evolution. For example, in a *de novo* act of creation, God created the first member (or species) of the cat family, and then over time the various species of the family continued to develop through the process of evolution.[69]

Fran, I contend that the most biblically and theologically viable and compelling theory of human origin is progressive creationism. For example, when God decided to create the first human, He did so directly and completely (Genesis 1:26–28; 2:7; 1 Corinthians 11:7; James 3:9). In other words, God did not create Adam out of a lower creature of an existing form of life. Nor did God solely create Adam's spiritual nature and infuse it into an already existing physical form of life. The Bible teaches that God made Adam from "the dust of the ground" (Genesis 2:7a). Then God "breathed into his nostrils the breath of life" (Genesis 2:7b), which resulted in Adam becoming a living being. In other words, God uniquely and supremely created both Adam's physical and spiritual nature. The fact that God personally created the physical and spiritual qualities of humanity gives prudence to the theological idea that He is also immensely concerned with the totality of our salvation, including both our body and our soul. It also prepares us for understanding the magnitude of God's decision to become a human being in order to save us (John 3:16).

---

[67] Erickson, p. 446.

[68] Erickson, p. 446.

[69] A similar example was used by Erickson, p. 446.

Fran wants you to explain the substantial, relational, and functional views on the *Imago Dei* in addition to the one you think is most compelling to teach within the gym.

FRAN, THERE ARE SEVERAL ways to understand what it means to say that humans are "made in the image of God" (Genesis 1:27). Each is unique and serves to paint a picture for the awesome implications of being an image bearer of our Creator. I want to share with you three traditional views of what the *Imago Dei* means (the image of God) in addition to two rather novel and more modern concepts. Finally, I want to explain the position that I find most compelling.

The first view is referred to as the *substantive view* and holds that human beings have a unique and definite characteristic or quality within our makeup; this same characteristic is what makes us "the image of God." In this sense, some people from the *substantive* camp would argue that the image of God in mankind is an aspect of our physicality or bodily makeup.[70] At the other end of the spectrum, but also from the substantive view, is the idea that the image of God in mankind has more to do the faculty of our reason (our mind).

The *relational view* of *Imago Dei* focuses more on a quality of mankind that is within our human nature. In this sense, the focus shifts from something substantial about our imaging God and instead brings attention to the manner in which humanity is intended to experience God within the context of a relationship.[71]

The relational view is also unique (and arguably more important) because it holds that the image of God within humans is best understood through a study of the *perfect person* of Jesus Christ who Himself is the "exact representation of God's being" (Hebrews 1:3). The relational view would also stress the importance of biblical revelation for understanding humanity. Only by studying the Word of God can we come to know humanity as originally created and intended, and Jesus is the fullest form of that revelation (Colossians 1:15). This also means that rather than imaging God in a structural manner, the image of God is more a matter of one's relationship to God as made possible through faith in Christ (John 14:6).

---

[70] Erickson, p. 460.

[71] Erickson, p. 464.

Finally, we come to the *functional view* of the *Imago Dei.* This view supports the idea that the image of God consists in something that we do. In this sense, humans image God in an objective and tangible way. The proponents of this view draw an association between being made in the image of God (Genesis 1:26a) and the subsequent *functional command* to "rule over the fish of the sea...." (Genesis 1:26b). The implication of Genesis 1:26 is that the exercise of rule and dominion is considered to be the image of God.[72]

Although these three views are widely held as foundational to understanding the *Imago Dei,* I want to share with you two additional more modern and rather novel concepts. The first is referred to as *divine presence* as illustrated by the theologian Marc Cortez. This view holds that the presence of God in humanity cannot be a function of something the human necessarily does (i.e., functional view), nor does it mean the image is reflected in a unique human capacity (i.e., substantive view). Cortez argues that such capacities or functions cannot define the image of God, since God is not dependent on mankind to manifest His presence.[73] In other words, God created human persons to be the physical means by which He would display and manifest His divine presence in the world, but He is not necessarily restricted to making His presence known only through humans. The *divine presence* view also holds that because humans are the primary means by which God manifests His presence, then the *Imago Dei* is intimately linked to the Holy Spirit.[74] This is significant because of the connection between God's presence and the Spirit throughout the Old Testament.

The final view I want to share with you is what we could refer to as *free imagers,* which was made popular by the work of theologian Michael Heiser. This view holds that the *Imago Dei* is not some unique attribute or ability within humanity. Rather, *it is a status* conferred by God to all humans, which mainly includes the responsibility of representing (or being an image bearer of) God. The attributes that God gives humanity are the *means to imaging,* but not the image status itself. In this sense, God's original intent was to equip and

---

[72] Erickson, p. 466.

[73] Marc Cortez, *Resourcing Theological Anthropology* (Grand Rapids, MI: Zondervan, 2017), p. 109.

[74] Cortez, p. 112.

arm His imagers with both the will (relational) and ability (functional) to carry out His decrees and to "extend Eden over all the earth." [75]

Fran, of all the views of the *Imago Dei* that I have shared with you, I believe the most compelling is the substantive view. The fundamental biblical reference for understanding the *Imago Dei* is Genesis 1:26–27, and this particular scripture holds that humanity's ability to image God is something unique to the fashion in which God created mankind. The words "image" and "likeness" seem to suggest that the image is satisfied in the way that God created us, and not continent upon something that we necessarily do. Along these same lines, it is important to note that, "although people look at the outward appearance, God looks at the heart" (2 Samuel 16:7). The application of this verse in the context of imaging God is that the *Imago Dei* refers to something that humans *are* rather than something that humans *have* or *do* (i.e., the "outward appearance").

By virtue of being a human, one is in the image of God.[76] Although exercising dominion and experiencing relationship are certainly very closely linked with imaging God, they are not the image itself. In fact, it is only through the *substantive view* of imaging God that dominion and relationship can then take place. In other words, although relationship and dominion (to include a human's ability to fulfill God's purposes for them) are important, *it is the image itself* that embodies the qualities required for the relationships and functions to take place.

---

[75] Michael Heiser, *The Unseen Realm* (Bellingham, WA: Lexham Press), p. 59.

[76] Erickson, p. 470.

Fran is well aware that in the Sport of CrossFit, there is a great emphasis placed upon the physical capacity of the human body. She is curious about what the "physical and spiritual construction" of a human being is.

FRAN, WHEN WE BEGIN to study and contemplate what a human being is, we are in fact asking a series of interrelated questions. For example, we ask the question of origin, in addition to meditating on the unique purpose and function of humanity. Another question that we must consider, and the focus of what I want to share with you here, is the constitution and makeup of the human being.

One view of the human constitution is referred to as *trichotomism*. This view holds that the human being is composed of three elements: a physical body, a soul, and a spirit. Certain passages from Scripture would seem to support this view. For example, in 1 Thessalonians 5:23, Paul prays that the "whole spirit, soul and body" would be kept blameless. This would suggest that the human is in fact made up of these three distinct parts, namely the "spirit, soul, and body."

The *dichotomist* view holds that the human is composed of only two elements: a material body and an immaterial component associated with the soul of the spirit.[77] This view further holds that the physical part of the human (their body) dies and returns to the ground. The spiritual part of the human, being immaterial, survives death. This immortal nature of the human is what sets them apart from all other creatures.[78] Scripture passages to support this view are numerous (Luke 12:4; 1 Corinthians 15:50) and include Christ's words on the cross, "Father, into your hands I commit my spirit" (Matthew 27:50; John 19:30; Luke 23:46).

The final view of the human constitution is referred to as *monism*. This view holds that humans are not to be thought of as existing in separate parts or entities. Rather, humans are a "radical unity" and must be treated and ministered to as such.[79] In the *monistic* view, to be human is to have a body, and the idea that a human can somehow continue to exist without one is not compatible with sound reason. In this view, it is understood that in the biblical

---

[77] Erickson, p. 478.

[78] Erickson, p. 478.

[79] Erickson, p. 481.

conception, a human being is a psychophysical unity, in other words, "flesh animated by the soul."[80]

Although these three views are the most common, there is one additional view of the human constitution that I want to bring to your attention. This view is referred to as *conditional unity* and has some unique contributions to make to our understanding of what makes a human. At the fundamental level, conditional unity holds that the "normal state" of a human is an embodied and unitary being. At death, however, the material body of the human decomposes while the immaterial aspect of the human lives on. In this sense, a human is a "unitary compound of material and immaterial elements" that are not always distinguishable.[81] However, this unity is also dissolvable, and this dissolution takes place at death. Yet this is not the end of the story, for at the resurrection the "compound of the body" will be formed again, and the immaterial (the soul) will once more become inseparably attached to it.

Fran, of the views discussed here, I am most in favor of the model of conditional unity. I believe that a human beings spiritual condition cannot be dealt with independently of their physical and mental conditions, and vice versa. In our walk with Jesus, we must remember that he came to save every part of us (1 Thessalonians 5:23)! In other words, every part of what makes us who we are—our body, our mind, our soul, our spirit—it is all precious to God. In the incarnation, Jesus became fully human—just like we are—because he wanted to redeem the *whole and totality of what we are* (Luke 19:10; Hebrews 2:5–18)

---

[80] Erickson, p. 482.
[81] Erickson, p. 492.

There is a lot of ethnic diversity and cultural background in the gym that Fran trains at. Fran wants to know what difference it makes to see human identity and sin from within a shame and honor society that is more dominant in the East compared to a guilt and innocence society more dominant in the West.

––––––––––––

FRAN, IN OUR CULTURE of the West, we tend to see things from within the context of guilt and innocence. Although this is particularly true in our country's legal system, the implications tend to run throughout our entire society. On the other hand, in Eastern cultures, there is much more emphasis placed upon shame and honor. Understanding our human identity and sense of sin from these two unique perspectives has immense implications for the way we share the Gospel of Jesus Christ.

The fundamental difference between shame-based and guilt-based cultures is that shame-based cultures tend to focus on external pressures from an individual or group, whereas guilt based cultures tend to focus more on internalized societal prohibitions and moral law. In other words, in the West, our understanding of right and wrong is internalized, whereas in the East, the same sense of right and wrong is predominantly the result of external pressure.[82]

The difference in the way we understand our human identity and sin within a shame-based culture, as opposed to one that is guilt based culture, is significant. In the west, sin would have the effect of creating a sense of internalized moral failure. In other words, even if no other person knew of my sin, I would nevertheless retain a "loss of innocence" and feeling of separation and alienation from God. Even apart from the ridicule of other people, I can still sense my own guilt and respond to it. On the other hand, in a shame-based culture, the same sinful act would result in a feeling of "loss of face" because I would view my sin as having resulted in a loss of standing or status within a group.[83] This means that reduced to the most fundamental differences, guilt tends to be inherently individualistic and private, whereas shame tends to be more corporate and public.

[82] Timothy Tennent, *Theology in the Context of World Christianity* (Grand Rapids, MI: Zondervan, 2007). p. 79.

[83] Tennent, p. 79.

Fran, let's look at how shame and guilt are portrayed within a particular account of the Bible. When Adam and Eve were first united in the Garden of Eden, they were "both naked and they felt no shame" (Genesis 2:25). This is a significant verse, for it tends to illustrate the fact that apart from sin, Adam and Eve were in the company of each other, and the company of God, in good standing, with a sense of both internal (guilt and innocence) and external (shame and honor) *Shalom* and righteousness. However, following their willful sin and disobedience to God, everything changed. Rather than walking with God in the garden, Adam hid from God because "he was naked and afraid" (Genesis 3:10). The effect of sin in Adam's life resulted *in both* his sense of guilt and moral failure (internalized) and loss of honor and shamefulness before God (externalized). This is extremely important to understand and is congruent with modern anthropological research on the effects of guilt and innocence, and shame and honor: no culture can be thought of *exclusively* one or the other.[84] This relatively recent anthological discovery is clearly evident in the case of Adam and Eve.

The account of Adam and Eve further reveals the interconnected effect that sin produces in our life. Following their sin, Adam and Eve felt a sense of guilt because they knew they had violated God's command. However, in addition to their sense of guilt, they also became self-aware of their nakedness, a sign of their vulnerability and shame. This means that sin produces *alienation from God and from other human beings*. When Adam and Eve realized they had sinned, they "made coverings for themselves" (Genesis 3:7) and tried to hide from God (Genesis 3:8). Their first act portrays the effect the sinful act had on their externalized sense of shame and honor (trying to *hide from each other*), and the latter act their internalized sense of guilt and innocence (trying to *hide from God.*)

Fran, lest you feel overwhelmed with the gravity of the effects of sin, let us now turn to the good news of Jesus Christ and His redemptive work on the cross. Jesus bore both our guilt (our willful disobedience to God) in addition to our shame (the fruit of a broken relationship).[85] From a cultural and missionary perspective, we must remember that in the Bible, responding to the Gospel of Jesus Christ was both an individual and corporate activity.

---

[84] Tennent, p. 101.

[85] Tennent, p. 100.

Although Jesus made it clear that seeking Him must take priority over one's own family and nation (Matthew 10:35–37), there are also examples of entire households and large groups of people turning to Christ (Acts 11:14; 18:8). This leads me to believe that the Gospel of Jesus Christ is not limited to social barriers or national boundaries. Jesus bore *our guilt* and *our shame*, and in the process he provides believers with a new identity (2 Corinthians 5:17) and participation in both His *righteousness* and *honor* (2 Corinthians 5:21).[86]

Fran tends to understand sin basically in the legal terms of a crime against God's Law. She asks you if any other models of God's Law might help her grasp the magnitude of sin in her life.

FRAN, ONE OF THE ways to understand sin is from the perspective of a crime against the law of God. For example, in the case of Adam and Eve, when they were told not to eat from the tree of the knowledge of good and evil (Genesis 2:17), they were given a "law" or "rule" by which God intended them to abide. In this sense, when Adam and Eve ate from the tree, they committed a sin because they violated the law and rule of God. The potential pitfall with understanding and defining sin solely in the context of a transgression of God's law is that we could mistakenly see the work of Jesus as only creating a legal loophole (i.e., Jesus gets me out of jail) and nothing else. Furthermore, our view and understanding of God would be limited to His mainly bureaucratic nature, and there would be an emphasis on trying to avoid sin (an impossibility) rather than relying on our savior Jesus Christ (our only hope for salvation, relationship, and adoption into the family of God).[87] Therefore, as important as the context of legal terminology is for understanding God's law, there are other concepts that I want to share with you.

Fran, when we broaden our understanding of sin, we begin to see the awesomeness of the saving grace of Jesus Christ. At the most fundamental level, sin causes separation and alienation from God. This was evident from the time our first parents sinned; their immediate reaction was to hide from God

---

[86] Tennent, p. 101.

[87] Dr. Adam Nigh, lecture, *Understanding the Nature of God*, Western Seminary, February 2020, TH502.

(Genesis 3:10). However, their sin also produced a sense of fear and shame and a need to shift blame away from themselves onto each other (Genesis 3:12), onto the tempter (Genesis 3:13), and even onto God Himself (Genesis 3:12). Furthermore, their sin produced a sense of intrinsic shame, which was evident in the newfound awareness of their nakedness (Genesis 3:7). From this perspective of sin, we begin to see that Jesus does far more then mitigate and reconcile our *legal transgressions* against God. Jesus restores our *very relationship* with God. He reconciles us with God (Acts 3:19; Romans 5:12) and adopts us back into His covenant family (Galatians 4:4–8).

You see, Fran, in many respects, the way we come to understand sin will influence the way we come to understand God and the saving work of Jesus Christ. Here are a few examples of what I mean: If sin is simply a matter of violating God's law, then my understanding of God could become that of Him as a tyrant, with Jesus serving the purpose of "bailing me out." Additionally, this could create a sense of "I can do whatever I want now that I'm saved" type of mentality. If my view of sin is a matter of making a mistake or going astray, then I could understand God as illusive, with Jesus serving the purpose of helping me find my way back.

When it all boils down, the important thing to remember, Fran, is that the essence of sin is anything that comes between you and God. In other words, sin is a failure to let God be God, and it is the placing of something else in the position of first place—a place that rightly belongs only to God.[88] The first thing you have to notice here, Fran, given this broad definition and understanding of sin, is how inescapable sin is in our life! To use the words of the Apostle Paul, "Sin is living inside of you" (Romans 7:17). That means that wherever you go, and whatever you do, you bring sin with you! And for this reason, avoiding sin is not a matter of trying harder, changing one's social conditions, having more knowledge, or acquiring more economic resources. You see, Fran, it's not a *thing* that can save you from your sin. Rather, it is a *person* who saves you and reconciles your relationship with God (2 Peter 1:11; Romans 6:23; Acts 4:12).

---

[88] Erickson, p. 530.

Fran asks you for help in understanding the results of sin in our various relationships. What are the effects of sin in her life and the life of her friends?

FRAN, PERHAPS ONE OF the best ways to understand the perilous effects of sin is to consider the result of sin in the various relationships we have in our life. By way of illustration, consider the implications of not achieving full hip extension in the basic "air squat" of the CrossFit program. If we equated "lack of hip extension in the squat" to a "sin," then every other movement that required hip extension would by default be subject to the same "sin." In other words, a variety of interrelated skills, such as gym jump, push-press, deadlift, kettlebell swing, and wallball, would be negatively affected. In this sense, the "sin" of a lack of hip extension would not exist in a vacuum, but would rather radiate throughout everything we did in the gym. And now as a showstopper, consider this: the founder of CrossFit once said, "Hip extension is necessary and sufficient for elite human performance." Therefore, the seemingly harmless "sin" of missing full hip extension in the squat would in fact jeopardize everything else we did in our athletic training.

If we press this illustration to the biblical effect of sin in our life, we begin to see the magnitude of the problem. Simply put, sin corrupts every area of our life and thus negatively affects every relationship as well. Even relationships we would normally associate as existing within God's covenant, such as marriage, are painfully tainted by sin. Fran, this means that sin negatively affects our relationship with God (Psalm 5:4; Isaiah 59:2), with other people (Numbers 32:23; Proverbs 4:23), with the world (Job 14:1–2), and even with ourselves (1 John 3:4; 1 Corinthians 6:19–20).

As depicted in the account of Adam and Eve, our sin creates a sense of shame and guilt in our relationship toward God (Genesis 3:10). Rather than enjoying fellowship with God, we try to "hide" from Him. Furthermore, in addition to a severed relationship with God, we attempt to shift the blame for our sin onto others, and even onto God Himself (Genesis 3:12). To use the modern axiom, once sin begins to roll, "it's all downhill from there!"

Fran, we have to come to grips with the severity of sin in our life and how sin negatively affects our relationship with others. If it is any indication just how bad things are, consider that in Hosea, God is said to actually hate sinners (Hosea 9:15; cf. Psalm 5:5). In other words, because God is unchanging, His reaction to sin in our life must always be one of disfavor.[89] To use another example from the CrossFit gym, consider the role of a judge in competition. By their very nature and inherent responsibility, the judge is categorically opposed to an athlete's failure to adhere to the standards of the workout. The dreaded "no rep" is a function of the athlete's behavior, not that of the judge. In the same sense, God is categorically opposed to our sinful nature, which is not a fault of His, but of our own!

In addition to negatively affecting my relationship with God, sin corrupts my relationship with other people. Sin creates a feeling of pride and sense of competition against others. This sense of competition inevitably leads to "fights and quarrels" with other people in an attempt to get what I want (James 4:1–2). Our society is also evidence of the tendency sin has to lead people to reject authority and to create a mindset of "us versus them." And perhaps worst of all, sin results in an inability to love God and to love others as I love myself (Mark 12:30–31).

Finally, at the polar extremes, sin affects my relationship with myself in addition to negatively affecting my relationship with the entire world. In my individual life, sin becomes much like a parasite, where it continues to feast upon more of its inherently corrupted nature. This means that one sin has the tendency to lead to another, in an ongoing and perpetual cycle of self-destruction. This was the case with David, who following his sin of adultery with Bathsheba, found it necessary to commit murder in an attempt to conceal what he had done (2 Samuel 11:1–22). At the other end of the spectrum, sin affects my relationship with the entire world, creating an unnecessary strain on everything that I do and a general sense of futility and fear (James 4:14; 1 Corinthians 3:19–20).

---

[89] Erickson, p. 550.

Fran, needless to say, sin is a major problem! Before we turn to the solution, let's revisit the illustration of "sin" in the CrossFit gym. Imagine if the athlete who was missing full hip extension had never been taught how to do a proper squat. In other words, they never had someone to model, or an example to follow. In this case, wouldn't their every attempt at a proper squat be difficult at best, and entirely impossible at worst? And because of their continual failure at "getting it right," what would their relationship be like with the judge, who continued to "no rep" their every attempt?

The good news is that in the theological sense, the judge also wants to be our savior—or in the case of the CrossFit studio, our coach. God knows that humanity's ability to "get it right" independent of Him is simply impossible. However, because God loves us, He makes a way for us to enter into a loving relationship with Him. And what's even more awesome is that this relationship is not a matter of us trying harder, nor is it a matter of "more practice" or any other self-meritorious attempt at getting it right. Rather, it is the free gift of grace through faith in Jesus Christ that releases us from our sinful nature and joins us into a new life in Christ (2 Corinthians 5:17).

Fran has heard some confusing information about Pelagianism. She wants to know the implications of this diversion from traditional Christian theology and why it has been considered heresy.

FRAN, ONE OF THE fundamental tenets of the Christian faith is that apart from the free gift of grace through faith in Jesus Christ, mankind is unable to save themselves from the detrimental effects of sin (Romans 3:10–18). In other words, because of mankind's fallen state, it's not that we need a great spiritual teacher, a great guru, or even a great set of spiritual "self-help" principles to follow. Rather, we need a savior. As disciples of Jesus Christ, we must guard ourselves against the illusion that we can proceed on the path independent of the one who we are following.

The Bible is abundantly clear that all humans are sinners. Although there are numerous examples that we could choose from (1 John 1:8; Ecclesiastes 7:20), consider the words of Paul in his letter to the Romans: "For all have sinned and fall short of the glory of God" (Romans 3:23) and "There is no one righteous, not even one" (Romans 3:10). Not only are humans sinners, but we actually *inherit our sinful nature at birth.* Paul explained this when he wrote that "sin entered the world through one man, and death through sin, and in this way death came to all people, because all sinned" (Romans 5:12). This means that our very nature as humans is an inclination toward sin, rather than away from it. And this is precisely why we need a savior. Apart from Jesus Christ, no amount of willpower, knowledge, or "self-help" can position us into right standing with God.

One of the proponents for the idea that we could in fact achieve right standing with God and live a life of perfect obedience to Him was a British monk named Pelagius.[90] Pelagius was concerned that there was an unnecessarily negative view of human nature. In other words, if humanity believed that they were born into a corrupted state of sin, what hope was there for good and decent behavior? Therefore, Pelagius emphasized that humans have free will, and that this state of fully activated free will allowed mankind to operate independently of controlling influences of the universe. This view, in addition to his argument that every human's soul was created specially by God for each individual (and was therefore untainted by any historical sin or guilt), motivated Pelagius to contend that there was no need for a special working of God's grace within the heart of every individual.[91]

Fran, notice that this view seems to suggest that salvation by works is *possible*—a position that Jesus Christ Himself adamantly taught was *impossible* (John 14:6; cf. Ephesians 2:8–9). And to make matters even worse for Pelagius, because he held that we are not sinners at birth, salvation by works was not an escape from sin that presently bound us; rather our good works maintained our inherently "right status and good standing" before God.[92] In other words, by our own effort and accomplishment, we are able to keep from falling into a sinful condition. This would also seem to suggest that if salvation were simply

---

[90] Erickson, p. 575.

[91] Erickson, p. 576.

[92] Erickson, p. 576.

a matter of "trying harder," Jesus would not have needed to die for our sins. This is a position that the Bible holds was the very mission of Christ's life on earth (John 3:16; 2 Corinthians 5:21; 1 Peter 2:21–25).

Fran, needless to say, the position of Pelagius is completely contradictory to what the Bible teaches and was ultimately condemned as heresy. As Paul explained in his letter to the Romans, all humans have a natural inclination toward sin because we are born into a corrupted and sinful nature. In this sense, our natural state is one of sin—not the absence of it (Romans 5:12–19). The good news, however, is that in the same way the sin of one person brought guilt and sin to all of humanity (Romans 5:12), the perfect obedience of one person brings grace and salvation to all of humanity (Romans 5:15–21). When we put our faith and hope in Jesus Christ, we are delivered from our sin through a new life in Christ (Romans 7:25).

CHAPTER FIVE

CHRISTOLOGY

CHAPTER SUMMARY:

IN THE HISTORY OF the Church, the most heated topic of debate has been understanding the person and work of Jesus Christ. The deity of Jesus is at the very pinnacle of controversy concerning the Christian faith. While some have overemphasized the deity of Christ at the neglect of His humanity, others have failed in the reverse order. The implications of the deity of Christ are immense. Christians can have real, direct, and personal knowledge of God through a relationship with Jesus (John 14:9). Furthermore, because Jesus was not merely a finite human, but rather an infinite God, His death is sufficient for all sinners who have ever lived.

Fran has heard some people in the gym talking about the "quest for the historical Jesus" movement. She asks you what this is all about and if there is any value in this movement to shaping her theology.

FRAN, IN OUR DAY and age, it is seldom that we come across people who outright reject the *historical* person of Jesus Christ. Evidence for this claim is plentiful—even the popular book of positive quotations *The Book of Courage* includes sayings of Jesus, complete with the historical association of his birthplace: "Jesus of Nazareth."[93] This is significant in two ways. On one hand, we should be encouraged to see that the words of Jesus are increasingly entering the mainstream. However, the words apart from accepting Jesus Himself as Lord and God are akin to simply parroting the wisdom words of any other spiritual teacher or guru.

Therefore, the great chasm of division begins when we attempt to determine the *deity* of Jesus Christ rather than His *historical and human* life. In this sense, the challenge we have in sharing the Gospel is that people we encounter may be very inclined to adopt the teachings of Jesus (after all, who would argue with the premise of the Golden Rule from Mark 12:31: *Love your neighbor as you love yourself?*) but to simultaneously reject the teacher himself.[94]

As a case in point, consider such popular books as *The Da Vinci Code*. Although this book did not claim to be factual or historical, it nevertheless impacted people's curiosity and imagination about Jesus Christ in a profound—albeit completely distorted—way. In fact, the book even became a national bestselling premier movie! This leads me to believe that both the "producer" and the "consumer" are interested in attempting to reconstruct the life, words, and teachings of Jesus.

Fran, it is important to understand that the manner in which these attempts have been made are disturbing—it's as if people have tried to "backdoor" or "sidestep" the biblical revelation of Jesus and create something more agreeable to *who they think Jesus is*. In this sense, the problem is that in the attempt to reconstruct the life and teachings of Jesus, very often the people reconstructing

---

[93] Matthew Kelly, *The Courage Book* (Cincinnati, OH: Beacon Publishing, 2003), p. 40.
[94] Erickson, p. 616.

Jesus create a figure strangely similar to the personal convictions that they bring to the table.[95] In other words, they energize an *idea about Jesus* already stored in their mind and then bring this idea to life, finding "evidence" to support their previously held beliefs.

One of the most concrete examples of the attempts to re-create or "find" the historical Jesus has been referred to as the "Search for the Historical Jesus Movement." The original "search" began in the nineteenth century, although the most recent is our best case study. In 1985, a group of scholars under the leadership of Robert Funk and John Crossan began to meet and lead group discussions about the actual words and deeds of Jesus. The group's goal was to determine by democratic vote the degree of authenticity of a particular passage. Although perhaps originally formulated with good intentions, this group tended to give more credence to the Gospel of Thomas rather than the four traditional Gospels of Matthew, Mark, Luke, and John. Needless to say, this is problematic and only increased the likelihood that the group created a false notion of Jesus that was more akin to the personal convictions of the researchers themselves.[96]

Another challenge with the "historical search" method is that many engaged in the search have a general expectation that the Jesus they find will be different than the Christ who appears in the four Gospels and the theological writings of the Apostle Paul.[97] The "historical search" movement has tended to sidestep, coincidently avoid, or altogether dismiss the deity of Christ in order to produce a Jesus who was basically a good moral teacher, and a Jewish Rabbi who embodied great spiritual truth.[98] However, He was not the miracle working and eternal Second Person of the Trinity. Needless to say, the product of this reasoning is dangerously akin to the modern Yogic teaching that Jesus was indeed a great man yet in the same category of other great men such as Lord Krishna or the Buddha.

---

[95] Erickson, p. 616.

[96] Erickson, p. 616.

[97] Erickson, p. 604.

[98] Erickson, p. 604.

Fran, my position on the matter is that searching for a "historical Jesus" is what we do when we faithfully study the Bible. In the Bible, we come "face to face" with the Word of God in addition to the incredible and miraculous account of the "Word becoming flesh" in the person of Jesus Christ (John 1:1–3, 14). In other words, if you want to know Jesus, just open your Bible! There is nothing wrong with applying sound principles and methodologies of historical research into the life and teaching of Jesus. However, we must ensure ourselves that the basis for our understanding of Jesus is made through a theologically systematic approach and that the mosaic of Jesus that we create is a composite of the biblical revelation found in the four Gospels in addition to the epistles of all of the other great biblical authors.

Fran is interested in the difference between studying the life of Jesus "from above" as opposed to "from below." Can you teach Fran more about the implications of these different approaches?

FRAN, WHEN WE ARE presented with an opportunity to share the Gospel with someone, we must carefully determine the strategy we are going to take. Some people will foreseeably be more inclined to listen and believe the historical evidences of Jesus's life and teachings. On the other hand, another person might not be as concerned with rational proof and would instead be more favorably disposed to hearing the Church's proclamation of Christ and reading from the Word of God. These two general strategies are referred to as "Christology from Above" and "Christology from Below." The position of "below" would tend to favor developing a picture of Jesus based on the historical facts of His life, what Jesus accomplished in history and what He continues to do in the world. On the other hand, the position of "above" would focus on the Church's proclamation regarding Christ and God's divine initiative in becoming a man.[99]

For greater clarity on these two theological positions, consider the following illustrations from within the context of the CrossFit studio. When a potential new athlete arrives at the doors of the gym, a Coach will need to

---

[99] Tennent, p. 108.

determine the manner in which they want to share the benefits of the training program. One approach, which we will call "CrossFit from below," would be to explain the science of the program. In other words, the Coach would focus their message on the chemical and hormonal changes in the muscle tissue of the body as a result of adhering to the methodology of moving large loads, a long distance, with as much speed as possible. An athlete with a predisposition to sound scientific facts, analysis, and "proof" would then access the validity of the Coach's claims, and make a decision to join the gym.

At the other end of the spectrum, the Coach may decide to explain all the intangible and more subjective benefits of the program, the joy of the community of CrossFit athletes, and the traditionally "preached message" that constantly varied functional movement at high intensity can change your life—just look inside the gym! In this sense, the potential athlete would make a decision not based on rational proof, but rather on the faithful testimony of the CrossFit Coach in addition to other members of the studio.

Fran, this analogy might help you understand the contribution of a theologian named Wolfhart Pannenberg, who was a proponent for a "Christology from Below" approach. Pannenberg realized that there were three significant problems with an "Above" approach: First, people today want rational proof for the *deity* of Christ, which implied that when sharing the Gospel, the deity of Christ cannot be presupposed. Second, the "Above" approach tends to neglect the historical features of Jesus of Nazareth, and His relationship to the Judaism of His day. Third, a true "Christology from Above" understanding of Jesus is only possible from the position of God Himself, not for mankind. From our perspective, we must begin "from below" and work our way up.[100]

It is important to note that for Pannenberg, history was unitary, not dualistic. According to Pannenberg, this meant that the life, teachings, and ministry of Jesus were included in every other type of event that ever occurred in human history. In this sense, Jesus is as much a part of human history as Abraham Lincoln, and therefore the same methods one could use to study Lincoln could be employed to study the life of Jesus Christ.

---

[100] Erickson, p. 610.

Of great importance to Pannenberg's argument for a "Christology from Below" approach to knowing Jesus was the Apostle Paul's first letter to the Church in Corinth, in which Paul provides a summation of the death and resurrection of Christ. In 1 Corinthians 15:1–11, Paul establishes specific evidences of Christ's life, but more significantly, Christ's death and resurrection. The death and resurrection of Jesus would validate that "Jesus was who he said he was." How were Jesus's claims proven? According to Pannenberg, the resurrection of Jesus, taken as a historical fact (1 Corinthians 15:5–8), would prove that God gave His approval to the claims of Jesus—and in this sense, both the historical facts of Jesus's resurrection, in addition to the theological truth of His deity, would be faithfully established.[101]

Fran, let's return for a moment to the analogy of the CrossFit gym. Is it possible that the CrossFit Coach could provide a combination of "historical evidence" for the program in addition to a more intangible form of "testimonial fact" about the benefits as well? If we are agreeable with this proposition, then we have a very sound means by which we can share the benefits of the program with a potential new athlete. Appling the analogy, we can see how a "Christology from Above" and a "Christology from Below" need not be mutually exclusive, but can in fact serve one another.

The greatest strength of the "Above" position is recognizing that the testimony of the people who knew Jesus—whose lives were touched by Him— deserves our closest attention, for of all the people in the world at that time, the people who wrote about Jesus and proclaimed His name knew Him best and could therefore best describe Him to others. The greatest strength of the "Below" position is its ability to create a tapestry and mosaic of Jesus's life in such a way that one is able to believe in Jesus Himself, not simply what the Gospel authors or Paul said about Him. In this sense, the Church's preached message of Christ (the "Above" position) is the key that unlocks the historical Jesus (the "Below" position) and allows the facts of His life to provide the evidence that He is the Son of God.[102]

---

[101] Erickson, p. 612.

[102] Erickson, p. 615.

Fran has heard rumors in the gym that much of the Bible is a myth. Is this true?

———————————

FRAN, I WANT YOU to imagine for a moment that when you read the Bible, you are akin to a detective looking for clues. Another illustration, if you prefer, could be that of an archeologist searching through an ancient city looking for evidence of civilization. In either case, the key to your success will be in appropriating the right tools of your trade. Perhaps fingerprint analysis for the detective, and a shovel for the archeologist.

By pressing this analogy into our biblical and theological inquiries into the Word of God, we have an apt illustration for appropriating the right "Bible reading tool" for the job. This tool is referred to as *hermeneutics*; it is concerned with a branch of knowledge that deals primarily with biblical interpretation. In order to understand the Scriptures, you want to use the right key or tool—and this is akin to using the right hermeneutic.

One of the key theologians who researched and wrote on the challenging issues of the Bible, in particular angels, demons, and the incarnation of Christ, is Rudolf Bultmann—specifically his program of demythologization. Bultmann contends that angels (and the supernatural world view in general) were merely a reflection of the popularly held ideas of the biblical day. Lacking the modern scientific knowledge afforded to our culture (for example, we "know" that demons do not cause disease) the people alive during the biblical times understood such phenomena in a similar fashion to what we now consider myth. Bultmann further argues that there is such a stark difference between our modern understanding and that of the biblical era that "it is impossible to use electric lights and the wireless and to avail ourselves of modern medical and surgical discoveries, and at the same time believe in the New Testament world of spirits and miracles."[103]

Bultmann concluded that much of the New Testament—in particular accounts of supernatural and miraculous events—were largely mythical in nature, by which he meant the attempt of human beings at the time to "give expression to the otherworldly in terms of symbolism drawn from the this-

---

[103] Erickson, p. 407.

worldly."[104] It is important to note that Bultmann did not argue that the events should be entirely discarded from biblical study or the formulation of our theology. Rather, the events must be "demythologized" or "reinterpreted" in such a fashion that is more agreeable to our modern understanding. In this sense, the hermeneutic employed in a careful reading of Scripture would be akin to putting ourselves into the minds and bodies of the biblical writers and asking ourselves, "What were the authors attempting to convey and express at the existential level?" In other words, rather than the *actual event*, the key is to understand *what had happened to those who had witnessed the event*.

Take for example the account of Jesus walking on water (Matthew 14:22–33) or Jesus calming the storm (Mark 4:35–41). According to Bultmann, in both of these instances, the key to understanding the Scripture is not to overly concern ourselves with what *actually happened*. Rather, what is important (once the Scripture is "demythologized") is to ask ourselves: "What impact did this have upon the disciples?" In this sense, the point of the story is that Jesus had made such a profound impact upon the 12 that when they retold the story, they would portray Jesus as the kind of person who "could walk on water" and "calm the storm at sea."[105]

Fran, for our purposes, I must challenge the work of Bultmann and argue that the biblical accounts of the miraculous—Jesus raising the dead, healing the sick, walking on water, and *Himself being raised from the dead*, appearing to His disciples in His resurrected body, and ascending before their very eyes into Heaven—must all be taken literally (Mark 5:21–43; Matthew 14:22–33; Luke 24:50–53). The reason for my position is that if we dismiss the supernatural (and scientifically unexplainable), then we simply take a posture of submitting ourselves to society's modern demand for rational proof and scientific evidence to substantiate one's belief. And this, of course, is completely contradictory to the words of Jesus (John 20:29).

Consider for a moment the words of the genius mind of Albert Einstein: "There are two ways to live your life. One as if nothing is a miracle. The other as if everything is a miracle." Einstein, despite his bend for mathematical and scientific proof, chose to see everything as a miracle. When we share the

---

[104] Erickson, p. 619.

[105] Erickson, p. 407.

Gospel, we are making the proclamation that God came to Earth, became a man, and lived among us (John 1:1–15). This is foundational to the Christian faith—and you can plainly see—this statement itself is a miracle! If we concede that the incarnation of Christ is merely a myth, we move Jesus into a long line of other great spiritual teachers, such as the Buddha, who, according to many world religions, is also an embodiment of God. Therefore, when sharing the message of Jesus Christ, I encourage you to consider the words of the Apostle John that "everything that Jesus did (and this includes the supernatural and miraculous) while on Earth was for the purpose of you believing in Him, and that by believing, you would have life in His name" (John 20:30–31).

Fran wants to know what Arianism is all about. Why was it rejected at the First Council of Nicea?

FRAN, THE CHRISTIAN PROCLAMATION that Jesus Christ is *fully God* and *fully Man*—in other words, the God-Man—is a statement of such extraordinary proportion that the human intellect can barely comprehend or understand it. Over the years, as the Church has faithfully attempted to understand exactly who Jesus is, and how He relates to the Father, there have been a few key deviant opponents that incidentally have helped solidify the Church's proclamation.[106]

One such attempt is known as Arianism, and although it was condemned as heresy, it continues to linger in a variety of forms, in particular with the faith of the Jehovah's Witness. The central premise in the Arian understanding is the absolute uniqueness and transcendence of God.[107] Because God is the only source—or cause—of all things, and is the only uncreated and internal Being in the entire universe, then God alone possesses the attributes of deity. If God were to share these unique attributes with anything or anyone else, God would by implication be divisible and subject to change—and this would suggest a duality or multiplicity of divine beings, and this is obviously in direct contradiction to the concept of monotheism and Oneness of God.[108]

---

[106] Erickson, p. 635.

[107] Erickson, p. 635.

[108] Erickson, p. 635.

Therefore, the Arian understanding of the relationship between God and Jesus is that the Father, while creating everything that is, worked through His unique agent of creation, which was the Word. In this sense, the Word was also a created being, and was not eternally existent with the Father. Thus, while the Word was a perfect creation, and certainly not in the same class as other created creatures, he would nevertheless owe his existence to the Father. Furthermore, this would imply that at one time, "the Word was not" because everything in the created order had a "starting point" within time.[109]

The second major departure from the Church's traditionally held proclamation of Christ was the Arian concept that Jesus did not have direct communication or knowledge with the Father. Because Jesus was a created being, he was totally different in essence from the Father and therefore subject to change and sin. In order to justify these claims, the Arians looked to such Scripture references that seemed to indicate that Jesus was "made by God" (Acts 2:36: "God has *made this Jesus....*") in addition to texts that alluded to Jesus's lack of knowledge, most notably Mark 13:32: "About that day or hour no one knows, not even the angels in heaven, nor the Son, but only the Father."

It is important to note that one of the biblical arguments the Arians used in favor of their position in fact supports the Church's proclamation about the humanity of Christ. For example, in Mark 13:32, the systematic treatment of the text illustrates that during His earthly time, Jesus—*being fully human*—took upon Himself the limitations of humanity. In this sense, for a short time, the deity of Jesus was experienced only in harmony with His humanity.[110]

Ultimately, in 325 AD, the Council of Nicea rejected the Arian view on the grounds that Jesus "is as much and as genuinely God as the Father."[111] The council reached this conclusion by noting first that the Arian position was in exact opposition to the Scriptures unified teaching on the deity of Christ—in particular the Gospel of John, (John 1:1–3) the Book of Hebrews (Hebrews 1:1–3), and the epistles of Paul (Colossians 1:15–20, 2:9). Furthermore, the Church pointed out that upon closer examination of the texts that the Arians thought were in favor of their position, a more systematic reading revealed

---

[109] Erickson, p. 635.

[110] Erickson, p. 637.

[111] Erickson, p. 637.

the evidence in fact favored the deity of Christ. For example, the Arian view of Colossians 1:15 that Jesus was "the firstborn over all creation" implied that Jesus was "created by the Father." However, this verse speaks to the fact that Jesus's "firstborn status" was in reference to His preeminent nature—or first rank—over creation.

Fran has heard some rumors in the gym about Apollinarianism in regards to the humanity of Jesus. She asks you what this was all about and why the early Church ultimately rejected the position.

FRAN, EQUALLY IMPORTANT TO the Church's proclamation of the deity of Jesus Christ is the fullness of His humanity. In this sense, Jesus is the God Man. Fully human (John 1:14; Philippians 2:8) while simultaneously fully God (Hebrews 1:1–3). While there have been departures from understanding the deity of Jesus, there have also been heresies regarding the fullness of His humanity.

One such example of an incorrect conceptualization of Jesus's humanity is known as Apollinarianism. It should be noted that with all due respect to Apollinarius, although he was wrong, his heart was in the right place: he was very concerned with maintaining the unity of Jesus Christ. However, as so often happens, his response to the heresy of Arianism (if you recall, this was the heresy that Jesus was "created by God" and was not eternally with the Father) became an overreaction.[112]

Apollinarius constructed a Christology based on a very narrow reading of the verse that many theologians do in fact use to establish the humanity of Christ—it's just that Apollinarius took it too far. In John 1:14, the Apostle wrote that "the Word became *flesh*" and according to Apollinarius, the "flesh" was the only aspect of human nature that Jesus took on. In other words, the "spark" that animated Jesus's "flesh" was divine—meaning that Jesus had a divine soul—but the remainder of His physicality was "flesh."[113] This meant that Jesus did not have a human will—in other words, the faculty of Christ's mind, will, and reason were *divine,* not *human.* So according to Apollinarius,

---

[112] Erickson, p. 652.

[113] Erickson, p. 652.

was Jesus human? Yes. However, Jesus was "just a bit different from other humans" because He lacked a human mind.[114] To concisely explain the view of Apollinarius, it was that the center of Jesus's consciousness was not human—*it was divine.*

Fran, needless to say, this view of the humanity of Jesus is very problematic, because the "human Jesus" that Apollinarius constructed turns out to be not very human at all! You see, what Apollinarius had failed to account for is that Jesus came to redeem humanity—*and all of it.* In other words, if Jesus did not have a human mind, soul, and center of consciousness, then how could He have saved the mind, soul, and center of consciousness of mankind? As a case in point, consider the implications of Hebrews 4:15—that Jesus is able to be our High Priest precisely because he *knows everything about us.* Jesus understands the nature of the human mind, and what it feels like to be tempted, because Jesus *had a human mind and experienced temptation.*

In addition, Apollinarius also fails to account for the abundance of Scripture that teaches the full range of human emotion, feelings, and mindful reactions that Jesus experienced during His lifetime. Even a brief summation of Scripture reveals that Jesus was very familiar with the full gauntlet of human thoughts, emotions, and feelings: Jesus wept, became angry, had compassion, and felt lonely (John 11:35; Mark 3:5; Matthew 18:11–13; Isaiah 53:3). Based on these reasons, the doctrine of Apollinarian was ultimately condemned at the Council of Constantinople in 381.

---

[114] Erickson, p. 652.

Fran asks you to briefly summarize the significance of the Chalcedonian Definition.

FRAN, CONSIDER FOR A moment the implications of the definition of the CrossFit program: "Constantly Varied—Functional Movement—Performed at High Intensity." The only way to fully comprehend and therefore participate in the program is to accept the absolute and complete *unity* of the program while simultaneously acknowledging that the *unity* is experienced through the application of three distinct entities. In other words, if you remove one part of the definition, you are left with something less than CrossFit. In this sense, the definition of CrossFit is broad, general, and inclusive and provides athletes with what we could term a "framework" or "boundaries" in which they can participate in the program.

This analogy is a helpful starting point for understanding the implications of what became known as the Chalcedonian Definition. As Professor of Theology Ian McFarland has wonderfully explained in a lecture on "Challenges on Christology," the challenge of the Church over the ages has been in rectifying the humanity and deity of Jesus.[115] In other words, the Church has been forced to explain how it is possible for both a fully *divine nature* and a fully *human nature* to harmoniously exist within the person of Jesus Christ. Interestingly, McFarland points out that the error in thinking was not often in regards to Christ's deity, but rather His humanity. Some heresies went so far as to claim that Jesus "left no footprints" because *He only seemed to be human.*[116] However, any denial of Christ's humanity would potentially mean, in the famous words of Pope Gregory of Nazianzus: "What is unassumed is unhealed." In other words, in order for Jesus to save humanity (John 3:16), Jesus had to be Himself fully human.

In order to unify the position on the humanity and deity of Christ, the Church realized it would need to issue a statement that would become the standard for all Christendom. Therefore, at the Chalcedon Council in 451, the Church established what became known as "The Chalcedonian Definition."

---

[115] Ian McFarland, lecture, *Challenges in Christology,* April 1, 2017.
[116] McFarland, April 1, 2017.

For our purposes, it is important to think of this definition in a similar way that we think of the broad and inclusive definition of CrossFit. In other words, rather than narrowly and *positively* describing the deity and humanity of Christ, the Chalcedonian Definition took a broad and essentially *negative* approach. By *negative* I mean that the definition explained what the two natures of Christ *were not* rather than what *they were:* They were "without confusion, without change, without division, and without separation." This means that the definition did not specifically set boundaries on different ways to conceptualize the deity and humanity of Christ. In the words of McFarland, "so long as there was no confusion or separation in the definition, there leaves a lot of freedom for talking about Jesus Christ."[117]

There is a lot of diversity and cultural background at the gym that Fran trains at. Fran asks you about the idea of Christ as Healer and Life-Giver within the context of African history and if there is any value in this for her.

FROM AN EVANGELICAL PERSPECTIVE, it is always a good idea to understand the background culture and "atmosphere" of the person with whom you intend to share the Gospel. For example, consider the brilliant approach of the Apostle Paul while in Athens. Aware that the city was full of idols and the cultural backdrop was consistent with discussing "the latest spiritual ideas" (Acts 17:16, 21), Paul capitalized on this opportunity to preach about the One True God the people were ignorant of (Acts 17:22–23). In other words, Paul saw an "open door" and boldly marched right through it.

In this context, I want to share with you a fascinating approach to sharing the Gospel that we can learn from the cultural atmosphere of Africa. Having personally visited and shared the Gospel in Kenya, I can attest that the idea of Christ as a "Healer" and "Life Giver" is an intriguing archetype in which the Gospel of Jesus Christ can be relevant, relatable, and immediately applicable.

---

[117] McFarland, 2017.

To begin, it is important to understand a significant difference between the theological thinking in the African Church compared to the Church in the Western hemisphere. The starting point for African Christology is what we would describe as "Christology from Below" as opposed to "Christology from Above." By "below," I mean that African thinkers tend to be more concerned with the person and work of Jesus Christ in a historical context (the Gospels of Matthew, Mark, Luke, and John) in addition to what Christ is continuing to do within the African Church.[118] In other words, the great theological discussions (and debates!) of the ecumenical councils regarding how the deity and humanity of Christ were united into one theanthropic person are not the central focus on African theologians or pastors.[119] Rather, the African Church is more interested in proclaiming the holistic and integrative application of the Gospel into the whole of African life.[120]

This backdrop is crucial to understanding the significance of presenting the Gospel within the context of Christ as a "Healer" and "Life Giver" in the African culture. When you consider the ravaging effects of the AIDS pandemic, in addition to the suffering, poverty, and malnutrition of a great majority of African people, it seems that a fundamental starting point to the Gospel message would be to focus on Jesus's earthly ministry and the numerous accounts of His healing and life-giving miracles. The African theologians point out that Jesus enters the lives of the African people as "someone familiar with suffering" (Isaiah 53:3) who came to "give life to the fullest (John 10:10). For a people who are starving and oftentimes without clean water, the message of a Savior who brings "the bread of life" (John 6:35) and living water (John 4:10) is very good news indeed!

It is also important to understand that in African culture and history there is not a sharp distinction between physical healing and spiritual healing. Whereas in the West, we tend to call on a doctor for physical illness and a pastor for spiritual illness, for the African, the physical and spiritual illness (and subsequent healing) are intimately connected. This is also a powerful launching pad for sharing the Gospel—the accounts of Jesus forgiving sins and

---

[118] Tennent, p. 113.

[119] Tennent, p. 113.

[120] Tennent, p. 113.

the resulting physical healing and bodily restoration are immediately relatable in the mind of the African (Mark 2:1–12). It is also significant to note that for the African, the healing of the individual implies not just restoration with God, but also the restoration and healing between other human beings. In this sense, healing is simultaneously physical and spiritual and is both individual and corporate.[121]

Fran, at this point, a good question to consider is "How does the cultural context of the Gospel in Africa relate to me?" My answer is *in every way!* Whenever we share the Gospel, it is imperative to remember that any image, metaphor, or illustration that we use will potentially fall short of capturing the comprehensive view of the Kingdom of God as any other approach.[122] As a case in point, an illustration of Christ as a "Coach" may relate well to someone with an athletic background, whereas Christ as a "Company Commander" would relate well to someone with military or law enforcement training. But to someone with neither a military or athletic background, an entirely new and more relatable illustration would become necessary. So the key takeaway for the Christian evangelist is that we must continually equip ourselves with a variety of images in preparation for sharing Christ with new believers. In this sense, the more we learn about the needs and shortcoming of different cultures, the more prepared we will be to present the good news of the One who came to bring light to the world (John 8:12).

---

[121] Tennent, p. 119.
[122] Tennent, p. 118.

CHAPTER SIX

THE ATONEMENT

CHAPTER SUMMARY:

THE MOST RECOGNIZABLE symbol of the Christian faith is the Cross. The significance of the Cross can be found in the atoning work of Christ. In this sense, the Cross serves as a transition from vague discussions of the Christian faith to actionable and relevant implications in the life of the believer. The theme of the atonement as revealed within the Bible involves sacrifice, propitiation, substitution, and reconciliation in the relationship between God and humanity. We will discover that the penal substitution theory of the atonement best describes the work of Christ and how a saving relationship with Jesus is the key to reconciliation with God.

Fran is aware that there are several different theories of the atonement. She asks you to explain the more prominent positions, beginning with the recapitulation theory of atonement.

TRADITIONALLY THERE HAVE BEEN FOUR different theories of the atonement. However, before going too much further in their differences, we first need to understand *what the atonement means* in order to appreciate its significance in the life of the believer. If we go immediately to the various theories, it's kind of like trying to learn how to perform a Snatch if we haven't first learned how to Deadlift.

In many respects, the most recognizable symbol of the Christian faith is the Cross, and in itself, the Cross is a brutal symbol of torture, agony, and death. Therefore, Christians need to be prepared to answer the question, "Why is a symbol of torture and agonizing death such a big part of the Christian faith and culture?" When we engage with these types of questions, we must move the nature of the inquiry from the limited scope of *what the Cross is*, to the broader and more significant theological matter of *what the Cross accomplished.* When we approach the question from this perspective, everything changes. In this sense, the Cross can become a pivotal point of transition from studying the *nature of Christ* to studying the *objective work that Christ did on our behalf.*[123]

Fran, at the most fundamental level, the atonement is what makes the salvation of the believer possible. Many of the world's greatest theological minds agree with the proposition that understanding the significance of the Cross is absolutely crucial to understanding the entirety of the Christian faith. For example, Emil Brunner said, "He who understands the Cross aright understands the Bible, and he understands Jesus Christ"; and Leon Morris wrote, "The atonement is the crucial doctrine of the faith. Unless we are right here it matters little what we are like elsewhere."[124]

---

[123] Erickson, p. 714.

[124] The quotes of Brunner and Morris were identified in Erickson's *Christian Theology*, p. 714.

Now that we have an appreciation for the significance of the Cross, we are better prepared to examine four different theories of the atonement: *recapitulation, penal substitution, Christus Victor,* and *moral influence.* As we move through these theories, I will draw on the imagery of a mosaic or tapestry of the atonement—these being the feet, the heart, the head, and the hands of Christ. In the mosaic's integrated and holistic beauty, we can begin to appreciate the magnitude of Christ's work on the Cross.[125]

The key figure behind the development of the *recapitulation theory* was Irenaeus. This view of the atonement identifies Jesus Christ as the new Adam, and through Christ's headship a new humanity is ushered into place. Just like the fallen and sinful state of humanity that was under the headship of Adam, a new faithful and righteous humanity will be brought about under the headship of Jesus (Romans 5:12–18). In this sense, Christ's first redemptive act can be seen in the incarnation itself. In order for Christ to redeem humanity, He first needed to become human (Hebrews 2:5–18).

There is an abundance of biblical support for the *recapitulation theory* of the atonement. One of the most significant Bible verses for this position is found in Paul's letter to the Romans. Here, Paul explains that in the same manner that Adam's *disobedience* resulted in "many becoming sinners," through the obedience of Christ, "many will be made righteous" (Romans 5:19). Another biblical text that explains this concept is found in 1 Corinthians 15:22. Here, Paul focuses on what Christ's atoning work accomplishes in the life of the believer, mainly that "As in Adam all die, so also in Christ all will be made alive." It is also important to note that when Paul explained the significance of the atonement in Ephesians, he settled on the phrase "summing up" or "gather together" (Ephesians 1:8–10). The Greek word Paul used was *anakephalaioō,* which translates as *recapitulate* in Latin.

---

[125] The "mosaic of the atonement" is from Dr. Nigh's lecture, *Theology II, Glorifying the Word of Life,* Western Theological Seminary.

Fran tells you that there are a lot of military and law enforcement professionals who train at her gym. She thinks the penal substitution theory of the atonement might be helpful in explaining the significance of the Cross and asks you for help.

FRAN, THE NEXT THEORY of the atonement that I would like to present is referred to as the *penal substitution theory*. Given my background in law enforcement, this theory is the easiest for me to understand and relate to. One of the major figures in the development and support of this position was Calvin, although there is evidence that suggests that this particular theory is dated back to the early Church Fathers, including Athanasius and Augustine.[126] Similar to the theory of *recapitulation,* the biblical support for the penal substitution theory of the atonement is plentiful.

As the name would imply, the penal substitution theory is best understood in the framework of God's Law. Therefore, we must begin our discussion of this particular theory of atonement by understanding the significance of God's moral and spiritual Law. Rather than thinking of the Law as something apart from God, it is far better to see the Law as the expression of God's very person, nature, and divine will.[127] This means that obedience to the Law is a testimony and demonstration of our love and obedience to God. In fact, this principle was very important to Jesus, who explained to His disciples in a variety of ways that if they loved Him, they should obey Him (John 14:15, 15:14). In this sense, obedience to the Law is akin to a demonstration of love obedience to God, and disobedience to the Law is akin to an attack on the very nature of God Himself. Following this logic, disobedience to the Law—as an attack on God's nature—needs to be punished, and the consequences of such transgressions carry serious consequences, especially death.[128]

---

[126] Erickson, p. 733.

[127] Erickson, p. 733.

[128] Erickson, p. 734.

The fact that violation of God's Law could potentially carry the punishment of death provides appreciation for what Jesus understood His atoning work would accomplish for humanity. For example, when Jesus said that "Greater love has no one than this: to lay down one's life for one's friends" (John 15:13; cf. 17:19), inasmuch as He was speaking on the eve of His death, He most certainly was referring to the substitution of Himself for mankind.[129] Even the sneering words of Caiaphas to the Sanhedrin (although it is unlikely that he realized the full implications of his utterance) provide support for the penal substitution: "It is better for you that one man die for the people than the whole nation perish" (John 11:49–50).

One of the most important biblical texts in support of the penal substitution theory is found in Isaiah 53:5. Here, the Prophet describes a "Suffering Servant" who would be "pierced for our transgressions and crushed for our iniquities." The significance of this verse in the context of Christ providing a substitution for a penalty that was ultimately due to mankind was certainly understood by John the Baptist, who, upon seeing Jesus, proclaimed, "Look, the Lamb of God, who takes away the sin of the world!" (John 1:29). John the Baptist's testimony speaks to the theology and doctrine that in His death, Christ would take the punishment that humanity deserved and bear it upon Himself. In the context of the mosaic of Christ's atoning work, in the penal substitution theory, we see the powerful imagery of the heart.

Fran wants you to explain the *Christus Victor* theory of atonement.

FRAN, AS WE CONTINUE our survey of the various theories of the atonement, we now turn our attention to the theory of *Christus Victor.* In the context of understanding the atonement as a mosaic, we move from the feet (the theory of *recapitulation*) to the heart (the theory of *penal substitution)* to the head (*Christus Victor*). The major historical figure associated with this particular theory was Gustaf Aulén, who taught that Christ's life, death, and resurrection were akin to Christ defeating God's enemies. In addition to Aulén, this particular theory was the primary way in which Augustine understood the

---

[129] Erickson, p. 734.

atonement.[130] The dominant theme and way of conceptualizing the *Christus Victor* theory was that Christ's death achieved a victory over Satan and deliverance of humankind from bondage to him.[131]

The biblical evidence in support of *Christus Victor* is immense, and in many respects continues to develop biblical passages used to support the penal substitution theory. For example, in Colossians, Paul wrote that the legal charges that stood against and condemned mankind (thus pointing to the penal substitution theory) had been taken away through Christ's death on the Cross (Colossians 2:13–14). And how exactly was this accomplished? According to Paul, this was achieved by Christ having "disarmed the powers and authorities" and "overcoming them through his death on the cross" (Colossians 1:15). In this sense, the death of Christ was in fact a victory over God's enemies.

This theory certainly provides a radical new framework for seeing the Cross not so much as an instrument of torture and death, but rather the means by which God saved the world by overcoming the powers of darkness (John 12:31–33; 1 Corinthians 15:55–57). Because Christ has triumphed over evil, there is no one (including Satan) who can now condemn the believer (1 John 3:8). Furthermore, this theory provides greater appreciation and understanding for the way that God can take something the enemy intended for harm (the Cross) and use it for good (triumphing over evil and redeeming mankind— refer to Genesis 50:20).

---

[130] Erickson, p. 723.
[131] Erickson, p. 723.

Fran tells you that many of her training partners at the gym are agreeable to concepts of ethics, morality, and setting a positive example. She thinks the moral influence theory of the atonement might be a helpful model to reach these people and asks you for help.

———————————

FRAN, IN THE CONTEXT of the mosaic of the atonement, we now arrive at the hands of Christ. In this sense, we seek to understand the atonement by investigating the moral example that Christ provided humanity. This particular theory portrays the atonement as a demonstration of God's love (John 3:16). The major historical figure associated with this theory was Peter Abelard, who emphasized that in the atonement, Christ exemplified the nature and extent of God's love for mankind. Later proponents of the theory, including Hastings Rashdall and Horace Bushnell, would continue to advance the notion that God's nature is essentially love, and that in the atoning work of Christ, mankind is able to witness the extent to which God would go to redeem humanity onto Himself.[132]

Unique in this theory is that humans should not fear God's justice and punishment. According to Bushnell, this view of God would minimize His enduring love for mankind and create within the human heart an attitude that would keep them apart from God.[133] In this sense, Bushnell regards sin as a "type of sickness" that must be healed, and Christ's atoning work served the purpose of correcting and healing this defect within us. The biblical support of this view of the atonement can be found in such passages as Luke 19:10, where Jesus says, "The Son of Man came to seek and to save the lost." Furthermore, Paul speaks to the moral influence of Christ's atoning work as "God having reconciled the world to Himself in Christ" (2 Corinthians 5:19). In a summary of the biblical texts in support of his position, Bushnell claims that in a word, Christ's atoning work "established the Kingdom of God, or of heaven, among men, and the gathering finally of a new-born world into it."[134]

---

[132] Erickson, p. 717.

[133] Erickson, p. 718.

[134] Erickson, p. 718.

The moral influence theory of the atonement also provides humanity with inspiration. Rather than an abstract conception of the holiness that humanity was created to embody, through Christ's example on the Cross it becomes real for us. In other words, rather than general theological ideas about God, humanity cries out for "a friend, whom we can feel as a man, and whom it will be sufficiently accurate for us to accept and love."[135] In the mosaic of the atonement, the moral influence theory exemplifies the hands of Christ and demonstrates one of the most powerful inducements for love and trust of God—that God suffered and died for humanity in order to reconcile us onto Himself (2 Corinthians 5:18–21; 1 John 4:10–11).

Fran is having a hard time wrapping her mind around the idea that God's justice could be satisfied by an innocent person being punished in place of the guilty. Can you help her out?

———————————————

FRAN, ON ONE HAND, the idea of an innocent person being punished in place of the guilty—the person who actually deserves the punishment— is repulsive and speaks against the moral fabric of our country. However, in certain instances, the practice of the "innocent" taking on the punishment of the "guilty" is more common than you might expect. Although I will ground my answer for you in Scripture and sound theological reasoning, let me first explain how the concept of "paying the debt" of another person happens right in our own back yard.

In the United States Military, the sense of individualism goes out the window from the very first day you take the oath of office. Instead of retaining even the faintest notion of "I am," the atmosphere and culture of the institution instill within you the concept of "We are." What any individual does or fails to do affects the entire unit, often referred to as a "body" of troops. In this sense, one person can achieve a certain level of acclaim that positively affects the entire body. On the other hand, that same person can also bring disfavor upon the entire unit. Now here is where things get interesting. If the entire unit, or "body," is subject to uniform punishment, it is a common practice

———

[135] Horace Bushnell, quoted in Erickson's *Christian Theology,* p. 719.

for one person to volunteer to "pay the price" individually—because that "individual" still represents the entire "body." Although only "one person" pays the price, that person is (in a theological sense) in a "headship role" and therefore represents the remainder of the collective body.

Although it might be helpful to press this illustration from the military to your specific question, we begin to see where its logic comes up short. In the case of the individual soldier "paying the price" for their comrades, as a member of the collective body, the individual soldier would still retain the guilt associated with the remainder of the troop. In this sense, although they volunteered to take the punishment on behalf of their fellow soldiers, individually they were still subject to the punishment in the first place. However, in the case of Jesus Christ, we know that Scripture tells us that He was without sin and lived a perfect life (1 Peter 2:22; 2 Corinthians 5:21). Therefore, to return to your question, how does it make sense that Jesus—an innocent person—could be punished for the guilt of mankind?

Fran, now we turn our attention to the bedrock of Scripture to formulate our answer to this challenging question. First of all, the idea of an innocent person suffering the punishment of the guilty would seem to suggest that the innocent person was an unwilling participant. In other words, what kind of person in their right mind would want to take on punishment of somebody else? However, what we find in the Bible is that Jesus was a *willing participant* and was intimately involved in the decision to lay down His life for His friends (John 15:13). Jesus explained to His disciples that nobody was forcing a punishment on Him. Rather, on His own accord and in perfect harmony with the Father, Jesus was willing to lay down His life in order to take it up again (John 10:17–18). These verses speak to the idea that Jesus was not compelled by the Father to lay down His life. Rather, Jesus did it voluntarily to save mankind and to reconcile humanity to God (John 3:16).

As an additional and super important point to consider, we must remember that our doctrine of the Trinity fundamentally shapes the way we see Jesus and the Father intimately involved in Christ's atoning work. Because the Father and the Son are One, Christ's work is also the Father's work, and the Father's the Son's (John 5:17–19; Romans 8:35, 39).[136] In this sense, the Father was

---

[136] Erickson, p. 746.

both the Judge *and the Person receiving the punishment*.[137] In addition, the Trinity also provides the theological framework to understand that in Christ's humanity, His atoning death is directly applicable to human beings. However, if Jesus were only a human, at the most, His death would have been sufficient to cover His own sins (of course, there were none), not the entire human race. But as the God Man, Jesus's death is of infinite worth.

This means it wasn't just an innocent person (or even a Divine person at that!) who was being punished for the guilty—it was the Creator Himself, the basis of all humanity, who took the collective guilt of humanity upon Himself in order to save us. Our Lord's sacrificial death, in perfect cooperation with the Father, atoned for the sins of the entire human race, and reconciled mankind onto God (John 3:16). To return to our analogy of the military, it is as if the Drill Instructor who orders the punishment on the body of troops removes his rank, has the troops stand at ease, and then pays the penalty himself.

Fran has a training partner at the gym who has been telling her that Jesus took our sickness on the Cross, so if we pray with confidence, then our sicknesses will be healed. Is it biblical to pray for healing from sickness?

FRAN, IMAGINE IF THERE were a giant net placed over the world right now—how many millions of prayers "going up to God" would be caught in the net—and of those millions, how many would pertain to healing and protection from the sickness that is currently plaguing our world? I suspect nearly all of them! Therefore, we must be prepared to answer people's questions about how Jesus's work on the Cross impacts human sickness and death.

In the Gospel of Matthew, we discover that Jesus healed Peter's mother-in-law from a fever by touching her hand (Matthew 8:14). Following this miraculous healing, many more sick people were brought to Jesus, and He healed them all (Matthew 8:15–16). Matthew then makes a connection between these healings and the Old Testament prophecy of Isaiah: "He took up our infirmities and carried our diseases" (Isaiah 53:4). Although not specifically quoted by Matthew, the next verse in Isaiah informs us that the same person who "carried our diseases" was also "pierced for our transgressions, he was

---

[137] Erickson, p. 746.

crushed for our iniquities; the punishment that brought us peace was on him, and by his wounds we are healed" (Isaiah 53:4). On this basis, it would appear that the purpose of Matthew's reference of the Old Testament prophet was to make a connection between Christ's death and the reversal of not just the curse of sin, but of sickness and disease as well.[138]

This leads us to a logical question: Is sickness and disease a curse? The Scriptures teach that as a result of the fall, a whole host of evils entered the world, of which illness, sickness, and disease were apart (Deuteronomy 28:22, Romans 8:20–23). This would certainly suggest that in this case, if Jesus's death removed us from the curse of the fall and sin (Galatians 3:13–14), then the believer should be able to ask for and receive divine healing. Therefore, it becomes imperative that we have a sound exegetical understanding of both Isaiah's and Matthew's reference of the prophet's words.

In addition to an exegesis of Isaiah 53:4 and Matthew 8:14–16, there is one additional step at hand—for once we have established the connection between the curse and sickness, we must determine whether there is also an intrinsic connection between the forgiveness of sin and physical healing. If we can establish a definitive connection and "once for all" pattern of Christ's healing as a direct result of forgiveness of sin, then the believer's right to divine healing can be firmly rooted in sound doctrine. Fran, I should mention here that I have always found it interesting (and encouraging as well!) that David himself recognized a connection between his physical ailments (Psalm 32:3–4) and the subsequent healing he received as a direct result of forgiveness of his sin (Psalm 32:5). In other words, according to David, the *cause of his physical suffering was his spiritual sin.* When David confessed his inequity, "the LORD forgave the guilt of his sin" (Psalm 32:5b) and his health was restored.

This being the case, there would certainly be reason to attribute physical sickness to sin. If this were so, the chronological sequence of events in the restoration of health would be to acknowledge sin, repent, receive the forgiveness of Christ, and prayerfully await the restoration of health. If only things could be so simple and straightforward! For when we look at the healing miracles of Christ, we are faced with the realization that He did not outright accept this view, nor did He reject it. In some instances of His healing, there

---

[138] Erickson, p. 764.

was a direct causation between the restoration of health and the forgiveness of sin (Mark 2:5). However, this was not always the case (John 9:2–3).

Fran, we now have sufficient "background data" to return to the foundation of your original question: Did Jesus Christ in fact "take up our infirmities and bear our diseases?" I would answer with a resounding, "Yes!" However, the manner in which He accomplished this was in the incarnation— God Himself making His dwelling among us (John 1:14). When God entered our sinful world, He entered into the very conditions that we seek to escape from—including our sickness, brokenness, sorrow, and disease. In this sense, the believer prays to a God who can relate and sympathize with our needs and our prayers. Is it proper, therefore, to pray to God for healing from sickness? Again, my answer is a resounding, "Yes!" In the long run, the work of Christ on the Cross does in fact cancel all the effects of the fall and saves us from the curse of sin. Some of these benefits will be experienced on Earth, while others will not be realized until the end of time (Romans 8:19–25). In the same fashion that the Apostle Paul had to surrender to the reality that he would live with "a thorn in his flesh" (2 Corinthians 12:1–10), so must we patiently await the day that we enter with resurrected bodies into the presence of God (1 Corinthians 15:35–58).[139]

---

[139] Erickson, p. 768.

In addition to CrossFit, Fran also participates in yoga at her gym, and many of her friends are Buddhists. She explains that according to her friends, the idea of grace through faith is also a prominent theme in True Pure Land Buddhism. This is a bit confusing for Fran, because she's heard several times in Church that salvation by grace through faith was a unique core tenant of Christianity. Can you help her out?

FRAN, I JUST LOVE our Lord's great commission to "go and make disciples of all nations" (Matthew 28:19a). The implicitness of Jesus's command is so clear—His disciples are to make more disciples. This being the case, I am increasingly inspired to see the "fingerprint" of Christ within the sacred texts of so many world religions. From an evangelical perspective, the faint glimmer of light within world religions apart from the Judeo–Christian faith means that God "has not left himself without testimony" (Acts 14:17). Much akin to a flicker of light eagerly awaiting an opportunity to be joined with an Eternal Flame, in the full radiance of God's glory in the person of Jesus Christ, every dim light can ultimately be brought to Life (Hebrews 1:1–3).

Fran, to anchor this theological position a bit more firmly, let me begin by stating that it is imperative that Christians with a heart for evangelism gain an understanding of other world religions. As we gain an understanding and appreciation for other world religions, we are more apt to discover "touch points" that allow us to formulate new ideas for how the Gospel can relate to the wide range of religiously held views apart from the Christian faith.[140] In other words, learning about other world religions can help us to create a bridge of hope between the Gospel and those people still searching for a relationship with the One True God.

Now Fran, let's turn our attention to one of the fundamental theological and doctrinal positions of the Christian faith: The concept of salvation by grace through faith in Jesus Christ (Galatians 3:22; Ephesians 2:8–9). I'm not sure about you, but I've attended several sermons in which the pastor seems to suggest that this doctrine is absolutely unique to the Christian faith. If that were the case, then I might not necessarily lead with that particular position when sharing the Gospel with people from a different religious background.

---

[140] Tennent, p. 157.

However, imagine if there were an existing world religion that was very familiar with the concept of grace through faith. If that were so, it would be an awesome "touch point" and "bridge of hope" to share the fullness of this biblical truth, and point people to the "name above every other name" on which salvation truly rests (Philippians 2:9). Well Fran, it turns out that Pure Land Buddhism does indeed retain a "glimmer of light" and a doctrine of salvation by grace through faith.[141]

Now that a "touch point" has been established between Christianity and Pure Land Buddhism, what do we do with it? I believe the first step is to appreciate the similarities while simultaneously being firm in their differences. When the Christian calls on the name of Jesus Christ, we are proclaiming that He is God Himself, who became incarnate as the God Man (Hebrews 1:1–3; Colossians 2:9). Jesus Christ was sent to "take away the sin of the world" (John 1:29), and apart from Christ, it is impossible for the believer to know God or enter into His presence (John 14:6). When the Christian thinks and speaks of salvation, at the most fundamental level we are referring to the fact that God Himself in the person of Jesus Christ stepped into human history (Colossians 2:9). As the God-Man, Jesus Christ is our Savior, and through His death on the Cross, Jesus removed the great chasm of divide between God and mankind (Isaiah 59:1–2; Romans 6:23). In other words, Jesus redeemed mankind onto God (John 3:16, 3:36).[142]

On the other hand, in the Buddhist mind, there is not an inherent sinful nature to begin with, nor does mankind rebel against a holy and personal God. The Buddhist rejects all first causes—including God.[143] This means that when a Pure Land Buddhist calls on the name of their "savior," they are calling on a *man who became exalted as a savior*, not the incarnate God-Man who actually came into the world to save it. Therefore, in the words of the great theologian Karl Barth, "in the end only one thing is really decisive for the distinction of truth and error ... that one thing is the name of Jesus Christ."[144]

---

[141] Tennent, p. 158.

[142] Tennent, p. 155.

[143] Tennent, p. 155.

[144] Tennent, p. 155.

This means that rather than Pure Land Buddhism undermining or distracting from the Christian doctrine of "salvation by grace through faith," it instead accentuates the believer's conviction in the power of the name of Jesus Christ and compels us to share the grace of the Gospel with those still searching for light.

PART THREE

THE BREATH OF GOD

CHAPTER SEVEN

SOTERIOLOGY

CHAPTER SUMMARY:

THE DOCTRINE OF SALVATION deals with the most crucial needs of the human person. This is especially true and glaringly apparent for those people who understand the biblical doctrine and teaching regarding the nature of sin. The questions of how salvation is to be obtained, and for whom and how many, are of extreme importance. Predestination treats the theological doctrine of God's choice of persons for either eternal life or eternal death. Salvation may be understood as taking place in three steps: effectual calling, conversion, and regeneration. The human's response to God's grace involves turning from a life of sin to a saving relationship with Jesus Christ. The objective aspects of salvation are union with Christ, justification, and adoption into the family of God.

Fran has heard a lot about the different models of election and is curious to hear about your position on the matter. Specifically, she asks you the difference between Calvinism, Arminianism and the middle position of "Calminian."

FRAN, ONE OF THE most challenging theological concepts to understand is that of *election.* Generally speaking, election refers to God's sovereign selection of some people for eternal life, whereas others for eternal death.[145] In other words, the treatment and study of election seeks to understand whether some people are singled out by God to be special benefactors of His grace. Historically, there have been several views on the matter, including the major ideas presented in Calvinism and Arminianism. As background context for these two views, Arminians believe that God chooses some people to receive salvation, and others He chooses to pass by. Those people whom God elected to receive salvation are people whom in His infinite knowledge God knew would positively respond to His offer of salvation in Jesus Christ (Romans 8:29).[146] This view includes what is referred to as *prevenient grace,* which holds that God has provided humanity with sufficient grace to either receive or reject the Gospel message. On the other hand, Calvinists believe that the entire human race is lost in sin and unable to positively respond to God's offer of grace. Therefore, Calvinists hold that God's offer of salvation to His elected people is *efficacious*, by which they mean that those whom God has chosen will certainly come in faith to Him (Ephesians 1:4–5).

Fran, I would like to present you with a unique model of election referred to as "Calminianism." This view is taught by Professor Gerry Breshears of Western Seminary. The view holds that God loves all people and draws them toward Himself (John 3:16). In order to accomplish this, God works "in different ways with different people, and in different ways with the same person at different times."[147] Needless to say, the Bible is rich with examples of the assortment of ways that God accomplishes this.

---

[145] Erickson, Millard, *Christian Theology* (Grand Rapids, MI: Baker Academic, 2013) p. 842.

[146] Erickson, p. 853.

[147] Dr. Gerry Breshears, "Soteriology" outline, Western Seminary TH503.

Take for example the incredible conversion of Saul (Acts 9:1–19). In this particular case, God's drawing was *effectual* to the extent of knocking Saul to the ground (Acts 9:4). However, at other times, God gently *opens people's heart* and works in such a way as to enable them to freely make the choice on their own (Acts 16:11–15). The unique and varied manner in which God draws people to Himself also includes working against people's intent (as we noticed in the case of Saul), while at other times working in special and cooperative ways with what people were already actively seeking (Acts 8:26–38, 10:1–16).

Fran, I tend to agree with the Calminian model of election. The totality of biblical evidence seems to suggest that God wants all people saved (John 3:16; 1 Timothy 2:3–6; 2 Peter 3:9). However, it is also true that in order for people to come to Christ, "the Father must draw them" (John 6:44). This being the case, it perfectly follows that the manner in which people are drawn toward God will be different from person to person. This is what Paul described in his letter to the Ephesians: "God chose us *who are* in Him before the creation of the world to be holy and blameless in His sight" (Ephesians 1:4).[148] This verse, when coupled with what Paul wrote to the Romans—"God works for the good of those who love Him, who have been called according to His purpose (Romans 8:28)—demonstrates that while all are chosen in Christ, *the way God works to draw people into Christ* will vary from person to person.

Fran wants to know more about the theological concepts of *effectual calling* and *prevenient grace*.

FRAN, THE BIBLE TEACHES that mankind is so hopelessly lost in our sin that we are essentially *dead* (Romans 3:10, 5:12; Ephesians 2:1). This being the case, *how does mankind respond positively to God's offer of grace?* One solution is the concept of a special or *effectual* calling upon people's lives, which draws them out of death and into life (John 5:24). Achieved entirely by God, the effectual calling upon someone's life is powerful enough as to counteract the effects of sin and to cause them to believe.[149]

---

[148] This translation of Ephesians 1:3 (noted in italics) was brought to my attention by Dr. Gerry Breshears.

[149] Erickson, p. 863.

The Calvinistic model holds that this effectual calling is only bestowed upon God's elect. Furthermore, the calling is so strong that it will always lead to an infallibly or efficaciously positive response on the part of the recipient. Another way of understanding this model is that the grace of God "invades the inner being of man so that he is compelled to accept and believe" God's offer of salvation.[150]

On the other hand, the Arminians hold that God grants everyone with *prevenient grace* sufficient enough to positively respond to His offer of salvation. Consequently, according to this view there is no need for a special or *effectual* grace to particular individuals. This view suggests that God takes the initiative in salvation (John 15:16) and that "in God's grace He makes it possible for all to be saved."[151]

Fran, I tend to favor the model of prevenient grace and believe that "the grace of God has appeared that offers salvation to *all people*" (Titus 2:11). If this were not the case, then seemingly nobody (or only God's elect) would be able to come to Christ (John 6:44). However, if we hold that God wants all people to be saved (John 3:16), then Christ's atoning death was sufficient to *draw all people to God* (John 12:32). I think the best way to treat Bible verses that seem to suggest mankind's response to God's offer of salvation depends on His prior decision (John 6:37, 6:44, 15:16) is to understand them in relation to particular purposes in His Kingdom, rather than to salvation. God's grace is offered to everyone—God does not show favoritism (Romans 2:11)—and it is sufficient enough to enable people to freely choose eternal life or death (Romans 2:4–10).

---

[150] Breshears.

[151] Breshears.

Some argue that both *justification* and *regeneration* are gifts of God that are by grace alone, through faith alone, in Christ alone. Can you help Fran understand what these theological concepts mean and their implications in the life of a believer?

———————————

FRAN, THE MOMENT THAT a believer "confesses with their mouth that Jesus is Lord, and believes that God raised him from the dead" (Romans 10: 9), a radical transformation takes place in their heart. Theologically, this is referred to as *regeneration* and speaks to the new spiritual vitality the believer experiences when they accept Christ.[152] The Bible emphatically teaches that regeneration is absolutely necessary for the believer because our innate human nature is in desperate need of transformation (Ro. 3:10–12). In addition, regeneration is a gift of God's grace—it is completely and entirely God's doing.

In addition to *regeneration*, when a new believer places their trust in Christ, they receive *justification*. As we discussed above, human nature is corrupt and dead to sin. Not only do we need to be regenerated, transformed, and "born again" (Ezekiel 11:19–20; John 3:5–8), but we also need to deal with the guilt of our sin. In other words, unless there is a supernatural and gracious move on God's part, mankind is liable to punishment for having failed to fulfill His expectations. Thankfully, when the believer comes to Jesus, in addition to being *regenerated,* they also receive God's free gift of being declared *righteous* in His sight, which is the theological meaning of *justification*. Justification is God's forgiveness of our sins and our acceptance into His family.

This means that both justification and regeneration are *gifts from God* that are by grace alone, by faith alone, in Christ alone at the time of conversion.[153] Fran, I believe there are three primary reasons why this is the case. First, the new heart achieved at the moment of conversion (our regeneration) enables the believer to be presented righteous before God (our justification). Second, Jesus emphasized the fact that believers would need to be born again. The "new life" achieved through the grace of God would entail a supernatural work, not something that mankind would be able to achieve on their own (John 3:5–8; 2 Corinthians 5:17).

———————————

[152] Erickson, p. 872.

[153] Dr. Gerry Breshears, "Soteriology" outline, TH503.

The reversal of the believer's natural sinful tendencies prior to regeneration is therefore a gift of God's grace. Similarly, our sin and liability for punishment is forgiven at the moment of conversion—it is not something that we can earn or achieve on our own. In other words, our "works" are never the basis of either our justification or regeneration. They are both gifts of God, by God, and through God. Finally, the Bible teaches that "the righteous person will entrust themselves to God" (Habakkuk 2:4) and that "the one who is justified will live by faith" (Romans 1:16–17). In this sense, our regeneration (being made new) and justification (our new forgiven self accepted into God's family) are intimately linked, and the basis of both actions are impossible to achieve independent of God Himself working in the life of the believer (John 1:14; Romans 5:1).

In the gym that Fran trains at, there are several Catholics. Can you help Fran understand the central differences between a Roman Catholic and an evangelical view of justification?

FRAN, IN MY CHILDHOOD, I attended a Catholic grade school and Catholic Church services on Sunday. Needless to say, my young and impressionable mind was filled with some very interesting (and conflicting!) ideas about justification. The longstanding tradition of the Roman Catholic Church was that the Church itself was the only channel of God's grace.[154] In this sense, the grace of God (which included justification) was functionally transmitted through the sacraments of the Church. In other words, a believer had to *do something* in addition to believing in God in order to receive God's grace. The *doing something* included such sacraments as baptism and Holy Communion.

In addition, justification was seen as a cooperative act between God and mankind. There were objective and tangible "works" that mankind could do to increase their justification and righteousness before God. Reversely, this meant that sin could result in losing an achieved status, and would therefore logically entail the subsequent necessity of more "works." The combined effect would create a "roller coaster ride" of increasing and decreasing merit during the believer's lifetime. Historically, many Catholics have appealed to such verses as James 2:24,

---

[154] Erickson, p. 837.

that states, "Faith workout works is dead" as evidence for the idea that certain things must be done in order to be justified and to retain that justification.

The evangelical view of justification is that the believer is justified by faith alone, through grace alone, in Christ alone. In no way whatsoever is this saving grace of God to be confused with a "work" on the part of the believer. In fact, this is exactly why Paul wrote that faith "is not by works so that no one can boast" (Ephesians 2:9). If justification were a *work*, then mankind could boast about it—and this is clearly antagonistic to the biblical teaching. In fact, numerous passages of Scripture indicate that justification is a gracious gift from God (Romans 6:23; Galatians 3:6). One of the strongest verses to solidify this point is when Paul wrote: "The gift of God is eternal life in Christ Jesus our Lord" (Romans 6:23). This means that justification is something that mankind *does not deserve* and *cannot earn.*

Fran wants to deepen her knowledge on the subject of *prevenient* and *effectual* grace. Can you help her unpack these theological principles within the context of Romans 2:4–7?

FRAN, MY STARTING POINT in developing a framework for salvation is that God wants all people to be saved (John 3:16; 1 Timothy 2:3–6; 2 Peter 3:9). This position provides a foundation for justifying God's indiscriminate offer of *prevenient grace* to all of mankind. Based on the fact that mankind is dead in our transgressions (Ephesians 2:1) and unable to accept Christ as Lord and Savior apart from God working supernaturally within his heart, then it logically follows that in order for God to work within us, His grace must be offered to the entire human race. The theologian Henry C. Thiessen wrote, "Since mankind is hopelessly dead in trespass and sins and can do nothing to obtain salvation, God graciously restores to *all men* sufficient ability to make a choice in the matter of submission to Him."[155]

A key distinction in this understanding of prevenient grace is that although God's grace is freely offered, and everyone is capable of accepting His offer of salvation, not everyone will. This is the exegetical unpacking of Romans 2:4–7.

---

[155] The quote of Thiessen was discovered in *Christian Theology* by Millard Erickson, p. 852.

Paul teaches that the "riches of God's kindness, forbearance and patience" (Romans 2:4) are reflections of His grace and are provided for the purpose of freely choosing His offer of salvation. Nevertheless, because of some peoples "stubbornness and unrepentant hearts" they will equally and freely choose to reject God's offer, and thus suffer the consequences of His judgment (Romans 2:5). By the same logic, all humans have sufficient grace to freely choose God's offer of salvation (what Paul referred to as "doing good" in verse 2:7) and to receive eternal life through faith in Jesus Christ (Romans 2:7).

Fran wants to know if there is a difference between a believer's *acceptance* and *approval* before God.

THERE IS A SUBTLE BUT EXTREMELY important distinction between a believer's *acceptance into God's family*, and God's *approval of the believer's faithfulness* in living out the life God has graciously given them.[156] The acceptance into God's family happens immediately at the time of conversion and is entirely dependent on the believer's acceptance of God's free gift of salvation through faith in Jesus Christ (2 Corinthians 5:17). On the other hand, approval and spiritual maturity (much akin to sanctification) is a lifelong process the believer participates in with the help of the Holy Spirit and the body of the Church (Philippians 2:12).

Fran, I think this distinction is valid and very important in the believer's life. Furthermore, I think they are logically sequential, with the first step being the acceptance into God's family. The acceptance and entry into God's family is a two-step process. On one hand, the believer is in Christ (Ephesians 2:10), and on the other hand Christ is in the believer (Colossians 1:27). The union with Christ and entry into God's family are given by grace through faith in Jesus. The same power of God, now within the believer, empowers and equips them for continued approval, growth, discipleship, and spiritual maturity (Ephesians 4:15; 2 Peter 3:18).

---

[156] Breshears.

Fran asks you about the nature of the heart within the context of the Bible. Why is the "heart" such an important concept for Christians to understand?

FRAN, IN THE BIBLE, the *heart* often refers to the innermost nature of the individual—the very seat of the human being's deepest and strongest emotions and desires.[157] The Bible teaches that our *heart* must be *sanctified* and made holy—which means "set apart" and "bearing an actual likeness to God."[158] On one hand, sanctification is something that happens at the point of conversion and acceptance into the family of God. On the other hand, the entire Christian life is a process of becoming increasingly conformed to the image and likeness of Jesus Christ (2 Corinthians 3:18). In other words, whereas justification and regeneration are instantaneous occurrences, sanctification is the process of God continually working in the believer's life, making us more like His Son (1 Thessalonians 5:23).

The Wesleyan model of sanctification teaches that the believer receives by faith an entirely cleansed heart. The new heart within the believer "frees them from sin" and tends to foster the idea in their mind that "Jesus will do it!"[159] On the other hand, the Keswick model is more akin to "an exchanged life" in which the Spirit of Christ dwelling within the believer's heart sustains them for moral victory. The traditional Reformed position is that believers experience gradual spiritual growth, increasing spiritual maturity and progressive capacity to be obedient to the Word of God.[160]

Fran, the model I tend to align with is referred to as the New Covenant, in which believers receive a new heart at the moment of conversion. The Holy Spirit indwells the believer's heart, enabling them to "walk in step with the spirit" (Galatians 5:25) and to progressively grow in grace, knowledge, faith, love, and "doing good" (Ephesians 4:15; 2 Peter 3:18). The believer is accepted into the family of God, in addition to enjoying fellowship in the body of the Church. The combined effect results in the believer becoming transformed by God and "sharing the diving qualities as fruit of the Spirit."[161]

---

[157] Walter A. Elwell, *Baker Encyclopedia of the Bible* (Grand Rapids, MI: Baker House, 1993), p. 2149.

[158] Erickson, p. 897.

[159] Breshears.

[160] Breshears.

[161] Breshears.

CHAPTER EIGHT

THE HOLY SPIRIT

CHAPTER SUMMARY:

THE HOLY SPIRIT OF GOD provides the crucial link between the believer and God. Due to the fact that the doctrine of the Third Person of the Trinity is not systematically described in Scripture, over the life of the Church, there have been difficulties in understanding His nature and work. The Holy Spirit is particularly at work in the life of Jesus and throughout the New Testament. The Holy Spirit guides believers from spiritual infancy to maturity and provides miraculous gifts that edify and build up the body of Christ.

Summarize the historical context of the *filoque* **controversy for Fran and help her understand its significance for the Trinitarian theology of the Spirit.**

FRAN, THE CHRISTIAN FAITH is unique in the entire world for making the claim that God is One—and yet there are three Persons who are in God. These three persons—God the Father, God the Son, and God the Holy Spirit—share equality within the Godhead. The equality of the three Persons within the Godhead is crucial for establishing the deity of Jesus Christ, which has historically been a point of great tension, even during the life of Jesus Himself! As important as the Trinity is within the context of Christology, it is also important within the Trinitarian theology of the Holy Spirit. One of the intriguing points of contention regarding the full deity of the Spirit is referred to as the *filoque* controversy.

Briefly summarized, the controversy can be understood by defining the meaning of the Latin word *filoque,* which translates as "and the Son." During the medieval period, the word appeared within Church doctrine in the establishment of the Nicene Creed that states: "We believe in the Holy Spirit, the Lord, the Giver of life, who proceeds from the Father (*filoque*) and the Son." Because this language is common with the Western Church, you might ask yourself, "What is the controversy?" Well, the issue that arose was whether the Spirit proceeded from the Father *and the Son* (Roman Church) or only from the Father (Eastern Church)?[162] Although the Eastern Church could have accepted language similar to *through the Son,* they argued that *and the Son* subverted the primacy of God the Father and the "secondness" of the Son.[163] The Eastern Church's insistence of the matter eventually led to a split between the Eastern and Western Churches.[164]

For our purposes, establishing the full deity of the Spirit, and the Spirit's equality with the Father and the Son, is tantamount to our doctrine of the Trinity. In order to uphold our view of the Trinity, we must assign full deity to the Spirit.

---

[162] Dr. Gerry Breshears, "Holy Spirit" outline, Western Seminary, TH503.

[163] Breshears

[164] Millard Erickson, *Christian Theology* (Grand Rapids, MI: Baker Academic, 2013), p. 778.

Fran, one of the ways we can do this is to look systematically at the way the Holy Spirit is treated within Scripture. What we discover is that the word "Spirit" is often used interchangeably with the word "God" (Luke 1:35; Acts 5:3,4; 1 Corinthians 3:16–17). I've found that Luke 1:35 is one of the best verses to help me teach the integrity and equality of the Trinity. In this one beautiful verse, Luke paints a picture of the mosaic of the Trinity, working harmoniously together, and sharing equality within the Godhead. Finally, when we look to the Scripture for statements that establish the doctrine of the Trinity, it becomes immediately apparent that the Spirit is treated with perfect equality to the Father and the Son (Matthew 28:19; 1 Corinthians 12:4–6; Hebrews 9:14).

Some argue that Acts 2 teaches that true believers in Jesus receive the Holy Spirit at a time well after their conversion to becoming Jesus followers. Is this true?

FRAN, SOME CHRISTIAN DENOMINATIONS teach that believers in Jesus Christ should expect (and look forward to) an experience of the Holy Spirit after their initial conversion. In the Pentecostal tradition, this experience is usually referred to as the "Baptism in the Spirit." This view further claims that objective evidences of the Holy Spirit baptism are speaking in tongues and empowerment for service in God's Kingdom. Those who hold this view substantiate their position by noting that in Acts 2, the disciples "were filled with the Holy Spirit and began to speak in other tongues as the Spirit enabled them" (Acts 2:4). Because the disciples had been followers of Jesus for nearly three years, in addition to the fact that in John 20:22, "Jesus breathed on them (the disciples) and said, 'Receive the Holy Spirit,'" the logical conclusion is that there is a distinct second baptism. In other words, John 20:22 clearly establishes one baptism, whereas Acts 2:4 establishes another. The difference in Acts 2:4 (the second baptism) is there is *objective evidence* of the Holy Spirit's work within the believer which is made manifest in *glossalilia*— speaking in unknown human languages.

Fran, I believe that when you "confess with your mouth that Jesus is Lord, and believe in your heart that God raised Jesus from the dead, you will be saved" (Romans 10:9). In this grace-empowered moment of conversion, you receive the gift of the Holy Spirit. The indwelling presence of the Spirit unites you to the Body of Christ—His Church—and initiates the process of sanctification. As the new believer lives out their faith in the Body of Christ, there is a continual filling of the Spirit that is evident in the believer experiencing an increase in the *fruit of the Spirit*.[165] However, I think it is a mistake to view these as second blessings. Rather, this is the actualization of what the believer receives at the moment of conversion.

Fran, I think a potential danger in expecting a distinct "second baptism"—and in particular a baptism that results in speaking in tongues—is that the believer could be led to doubt the validity of their initial conversion experience. In other words, the believer could be torn between the conflicting views that they should expect a second distinct work of grace from God, or whether the indwelling gift of the Spirit at the moment of conversion was sufficient. In addition, there could be subconscious pressure to manifest or exaggerate a second baptismal experience to fit in with social pressure with the Church.

Some of the Christians that Fran trains with at her gym attend very charismatic Churches. What are three "big ideas" about the Holy Spirit within Pentecostalism?

FRAN, TIMOTHY TENNENT, in his masterful book *Theology in the Context of World Christianity,* provides a comprehensive treatment on the doctrine of the Holy Spirit within the Pentecostal faith. In his discussion, there are three "takeaways" that can help shape our understanding of the role of the Holy Spirit within the life of the believer.

The first big idea presented by Tennent is of immense importance. Given that many Christians assume "that denomination is *different* than mine," we often fall victim to focusing on our differences, rather than our similarities. Tennent makes the point that this is a big mistake, in particular within the context of Pentecostalism. Tennent points out that Pentecostals fully affirm the authority

----

[165] Breshears.

and inspiration of the Bible as well as the centrality of Christ's atoning work on the cross for salvation and reconciliation with God. They also affirm the historic reality of the resurrection of Jesus and teach the importance of repentance, conversion, and living a holy and sanctified life. Furthermore, although most Pentecostal Churches do not adhere to creeds, they would nevertheless be able to affirm every statement of the Apostles' or Nicene Creed.[166]

Another important point Tennent makes is that the believer never witnesses or evangelizes alone, because they are always "accompanied by God the Evangelist, who speaks and works through them by the power of the Holy Spirit."[167] This is a particularly empowering consideration, especially within the context of the Great Commission to "go and make disciples of all the nations." Speaking from personal experience, my tendency has been to think, "I need more education before I can 'go and make disciples.'" However, in adopting the Pentecostal view that the Holy Spirit is present with me and prepared to manifest His power alongside me, I have a renewed sense of purpose and potential to lead others to Christ.

Fran, it's the same thing within the CrossFit community! At the Level I Course, attendees are encouraged to "go home, knock on your neighbor's door, and teach them how to squat." The new CrossFit athlete does not need to concern themselves with credentials—they have the backing of the entire CrossFit community to help them. In this sense, how much more inspired should Christians be to "knock on our neighbor's door and teach them about Christ!" Much like Tennent pointed out, with God the Evangelist present, success in leading others to Jesus is not contingent upon financial backing, big fancy Churches, detailed planning, or even seminary degrees! The important thing to remember is that God Himself is *with us*, and He is opening doors and hearts *for us*.

The third takeaway offered by Tennent is the contrast between the *Homogenous Unit Principle* and the Pentecostal approach to evangelism and mission work. Within the CrossFit culture, Tennent's observation has immense implication and relevance. The *Homogenous Unit Principle* is a proven sociological fact that people prefer not to cross social and ethnic

---

[166] Timothy Tennent, *Christian Theology in the Context of World Christianity* (Grand Rapids, MI: Zondervan, 2007), p. 166.

[167] Tennent, p. 182.

barriers when becoming a Christian.[168] In addition, this principle holds that people prefer to worship alongside people who are like themselves in cultural, socioeconomic, and a variety of other ways. This is the reason why the Faith Rx'd movement in the CrossFit community is so strong—CrossFit athletes are more inclined to pursue a relationship with Jesus Christ when in the company of other CrossFit athletes.

For this very reason, the Pentecostal tradition has largely been reluctant to embrace or employ the *Homogeneous Unit Principle* in their evangelistic and missionary work. Rather, the Pentecostal would find inspiration in the account of Acts 10, in which Peter and Cornelius—two people completely separated in nearly every conceivable way—nevertheless found congruency and unity through the power of the Holy Spirit (Acts 10:44). According to the Pentecostal tradition of mission work, the Holy Spirit should empower the believer to transcend the normal social and ethnic barriers—in addition to any preconceived barrier to the Gospel message of Unity in Christ.

Fran wants to know the difference between Cessationism and Functional Cessationism.

FRAN, OVER THE YEARS there have been differing views on the active role of the Holy Spirit continuing to perform miracles, divine healing, prophecy, and most notably, speaking in tongues. Generally speaking, four different views have been proposed to include *Cessationism, Functional Cessationism, Continuationism,* and *Word Faith.* In the broadest sense, we can understand these four positions in two general categories: Continuationism—Word Faith; and Cessationism—Functional Cessationism.

Continuationism holds that while Scripture is God's only trustworthy voice, He continues to speak to Churches and individuals through His Spirit. These unique revelations of His Word must be tested and weighed against the Bible. In addition, God continues to perform miracles (which may include speaking in tongues) and believers should pray and expect these miracles to be a present reality within their life and Church. The Word-Faith movement takes an even more liberal interpretation of the Holy Spirit's active work in the world and holds that the

---

[168] Tennent, p. 188.

atonement of Jesus includes healing from every kind of disease. By participating with the Spirit and "speaking faith," believers should expect to experience God's Kingdom in emotional, financial, relational, and spiritual realities.[169]

Fran, lets compare and contrast the categories of Cessationism and Functional Cessationism. The Functional Cessationist would hold that although the sign-gifts of speaking in tongues and miraculous healing most notably authenticated the Apostles (Acts 5:15, 19:12), there is no reason to believe that these gifts have ceased today (John 14:12–14; 1 Corinthians 12:31,14:1–18). However, abuses and exaggerations of continuing miraculous experiences with the Holy Spirit are so rampant and abusive that it is better to rely on the revealed wisdom of the Bible.[170] At the other end of the spectrum, many notable theologians believe in Cessationism and that the diffusion of miraculous gifts by the Holy Spirit was confined to the apostolic Church and subsequently passed away with it.[171]

Fran, I lean toward the Functional Cessationism view and argue that although the Bible is God's only trustworthy voice, believers should "let the Holy Spirit guide our lives" (Galatians 5:16) and leave room within the traditionally held Western Enlightenment worldview that tends to create a wall between the experiential framework of the senses and the supernatural framework of the biblical authors.[172] In other words, when guided by the Bible, believers have more to gain than lose in opening our mind to the idea that the same Holy Spirit who acted supernaturally in the lives of the Apostles and early Church is active and alive in similar ways today.

---

[169] Dr. Gerry Breshears, "Holy Spirit" outline, Western Seminary, TH503.

[170] Breshears.

[171] B. B. Warfield in his book *Counterfeit Miracles,* as identified in *Christian Theology,* p. 172.

[172] Tennent, p. 178.

Fran wants to know if an evangelical could hold that there is continuing special revelation, while at the same time affirming that the canon of Scripture is closed. Biblically speaking, is it possible that there is continuing special revelation beyond the canonical books of the Holy Bible?

FRAN, IT IS IMPORTANT to make the distinction between the contention that the Holy Spirit is actively working in the Church and God's people, and the fact that the canon of Scripture is closed. Or to explain this in another way, although the canon of Scripture is closed—and inspiration ceased—this does not discount the fact that the Holy Spirit may continue to work in supernatural ways within the Body of Christ.

Fran, I do not believe that it is possible for an evangelical to hold on one hand that the canon of Scripture is closed, and on the other that there is continuing special revelation. We must make the distinction between the supreme and independent authoritative Word of God contained within the Bible, and other forms of prophecy that may continue in the Church today. Evangelicals hold that special revelation was received through the power of the Holy Spirit by the authors of Scripture—this makes it authoritative, infallible, and "God's Word" (2 Timothy 3:16–17; 2 Peter 1:20–21). When the canon of Scripture was closed, this specific type of special revelation also ceased. In this sense, we cannot "add to the Bible" (Deuteronomy 12:32; Proverbs 30:5–6; Revelation 22:18–19).

Fran, I want to point out that although the canon of Scripture is closed—which means there will not be any *new revelation*—God continues to reveal Himself to believers today. This means that we should not discount the fact that prophecy may still occur in the Church, and that believers may experience "Spirit empowered proclamations of the Word of God that press deep into peoples hearts."[173] However, in modern times, we must make a distinction between the infallible Word of God contained within Scripture and "Words from God" that believers may experience through the indwelling power of the Holy Spirit. Unlike the Bible, these *Words of Wisdom* (Acts 6:3; Galatians 2:11–21), *Words of Knowledge* (John 4:17–18), and *Prophecies* must be tested

---

[173] Dr. Gerry Breshears, position paper, *Spiritual Gifts,* Western Seminary.

in a variety of ways, most notably ensuring congruency and consistency with what the Bible already says (Deuteronomy 13:1–11; 1 Kings 13:15–18).[174]

Fran asks for your insights and understanding of Paul's exhortation in 1 Corinthians 14:1. How would Paul's teaching relate to ministry inside the gym?

FRAN, IN THE CHURCH today there is a lot of discussion—and enthusiasm—around gifts of the Holy Spirit. As a result, some people seem to be more interested in pursuing the *gifts of the Spirit* rather than the Holy Spirit Himself; the gift given to *all believers* at conversion (Acts 2:33; Romans 8:15). Nevertheless, evangelicals must also remember that in Paul's first letter to the Corinthians, he wrote that believers should "Follow the way of love and eagerly desire gifts of the Spirit, especially prophecy" (1 Corinthians 14:1). Based on this verse, one could be led to think that seeking the "gifts of the Spirit" should be first priority in a believer's life. So how do we balance on one hand the idea that the Holy Spirit is freely given at conversion, and on the other hand the idea that we are called to eagerly desire more of the Spirit?

To begin, it is important to note that in verse 14:1, the Greek word that Paul used for "Spirit" is in fact *pneumatikos*, which is translated as *spirituals* and, in the context of the verse, means *spiritual gifts*. Whereas in 1 Corinthians 12:1, "Now about the gifts of the Spirit," Paul uses the Greek word *charisma* for Spirit, which on its own has nothing to do with the Spirit; rather, it designates a variety of ways that God's grace is evidenced among His people. Given that Paul continues his exposition on spiritual gifts throughout Chapters 12 through 14, it is important that we see the "big picture" of what Paul is teaching, and most importantly filter our view of spiritual gifts through the lens of love (Chapter 13). In this sense, "gifts of the Spirit" (12:1 and 14:1) likely means something along the lines of "concrete expressions of grace manifested through the Spirit's empowering."[175]

---

[174] Dr. Gerry Breshears, "Holy Spirit" outline, Western Seminary, TH503.

[175] Gerald F. Hawthorne, *Dictionary of Paul and His Letters* (Downers Grove, IL: InterVarsity Press, 1993), p. 340.

Verse 14:1 is best understood in the context of Paul summarizing Chapter 13, in which he demonstrates love as the essential and primary fruit of the Spirit. In this sense, Paul is instructing the Corinthians to "pursue more love." This also means that according to Paul, love is the foundational quality that should be growing in the life of every Christian. To the extent that Christians are growing in love, then it is appropriate for them to also desire other spiritual gifts. It is interesting to note that of all the gifts Paul could emphasize or reference, he specifically settled on the gift of prophecy, which we will discuss in depth below.

Fran, in our ministry within the CrossFit gym, Paul's exhortation in verse 14:1 could be seen as a three-step movement in the Christian life. The first step is to follow the way of love. This is a reminder that even if a believer has every spiritual gift under the sun—but they lack love—then "they have nothing" (1 Corinthians 13:1–3). The second step is to eagerly desire the variety of gifts, services, and workings that are manifested in the believer's life by the Holy Spirit for the purpose of "making disciples of all the nations" (Matthew 28:19–20). This is an important qualification: the gifts of the Spirit were not meant to edify the believer—they were intended to edify the Church. Logically, this leads us to the third step, desiring the gift of prophecy. According to Paul, the gift of prophecy speaks words that communicate the truth of God's Word into people's lives. Prophecy edifies the entire Body of Christ and thus correlates perfectly to the reason why spiritual gifts are given in the first place (1 Corinthians 12:7).

Many of Fran's workout partners talk about being "filled with the Holy Spirit." Can you help Fran understand the biblical and theological implications of what this filling means?

———————

FRAN, MY POSITION ON being *filled with the Holy Spirit* is that this supernatural gift from God occurs in the believer's life at the moment of conversion. A key passage for this position is 1 Corinthians 12:13, where Paul writes: "For we were all baptized by one Spirit so as to form one body—whether Jews or Gentiles, slave or free—and we were all given one Spirit to drink." In this theologically packed verse, Paul makes four remarkable points: First, the baptism applies to all believers; second, all believers are baptized by the same Spirit; third, believers are baptized into the Body of Christ; and fourth, the baptism and union with the Body of Christ take place at the moment of conversion. This means that when a new believer "confesses with their mouth that Jesus Christ is Lord, and believes in their heart that God raised Jesus from the dead" (Romans 10:9), they receive the indwelling power of the Holy Spirit (John 14:17), a new heart (Titus 3:5), and are incorporated into the Body of Christ (1 Corinthians 12:13).[176]

Following the initial conversion experience and the receipt of the Holy Spirit's indwelling presence, the believer is called to a life of increasing sanctification and growing Christlikeness (2 Thessalonians 2:13; Colossians 3:1, 5). This means that although the Holy Spirit comes to indwell every person at conversion, there is an ongoing experience throughout the believer's new life in Christ of being continually *filled with the Spirit.* This subsequent filling may be gradual or rather dramatic (1 Corinthians 12:7–11) and occurs as a result of living out the reality of being baptized by the Spirit. This perpetual filling is not to be confused with distinct second blessings of the Holy Spirit, but rather "an actualization of what we have already received at conversion."[177]

———————

[176] Breshears.

[177] Breshears.

CHAPTER NINE

THE CHURCH

CHAPTER SUMMARY:

THE CHURCH IS THE visible form of the corporate relationship between followers of Jesus Christ. In the New Testament, a variety of images are used to describe the Church, including the people of God, the body of Christ, and the Temple of the Holy Spirit. The purpose of the Church is to carry out Christ's ministry to the world (Matthew 28:19–20). To remain relevant and effective, the Church must be willing to serve, adaptable to an ever-changing environment, and steadfast in the proclamation of the Gospel message. Different leadership roles within the Church are meant to guide the body of believers to a sound understanding of doctrine and to maintain an upright and moral life. The two rites of the Church, baptism and the Lord's Supper, play a significant role in the life of the Church and the individual believer.

Fran is interested in the different ways that the Church can interact with the CrossFit culture and the local gym.

———————————

FRAN, OVER THE YEARS, there have been several attempts to explain and contextualize the relationship between the Church and culture. For example, the great theologian H. Richard Niebuhr proposed that there were seven distinct models of the way that the Church interacted with modern culture: the Church against culture; the Church over culture; the Church alongside culture; the Church transforming culture; the Church lost in culture; the culture against the Church; and the Church speaking prophetically into the culture.[178]

In addition to the work of Niebuhr, the Bible offers several models for understanding the unique way that the Church interacts with culture. For our purposes, it is important to consider the different ways that a particular model might shape the ministry context of the Church. For example, consider the implications of adopting what we could define as the "Noah" model of the Church. In this context, the Church could potentially be seen as a "modern-day ark" that is used to escape from the culture. On the other hand, the Church could be seen within the framework of the "Moses" model in which people confront culture and then exit (i.e., "Exodus") from it. At the other end of the spectrum, the Church could be seen as a "David" or "Joshua" model, in which the intention of the Church is to invade, conquer, subdue, and rule over culture.[179] Fran, you can clearly see from these varying models that the particular context in which the Church relates to culture significantly influences how a Church proclaims the Gospel of Jesus Christ.

Fran, in the unique ministry context of the Church alongside the CrossFit community, I think one of the most powerful biblical models to consider is what we could refer to as the "Daniel" model. In this sense, a Christian athlete operates as an anointed ambassador of the Kingdom of God within the CrossFit gym. I think this particular model is very consistent with our Lord's command to "go and make disciples of all the nations" (Matthew 28:19a).

---

[178] Dr. Gerry Breshears, "Ecclesiology" outline, Western Seminary, TH503.

[179] Dr. Gerry Breshears, "Holy Spirit" outline, Western Seminary, TH503.

In other words, the CrossFit culture is a "micro-nation" in which a Christian athlete can go forth and teach their peers to "obey everything the Lord has commanded" (Matthew 28:20b—my interpretation).[180]

In CrossFit, Fran is aware that certain leadership positions carry with them a title, such as "Flow Master" or "Coach." She is curious about the different leadership titles of the New Testament, specifically the roles of the "Elder" and "Pastor."

FRAN, IN THE BIBLE, it says: "Whoever desires to be an *episkopē* desires a noble task (1 Timothy 3:1). The Greek word *episkopē* translates as "overseer" and refers to the office of elder in the local Church. In his first letter to Timothy, the Apostle Paul had a great deal to say about this particular leadership role (1 Timothy 3:1–7), including the fact that an elder must be above reproach, faithful to his wife, temperate, self-controlled, and able to teach the Word of God (1 Timothy 3:2). Needless to say, an elder is an extremely important leadership position in the Church.

Fran, reflect on the leadership role of a pastor in your Church. What does a pastor do? In the book *When God Doesn't Answer Your Prayer,* author Jerry Sittser quoted a Nigerian pastor who said that very often people think a pastor "is the official Christian of the Church, and that he performs for you Sunday after Sunday."[181] This being the case, it is imperative that we have a biblical and theological understanding of the role of the pastor—and I propose that this is best accomplished by understanding the office of the elder (or overseer). In the Bible, we observe that an elder is the highest office of the local Church and is charged with the responsibility of oversight of the doctrinal soundness and spiritual health of the congregation.[182] The specific duties of the elder revolve around the two most important responsibilities of their respective office: pastoral care (often referred to as *shepherding*) and guiding and guarding the teaching of the Church. This combination of

---

[180] My current ministry context is Law Enforcement Chaplaincy and the establishment of a Church within my CrossFit studio in Santa Cruz, CA.

[181] Identified in Dr. Breshears's notes on "Church," Western Seminary, TH503.

[182] Breshears.

pastoral shepherding and doctrinal oversight are beautifully taught in Acts 20:28 and 1 Peter 5:1–2.

Fran is very curious about the authority of the Church and those people who hold office. Can you summarize for her the difference between official, moral, and perceived authority and their relationship to how power is utilized in leadership?

FRAN, UNDERSTANDING THE DIFFERENCE between biblical and secular models of authority is extremely important. Based on my experiences in the U.S. Army and civilian law enforcement, I have learned that there are significant variances between how authority is perceived. Given the fact that there is such a wide range of contexts for how authority is portrayed and experienced (for example, the authority of a Little League baseball umpire as opposed to a Supreme Court judge), let's begin with a basic definition of what authority is within the framework of the Bible. Throughout the Bible, we learn that authority refers to the right to make decisions, rule over people, and direct the behavior of other persons.[183] Although these qualities of authority might sound familiar within the context of our secular society, the Bible recognizes authority in a unique way—rather than *commanding others,* a biblical authority figure (i.e., a "leader") leads others by equipping, empowering, unifying, and shepherding them.

Fran, I think it is imperative to understand the authority of a pastor within the context of established Church offices. Certain offices of the Church carry with them specific responsibilities, and in order to accomplish these responsibilities and objectives, the Church grants authority to the person holding the office. However, as one of my military mentors once told me, "It's not the rank that makes the person; the person makes the rank." In this sense, the authority of the pastor is a combination of *ex officio* (the legal authority of the office), *ex persona* (the moral authority of the leader), and *ex charismata* (the perceived authority of the leader).[184]

---

[183] Breshears.

[184] Dr. Breshears, notes on "Leadership Roles," TH503.

The pastor is entrusted by the Church to make decisions, direct the cooperate body of the Church, and shape the behavior of Church members.[185] However, rather than "lording it over them" (1 Peter 5:3), pastors are to exercise their authority by equipping, inspiring, empowering, unifying, edifying, exemplifying, and "shepherding" the Church (Ephesians 4:3, 4:11–12; 2 Timothy 2:24–25; 1 Peter 5:1–4). Furthermore, a distinction must be made between a pastor's serving in a position *of authority* as opposed to their being *an authoritarian.* The pastor's authority flows from their character and wisdom rather than an abuse of (or reliance upon) their position of power. By exercising a combination of their spiritual gifts alongside the established position of authority they hold, pastors guide and guard the Church and lead in the decision-making process (Acts 6:2–3, 15:22; 20:28; Titus 1:5–9). Rather than handling all of the ministry tasks of the Church himself, the pastor seeks to empower, build up, and equip others to function successfully in a variety of leadership roles (Ephesians 4:12). In fact, one of the greatest signs of a pastor's authentic authority is their ability to share that authority with others instead of always seeking to be "center stage" in the eyes of the congregation.

Fran is interested in how Jesus Christ is "present" within the communion meal. Can you explain your perspective on "real presence" while also providing contrast with other positions?

FRAN, THE LORD'S SUPPER is a vital part of the Christian faith. Whereas baptism is the initiatory rite, the Lord's Supper is the continuing right of the local Church.[186] Although there are several points of agreement among various Christian groups (the establishment by Christ; the necessity of repetition; a form of proclamation; a spiritual benefit for the partaker; restriction to followers of Christ; and the horizontal dimension of the rite), there are also significant differences.[187] One of the most disputed matters regarding the Lord's Supper is the presence of Christ. The specific issue pertains to whether (and in what sense and degree) the actual *body* and *blood* of Christ are effectually

---

[185] Dr. Gerry Breshears, "Ecclesiology" outline, Western Seminary, TH503.

[186] Millard Erickson, *Christian Theology* (Grand Rapids, MI: Baker Academic, 2013), p. 1034.

[187] Erickson, p. 1038.

present in the elements of the communion. In other words, how are Christians to faithfully understand what Jesus meant when He said, "This is my body" and "This is my blood"? (Matthew 26:26–28).

There have traditionally been four answers given to this complex theological question: The bread and wine *are* the physical body and blood of Christ; the bread and wine *contain* the physical body and blood; the bread and wine *spiritually contain* the body and blood; and the bread and wine *represent* the body and blood.[188]

Fran, I was raised in a traditional Roman Catholic Church. On Sundays during communion, the priest who administered the elements would effect an actual metaphysical change in the bread and wine. Referred to as the doctrine of *transubstantiation,* the belief was that the whole of Christ was fully present with each of the particles of the elements of communion. In this sense, "the real presence of Christ" within the elements of communion meant that everyone in the Church would literally partake in the body and blood of Christ.

Although I certainly appreciate the historical tradition of the Catholic Church, I propose that in order to understand what Jesus meant when He said, "This is my body" and "This is my blood," we must exegete His words within the larger context of the other unique metaphors He used to describe the relationship between individual believers and their Lord. For example, Jesus characterized Himself as a *vine*, a *shepherd*, and *the bread of life* (John 6:35, 10:11–18, 15:5). In keeping with the figurative language of Jesus, we could understand Him to have meant, "This bread represents my body, and this cup represents my blood." In this sense, through the power of the Holy Spirit, Jesus is present in a very special way as the sacramental meal occurs. Although there is nothing *special about the elements* of communion (the bread and wine), the Lord's Supper is a time of *special relationship and communion* with Christ because He promised to be especially with us when we gather as a body of believers (Matthew 18:20). In other words, "we should think of the sacrament not so much in terms of Christ's presence as in terms of his promise and the potential for a closer relationship with Him."[189]

---

[188] Erickson, p. 1039.

[189] Erickson, p. 1047.

Fran is interested in the different positions on who should be invited to participate in communion. Can you provide her with biblical evidence that can equip her to answer this question within her gym?

FRAN, I BELIEVE THAT due to the fact that the Lord's Supper signifies a special relationship between the individual believer and their Lord, it follows that a personal and saving relationship with God be a prerequisite for participation in the communion meal. Furthermore, given that Paul specifically addressed the importance of the individual believer being able to discern for themselves the spiritual significance of the meal (1 Corinthians 11:29), it logically follows that the communion meal should be withheld from nonbelievers. It is also important to note that Paul stressed that people in the Church who were blatantly living a life of sin should be removed from the Body of Christ (1 Corinthians 5:1–5). This would suggest that if Paul argued for the removal of people entertaining a sinful lifestyle (thus also withholding the Lord's Supper from them), then as a first step in Church discipline and entry into the Body of Christ, the Lord's Supper should likewise be withheld from nonbelievers.

Fran, I recognize that my view might be less than inviting for the modern "seeker sensitive" approach that many Churches are taking to evangelism. A strong argument for a more welcoming position is based on the fact that the Lord's Supper is a special time of fellowship with Christ and with His Church, and that everyone present should be invited to participate as a means of welcoming potential new believers into the family of God. In either case, I think given Paul's exhortation for "self-examination" (2 Corinthians 13:5), the most important qualification is to explain the meaning of the Lord's Supper, emphasize the significance of a personal relationship with Jesus Christ, and then leave the decision to participate up to the individuals gathered in the Church.

One aspect of CrossFit that Fran really loves is that it's a merit-based community. Fran is concerned about what appears to be biblical restrictions on women in leadership positions within the Church. Can you summarize for Fran the three evangelical views on women in leadership, and which one you lean toward?

———————

FRAN, THE THREE MAIN views on women in leadership (not to be confused with women in ministry—everyone in the Church is *in ministry*) are the egalitarian, the male elder, and the male teacher positions. The egalitarian position holds that all roles and offices are open to all persons, whereas the male elder position restricts the office of elder to just men. The male teacher position is the most restrictive and holds that women should not teach or have any authority over men in the Church.[190]

I lean toward the male teacher position and believe that women can minister in a variety of ministries that are open to any other male in alignment with their spiritual gifting and qualifications established by the local Church. However, these respective ministries should not include teaching the corporate body of the Church, teaching the Bible to men, or exercising authority over men in the Church. These elder-type positions are to be specifically reserved for men (1 Timothy 2:11, 3:1–7; Titus 1:6–9).

In implementation, the elder leadership positions reserved for men must by no means be interpreted to suggest male favoritism or male-gender superiority. The creation account of Genesis 1:26–27 firmly establishes that men and women are equally created in God's image. Furthermore, in Galatians 3:28, Paul teaches that in the context of God's salvation, there is no distinction between male and female "for you are all one in Christ." This means that it is through faith in Christ that people become "children of God" (Galatians 3:26): race, economic status, and gender are of no consequence in His Kingdom. Men and women were both fully created in God's image and are perfectly equal in dignity, value, and essence.[191]

———————

[190] Breshears, notes on "Male/Female Roles," TH503.

[191] Dr. Gerry Breshears, *Women in Leadership Roles and Ordination Study Packet*, p. 16.

This being the case, as Genesis 2 describes, the humanity and functions of men and women are to be experienced differently, with the female functioning in a subordinate role to male leadership and authority (Genesis 3:16). However, the leadership and authority of men must be seen, understood, and applied within the context of the Church's submission to Christ (Ephesians 5:22–23). This means that men are to lead and exercise authority in a Christlike manner and not lord their position over women. The role distinctions and male headship described in Genesis 2 (in addition to the more overt statement in Genesis 3:16) and later elaborated on by Paul (1 Corinthians 11:8–10; 1 Timothy 2:13) must not be contextualized in such a way as to imply a lack of female dignity, value, essence or *Imago Dei*. Rather, these distinctions must be understood in the context of 1 Timothy 2:8–15.

For example, the requirement for women to learn in "quietness and full submission" and to "not exercise authority over a man" (1 Timothy 2:11–12), is to be seen as a distinction between appropriate male and female roles, offices, and responsibilities within the Church—not in degrees of essence or standing before God. Furthermore, the requirement for women to "be silent in Church" (1 Corinthians 14:34), and that it would be "disgraceful for a woman to speak in Church" (1 Corinthians 14:35), must be understood in the context of the judging and interpretation of prophecy—a role reserved for male elders.[192] Both men (1 Timothy 2:8) and women (1 Timothy 2:9; 1 Corinthians 11:4–5) are to worship in such a way as to edify the body of believers and to maintain harmony and good order.

Fran, although I hold the male elder position, there are a few key strengths to the egalitarian position that should be recognized. Of most significance is the fact that Jesus Himself affirmed women and included them in His entourage throughout Galilee and Judea (Luke 8:1–3). In addition, Jesus refused to rebuke Mary for taking the traditionally male-reserved position of discipleship at a rabbi's feet (Luke 10:38–42). In this sense, Jesus can be seen overturning the socially normative practices of His time, and in the establishment of His Church, it follows that He expected believers to do the same. Because Jesus used the example of both men and women in His parables to represent God (Luke 13:20–21), in addition to the fact that Jesus commissioned women to

---

[192] Dr. Gerry Breshears, "Holy Spirit" outline, Western Seminary, TH503.

go and tell of His resurrection (John 20:17), Jesus clearly demonstrates His intention to allow women to continue to teach and spread the Gospel.[193]

Fran has seen a lot of differences in the ways that Christian denominations experience worship and praise God. Can you help her understand the different dimensions of worship?

———————————

FRAN, IT IS SIGNIFICANT that throughout the entire Bible, the worship (or exaltation) of God is a reoccurring and major theme. Whereas teaching and edification tend to focus on and benefit the believer, worship concentrates and focuses on the Lord.[194] In ministry application, it is important to remember that in addition to worship and instruction, the Church also has a mission to evangelize non-Christians (Matthew 28:19–20). In this sense, the Church comes together for distinct purposes, and in many respects it is good to keep some degree of separation among these different activities lest one be crowded out in favor of another.[195] For example, if the Church were solely focused on instruction from the pulpit, then worship of God would tend to suffer. On the other hand, if worship of God were the sole focus of the Church, then the mandate to "go make disciples of all nations" (Matthew 28:19a) would tend to be neglected.

This being the case, it is important to understand the "four dimensions of worship." Succinctly explained, the four dimensions are adoration of God (Psalm 145; Luke 17:15–18); service onto God's Kingdom (Psalm 37:3; Matthew 25:35–40); Sacrifice (Psalm 51:15–19), and participation and unity in Christ (Psalm 149; John 17:21–23).[196] In this sense, there is certainly a wide range of ways that we can worship God!

---

[193] Dr. Gerry Breshears, *Women in Leadership Roles and Ordination Study Packet,* p. 10.

[194] Erickson, p. 977.

[195] Erickson, p. 977.

[196] Dr. Gerry Breshears, "Worship" outline, Western Seminary, TH503.

Everything from "walking and jumping and praising God" (Acts 3:8) to being still and silent before God's mighty presence (Psalm 46:10; Lamentations 3:28) qualifies as worship. This means that worship is a "whole person thing, a whole body thing, and a whole life thing."[197]

Fran, practically speaking, I believe that worship of God should be a "whole life thing." In other words, as Christians, we are called to be disciples of Jesus 24 hours a day, 365 days a year. At the other end of the spectrum, some people think that being a Christian and following Jesus is a one-hour-a-week thing—and that that particular hour is reserved for Sunday! However, when we look to such biblical superheroes as David, we see something altogether different. David longed to have his mind and heart focused on God "day and night" (Psalm 119:97). David's entire life was consumed by worship of God. In other words, David's "one thing" was that he would "dwell in the house of the Lord all the days of his life" (Psalm 27:4). Following David's awesome example, as Christians, the thought of God should "always be just to the side and ready to take the place of what you are concentrating on."[198]

---

[197] Breshears.

[198] Donald Whitney, *Spiritual Disciplines for the Christian Life* (New York, NY: NavPress, 2016), p. 51.

CHAPTER TEN

ESCHATOLOGY

CHAPTER SUMMARY:

THE STUDY OF ESCHATOLOGY does not exclusively pertain to the future. Jesus Christ introduced a new age that He achieved by His victory over the powers of evil and darkness. This means that although the war has already been won, the battle is still being enacted within history. Therefore, the doctrine of eschatology should inspire watchfulness, alertness, and a sense of positive expectancy in the life of the believer. The incentives to a proper understanding of eschatology are purity of life, diligence in the service to the Kingdom of God, and hope for the future.

Fran tells you that some people at her CrossFit gym believe that when you die, you become "worm food" and just cease to exist. Can you help Fran understand the biblical and theological implications of death?

———————————

FRAN, I AM SURE you are aware that one of the undeniable facts of *human life* is that it ends in *human death*. Reasoning from this fact, some people hold the view that following death, human beings simply cease to exist. The eschatological idea of heaven or hell is therefore of no concern, for the world is all there is. In other words, the temporal reality of what people can hear, see, touch, taste, and feel is all that matters—any concept of eternity is a figment of the human imagination. In many respects, this view would fall into the eschatological category of what is referred to as annihilationism. This doctrine holds that although man was created immortal, those who continue in sin are deprived of their immortal inheritance and are reduced to a state of nonexistence. In this sense, they are annihilated.[199]

Fran, the study of eschatology is a difficult topic, in particular because this doctrine forces us to come to grips with the discussion of either eternal punishment or eternal blessedness. In either case, the key word here is *eternal*. This is why Jesus said, "Do not be afraid of those who kill the body but cannot kill the soul. Rather, be afraid of the One who can destroy both soul and body in hell" (Matthew 10:28). Jesus clearly taught that although physical death is the cessation of life in our physical body, this is not the end of our existence.

The Bible is very clear on the subject: The end of human life on earth is not the end of existence. Death is simply a transition from one mode of existence to another—it is not extinction.[200] The author of Hebrews wrote, "People are destined to die once, and after that to face the judgment" (Hebrews 9:27). The only logical reason why the author would speak to "judgment" is if something followed death. Using the logic of the author of Hebrews, if there were no continued state of existence following death, then there would be nothing to face, and subsequently no judgment. However, eternal judgment

---

[199] Anthony Hoekema, *The Bible and the Future* (Grand Rapids, MI: William Eerdmans Publishing Company, 1979), p. 266.

[200] Millard Erickson, *Christian Theology* (Grand Rapids, MI: Baker Academic, 2013), p. 1073.

is a huge concern to the biblical authors and was a resounding theme in the teaching of Jesus.

Fran, the Bible teaches that death is to be considered an enemy. It is not a natural part of living (1 Corinthians 15:26). This is precisely why believers in Jesus Christ have hope for eternal life—Jesus *conquered death* through His death and resurrection, and believers now (and for eternity) live with Him (1 Corinthians 15:50–58). This means that as believers in Jesus Christ, the idea of "worm food" or "nonexistence" is a completely foreign and non-biblical concept. For the believer, life after death means that we will continue to exist in the presence of Jesus, along with those who love Him, and will together serve for eternity in His Kingdom (Matthew 25:23).

Fran is very interested in learning more about the Kingdom of God. Can you help her grasp the essence of Jesus Christ's teaching on the Kingdom?

FRAN, ACCORDING TO THE Gospel of Matthew, the very first word that our Lord spoke at the inception of His public ministry was *metanoeō*. In context, Jesus said, "*metanoeō* for the Kingdom of Heaven has come near" (Matthew 4:17). The Greek word *metanoeō* means: "To change your mind *for the better.*" In this sense, Jesus said, "Change your mind for the better, because I am here." Fran, I am so encouraged by this verse and hope that you are as well! I believe that this verse contains a fundamental principle of the Christian faith that can completely transform your life. Speaking about Himself, Jesus explained that in order to have a relationship with Him, your thoughts about Him would need to change—and they would specifically *need to change for the better.* In addition, your thoughts about His Kingdom would need to change as well.

In many respects, the center of Jesus's message was the Kingdom of God (Mark 1:14–15). Although Jesus was the Son of God and had the supreme authority to usher in this Kingdom (not to mention explain what it was), the four Gospels reveal that our Lord meant one thing by the Kingdom, and His disciples who listened to Him meant another. In Acts 1:6–8, we are witness to how pressing of an issue the Kingdom was to the disciples; "Lord, are you going to restore the Kingdom of Israel at this time?" (Acts 1:6). For the Jewish people (whom the disciples represented), the concept of God's Kingdom was a prominent theme throughout the Old Testament (Exodus 15:18; Psalm 29:10; Isaiah 43:15). The basic idea was that the Jewish people were God's chosen people, and although they endured a long history of persecution, the day would come that God would intervene into human history to establish His reign. In this sense, God's Kingdom was understood in the context of a messianic Kingdom centered in Jerusalem (Luke 19:11).

Fran, I believe that when Jesus spoke to the "nearness of God's Kingdom," He was referring to Himself. In other words, the Kingdom had drawn near *spatially* and *physically* in the very person of Jesus Christ. Simply stated, the Kingdom had drawn near, because the King had arrived! But there was also a spiritual–eternal aspect to the Kingdom. Although the disciples thought the Kingdom would be achieved through physical conquest, in His death, Jesus taught that the establishment of the Kingdom would be through sacrifice. Although there was a present reality to the Kingdom, it would not be consummated until Jesus returned in power and glory.

Fran, perhaps the best way to understand the Kingdom is to see it through the lens of the Lord's Prayer (Matthew 6:9–13). In this prayer, we see that by the Kingdom, Jesus meant a society upon earth where the will of God's would be done "as perfectly on earth as it is in heaven" (Matthew 6:10). This means it would be a Kingdom founded on love, not human power. In his commentary on the Gospel of Matthew, scholar David Hill explained that God's Kingdom means, "the establishment on earth of the sovereign rule and authority of God."[201] In this sense, Jesus offers us a window to see *now* what we can anticipate *when He returns*. This was exactly the stance of the early Church, which saw it's "dual citizenship" in covenant relationship to the King in heaven, who at His return would establish His Kingdom on earth (Philippians 3:20).

---

[201] David Hill, *The Gospel of Matthew* (London, UK: New Century Bible Commentary, 1962), p. 90.

Fran wants to know about the state that humans experience after death. She tells you that some evangelicals affirm that believers go to be with Jesus after they die, where they abide in a sleep-like peaceful existence. Is this view biblically accurate?

FRAN, I BELIEVE THAT at death, the bodies of mankind will return to dust (Genesis 3:19; Acts 13:36). However, this is far from the end of the story! The good news of the Gospel is that at death, the souls of believers will pass immediately into the presence of Jesus Christ (Luke 23:43) to remain in joyful fellowship with Him while awaiting the full redemption (or resurrection) of our bodies (2 Corinthians 5:1, 6). Although there are numerous places in Scripture that speak to what could be described as "soul sleep" (Acts 7:60, 13:36), these references are better understood in the context of physical death. For example, Jesus said of His friend Lazarus that he had fallen asleep (John 11:11) and then continued to explain to His disciples that by "sleep," He meant "death" (John 11:14).

In our Lord's parable about the rich man and Lazarus, Jesus taught that upon death there will be a personal, conscious existence that both the believer and nonbeliever would experience up until their resurrection (Luke 16:19–31). Furthermore, how could the notion "soul sleep" be maintained given our Lord's promise to the thief on the cross: "Truly I tell you, *today you will be with me in paradise* (Luke 23:43—my emphasis)? The obvious answer is, "It can't!" In this immensely encouraging verse from Scripture, it becomes clear that both Jesus and the thief would pass from one state of existence into another—and that in this state they would be enjoying paradise together. Weighing all of the biblical data, it is best to understand "sleep" as a euphemism for the cessation of life, rather than as literal description of the condition of the dead prior to resurrection.[202]

---

[202] Erickson, p. 1080.

Fran wonders why Jesus did not come within a generation as He seemed to promise in Matthew 24:34. Can we know the exact time and place of our Lord's return?

FRAN, THE BASIS OF Christian hope amid the trials and tribulations of the world is that Jesus Christ overcame the world (John 16:33) and that He will return in glory to establish His Kingdom on earth (Mark 8:38). This being the case, wouldn't it be wonderful to know the exact time and day of our Lord's return? We can be certain of one thing—Christians alive today are not the first people to wrestle with this question!

Fran, you've brought up a really good question. When Jesus said, "This generation will certainly not pass away until all these things have happened," He seemed to suggest that the *Parousia* (second coming of our Lord) would take place within the generation of the group of disciples He was addressing. However, this interpretation would be incorrect for several reasons. First, just a few moments after Jesus referred to "this generation," He further elaborated on the second coming and said, "But about that day or hour no one knows" (Matthew 24:36). Given this fact, it is better to understand the "generation" that Jesus spoke to as encompassing the generation of the living people at that time in history who would experience the distress He described in Matthew 24:4–28.[203] In this sense, Jesus did not mean that *all distress* must end within that time, but only that "all these things" (the specific events of 24:4–28, including the fall of Jerusalem) would happen within a generation of AD 30. The unified message of the Bible is clear on the matter of our Lord's second coming: there is no mention of a specific time or day given as to when the *distress in general* will cease, other than the *Parousia* itself—and "only the Father" knows when this will be (Matthew 24:36).[204]

---

[203] Tremper Longman, *The Expositor's Bible Commentary, Edition 9* (Grand Rapids, MI: Zondervan, 2010), p. 569.

[204] Longman, p. 569.

Fran, as mentioned before, Christians alive today are essentially echoing the inherent curiosity of our Lord's first disciples when we ask, "Jesus, when are you coming back?" At our Lord's discourse on the Mount of Olives, His disciples asked Him, "What will be the sign of your coming and of the end of the age?" (Matthew 24:3). These words show how much vested interest the disciples had in Jesus's return—just like we do today! In this sense, the question still remains: What will be day of our Lord's return? A few things we can be certain of: it will be sudden and unexpected (Matthew 25:13), and when it does happen, it will be like lightening in the sky, obvious to everyone who sees it (Matthew 24:27). Therefore, Christians today are called to be watchful and hopeful (Matthew 24:42-51) as we prayerfully await our Lord's triumphant return.

Some of Fran's workout partners at her CrossFit gym are of the Jewish faith and have family in Israel. Fran asks you if there is a national future for Israel as a fulfillment of God's promises.

FRAN, I BELIEVE THAT the totality of biblical evidence supports the idea that there will be a national future for Israel. In fact, Jesus taught that the future of Israel would take place in accordance with the fulfillment of God's promises (Luke 24:44)., Whenever we read the Bible, it is important to do everything we can to put ourselves "into the mind" of the original audience. This being the case, it is interesting to note that on the road to Emmaus, two of Jesus's disciples recapitulated a full explanation of the Old Testament and the Kingdom (Luke 24:19–20), but still made mention of their hope for a restoration of Israel (Luke 24:21). The reason for this was that in the mind of the disciples, they saw the coming of God's Kingdom as fulfillment of the new covenant that included the restoration of Israel (Ezekiel 36:22).[205] Although it might appear that Israel had been set aside, there nevertheless remained a hope and promise of their restoration (Romans 11:25–29).

---

[205] Dr. Gerry Breshears, "Eschatology" outline, Western Seminary, TH503.

In contrast to the view of a national future for Israel, there is an alternative position referred to as *Replacement Theology*. These teachings hold that the New Testament Church has replaced Israel and will receive all the promises of the Old Testament, to include land and national promises. However, when interpreted in the proper context, God's promises to Israel of "land and seed" (Genesis 12:1–3) will be fulfilled independently of the New Testament Church. The strongest argument for this position is that if Jesus had intended to reinterpret the Kingdom of God as anything other than the fulfillment of Old Testament prophecy, He certainly would have done so. However, rather than a *reinterpretation*, Jesus provided a *reinforcement* of the Old Testament within the context of future state of Israel (Mark 10:35–45; Acts 1:3–8).[206] This is precisely why in his letter to the Romans, Paul explained that Israel's "hardening of heart" (Romans 11:25) was only temporary, and that in the long run, "God's gifts and his call are irrevocable" (Romans 11:29).

Fran asks you to summarize the positions on the Church's attitude toward history, culture, and society.

FRAN, THROUGHOUT THE COURSE of history there have been two general approaches to solving the problems of the world. On one hand, some people believe there is a *political solution to every problem*. On the other hand, some people believe there is a *spiritual solution to every problem*. Needless to say, the Christian solution to every problem is spiritual and is found in the person of Jesus Christ. It is imperative to remember that Jesus never promised that problems would cease (John 16:33). Rather, our Lord demonstrated that He had overcome the world (1 Corinthians 15:55–57), and promised to be with us forever (Matthew 28:20).

This being the case, there have traditionally been five views (we could also refer to them as positions or attitudes) that question the Christians' relationship toward history, culture, and society. In other words, what is the Christian relationship to the State? Are we meant to see ourselves as a citizen, a resident alien, someone just passing through, or a captive in enemy territory? The way we answer this question has profound implications for how we share the Gospel and live out our lives.

---

[206] Breshears.

The first view has been referred to as *triumphant*. In this view, the Gospel will prevail and everyone will come to Christ. The second view is *transforming* and holds that over time, Christians will penetrate society and transform (or convert) the values, ethics, relations, and goals from secular to sacred. In this sense, Christians will transform secular culture into the service of the Kingdom of God. The third view is *prophetic* and holds that Christians will proclaim the Gospel and "make disciples of all the nations" (Matthew 28:19–20). In the process, the Church will proclaim righteousness in the culture while simultaneously exposing evil. The fourth view was held by renowned evangelist Billy Graham and is referred to as *ambivalent*. This view focuses on the proclamation of the Gospel, and that as a result of a revival of Christian conversion, society will improve as a secondary effect. The final view is referred to as *negativism* and holds that only Christ, upon His second coming, can transform society. This is also referred to as the "lifeboat view" in the sense that Christians try to save people (or rescue them) from the world and bring them into the Church.[207]

Fran, I tend to favor the view held by Billy Graham that is referred to as *ambivalent*. In order to make my case, allow me to share an analogy from the CrossFit culture. In 20 years of teaching CrossFit, I've noticed that when people are "converted" to CrossFit (in other words, they join a CrossFit gym and participate daily in the exercise program), a curious thing happens: Their entire world begins to change! All of a sudden they eat differently; change their sleep pattern (getting more rest); associate with other people who do CrossFit; buy new apparel, new shoes, new fitness equipment—Fran, do you get my point? One variable (starting CrossFit) changes everything! I believe it can be the same thing with the proclamation of the Gospel and a revival within our society. As people come to Christ, their entire world begins to change. Rather than trying to change society, I feel strongly that a Christian's first priority should be to bring more people to Christ. This is in perfect alignment with our Lord's instruction to "seek first the Kingdom of God" and then everything else will fall perfectly into place (Matthew 6:33).

---

[207] The five models of "Christians Attitude Toward History" were identified in Gerry Breshears's "Eschatology" outline.

Fran asks you to summarize the progressive dispensational premillennial view of the end of times.

FRAN, I BELIEVE THE key to understanding the progressive dispensational premillennial view is establishing a proper hermeneutic for Old Testament prophecy. This being the case, all Scripture (in particular the Old Testament) must be interpreted according to the intent of the author and original audience. This means that the promises given by God to the Jewish people (Genesis 12:1–3, Isaiah 11:11–12, Jeremiah 31:31–37) must be interpreted literally. Given that the Old Testament promised Messianic hope for the Jewish people, this means that the coming King will judge Israel's enemies, re-gather God's people, pour out the Spirit, reign personally from Jerusalem, and be worshipped by all the nations.[208]

This view also holds that the covenant that God gave to Abraham (Genesis 12:1–3) was foundational and unconditional. Although there were periods of punishment, the promises to Israel are irrevocable (Romans 11:27–32). Furthermore, the universal Kingship of God is everlasting and over all creation. Although Israel as a nation rejected both Jesus and His Kingdom, there is no biblical teaching that the arrival of the Kingdom was conditioned upon Israel's receptivity of Christ. In the context of the Kingdom, many theologians use the word "postponed" to describe the fact that the fullness of the Messianic Kingdom ushered in by Jesus was not established in its fullness at the first coming, but will be fulfilled at our Lord's return. In this sense, Jesus is King now in the same way that David was King between his anointing and his appointing (or reign). Jesus is the anointed King waiting in Heaven until the time that He will return to establish His Messianic Kingdom in its fullness.[209]

---

[208] Breshears.

[209] Breshears.

PART FOUR

ANSWERING HARD QUESTIONS FROM THE GYM

SECTION SUMMARY:

THE STUDY OF THEOLOGY is an exciting, life-changing, and immensely rewarding journey that beckons each and every human being alive today. As the study of theology progresses, the inquisitive nature of our mind begins to shift from the fundamental question of our origins to more complex issues regarding the nature of gender, leadership roles within the Church, and issues of cohabitation and marriage. These are the "Hard questions from the Gym" that Christian leaders must be prepared to thoughtfully, biblically, and compassionately respond to.

What are two common misperceptions of Jesus? Why do people cling to them?

THE CHRISTIAN PROCLAMATION THAT Jesus Christ is *fully God* (Colossians 1:15, 2:9; Hebrews 1:1–3) and *fully Man* (Luke 2:52; Hebrews 4:15) is a statement of such extraordinary proportions that the human intellect can barely comprehend or understand it. Despite the biblical account of who Jesus is, many people hold misperceptions and incorrect ideas about Him. The historical context for these misperceptions is significant, for they tend to show mankind's general reluctance to accept Jesus Christ for *who He says He is* (John 9:17, 35-41).

It seems that the basis for two of the common misperceptions about Jesus stem from Arianism. Although it was condemned as heresy, Arianism continues to linger in a variety of forms, in particular with the faith of the Jehovah's Witness. The central premise in the Arian misunderstanding of Jesus is the absolute uniqueness and transcendence of God.[210] Because God is the only source—or cause—of all things, and is the only uncreated and eternal Being in the entire universe, then God alone possesses the attributes of deity. If God were to share these unique attributes with anything or anyone else, God would by implication be divisible and subject to change—and this would suggest a duality or multiplicity of divine beings: a direct contradiction to the concept of monotheism and Oneness of God.[211]

Therefore, the Arian understanding of the relationship between God and Jesus is that the Father, while creating everything that is, worked through His unique agent of creation, which was the Word. In this sense, the first common misperception of Jesus is that He was also a created being and not eternally existent with the Father. Thus, while Jesus was a perfect creation, and certainly not in the same class as other created creatures, He would nevertheless owe His existence to the Father. Furthermore, this would imply that at one time "the Word was not" because everything in the created order had a "starting point" within time.[212]

---

[210] Erickson, p. 635.

[211] Erickson, p. 635.

[212] Erickson, p. 635.

The second common misperception of Jesus is that He did not have direct communication or knowledge with the Father. Because Jesus was a created being, He was totally different in essence from the Father and therefore did not share the same mind as God. In order to justify these claims, the Arians looked to Scripture references that seemed to indicate Jesus was "made by God" (Acts 2:36) in addition to texts which alluded to Jesus's lack of knowledge, most notably Mark 13:32: "About that day or hour no one knows, not even the angles in heaven, nor the Son, but only the Father."

In ministry application, many people cling to misperceptions of Jesus because they want to impose upon Him *who they think Jesus is*. As a biblical case study, when the disciples took Jesus into their boat "just as He was" (Mark 4:36) they imposed upon Him the wrong idea about *who they thought Jesus was* (Mark 4:35–41). However, when Jesus calmed the storm and saved their lives (Mark 4:37–38) the disciples began to sense there remained a great deal still to learn about *who Jesus actually was* (Mark 4:41). This means that for some people, the person who they think Jesus is, and the person He turns out to be, might be altogether different. As a minister of God's Word, my calling is to help people see that Jesus Christ is the "radiance of God's glory and the exact representation of His being" (Hebrews 1:3). Only when people receive Jesus into their heart according to the terms that He has set will they be able to understand the fullness of who He is.

Do we have to believe that Jesus is God incarnate as opposed to a prophet or wise teacher? How can Fran help people at her CrossFit gym see what difference it makes?

THE DISCIPLES WERE THE first to discover that mankind must learn to see both the *humanity* and *deity* of Jesus. On one hand, studying the human nature of Jesus is significant, for Jesus alone must fully embody what humanity was meant to be (Hebrews 5:8–9).[213] On the other hand, because Jesus is the "image of the invisible God" (Colossians 1:15) and the "exact representation of God's being" (Hebrews 1:3), mankind must also see Jesus in the fullness of His deity (Colossians 2:9). To only believe that Jesus was a great prophet or teacher (in other words, a denial of His divinity) would be to reduce Jesus to a long lineage of other-world religious spiritual teachers and prophets.

However, the disciples and great biblical saints did more than proclaim the fact that Jesus was a great teacher. Rather, they *rubbed Jesus into their eyes* (John 9:6), they *plugged Jesus into their ears* (Mark 7:33), they *submerged themselves in Him* (John 9:7), they *attached themselves to Him* (John 15:1–5), and they *ate His flesh and drank His blood* (John 6:56). In other words, the believer's *submersion into God* and *consumption of God* meant that God Himself would take up residence within the psychosomatic unity of their being.

In ministry application, I would emphasize the fact that a narrow focus on Jesus's teaching or prophecy means that we accept His *teaching* absent a relationship with the *Teacher Himself*. Although believers are certainly desirous of modeling the life of Jesus, this cannot be achieved by parroting His sayings or attempting to model His behavior. In fact, an exclusive emphasis on following the teaching of Jesus is little more than attempting to achieve our salvation by what we do (*adherence to the teaching*), rather than whom we know (*a saving relationship with the Teacher*).

The Bible holds that by proclaiming Jesus as Lord and God (John 6:69, 20:28), believers can be transformed into His image (2 Corinthians 3:18) through the process of "putting on the new self" (Colossians 3:10). When we

---

[213] T. Desmond Alexander, *New Dictionary of Biblical Theology* (Downers Grove, IL: InterVarsity) p. 566.

move beyond the teaching to a saving relationship with the Teacher—God Himself in the person of Jesus Christ—then "our lives gradually become brighter and more beautiful as God enters our lives and we become like Him" (2 Corinthians 3:18 MSG). Finally, and arguably most important, the believer's confession of faith in Jesus as Lord and God (not prophet and teacher) leads to the forgiveness of our sins, the gift of the Holy Spirit, and reconciliation into the family of God (Acts 2:38).

At the gym where Fran trains, she often hears the rhetorical statement, "What would Jesus do?" This has led Fran to contemplate the question, "How human is Jesus?" She comes to you and asks, "Can we really be like Him?"

JESUS ACCOMPLISHED A UNIQUE two-fold work during His life on earth. On one hand, Jesus revealed in His person the likeness and image of God, so that mankind might finally understand what a life in that likeness and image was (Colossians 2:9; 1 John 1:1–3).[214] Yet Jesus did more than provide humanity with the exact image and representation of God (Colossians 1:15; Hebrews 1:1–3)—Jesus also provided humanity with an image of the ideal human being (Luke 2:52; Hebrews 5:7–9; 1 Corinthians 11:1). Mankind now lives in the shadow of our Lord's first disciples to whom He declared: "Look at my hands and my feet. It is I myself! Touch me and see; a ghost does not have flesh and bones, as you see I have" (Luke 24:39). The Apostle John's testimony that he *heard, saw,* and *touched Jesus* (John 1:1) is further evidence that Jesus "ate with them, he bled, he slept, he cried. If Jesus was not human, then surely no one ever has been."[215] Because during Jesus's life and ministry He was both *fully God* and *fully man*, in His human nature we see the perfect example of the person we are called to follow and be like (Philippians 2:5; 1 John 2:6).

In ministry application, proclaiming the humanity of Jesus Christ is a delicate matter. On one hand, it is imperative that people understand that Jesus was *fully human*. Jesus's intercessory ministry depends on the fact that He was truly one of us and, during His lifetime, experienced the full range of human

---

[214] Andrew Murray, *The Essential Works of Andrew Murray* (Uhrichsville, OH: Barbour Books, 1962), p. 1380.

[215] Erickson, p. 650.

temptations and trials (Hebrews 4:15). Because Jesus was *fully human,* He knows us and can empathize with our human struggles.[216] On the other hand, it is equally imperative that mankind understand that not only was Jesus fully human, He was the *ideal and perfect human,* and in this sense *more human than any other human being who has ever lived.*

The question now gains immense relevance—can we really become like Jesus? This is a critical ministry question with astounding implications. Becoming like Jesus is indeed possible, but only through a combination of *union with Him* and *obedience to His Commandments* (John 14:15, 15:4–5). This means that becoming like Jesus is not achieved in the manner that many people think—*by narrowly focusing on what He said and did.* Strict adherence to religious customs and traditions was not what Jesus required of His followers (John 3:1–7). Jesus knew that the change in mankind required to *become like Him* was so great that Jesus Himself would need to take up residence within the believer (Luke 19:5). In order to become like Jesus, a complete death of the *old man* (Romans 1:18–20) and resurrection of the *new man* would need to take place (Romans 3:21–26). Being the very embodiment of the power by which God makes and sustains the world, Jesus promised that when *grafted onto Him,* we would *become like Him* and our new life would begin (John 15:5; Philippians 4:13). Through faith in Jesus, His life flows into our inner nature (Romans 12:2), giving us spiritual strength and empowering us to become like Him (2 Corinthians 4:16).

---

[216] Erickson, p. 645.

Fran is concerned that gender plays a role in the different types of leadership and ministry roles within the Church. Can you help her understand the Pauline doctrine on gender and ministry in addition to the broader picture of female leadership in the Bible?

———————————

LYDIA, PHOEBE, AND PRISCILLA were names to be reckoned with in the formative days of the first Christian house-Churches. In the account of his own ministry efforts, the Apostle Paul indicates that women were not only among his converts; they were also his colleagues in the work of sharing the Gospel of Jesus Christ. For example, in Romans 16:1-2, Paul speaks to the ministry and leadership role of Phoebe: "I commend to you our sister Phoebe, a deacon of the Church at Cenchreae, that you may receive her in the Lord as befits the saints, and help her in whatever she may require from you, for she has been a helper of many, and of myself as well."

In the Greek text, Paul refers to Phoebe as a *diakonos,* which we have translated in our English Bible as "deacon." This term is not one of endearment for the character of Phoebe, but is rather a definition (or description) of her leadership function within the Church. Furthermore, the term "deacon" that Paul applies to Phoebe is the same term he applies to himself and to other male colleagues in his ministry. This is all to say that Phoebe was no minor figure during the formative years of the Christian faith. She had a position within the Church of a leader and was taken seriously by Paul.

In addition to Paul's letter to the Romans, the presence of women within Jesus's inner circle is of equal significance and tends to demonstrate His approval of the equality of gender in ministry leadership roles and functions. Although the Catholic faith makes much of the fact that Jesus did not call women to be among His twelve disciples (the Pope has said on numerous occasions that the question of the ordination of women to the priesthood is settled given that Jesus did not call women to serve as His disciples), it remains undeniable that Jesus's inclusion of women was eons ahead of the socially normative practices of His time. Given what biblical scholars and historians tell us of the secular and religious culture during the time of our Lord's ministry, it is nothing less than revolutionary the precedence and presence that women had in the earliest recorded Christian communities.

Perhaps the most compelling (and sadly overlooked) account of the case for women in ministry leadership positions is that of Mary Magdalene, who in the Gospel according to John had the astonishing privilege of being the first to see the risen Jesus, and the first to tell others about Him: "Mary Magdalene went and said to the disciples, 'I have seen the Lord,' and she told them that he had said these things to her" (John 20:18). The implications for this single line of Scripture are immense, for they prominently position Mary as the first apostle of the resurrection!

In light of the aforementioned background, how are we to balance those parts of the Bible that proclaim the principles of equality and participation (Galatians 3:27-29) alongside the seemingly gender-biased declaration of Paul: "I permit no woman to teach or to have authority over men" (1 Timothy 2:11)? In other words, what does the Bible systematically reveal about the ministry roles that women can have, and how are these roles reconciled with the likes of Mary Magdalene and Deacon Phoebe?

In 1 Timothy 2:12 the Apostle Paul commands that a woman is forbidden to "teach or to exercise authority over a man" in the Church. Although some have suggested that Paul had only Timothy's immediate ministry context in mind, the reasoning Paul uses—that man was created first, then Eve, and that she was deceived first while he overtly rebelled first—excludes such a possibility. Paul bases his rule for Timothy's Church in the created order of things, which means it applies to all Churches. Furthermore, it is important to note that the grammar Paul uses in 1 Timothy 2:11-12 indicates that he has in mind two different things he wants to forbid; namely "teaching" and "authority". In other words, Paul is making the point that there is a certain kind of teaching that was to be reserved for men in the assembled Church.

Momentarily setting aside these female restrictions, we must heed the exhortation that the Bible makes on the fact that women are given the gift and responsibility to teach in God's kingdom. For example, in Paul's letter to Titus, he commands that women are to teach other women (Titus 2:3–5). In addition, throughout both the Old and New Testament, women are seen instructing and teaching mixed audiences—and doing so both publicly and privately. In the Old Testament, Deborah dispensed wisdom to Israel by her tree (Judges 4:4), and both Miriam's and Deborah's songs were given publicly to instruct and edify Israel (Exodus 15; Judges 5). In the New Testament, Priscilla instructed Apollos in matters of the Christian faith (Acts 18:26). Women prophesied publicly in the New Testament Church (Acts 2:11, 17; 1 Corinthians 11:5; 14:26), and the whole congregation (including men!) received edification from those prophecies (1 Corinthians 14:31; Romans 15:14). This being the case, what did Paul have in mind when he forbade women from teaching and exercising authority?

Weighing 1 Timothy 2:11-12 alongside the Gospel principle of equality in Christ (Galatians 3:27-29), it seems the only logical conclusion is that the kind of teaching restricted to men is the official, specially recognized office of teaching in the assembled Church. In other words, the "authority" and "teaching" that Paul reserves for men is that specific office that bears the authority of the Church and fulfills the Church's official responsibility to preserve and pass on the faith from generation to generation (Jude 3). This means that women can minister in a variety of capacities that are open to any other male in alignment with their spiritual gifting and qualifications established by the local Church. However, these respective ministries should not include teaching the corporate body of the Church or exercising authority over men in the Church. These elder-type positions are to be specifically reserved for men (1 Timothy 2:11, 3:1–7; Titus 1:6–9).

In implementation, the elder leadership positions reserved for men must by no means be interpreted to suggest male favoritism or male-gender superiority. The creation account of Genesis 1:26–27 firmly establish that men and women are equally created in God's image. Furthermore, in Galatians 3:28, Paul teaches that in the context of God's salvation, there is no distinction between male and female, "for you are all one in Christ." This means that it is through faith in Christ that people become "children of God" (Galatians 3:26)— race, economic status, and gender is of no consequence in His Kingdom. Men and women were both fully created in God's image and are perfectly equal in dignity, value, and essence.[217]

All of this being said, it is significant to note that Genesis 2 describes the functions of men and women were to be experienced differently, with the female functioning in a subordinate role to male leadership and authority

---

[217] Dr. Gerry Breshears, *Women In Leadership Roles and Ordination Study Packet,* p. 16.

(Genesis 3:16). However, the leadership and authority of men must be seen, understood, and applied within the context of the Church's submission to Christ (Ephesians 5:22–23). This means that men are to lead and exercise authority in a Christlike manner and not lord their position over women (or anyone else for that matter). The role distinctions and male headship described in Genesis 2 (in addition to the more overt statement in Genesis 3:16) and later elaborated on by Paul (1 Corinthians 11:810; 1 Timothy 2:13) must not be contextualized or interpreted in such a way as to imply a lack of female dignity, value, essence or *Imago Dei*. Rather, these distinctions must be understood in the context of 1 Timothy 2:8–15.

For example, the requirements for women to learn in "quietness and full submission" and to "not exercise authority over a man" (1 Timothy 2:11–12) are to be seen as a distinction between appropriate male and female roles, offices, and responsibilities within the Church—not in degrees of essence or standing before God. Furthermore, the requirement for women to "be silent in Church" (1 Corinthians 14:34) and that it would be "disgraceful for a woman to speak in Church" (1 Corinthians 14:35) must be understood in the specific context of judging and interpretation of prophecy—a role reserved for male elders.[218] Both men (1 Timothy 2:8) and women (1 Timothy 2:9; 1 Corinthians 11:4–5) are to worship in such a way as to edify the body of believers and to maintain harmony and good order in the Church.

In concluding this challenging topic, it is worth reiterating that Paul is not saying that women cannot teach in Church. Rather, Paul emphasizes that women should not teach in an "elder like way." For a woman to teach like an elder would be to go against the spirit of the order that Paul exhorts in 1 Timothy 2:12-14. This logically begs the question—what is an "elder like way?" It seems that Paul might have intended the answer to that question to remain within a bit of a "theological gray area". However, this gray area is certainly on the canvas of the beautiful and colorful mosaic that God ordained from the creation of the universe, for it tends to encourage the much-needed autonomy within each congregation to prayerfully decide how best to interpret and apply it.

---

[218] Breshears.

What kind of authority does a pastor possess? How should a pastor express their authority? What is the difference between *authority* and *authoritarian*?

THE AUTHORITY OF A pastor must be understood within the context of established Church offices. Certain offices of the Church carry with them specific responsibilities; in order to accomplish these responsibilities and objectives, the Church grants authority to the person holding the office. However, as one of my military mentors once told me, "It's not the rank that makes the person; the person makes the rank." In this sense, the authority of the pastor is a combination of *ex officio* (the legal authority of the office), *ex persona* (the moral authority of the leader), and *ex charismata* (the perceived authority of the leader).[219]

The pastor is entrusted by the Church to make decisions, direct the cooperate body of the Church, and shape the behavior of Church members.[220] However, rather than "lording it over them" (1 Peter 5:3), pastors are to exercise their authority by equipping, inspiring, empowering, unifying, edifying, exemplifying, and "shepherding" the Church (Ephesians 4:3, 4:11–12; 2 Timothy 2:24–25; 1 Peter 5:1–4). Furthermore, a distinction must be made between a pastor's serving in a position *of authority* as opposed to being *an authoritarian*. The pastor's authority flows from their character and wisdom rather than an abuse of (or reliance upon) their position of power. By exercising a combination of their spiritual gifts alongside the established position of authority they hold, pastors guide and guard the Church and lead in the decision-making process (Acts 6:2–3, 15:22; 20:28; Titus 1:5–9). Rather than handling all of the ministry tasks of the Church himself, the pastor seeks to empower, build up, and equip others to function successfully in a variety of leadership roles (Ephesians 4:12). In fact, one of the greatest signs of a pastor's authentic authority is their ability to share that authority with others instead of always seeking to be "center stage" in the eyes of the congregation.

---

[219] Dr. Breshears, ecclesiology notes on "Leadership Roles" Western Seminary, TH503.
[220] Breshears.

Fran wants to know how many parts there are to a human being? What difference does it make in the CrossFit culture?

————————————————

I BELIEVE THAT A human being is composed of a "conditional unity" of two parts—a *material element* and an *immaterial element*.[221] The two fundamental elements of the human being (the material part includes the body and the immaterial component consists of the soul or spirit) are taught at several places in Scripture, including Matthew 6:25 and 10:28 (in reference to *body* and *soul*) and Ecclesiastes 12:7 and 1 Corinthians 5:3 (in reference to *body* and *spirit*). In this sense, the soul and spirit of the human constitution would be categorically seen as *immaterial*, whereas the body of the human as *material*. The concept of conditional unity is also seen in Scripture passages that indicate an intermediate state between death and resurrection (Luke 16:19–31, 23:43; 2 Corinthians 5:8).[222]

In implementation within the ministry context of fitness training (for example, a Christian faith-based CrossFit studio), the concept of "conditional unity" is breathtaking. In the incarnation, Jesus Christ became *fully human,* which means He came to redeem the totality of who we are. In this sense, the Gospel is an appeal to the entire person.[223] A human being's physical body, mind, emotions, and intellect are all precious to God and components of our sanctification. In other words, there is not one particular "part" of a human that is more subject to sin than any other "part." Much like a fully metastasized cancerous cell, total depravity means that sin has infected every part of the human being. However, on the positive application, this means that God is at work renewing the totality of what we are.

In this sense, activities such as exercise, rest, healthy nutrition, and proper weightlifting technique (ensuring the bodily safety and health of the athlete) are just as important as instilling biblically grounded theological ideas, a positive mental attitude, constructive emotions, and proper interpersonal relationships within the fitness studio. In other words, sanctification cannot be thought of as involving only one part of human nature. God is renewing the entirety of *who*

---

[221] Millard Erickson, *Christian Theology* (Grand Rapids, MI: Baker Academic, 2013), p. 492.

[222] Erickson, p. 483.

[223] Erickson, p. 493.

and *what* we are; as such, the model of "conditional unity" supports our ministry efforts in treating a human's physical, spiritual, and psychological condition in an integrated and holistic manner.

What is the balance between the inaugural and the ongoing work of the Spirit in a believer? How would you help Fran define baptism in the Holy Spirit?

FRAN, MY POSITION ON the inaugural *baptism with the Holy Spirit* is that this supernatural gift from God occurs in the believer's life at the moment of conversion. A key passage for this position is 1 Corinthians 12:13, where Paul writes: "For we were all baptized by one Spirit so as to form one body—whether Jews or Gentiles, slave or free—and we were all given one Spirit to drink." In this theologically packed verse, Paul makes four remarkable points: First, the baptism applies to all believers; second, all believers are baptized by the same Spirit; third, believers are baptized into the Body of Christ; and fourth, the baptism and union with the Body of Christ take place at the moment of conversion. This means that when a new believer "confesses with their mouth that Jesus Christ is Lord, and believes in their heart that God raised Jesus from the dead" (Romans 10:9), they receive the indwelling power of the Holy Spirit (John 14:17), receive a new heart (Titus 3:5), and are incorporated into the Body of Christ (1 Corinthians 12:13).[224]

Following the initial conversion experience and the receipt of the Holy Spirit's indwelling presence, the believer is called to a life of increasing sanctification and growing Christlikeness (2 Thessalonians 2:13; Colossians 3:1, 5). This means that although the Holy Spirit comes to indwell every person at conversion, there is an *ongoing experience* throughout the believer's new life in Christ of being continually *filled with the Spirit.* This subsequent filling may be gradual or rather dramatic (1 Corinthians 12:7–11) and occurs as a result of living out the reality of being baptized by the Spirit.[225] This perpetual filling is not to be confused with distinct second blessings of the Holy Spirit, but rather "an actualization of what we have already received at conversion."[226]

---

[224] Dr. Gerry Breshears, position paper, *Spiritual Gifts,* Western Seminary, TH503.
[225] Dr. Gerry Breshears, "Holy Spirit" outline, Western Seminary, TH503.
[226] Breshears.

In ministry application, I believe that when you "confess with your mouth that Jesus is Lord, and believe in your heart that God raised Jesus from the dead, you will be saved" (Romans 10:9). In this grace-empowered moment of conversion, you receive the gift of the Holy Spirit. The indwelling presence of the Spirit unites you to the Body of Christ—His Church—and initiates the process of sanctification. As the new believer lives out their faith in the Body of Christ, there is a continual filling of the Spirit that is evident in the believer experiencing an increase in the *fruit of the Spirit*.[227] However, I do not view this as a distinct second blessing. Rather, this is the perpetual actualization (or manifestation) of what the believer receives at the moment of conversion.

Fran wants to know your assessment of the phenomenon that much of the current global Church growth seems to be driven by Pentecostalism. What do you tell her?

IN HIS MASTERFUL BOOK *Theology in the Context of World Christianity,* Timothy Tennent provides a comprehensive treatment on the doctrine of the Holy Spirit within the Pentecostal faith and rationale for the fact that Pentecostalism drives much of the current global Church. Given that my denominational background is predominately Conservative Baptist, my assessment of this phenomenon was significantly shaped by three of the foundational ideas presented in Tennent's book.

The first big idea presented by Tennent is of immense importance. Given that many Christians assume "that denomination is *different* than mine," we often fall victim to focusing on our differences, rather than our similarities. Tennent makes the point that this is a big mistake, in particular within the context of Pentecostalism. Tennent points out that Pentecostals fully affirm the authority and inspiration of the Bible and affirm the centrality of Christ's atoning work on the cross for salvation and reconciliation with God. They also affirm the historic reality of the resurrection of Jesus and teach the importance of repentance, conversion, and living a holy and sanctified life.

---

[227] Breshears.

Furthermore, although most Pentecostal Churches do not adhere to creeds, they would nevertheless be able to affirm every statement of the Apostles' or Nicene Creed.[228]

Another important point Tennent makes is that the believer never witnesses or evangelizes alone, because they are always "accompanied by God the Evangelist, who speaks and works through them by the power of the Holy Spirit."[229] This is a particularly empowering consideration, especially within the context of the Great Commission to "go and make disciples of all the nations" (Matthew 28:19). Speaking from personal experience, my tendency has been to think, "I need more education before I can 'go and make disciples.'" However, in adopting the Pentecostal view that the Holy Spirit is present with me and prepared to manifest His power alongside me, then I have a renewed sense of purpose and potential to lead others to Christ.

In ministry implementation within the fitness industry, Tennent's observations run parallel to the CrossFit community. For example, at the Level I CrossFit course, attendees are encouraged to "go home, knock on your neighbors' door, and teach them how to squat." The new CrossFit athlete does not need to concern themselves with credentials—they have the backing of the entire CrossFit community to help them. In this sense, how much more inspired should Christians be to "knock on our neighbors door and teach them about Christ"? Much like Tennent pointed out, with God the Evangelist present, success in leading others to Jesus is not contingent upon financial backing, fancy Churches, detailed planning, or even seminary degrees (although I feel strongly that ministry leaders should attend seminary). The important thing to remember is that God Himself is *with us*, and He is opening doors and hearts *for us*.

The third rational for the growth of Pentecostalism described by Tennent is the contrast between the *Homogenous Unit Principle* and the Pentecostal approach to evangelism and mission work. Returning to my specific ministry context of the CrossFit culture, Tennent's observation has immense implication and relevance. The Homogenous Unit Principle is a proven sociological fact that people prefer not to cross social and ethnic barriers when becoming a Christian.[230]

---

[228] Timothy Tennent, *Christian Theology with the Context of World Christianity* (Grand Rapids, MI: Zondervan, 2007), p. 166.

[229] Tennent, p. 182.

[230] Tennent, p. 188.

In addition, this principle holds that individuals prefer to worship alongside those who are like themselves in cultural, socioeconomic, and numerous other ways (including a lifestyle of fitness). This is the reason why the Faith Rx'd movement in the CrossFit community is so strong—CrossFit athletes are more inclined to pursue a relationship with Jesus Christ when in the company of other CrossFit athletes.[231]

For this very reason, the Pentecostal tradition has largely been reluctant to embrace or employ the Homogeneous Unit Principle in their evangelistic and missionary work. Rather, the Pentecostal would find inspiration in the account of Acts 10, in which Peter and Cornelius—two people completely separated in nearly every conceivable way—nevertheless found congruency and unity through the power of the Holy Spirit (Acts 10:44). According to the Pentecostal tradition of mission work, the Holy Spirit should empower the believer to transcend the normal social and ethnic barriers—in addition to any preconceived barrier to the Gospel message of Unity in Christ.

Fran wants to know how she should biblically and theologically pastor someone dealing with same-sex attraction or struggling with gender identity as part of the discipleship process.

DISCIPLING SOMEONE WITH SAME-SEX attraction (assuming the attraction leads to a desire for a homosexual relationship) needs to be a very delicate process. On one hand, biblical leaders have a pastoral obligation to confront the person with the reality of what the Scriptures teach on the subject: The Bible condemns sexual relations between people of the same sex (Leviticus 18:22, 20:13; Romans 1:24–27; 1 Corinthians 6:9). On the other hand, if homosexual orientation and same-sex *attraction* (as opposed to same-sex *sexual activities*) are a pattern of temptation in the person's life—the *temptation itself,* if not overtly acted upon, is not necessarily sinful. Jesus Himself "in every respect has been tempted as we are, yet without sin" (Hebrews 4:15). I believe that people dealing with same-sex attraction and homosexuality can have confidence that God's grace can "wash and sanctify" His people (1 Corinthians 6:9-11).

---

[231] FaithRxd.com is a worldwide Christian evangelical movement specifically targeting the CrossFit community.

When we put our faith in Jesus we receive Christ's resurrection life and the gift of the Holy Spirit. The Holy Spirit empowers the believer to live a sexually pure life with the help of discipleship and the body of Christ.[232]

Based on the fact that all humans suffer in varying degree with temptation, the discipleship process must include a measure of sympathy for the person dealing with sexual sin. Whereas some Christians experience temptation for alcohol abuse and need pastoral support in overcoming this particular sin, Christians dealing with same-sex attraction need love, prayer, and a sense of hope. Nevertheless, if the person is reluctant to heed and obey God's commands, then a sharp rebuke may be necessary in order to motivate and encourage the person's repentance and change their behavior. Furthermore, and again with a degree of compassion, I think it would be prudent to point out to the person that although all people struggle with temptation and sin—the Bible seems to indicate that sexual sin is judged quite severely.

For example, Paul writes, "every other sin a person commits is outside the body, but the sexually immoral person sins against his own body" (1 Corinthians 6:18). The theological point that Paul makes would need to be stressed in the discipleship process: sexual sin is an overt offense against the persons own body, which is the temple of the Holy Spirit (1 Corinthians 6:19). In this sense, if the discipled person longs for a relationship with Jesus Christ, then they must earnestly pray for God's grace and power in overcoming any tendency toward same-sex attraction or homosexuality.

In addition to the sexual sin associated with homosexuality, gender differentiation is an aspect of the image of God, and was the first distinction of the human species mentioned after the creation of mankind (Genesis 1:27). This particular verse clearly teaches that gender is part of God's plan to add richness and diversity to human life. Furthermore, gender and sexuality are a fundamental aspect of the cultural mandate to "be fruitful and multiply and fill the earth" (Genesis 1:28). There must be reproduction if there is to be dominion, and in this sense, the sexual relationship within the context of a covenant of marriage between people of two different genders is clearly part of God's plan for humanity.

---

[232] Dr. Gerry Breshears, position paper, *Sexuality in an Equal Marriage Environment*, TH503 resources.

Fran wants to know how she should biblically and theologically respond to issues such as cohabitation and gay marriage.

THE BIBLE CLEARLY ESTABLISHES that: "Marriage is defined by God as the publicly pledged, permanent, exclusive, covenantal union of *one man* and *one woman.*"[233] One possible response to the issue is to emphasize that the biblical concept of a family began when God created humankind "male and female" (Genesis 1:27). The two genders were designed for marriage (Genesis 2:24), and in their sexual union and distinctiveness they felt no shame (Genesis 2:25). In the New Testament, it is significant that Jesus Christ referenced and approved of the original design of marriage (Matthew 19:4–5; cf. Ephesians 5:28–31). Furthermore, although Jesus's command, "What God has joined together, let no one separate" (Matthew 19:6) dealt specifically with divorce, it is logical to trace the institution of marriage that our Lord desired to uphold and protect to be a union between a husband and wife (male and female). The covenant relationship between a husband and a wife that Jesus sought to protect is a picture of God's love for His people (Ephesians 5:25–33).

In ministry application within the CrossFit culture, it is helpful to unpack Ephesians 5:22–23 to explain that the difference between a man and woman is essential to understanding the meaning of a marriage. Paul explains that marriage is a God-ordained institution that is meant to be analogous to the relationship between Christ and His Church.[234] In Paul's analogy, man represents Christ, and the woman represents the Church. In this sense, it is imperative that these unique roles never be confused with each other. However, in a gay marriage, there is no biological distinction between the marriage partners. Although one partner may "play the part" of adopting a more submissive role (in this sense portraying the biblical role of the wife), there is no clear difference between the "bride and bridegroom."[235]

---

[233] Dr. Gerry Breshears, position paper, *Sexuality in an Equal Marriage Environment*, TH503 resources.

[234] Tremper Longman, *The Expositor's Bible Commentary, Volume 12* (Grand Rapids, MI: Zondervan, 2006), p. 150.

[235] John Frame, *The Doctrine of the Christian Life* (Phillipsburg, NJ: P&R Publishing, 2008), p. 759.

In the marriage analogy offered by Paul, the "husband is the head of the wife as Christ is the head of the Church" (Ephesians 5:23). In describing the husband as the "head," Paul clearly establishes the male leadership role and headship responsibility within the marriage. In this sense, a male husband is the "head of his wife" as the male Jesus Christ is the "head of His Church." However, in a gay marriage, physically the roles of either party are interchangeable, and in the context of the biblical view of marriage, this means that God and man are interchangeable. Not only is this notion wrong, it is "the root of all sin—the primal heresy."[236]

Fran wants to know if preaching and ministry within the CrossFit culture should always include a specific proclamation of the Gospel.

WITHIN THE CONTEXT of the CrossFit gym, it is imperative to include a proclamation of the Gospel whenever athletes gather together for ministry purposes. There are two primary reasons for this: first, athletes at a fitness studio are already inundated with *good information.* They receive an abundance of coaching cues on their physical technique, mindset, and nutrition. In this sense, when athletes gather with you for an evening of ministry, the last thing they need is more *good information.* Rather, they need to hear the *good news of Jesus Christ*—the Gospel. Second, I have discovered that many people in the CrossFit culture are very agreeable to hearing about the *lessons of Jesus Christ.* However, these same people make a distinction between the *teaching of Jesus* and the *person of Jesus Christ.* This being the case, many people are happy to follow the *teaching* of Jesus, but resist *worshiping* Jesus as Lord and God.

For the reasons stated above, I believe that every preaching opportunity that God gives a CrossFit athlete or coach is an ordained time to share more than just good information. Rather, preaching should always include the proclamation of the *euangelion*—the *good news* that in the life, death, and resurrection of Jesus Christ, the faithful believer can be reconciled with God (2 Corinthians 5:11–21; 1 Peter 2:24) and transformed into His image (2 Corinthians 3:18). The athletes in the CrossFit culture need to constantly hear

---

[236] Frame, p. 759.

the Gospel—that through the process of "putting on the new self" (Colossians 3:10) they can "gradually become brighter and more beautiful as God enters our lives and we become like Him" (2 Corinthians 3:18 MSG; cf. Acts 2:38–47).

Within the context of the CrossFit culture, the proclamation of the Gospel is also an opportunity to help people see that Jesus is far more than just a *good teacher* providing *good information*. In fact, I believe this was the same first-step and tactic that the Apostle Peter took. For example, in Acts 2, the Apostle Peter declared that Jesus was "a man accredited by God to you by miracles, wonders and signs" (Acts 2:22). Apart from simply being another prophet or religious teacher, Jesus walked the earth in "the fullness of the deity in bodily form" (Colossians 2:9) and was "the radiance of God's glory and the exact representation of His being" (Hebrews 1:3). Peter's declaration in Acts 2 is echoed throughout the New Testament—Jesus was the God-Man to whom all religions point (John 14:6) and to whom all the prophets testified (John 5:39; Hebrews 1:1–3). In ministry application, although the *teachings of Jesus* are certainly worthy of our attentiveness and obedience, even more important is establishing a saving relationship with the One who is "the way, the truth and the life" (John 14:6). I believe this is best accomplished by sharing the *euangelion*—the good news that the Gospel "is the power of God that brings salvation to everyone who believes" (Romans 1:16).

Fran wants to know if the Lord's Supper should be a meal for Christians only. What does Paul mean when he speaks about "examining oneself"?

DUE TO THE FACT THAT the Lord's Supper signifies a special relationship between the individual believer and our Lord (Matthew 26:26–28; 1 Corinthians 11:26), it follows that a personal and saving relationship with God be a prerequisite for participation in the communion meal. Furthermore, given that Paul specifically addressed the importance of the individual believer being able to discern for themselves the spiritual significance of the meal (1 Corinthians 11:29), the logical entailment is that the communion meal should be withheld from nonbelievers. It is also important to note that Paul stressed that people in the Church who were blatantly living a life of sin should be removed from the Body of Christ (1 Corinthians 5:1–5). This would suggest that if Paul argued for the removal of people entertaining a sinful lifestyle (thus also withholding the Lord's Supper from them), then as a first step in Church discipline and entry into the Body of Christ, the Lord's Supper should likewise be withheld from nonbelievers.

In ministry implementation, this particular view might be less than inviting for the modern "seeker sensitive" approach that many Churches are taking to evangelism. For example, many Christians believe that because the Lord's Supper is a special time of fellowship with Christ and His Church, everyone present in the congregation should be invited to participate as a means of welcoming potential new believers into the family of God. However, I think given Paul's exhortation for "self-examination" (1 Corinthians 11:28; 2 Corinthians 13:5), the most important qualification for partaking in the communion meal is a proper understanding of the meals significance. Unless the participant recognizes that the meal represents the body and blood of Jesus (the "proper examination" that Paul speaks to) they risk "eating and drinking judgment on themselves" (1 Corinthians 11:29). In 1 Corinthians 11:23–26, Paul recapitulates the fact that the Lord's Supper is "about Jesus and is eaten both with Him and for Him."[237]

---

[237] Dr. Gerry Breshears, "Ecclesiology" outline, Western Seminary, TH503.

In this sense, Paul emphasizes the significance of a personal and saving relationship with Jesus Christ, implying that the Lord's Supper is only fitting and appropriate for Christians to partake in. Furthermore, Paul stresses that the communion meal is a time to "examine" both the horizontal and vertical relationship with the Body of Christ. In other words, the communion meal is "a time to reflect not only on whether we are serving the Lord worthily but also on how we are treating fellow members of the same Church body, who *worship the same Lord.*"[238]

Fran is a bit confused about the role of baptism in the believer's life and wants you to explain your understanding in terms of Romans 6:1–6.

WHEN THE APOSTLE PAUL wrote, "One died for all, and therefore all died" (2 Corinthians 5:14; cf. Romans 6:3), he spoke to the idea that Christ's redeeming work on the cross was not only substitutionary, it was also representative.[239] As Paul elaborates in Romans 6:1–6, this means that Christians are viewed as being identified with Jesus in His death, burial, and resurrection. As a result of their salvation by grace through faith (Ephesians 2:8–9), Christians should see themselves as dead to sin (Romans 6:2) and "alive to God in Christ" (Romans 6:11). The best visual, symbolic, and spiritual portrayal of the "death to the old self" (Romans 6:6) and subsequent "new life in Christ" (Romans 6:4) is the believer's participation in water baptism.

When the believer is *immersed* into baptismal waters, they are symbolically "buried with Christ" (Romans 6:4a). The symbolic burial with Christ attests to the reality of death and expresses the end of the believer's old life that was governed by sin.[240] The resultant death into the baptismal water is then contrasted with the glorious effect of rising up out of the water (Romans 6:3–4). Paul explains that in the same way God raised Jesus from the dead, the believer's *emersion* from the baptismal waters represents God's gift of new resurrection life (Romans 6:5).

---

[238] Tremper Longman, *The Expositor's Bible Commentary, Volume 11* (Grand Rapids, MI: Zondervan, 2008), p. 361. My emphasis in italics.

[239] Longman, p. 105.

[240] Longman, p. 105.

In ministry implementation, this means that the believer's water baptism is a visible sign and public declaration of who they are in Christ (Romans 6:6). Pastoral counseling and preaching should focus on helping believers understand that the physical sign of their baptism represents spiritual realities. When they were brought up from the waters, their new life in Christ began, and they are "no longer slaves to sin" (Romans 6:6). The believer's death to sin and "resurrection like his" (Romans 6:5b) is the basis for our sanctification and new life of discipleship with Jesus and the Body of Christ (Romans 6:5).

Fran wants to know who the proper subjects for baptism are and what the preferred mode is.

THE BIBLE ESTABLISHES THAT BAPTISM is the beginning of the Christian life. This being the case, baptism by immersion into water is an outward symbol of the believer's inward change of heart—a physical demonstration of their faith in Jesus and "death to sin but resurrection to God in Christ Jesus" (Romans 6:11). Baptism is also a sign of the believer's entry into the fellowship of the visible Body of Christ (Acts 2:41–42), and serves the purpose of distinguishing between those who believe in Christ and the rest of the world.

In Romans 6:1–11, Paul emphasized that there is a strong connection between the believer's baptism and their subsequent union with Christ in His death and resurrection. Although salvation does not depend on one's being baptized, the act of water baptism symbolizes the "death of the old self" (Romans 6:6), the "resurrection like his" (Romans 6:5b), and is a natural "accompaniment and completion of faith."[241] Due to the spiritual significance of the act of water baptism, I hold that the proper subject for baptism is someone who fully understands the graphic picture of what the act conveys. In other words, baptism should be a visual sign of the believer's repentance of sin and trust in Christ, and a confession of faith in His atoning work (Acts 2:38, 22:16).

---

[241] Millard Erickson, *Christian Theology* (Grand Rapids, MI: Zondervan), p. 1028.

Based on the fact that the believer's baptism is symbolic of their union with Christ (Romans 6:5, 11), the believer's baptism should mirror that of our Savior. Just as the establishment and model of the Lord's Supper goes back to Jesus Himself, it is important to note that when baptized by John, Jesus "came up out of the water" (Mark 1:10). The complete immersion of Jesus in this particular verse is unmistakable, and the logical entailment is that His disciples should follow His example (1 Corinthians 11:1). Other evidence of baptismal immersion into water is abundant, including the fact that John specifically chose the location of Aenon to perform his baptisms because "there was plenty of water" (John 3:23), and when Philip baptized the Ethiopian eunuch, *they both went down into the water, and then came up out of the water* (Acts 8:36–29—italic emphasis and interpretation mine).

In addition to the biblical examples of the *mode of baptism*, it is also significant that the Apostle Paul seems to suggest that the *act of baptism* is intended to symbolize a particular effect on the believer. In Romans 6:3–5, Paul connects the dots by explaining that the lowering into water symbolizes our lowering into the grave of sin and death (Romans 6:3). Following this logic, coming up out of the water symbolizes that "just as Christ was raised from the dead through the glory of the Father, we too may live a new life" (Romans 6:4). In other words, the mode of baptism by immersion into water (and the subsequent emersion from the water) is meant to symbolize "our union with Christ in a death like His, and a union with Christ in a resurrection like His" (Romans 6:5—my interpretation). In this sense, baptism by immersion into water best symbolizes the biblical picture of the believer's death to sin and resurrection with Jesus Christ. Water baptism is "an immersion that is a sort of burial, and an emergence that is a sort of resurrection."[242]

---

[242] Erickson, p. 1031.

PART FIVE

CASE STUDIES FROM THE GYM

SECTION SUMMARY:

THE FOLLOWING CASE STUDIES from the gym are challenging theological and doctrinal examinations of modern issues facing the Christian faith. Each of the following topics are covered within a systematic framework, including a statement of the gym owner's (pastor's) position on the matter, biblical evidence to support their claims, and a critical examination of the leading positions of criticism and opposition.

CHAPTER 11

WHAT IS THE NATURE OF ORIGINAL SIN?

Fran wants to know more about the concept of original sin. Fran asks you to state the basic nature of sin and guilt, how sin is passed from Adam to us, and how this affects the free will of unregenerate people to accept or reject the Gospel.

UNDERSTANDING THE POSITION:

THE BIBLE TEACHES THAT the entire human race originated from one human pair (Genesis 1:27–28, 2:21–24). This means that Adam served as both the *first* and *universal* human through whom all forthcoming humans would trace their ancestry (Acts 17:26). Because of Adam's original sin and natural headship to the human race, all humans likewise share in his guilt and at birth inherit a corrupted nature and inclination toward sin (Psalm 51:5; Romans 5:12–19). As a result of mankind's inherently sinful nature, it is only through the irresistible grace and unmerited favor of God that we are able to positively respond to the Gospel of Jesus Christ (Acts 20:21; Ephesians 1:4–7; Titus 3:4–7).

SUPPORT FOR THE POSITION:

FRAN, ALLOW ME TO begin by admitting how challenging this theological concept is to grasp. I imagine your first response when you hear "Hey Fran, did you know you were sinful from birth" is one of shock, awe, and possibly even outright rejection. And this, of course, is the anticipated response that the Bible prepares us for. Because of our inherently corrupted sinful nature, the Bible warns us of our three most likely responses: We will deny our sin; shift the blame onto others; or, in extreme cases, even blame God (ref. Genesis 3:1–24). And don't take offense at this proposition—this was exactly what happened with our first parents! Not only did Adam blame Eve for enticing him to eat from the forbidden tree, but he also blamed God for "putting the woman there with him" (Genesis 3:12).

So you see Fran, we have a very big problem on our hands! As we unpack the idea of original sin, there are three general movements that will be introduced. The first is to understand the role that our original parents now play in the depraved and sinful life of humanity. Secondly, we investigate the implications of sin on mankind's interconnectedness and relationship to our first parents. In other words, because all humans are connected to one original pair, it logically follows that all humans inherit a sinful nature. And finally, we turn our attention to the parallel relationship that Adam had to our sinful nature, and that Jesus Christ has to our redeemed lives.

The universality of the human race, and thus the predisposition of the entire human race to sin, is taught at several places in the Bible. In the Old Testament, one description in particular is vivid: "The LORD saw how great the wickedness of the human race had become on earth" (Genesis 6:5). In the Psalms, we read a similar sentiment: "All have turned away, they have become corrupt, there is no one who does good, not even one" (Psalm 14:3). The New Testament teaching is equally convicting, perhaps most strikingly with the words of Paul, "There is no one righteous, not even one; there is no one who understands, there is no one who seeks God" (Romans 3:10–12). As if that were not enough, Paul then goes on to write, "All have sinned and fall short of the glory of God" (Romans 3:23).

Fran, you might be wondering, "How did this get so bad?" That is a very good question to contemplate. The answer is that because all humans share the same original parents, we likewise inherit the original sin and guilt of our first parents (Romans 5:12). The theological principle involved is referred to as "natural headship," which simply means that the totality of our human nature, including our physical and spiritual essence, has been received from our immediate parents and more distant ancestors through the original first pair of humans.[243] On this basis, we really were "present within Adam" at the time of his first sin and therefore inherit at birth the associated guilt and condemnation for our transgression (Jeremiah 17:9; Romans 5:18; 1 John 1:8).

Now Fran, lest you be overwhelmed by the negative implications of headship and "inherited guilt," let me now present how the principle of headship is in fact critical to the good news of Jesus Christ. You see Fran, the same person who explained that *sin entered the human race through one man* (Romans 5:12) paralleled this thought by explaining that *grace entered*

---

[243] Erickson, p. 580.

the human race through one man as well, and that one man is Jesus Christ (Romans 5:15, 17). What is the evidence that sin is within the human race? Well that's simple: "As in Adam all men die" (1 Corinthians 15:22a). In other words, the punishment for sin is evident in the death of mankind (Romans 6:23a). However, through the saving work of Jesus, this also means, "In Christ all will be made alive" (1 Corinthians 15:22b; Romans 6:23b). And what's the evidence that through faith in Jesus Christ we can inherit eternal life?

The answer is simultaneously simple, profound, and miraculous: that God raised Jesus from the dead (Acts 13:30, 2:24), and that through faith in Jesus, we can also "achieve victory over sin and death" (1 Corinthians 15:56) because "God so loved the world that He sent His one and only son, that *whoever believes in him* would not die, but would have eternal life" (John 3:16—my use of italics is to emphasize that all are offered the free gift of grace).

Fran, I imagine a question you might be asking yourself is this: If mankind is inherently sinful at birth, how can we possibly respond affirmatively and believe in the Gospel of Jesus Christ? This too is a great question and comes with a very encouraging answer. The Bible teaches that *before someone believes,* God draws that person to Christ (John. 6:44, 12:32). Additionally, God will supernaturally work in the human heart to persuade the unbeliever of truth, sin, righteousness, and the saving work of His Son (John 16:8–11).

Here is something fairly radical and encouraging to consider about the power of Jesus Christ to turn people from their sinful ways. If you recall, many of the Bible verses that I have referenced thus far were written by the Apostle Paul. But remember, "Before Paul became Paul he was Saul." And what was Saul up to before his remarkable conversion? He was persecuting those who followed Jesus Christ! That's why Paul himself declared that of all the sinners in the world, he was the worst (1 Timothy 1:15).

Yet nevertheless, the grace of Jesus was more then sufficient to transform the heart of Saul into the Apostle Paul. And according to Paul, this same grace that was demonstrated in his life was to serve as an example to everyone else (1 Timothy 1:16). The experience of Paul is consistent with the very words of Jesus, who explained on numerous occasions that he had not come to save the righteous, because there are none, but the sinners—because that's clearly the rest of humanity! (Ref. Matthew 9:13; Mark 2;17)

OPPOSITION TO THE POSITION:

FRAN, I WANT TO make you aware of an alternate position that some have taken in regard to original sin, and thus the redeeming work of Jesus Christ. One such view is referred to as Pelagianism; it was developed by a British monk whose primary concern was for people to live good and decent lives.[244] Pelagius was concerned that by focusing on the view of inherited sin, humans would be inclined to adopt a generally negative conception of their natural state. Therefore, the solution was to develop (or attempt to develop) a theology that strongly emphasized free will and the ability of a human being, through their own effort, to perfectly fulfill God's commands and live a life free of sin.[245] By implication, this means that humans would not need the gift of grace offered in the Gospel of Jesus Christ, since through their own means and willpower mankind would be able to achieve righteousness before God.

RESPONSE TO OPPOSITION:

FRAN, NEEDLESS TO SAY, the view of Pelagius is directly contradictory to the biblical teaching of both the sinful interconnectedness of the entire human race (1 Corinthians 15:21–22), and the total depravity that mankind now experiences (Romans 3:23). The idea that any amount of work (to include the "work" of faith itself!) could somehow result in righteousness flies in the face of the teachings of Jesus (John 14:6; Ephesians 2:9). In other words, even the decision to have faith is not a "work" that becomes the cause of our salvation. God is the cause of our salvation, and faith is the means by which God determined *all people* could receive His grace (John 3:16; Ephesians 1:7, 2:8–9).

---

[244] Erickson, p. 575.
[245] Erickson, p. 576.

CHAPTER 12

IS THE BIBLE TRUE?

Fran wants you to elaborate on the concept of biblical inerrancy. What does this entail, and what is the significance within the gym? Fran wants you to explain what the other views are and then provide application for her life.

UNDERSTANDING THE POSITION:

THE BIBLE IS THE inerrant Word of God and is truthful in all that it teaches (Psalm 18:30; 119:137–138, 142).[246] The Bible is the supreme and truthful rule for Christian doctrine and faith (Matthew 28:18–20), in addition to our guide for life to include our thoughts (Philippians 4:8), words (Titus 2:8; James 3:3–12), and actions (Philippians 4:9; 1 Peter 4:10).

SUPPORT OF THE POSITION:

FRAN, IT IS HELPFUL to understand what is meant by the word *inerrancy.* This theological word and concept teach that the Bible is truthful in all of its teachings.[247] In order to justify my view, I will offer you three arguments in support of my position.

First, we begin with the fact that "All Scripture is God-breathed" (2 Timothy 3:16a) and divinely given to us by God (2 Peter 2:21) to be our supreme guide to understanding our faith (John 10:35) and directing our behavior (2 Timothy 3:16–17). Because God cannot lie (Titus 1:2; John 17:17), and because we have the assurance that God wants what is best for us (Jeremiah 29:11), we therefore conclude that God gave us His Word contained within the Bible to "direct our steps" (Psalm 37:23) and to ensure our eternity with Him (Ephesians 1:18–19).

Secondly, we believe that the written Word of God encapsulated within the Bible was given to the human authors through the power and inspiration of the Holy Spirit (1 Corinthians 2:10, 2:13; 2 Peter 2:21). This means that the

---

[246] Erickson, p. 188.

[247] Erickson, p. 189.

Holy Spirit directed the thoughts and subsequently written words of the human authors in such a way that they composed God's Word without error (2 Peter 3:15–16). Therefore, the words written by the human authors convey God's truth for mankind (John 17:17; 1 Corinthians 2:10–13).

Third, and perhaps most importantly, is the fact that the "Word of God became flesh and made his dwelling among us" (John 1:14a). This means that although the various authors of the Bible, when "carried along by the Holy Spirit" (2 Peter 2:21), recorded the Word of God, the most accurate representation of God's Word was in the life of Jesus Christ (Hebrews 1:1–3). Through the power of the Holy Spirit (1 Corinthians 2:10–12), the believer may now embrace the truthfulness of God's Word through a relationship with His Son, Jesus Christ (Matthew 7:24; John 5:24). We further note that Jesus Christ Himself and the Apostles provided authority and justification for believing, trusting, and following the Word of God (Matthew 5:17–19; John 14:15; 2 Peter 3:15–16).

OPPOSITION TO THE POSITION:

IN ORDER FOR THE Bible to make the claim of inerrancy, there must be absolute continuity between all historical and chronological accounts within its various books and contents. The contradictions between the authors' reports of identical historical and chronological events clearly demonstrate that a theologian cannot maintain the argument for the inerrancy of the Bible.

If the Bible is inerrant in all that it teaches, how then can we explain the significant discrepancies in similar historical and chronological accounts of the Bible? Consider and explain these two examples: In 2 Samuel 10:18, we read that David killed 700 enemy charioteers (and even this seems exaggerated— how can a *man on foot* overcome and kill *700 troops in an armored chariot?*), yet the same account of the battle in 1 Chronicles 19:18 lists the enemy charioteers at 7,000 (refer to my previous concern of exaggeration!). Then there is the problem with the chronology of the Gospels. How do you explain the fact that the Gospel according to Matthew lists Jesus's temple cleansing near the end of His public ministry (Mathew 11:15–17), while John's Gospel lists the same event at the beginning of Jesus's ministry (John 2:14–16)?

RESPONSE TO THE OPPOSITION:

IT IS IMPORTANT TO understand the inerrancy of the Bible in terms of the cultural setting in which the biblical author recorded their message.[248] In other words, we cannot enforce the modern expectations for the exactness of numeric and chronological accounting to biblical times. Furthermore, we must understand and read each numeric and chronological account in the Bible from the perspective in which the original author intended.[249]

Let us begin with the concern regarding the seeming numeric discrepancy in the account of the enemy charioteers. In this case, the biblical writer intended to convey the point that David engaged with and killed *a large number of enemy forces*. The point of the written record was not for the purpose of serving as an official military document. Rather, the author's aim was to give some idea of the size and scope of the enemy forces killed by David. Furthermore, because even David acknowledged that "the battle is the LORD's" (1 Samuel 17:47), the point was not that David killed even a single enemy soldier, but rather that everyone who was gathered on the battlefield that particular day, and everyone who would subsequently read about the battle, would come to know the faithfulness of God.

Turning our attention to the seeming contradiction in the chronological discrepancy between the Gospel of Matthew and John, we may account for this by acknowledging that Jesus cleared the temple twice during His lifetime. Matthew accounts for the later event, and John for the first. Because of our belief in the doctrine of the divinely inspired Scriptures (2 Peter 1:20–21), we assert that God's Word is inerrant in all its teachings. Therefore, any seeming discrepancy between Matthew and John, or any other part of the Gospels, can be resolved through the harmonistic approach outlined in the example above.[250]

---

[248] Erickson, p. 203.

[249] Erickson, p. 203.

[250] Erickson, p. 199.

Another concern that someone might have in regards to the inerrancy of Scripture is the biblical reports of scientific matters. It must be understood once again that the original author had a specific purpose in mind, commonly referred to as "the author's intent," with whatever they recorded or described. In this sense, it is important to account for scientific matters in the phenomenal rather than a purely technical manner.[251] We may therefore conclude that the original author recorded things according to how they appeared to the eye. Additionally, the author recorded their observations in the most agreeable means by which the subsequent reader could frame, visualize, and conceptualize what they (empowered by the Holy Spirit) had intended to convey.

---

[251] Erickson, p. 204.

CHAPTER 13

WHO WORSHIPS GOD?

Fran wants to know if Christians and Muslims worship the same God. This is a very important topic for her because she trains at a gym with a variety of spiritual views and religious backgrounds.

STATEMENT OF THE POSITION:

THE BIBLE ESTABLISHES THAT the Father of Jesus is *not* the God of Muhammad. In other words, Christians and Muslims do not worship the *same* God.

SUPPORT FOR THE POSITION:

FRAN, IT IS FUNDAMENTAL to the Christian faith to define God in the manner in which He has most perfectly and supremely revealed Himself. The Christian holds that Jesus Christ is Himself God and the exact representation of His being (Hebrews 1:3; Colossians 1:19, 2:9). Furthermore, we believe that Jesus is the *only way to know God* (John 14:6). Jesus is "The way, the truth and the life" (John 14:6a), and no person can come to know God *except through Him* (John 14:6b).

In many respects, the realization that Jesus was God became the bedrock and cornerstone of the Gospel or "good news" that the Apostle Paul so adamantly and passionately proclaimed (1 Corinthians 8:6; Romans 10:13). According to the Apostle Paul, Jesus Christ was with God the Father in eternity (2 Timothy 1:9; cf. John 1:1–3). In the life, death, and resurrection of Jesus, eternal life and reconciliation with God become available to all who have faith in His name (2 Timothy 1:10, 2:8–10; Romans 10:13).

You see Fran, when the Christian says, "I worship God," what they in fact mean is that they worship the God who revealed Himself and became incarnate in Jesus Christ.[252] The Christian worships Jesus as God, who is the "Word become flesh" and who, as God in the flesh, died for our sins.[253] The proclamations of the Christian faith are the lifeblood of what we believe. When

---

[252] Tennent, p. 38.
[253] Tennent, p. 38.

the Christian declares to be true the words of the Apostle Paul—"In Jesus all the fullness of the Deity lives in bodily form (Colossians 2:9)—we are drawing up our battle lines. We are standing alongside the Apostle John when he wrote that "No one who denies the Son has the Father; whoever acknowledges the Son has the Father also" (1 John 2:23).

OPPOSITION TO THE POSITION:

THE CHRISTIAN AND THE Muslim both make the claim to *believe* in and *worship* One True God. In other words, Islam and Christianity are both monotheistic religions and *believe there is only One God*. Because both religions hold to *believe* in and *worship* this One God, they must concede they are *worshiping* and *believing* in the *same* God.

RESPONSE TO THE OPPOSITION:

THE CHRISTIAN AND THE Muslim are in agreement to the claim we collectively make to worship only One God. In other words, monotheism is central to the doctrine of both religions. We will see, however, that this monotheistic argument is not sufficient to establish that the One True God we both lay claim to worship is in fact the *same Being*.

The worship of One God, as opposed to several gods, was an important distinction between the people groups and religions of the old world. For example, when the Apostle Paul was in Athens, he became greatly distressed when he discovered that the inhabitants of the city worshiped several gods (Acts 17:1). Although Paul conceded the people were "very religious" (Acts 18:22), he explained to them that their religion was so completely distorted that they even worshipped an "unknown god" (Acts 18:23). Therefore, for both the Christian and Muslim faiths to ascend the spiritual ladder from worshipping several gods to One True God is a monumental leap forward when compared to the pagan philosophical views of biblical times. However, we must not stop there.

The Christian holds that the Father of Jesus is the only God there is (2 Corinthians 11:31). The Muslim holds there is only One True God (Surah 112:1). How are we to reconcile what on the surface might appear to be the worship of the same God? In the analogy of drawn-up battle lines, the key terrain features of the battleground are determined not through an ontological argument, but rather by describing the object of belief and worship of the Christian and Muslim faith.[254]

Although the Christian and Muslim agree that the object of their belief shares certain attributes, such as self-existence and omnipotence, there are also significant differences.[255] The age-old adage "We are more alike than we are different"[256] may hold true in certain contexts of evangelism. However, in this particular case, the differences form a chasm that cannot be easily crossed.

The Christian holds that without Jesus, any knowledge of God becomes impossible (Matthew 11:27; John 14:6). We believe that the eternal God of Heaven entered the human race as Jesus of Nazareth (Luke 1:30–35), died for our sins, and through faith in Jesus Christ reconciles mankind onto Himself (John 3:16).

The Muslim, on the other hand, holds that the God of Muhammad as described in the Quran is an *absolutely independent being who is not begotten, nor who begets* (Surah 112:1–4). And for the Muslim, this particular monotheistic view of God becomes the impassable chasm between their understanding of God and the Christian Trinitarian view of God. The Christian holds that Jesus Christ *is begotten of the Father,* and that Jesus is Himself God (John 1:1, 14, 8:58, 20:28; Colossians 2:9; Hebrews 1:3, 8). The Trinitarian view of God as One Being is simultaneously a monotheistic view of this same particular Supreme Being. However, the Christian holds that this One magnificent being is in fact *One Being in three Persons*: The Father, Son, and Holy Spirit.

Fran, let me conclude with this: the reason why the Apostle John wrote his Gospel was so "that you may believe that Jesus is the Christ, the Son of God, and that by believing you may have life in his name" (John 20:31). John's invitation to believe in the Son of God, at the most fundamental and

---

[254] Erickson, p. 271.

[255] Erickson, p. 271.

[256] Maya Angelou has historically been credited with this saying.

foundational level, is a simultaneous call to a Trinitarian faith.[257] Jesus is the *Son of God*. Therefore, God is the *Father* of Jesus. And Jesus is the *Christ*, the One anointed with the *Spirit*. The Christian view of God is therefore a Trinitarian view. So you see, for these reasons, we must conclude that the Father of Jesus is not the God of Muhammad.

---

[257] Reeves, p. 37.

CHAPTER 14

WHAT IS THE ETERNAL DESTINY OF HUMANS?

Fran wants to understand God's election as it pertains to human destinies. Furthermore, she asks for your help in understanding biblical passages that seem to suggest that God decided human beings would do evil, such as Joseph's conversation with his brother in Genesis 50, and God hardening Pharaoh's heart in Exodus 7–10.

UNDERSTANDING THE POSITION:

FRAN, THE BIBLE ABOUNDS with evidence that the plan of God is unconditional rather than conditional on human choice.[258] On the other hand, there is no biblical evidence that seems to suggest that God works within human free will in order to accomplish His purposes. Put another way, God does not decide what He is going to do and then find a human who would be agreeable to His plans. God decides ahead of time His plans and purposes and then carries out those plans and purposes within His creation.

This is why the Apostle Paul could write so emphatically that "God has mercy on whom he wants to have mercy, and he hardens whom he wants to harden" (Romans 9:18). Jesus Christ Himself told His disciples that they did not choose to follow Him; rather Jesus chose them (John 15:16a). Furthermore, in addition to choosing His disciples, God had also predetermined what they were going to do as a result of His selection: "That they might go and bear fruit—fruit that will last" (John 15:16b). The totality of the biblical evidence aligns with the notion that God renders it certain that people will act in a particular way in the accomplishment of His purposes.[259] However, would not this conclusion challenge the basic precepts of human free will? If God has chosen ahead of time what I will do, am I not reduced to an automated human being? The answer to this question and similar challenges is revealed in finding a more meaningful definition of what in fact constitutes free will in the first place.

In other words, although I am free to make my own decisions, those decisions that I am seemingly free to make are still made within the framework of certain predetermined conditions. These predetermined conditions ultimately affect what I perceive to be my own free will.

---

[258] Erickson, p. 327.
[259] Erickson, p. 327.

One illustration from the CrossFit culture may help make sense of this principle. Imagine a barbell is resting on the ground. I have the free will to lift the barbell and bring it over my head. I may either choose to do so, or not. However, if I do decide to lift the barbell overhead, the way in which my body was designed to perform this task will reduce the means by which I lift the barbell to only one mechanical action. And who created my body and the mechanical means by which I am able to produce force and productively apply strength? God did! And therefore, in the performance of lifting barbells, I am free to either partake in lifting weights or not, but I am not free to determine the most efficient and effective (not to mention safe) means to perform the task.

Another illustration is from the brilliant mind of C. S. Lewis. He used the illustration of an ocean liner carrying passengers from one location to another predetermined location. Along the way and across the ocean, the passengers on board the vessel are free to do what they wish. However, there are obviously certain conditions, constrictions, and a general framework within which the passengers must live and operate. After all, the passengers are on a boat in the middle of the ocean! So you see, the passengers all maintain a sense of free will, yet at the same time the vessel is moving swiftly along a predetermined route to a predetermined location over which they do not have any say or "will." Therefore, once again we see the principle involved: human free will is indeed free, yet still compatible and in alignment with God's predetermined and sovereign will. To use a modern term of speech, God determines and renders certain everything that occurs, and humans are along for the ride!

Fran, let's look a bit more closely at two intriguing biblical narratives to gain a greater appreciation for my position in light of sin and evil in the world. In Genesis 50, it appears that as a component of God's will, humans are forced into sinful actions. But wouldn't this be in direct opposition and conflict with our understanding of God's inherent goodness? How can a good God direct evil human behavior? The key is a broader interpretation and a "higher perspective" of what in fact the biblical author was revealing about God. When Joseph explained to his brothers that "what you intended for harm, God intended for good" (Genesis 50:19), he revealed that what his brothers perceived as sinful was in fact part of God's plan for good and was predetermined by Him. This is why Joseph comforted his brothers and helped them see that from the "highest perspective" (the "highest perspective" in this sense is God as articulated in Genesis 50:19: "Don't be afraid. Am I in the place of God?"), the actions of his brothers were not sinful at all. In fact, the actions that they performed were part of God's plan to "accomplish what is now being done, the saving of many lives" (Genesis 50:20).

Another biblical narrative that would on the surface seem to indicate that God were in effect directing sinful human behavior is the account of the hardening of Pharaoh's heart (Exodus 7:4). However, similar to the "higher perspective" hermeneutic that I proposed in the account of Joseph's brothers, we should note here that the "big picture" plan of God was to deliver Israel out of bondage while at the same time making the Egyptians witness to His power. For the Old Testament reader of the Exodus account and Israel's escape from slavery, it was clear that God not only created the world but was also directing human history. In this sense, Pharaoh served God's greater purpose by creating a series of conditions that would subsequently allow the Israelites "to tell your children and grandchildren how God performed signs among them" (Genesis 10:2). Based on this understanding of the biblical record, God permits sin to exist for the greater purposes of humanity. In other words, as the ultimate director of human history, God can "redirect" or "reverse" sin in such a way that it ultimate results in good.[260]

OPPOSITION TO THE POSITION:

THE ARMINIAN VIEW OF God's election of human destiny would contend that God gave humans free will with the expectation that they would exercise it without constraint. If this were not the case, then we would not see the "whosoever will" invitations within the Bible. These verses, such as, "Come to me, all you who are weary and burdened, and I will give you rest" (Matthew 11:28), carry within them the human's implied freedom to either choose Jesus or to deny Him. Therefore, the freedom of the human to make an independent choice would be inconsistent with the position that God's decisions have rendered the future certain and fixed.[261]

---

[260] Erickson, p. 326.
[261] Erickson, p. 326.

RESPONSE TO THE OPPOSITION:

THE ARMINIAN OPPOSITION IS largely based on their unique understanding of God's foreknowledge. The Arminian looked to Romans 8:29 and Paul's statement that "For those God foreknew he also predestined" and, from this verse, reaches the conclusion that God's determination of human destiny is a result of His foreknowledge.[262] In this sense, those whom God foreknew would receive Jesus Christ as their Lord and savior are the same ones that God predetermined would be saved. This means that human freedom was at the center of God's decision-making process in regard to human destiny.

The problem with this view is that it does not take into consideration what Paul adamantly emphasized: that no human being was without sin (reference Romans 3:23)! Paul made it clear that salvation was not a matter of anything that a human being could do, including exercising their free will. In fact, the exercise of free will would often result in "ignorance of God" and in humans choosing sin rather than God's grace (Acts 17:30). This is why Paul taught that we are saved by grace through faith in Christ alone (Ephesians 2:8–9). Furthermore, if we hold to the notion of the Arminian understanding of Romans 8:29, mainly God's foreknowledge as based on a favorable response on the part of Israel, then God's choice would have clearly been wrong.[263] Therefore, we must look for an alternative understanding of the text.

A far better understanding of foreknowledge is to link it directly to the will of God. This is made clear in Acts 2:23, in which Luke wrote, "Jesus was handed over by God's deliberate plan and foreknowledge." Another strong indication that foreknowledge is linked with God's will is that Jesus Christ Himself was foreknown even before the foundation of the world (1 Peter 1:20). Therefore, based on a more systematic understanding and treatment of foreknowledge, we must conclude that God's plan is unconditional rather than conditional on human choice.[264]

---

[262] Erickson, p. 327.

[263] Erickson, p. 327.

[264] Erickson, p. 327.

CHAPTER 15

HOW HUMAN WAS JESUS?

Fran wants you to explain what it means that "Christ emptied Himself" at the incarnation. What are the implications for the different views on this topic within the box?

UNDERSTANDING THE POSITION:

THE APOSTLE PAUL'S USE OF the word *kenosis* ("made himself nothing") in Philippians 2:7 meant that during Jesus's earthly life, while His divine nature and equality with God were maintained, He temporarily renounced and voided Himself of certain divine privileges in order to reveal the true nature and love of God to mankind (John 3:16). This means that during His earthly ministry, Jesus freely accepted the psychosomatic limitations of humanity (Philippians 2:8). However, the humanity of Jesus never resulted in the loss of His divine nature or attributes (Colossians 2:9). In this sense, while in the presence of His disciples, Jesus was fully human, and He was fully God.

SUPPORT FOR THE POSITION:

FRAN, AT FIRST GLANCE, it would be easy to take the word *kenosis* in Philippians 2:7—"made himself nothing" or the similar translation "emptied himself"—to mean that while on Earth, Jesus divested Himself of His divine nature and attributes in order to live a fully human life. However, this would be in direct contradiction to the fundamental belief and proclamation of the Church that Jesus's divine and human natures were "indivisible and inseparable" and that the properties of each nature were upheld in the One person of Jesus Christ.[265] Therefore, we must proceed with a more systematic and comprehensive evaluation of what Paul meant in his use of the word *kenosis*.

There is a wonderful story from the Brazilian Jiu Jitsu community that serves as an apt starting point for our discussion on this critical theological issue. Legend has it that a world champion Jiu Jitsu black belt once donned a crisp new beginner's uniform and white belt and humbly walked into a Jiu

---

[265] Erickson, p. 665 (Chalcedonian Definition).

Jitsu studio where he was unknown. Many of the more advanced students saw this as an opportunity to display their martial prowess, only to discover that this new "white belt" was able to easily counter their every attack. In other words, the world champion emptied himself of his rank (his black belt and world champion uniform) while simultaneously maintaining his skill and "black-belt attributes and world champion nature."

Let's apply this story to the biblical account of Jesus washing the feet of His disciples. Following the evening meal, Jesus got up from the table, wrapped a towel around His waist, and proceeded to wash His disciples' feet and dry them with the towel that was wrapped around Him (John 13:1–5). We need to understand the significance of this act in relation to Paul's use of the word *kenosis*. Here we have the "King of Kings and Lord of Lords" (1 Timothy 6:15; Revelation 17:14) washing the feet of His disciples? Shouldn't this be the other way around? Common sense would dictate that the disciples (the servants) should wash the feet of Jesus (the King)! And herein I believe we have the key to understanding what Paul meant when he wrote that Jesus "made himself nothing."

During His life on Earth, Jesus never ceased to maintain the nature of God. However, Jesus became "functionally subordinated to the Father" for the purpose of revealing "the radiance of God's glory and the exact representation of His being" (Hebrews 1:3).[266] In this sense, Jesus "emptied Himself" of certain divine rights. Rather than enjoying the privilege of having His disciples tend to Him, Jesus "emptied himself" and *served those who should have been serving Him.* Jesus took up the cross, not the crown. By "making himself nothing," I believe that Paul was referring to the fact that for Jesus, this meant giving up certain privileges, serving as a slave, obeying the Father, and dying a slave's death on a cross. In other words, although it would seem that "making himself nothing" would result in a loss of divinity, it was in fact the "making nothing" or "emptying himself" that revealed the true nature and love of God.

---

[266] Erickson, p. 670.

OPPOSITION TO THE POSITION:

OVER THE COURSE OF history, there have been many attempts to understand the relationship of Jesus Christ to the Father and to conceptualize the seemingly impossible notion that a divine and human nature can simultaneously exist within one person. Based on Paul's use of the word *kenosis,* one view has held that the Second Person of the Trinity—the Incarnate Son—laid aside His "distinctly divine attributes" in order to take on human qualities instead.[267] This view is commonly referred to as *kenoticism* and in a sense implies that at the incarnation, there was an exchange of divine nature for human characteristics. Although Jesus was God in eternity, during His ministry on Earth, He "emptied himself" of His divine nature. In the words of the theologian Millard Erickson, this meant that "Jesus is God and a human in the same respect, but not at the same time." This view would also suggest that at the incarnation, Jesus temporarily laid down or "emptied himself" of His divine attributes with the expectation and anticipation of winning them back again.

RESPONSE TO THE OPPOSITION:

FRAN, I DISAGREE WITH *kenoticism* and the idea that somehow Jesus "emptied himself" of the form of God during His life on Earth. I feel that a better and more comprehensive approach to understanding what Paul meant in his use of the word *kenosis* is to relate Philippians 2:7 to Paul's other epistles, in which the deity of Christ is taught (Colossians 1:15–20, 2:9). Furthermore, it is imperative to see that in Philippians, although Paul says Jesus "emptied himself," nowhere in the epistle does he even remotely imply that Jesus ceased to possess His divine nature (and this is true in all of Paul's epistles). The strongest biblical evidence for this claim is in Colossians 2:9, when Paul wrote that "in Christ all the fullness of the Deity lives in bodily form." In other words, we must understand the phrase "emptied himself" in light of the fact that Jesus also maintained the "fullness of Deity." The combination of Christ having "emptied himself" while simultaneously maintaining the "fullness of his Deity" is what has led some of the greatest theological minds to proclaim

[267] Erickson, p. 668.

that the two natures of Christ (His humanity and His deity) exist in One person—*not parted or divided into two persons, but one and the same Son.*"[268]

Fran, I also think it is important from an anthropological perspective to understand kenosis in the context of Christ's humanity. In other words, kenosis must be seen in accordance with Paul's explanation of Christ "being made in human likeness" (Philippians 2:7b). This is further made clear in verse 8, when Paul explains that Jesus Christ, although fully God, "was found in appearance as a man." This is nearly the same point that Paul was making in his letter to the Romans that "God sent His own Son in the likeness of sinful man" (Romans 8:3). Paul argues that although Jesus Christ was fully God during His life and ministry, Jesus was also fully recognizable as a human being. In this sense, Jesus was God living out a fully human life.

---

[268] Erickson, p. 665 (Chalcedonian Definition).

CHAPTER 16

WAS THE GOSPEL PREACHED IN HELL?

Fran has overheard conversations about Christ's descent into hell. She comes to you a bit confused and asks if it is biblically and theologically correct to say that Christ descended into hell and, if so, what did He accomplish by doing so?

UNDERSTANDING THE POSITION:

THE BIBLE TEACHES THAT Jesus Christ proclaimed the good news of God's grace to the sinners of His day while on Earth. Jesus's proclamation of the Gospel was received by people who rejected it and subsequently died (1Peter 4:6), in addition to persons who were already spiritually dead (Ephesians 2:1, 5). Our Lord's Heavenly descent from Glory involved leaving His seat at the Right Hand of the Father at the incarnation and becoming man (Hebrews 1:1–3; Colossians 2:9), and His death and burial in a borrowed tomb (Luke 23:50–56; 1 Corinthians 15:3–4). However, we do not believe that any further descent into an underworld, whether hell or Hades, can be adequately biblically or theologically supported.

SUPPORT OF THE POSITION:

FRAN, IN DISCUSSING WHETHER or not Jesus descended into hell or Hades, it is important to "locate" exactly where in our theological construction this particular question resides. In other words, once we understand our terrain, it is far easier to establish our boundary lines and reach an adequate final destination. Most theologians believe that the stages of Christ's work were accomplished in two basic movements, often referred to as Christ's *humiliation* and the state of His *exaltation*.[269] Within these two movements there is a series of what we could refer to as "stages of Christ's work": these consist of a series of steps down from Christ's eternal position with the Father (Hebrews 1:1–3, John 1:1), followed by a series of steps back up to His previous Glory at the Father's Right Hand (Acts 7:55–56).

---

[269] Erickson, p. 702.

In many respects, the first step of Christ's humiliation was at the incarnation, when "The Word became flesh" (John 1:14a). This realization should open our heart to the immense love that God has for His children! Just think of everything that Christ left behind in order to become human and "make his adobe among us" (John. 1:14b)—from a position of "equality with God" in Heaven (Philippians 2:16) to being born in the dirt and filth of a manger!

The next step down in Christ's humiliation took place at His death on the Cross. As an instrument of torture, the Cross was not only meant to kill its victim, but also to publically humiliate them. This means that the physical torment Jesus experienced on the Cross was just as painful as the mental and emotional suffering inflicted upon Him. The final step in Christ's humiliation was His death and burial. Although Jesus came to Earth as the "giver of life "(Psalm 36:9; John 14:6), He became subject to the most agonizing death conceivable. Those who gathered at the Cross mocked Jesus and offered a series of scoffing remarks: "He saved others; let him save himself if he is God's Messiah, the Chosen One" (Luke 23:35). To the unbelieving (and even to Christ's own disciples!), it seemed that sin and evil had achieved a victory.

However, the story and "stages of Christ's work" now progress onward and upward in an awesome way. Fran, we now turn the corner of the basic movements of Christ's work and begin to ascend the steps of His exaltation and return to Glory. In many respects, the resurrection of Christ was the catalyst that propelled the entire Christian faith into the worldwide prominence that it enjoys today. Fran, consider this—at the arrest of Jesus, His friends and closest disciples not only deserted Him, but also outright rejected that they even knew Him! (Luke 22:54–62). But then, something radical happened. These same people who were "naked and afraid" (Mark 14:51–52) became utterly and completely transformed—they became fearless in proclaiming the Gospel. What happened? It was simple, yet miraculous! They came face-to-face with the resurrected Christ (1 Corinthians 15:1–8).

As magnificent as the resurrection was, this was just the beginning of Christ's return to Glory. The next step of Christ's exalting work involves His ascension into Heaven and seat at the Father's Right Hand (Acts 1:9–11, 5:31; Matthew 26:64). This step in Christ's work was critical: He is now preparing a place for the believers' future home (John 14:2–3) and, from His place of Glory, Jesus is able to send the Holy Spirit (John 14:17). Through the power of the Holy Spirit, the Kingdom of God can now advance on Earth—believers today are empowered to do the works that Jesus had been doing (John 14:12). The final stage of Christ's exalting work still remains to be seen: His return in the future to judge the living and the dead (2 Timothy 4:1).

OPPOSITION TO THE POSITION:

SOME THEOLOGIANS CONTEND THAT there was one additional step in Christ's humiliation: a final descent into hell or Hades. This conclusion is reached by compiling various biblical texts (Psalm 16:10; Ephesians 4:8–10; 1 Timothy 3:16; 1 Peter 3:18–19, 4:4–6) that seem to suggest that between Christ's death on Friday and resurrection on Sunday, He descended into hell. This descent was understood to accomplish a variety of ends: 1) The Roman Catholic view suggests that Christ went to the *limbus partum,* preached the Gospel to the saints who had already lived and died, and then led them from that place into Heaven. 2) The Lutheran view is that Jesus descended into Hades not to proclaim the Gospel, but rather to announce His complete victory over Satan and decree a sentence of condemnation. 3)

The traditional Anglican view is that Jesus went to a specific part of Hades called Paradise and there proclaimed to the righteous a more complete exposition of the Truth.[270] From a theological perspective, the totality of these positions would be agreeable with the concept that Jesus came to save *all of humanity.* In order to reconcile mankind onto God, it necessitated the proclamation of the Gospel in every conceivable natural and supernatural realm and spiritual state wherein mankind resided.

---

[270] These three views of Christ's descent into Hades were identified in Erickson, *Christian Theology,* p. 708.

RESPONSE TO THE OPPOSITION:

FRAN, UPON A CLOSER inspection of the biblical texts used to support a final step of Christ's humiliation into the realm of Hades, we will discover that they lack congruency and do not form a convincing doctrine. On the other hand, when interpreted correctly, these same verses speak to the beautiful magnitude of Christ's work and encourage the modern-day evangelist to proclaim the Gospel to the ends of the Earth (Mark 16:15).

Fran, I'd first like to point out that there is no specific biblical text that conclusively or completely treats the doctrine of Christ's descent into Hades.[271] However, neither is there a single biblical text that treats the doctrine of the Trinity! Therefore, we simply can't throw out the argument on the basis that not one single text clearly and unambiguously makes the case for a final step in the humiliation of Christ into hell. Rather, we must look carefully at those texts that are used to make this position to determine their adequacy or lack therein.

I'd like to wrestle with what many biblical scholars consider to be the most challenging and difficult of the texts in support of the descent into Hades. If we can unravel the mystery of this particular text, we then have a "key" to understand the latter. The text I am referring to is 1 Peter 3:18–19, specifically when Peter wrote that Jesus "went and preached to the spirits in prison." The Roman Catholic, Lutheran, and Anglican Churches base their doctrines of Hades on this particular text—you can refer to their specific views in the Defend Section above. I propose a fourth interpretation of this verse, in addition to what Peter wrote in verses 4:4–6.

I believe the key to a sound exegetical interpretation is to consider the totality of Peter's train of thought by continuing into verse 20. I argue that "Christ's proclamation to the people of the days of Noah" (1 Peter 3:20) is figurative or illustrative and meant to symbolize the sinful people of Christ's days on Earth.[272] These people responded and behaved exactly the same way that the people did during the days of Noah—they were unresponsive, rebellious, and sinful. This same line of reasoning can then be extended into verse 4:6 as

---

[271] Erickson, p. 706

[272] This interpretation was brought to my attention in Millard Erickson's book *Christian Theology*.

a general reference to Christ's proclamation of the Gospel message, "either to persons who had since died or to people who were already spiritually dead (cf. Ephesians 2:1. 5; Colossians 2:13)."[273]

Unraveling these particular verses from 1 Peter (notably the strongest in support of the opposition) demonstrates that there is insufficient evidence to develop a definitive doctrine of Christ's decent into hell or Hades. From a theological perspective, the totality of biblical texts that speak to Christ's "descent" are meant to refer to Christ's descent from Heaven to Earth; not to another location beneath it. Furthermore, the "fourth model" of interpretation is much more congruent with the realization that nowhere else in Scripture is there even a hint of a second chance of Gospel proclamation to the dead.[274]

---

[273] Erickson, p. 709.
[274] Erickson, p. 709.

CHAPTER 17

CAN A BELIEVER LOSE THEIR FAITH?

Fran asks about your position on the Perseverance of the Believer. She asks, "Can a truly regenerate person lose his or her salvation?"

UNDERSTANDING THE POSITION:

OUR UNDERSTANDING OF SCRIPTURE IS that a truly regenerate person cannot lose their salvation. Those people who in faith "confess with their mouth that Jesus is Lord, and believe in their heart that God raised him from the dead" (Romans 10:9), will be accepted by God, indwelt by the Holy Spirit, and empowered by the grace of God to preserve into eternal salvation.

SUPPORT FOR THE POSITION:

FRAN, THE THEOLOGICAL DOCTRINE of *perseverance* is extremely important in the practical life of the Christian. For example, if a believer were uncertain about the status of their eternal salvation, they would be inclined toward a life of great anxiety and spiritual stress. The question on their mind would likely be, "Am I good enough?" Needless to say, the negative implications and connotation of the question would compel the believer toward a life of merit-based religious behavior—they would gravitate toward a Mosaic religious model of "working for their salvation." On the other hand, a believer who was adamant that their salvation was perfectly secure and entirely independent of anything they did or failed to do might become indifferent to our Lord's insistence that "if you love me, you must obey me" (John 14:15). Fran, it seems we are at a bit of a crossroads here! What are we to think?

In order to develop our position, we must survey the key biblical teaching on the matter, with a special emphasis on the words of Jesus Christ. Let's begin with one of my favorite verses: John 10:27–30. The context for the verse is our Lord's vivid imagery of a shepherd and a flock of sheep. Fran, did you know that sheep are the only animal without any means of self-preservation? In other words, they cannot defend themselves! They are entirely dependent on their shepherd. The implications are profound: believers are entirely dependent *on our shepherd* Jesus Christ. In addition to being unable to defend themselves, sheep have very bad eyesight and are prone to wandering off and getting lost. Once again, the implications are staggering. Jesus assures His "flock of sheep" that He has given them *eternal life* and that nobody will be able to *snatch them out of His hand* (John 10:28). This is a very strong argument for the assurance that believers can have in their salvation. Jesus Christ Himself promised that *nothing* would be able to come between Him and His flock.

Another encouraging illustration that our Lord used to emphasize the point of eternal security and the perseverance of the believer is that of a "vine and branch" depicted in John 15. Here, we see that our Lord turns to the practice of viniculture to explain the theological principle of Union with Christ. When a believer receives Jesus into their heart as Lord and Savior, they are joined with Christ and receive a regenerated heart—in other words, new life! The believer's union with Christ will empower them to keep our Lord's commands (John 15:10) and to "remain in him, even as he remains in the believer" (John 15:4).

Another extremely compelling treatment on the matter is found in the words of the Apostle Paul in his letter to the Romans. Fran, it's likely that you've heard this verse but might not have understood the context: "For I am convinced that neither death nor life, neither angles nor demons, neither the present nor the future, nor any powers, neither height nor depth, nor anything else in all creation, will be able to separate us from the love of God that is in Christ Jesus our Lord" (Romans 8:38–39). That is such a confidence booster! Fran, what this verse teaches is that although the believer may experience seasons of "present sufferings," we are assured that because God is with us, *no-body* and *no-thing* can be against us (Romans 8:18, 31). When we put our trust in Jesus Christ, we have the assurance that our Good Shepherd will protect us and keep our salvation tightly held in the palm of His hand. This assurance provides us with the confidence to stand alongside Paul and declare, "Because I have believed (in Jesus Christ) I am convinced that he is able to guard what I have entrusted to him (our salvation) until that day" (2 Timothy 1:12).

Fran, the book of Hebrews, Chapters 6 and 10, also emphasizes the assurance that the believer can have in their eternal salvation. The context for these verses is the theological doctrine of regeneration and the new birth that the believer experiences at the time of their conversion. The Apostle John explained that when a believer puts their trust in Jesus Christ, they are "born of God." This means that "because God's seed (the Holy Spirit) remains in them, they cannot go on sinning, because they have been born of God" (1 John 3:9). Fran, let me unpack this a bit for you. The *new life* that the believer receives at the moment of regeneration and conversion is actually an *eternal life* deposited by God within the believer's heart. By definition, something *eternal* is not subject to death! This is why in the same letter, John is able to "write these things to you who believe in the name of the Son of God so that you may know that you have eternal life" (1 John 5:13).

The context of the *eternal life* within the believer helps explain the essence of Hebrews verse 6:4. Here we read the author's contention that it is impossible for those who have once been enlightened (referring to regeneration, conversion, and the new life of the Holy Spirit) to fall away. The point the author makes is that although *logically* one could fall away—it is in fact *impossible* to do so! Therefore, the author encourages believers to be diligent to the very end, "so that what you hope for may be fully realized" (Hebrews 6:11). This same point is made later in the same letter when the author explained that believers can enjoy confidence in their eternal salvation because they put their faith in Jesus (Hebrews 10:19). There is no longer any "work" that the believer needs to do to ensure their salvation—the "work" has been fully accomplished by Christ's atoning death (Hebrews 10:20–22). Although seasons of temptation and testing will come and go, the believer can be certain that "God is faithful" and will always provide a way out (1 Co. 10:13). The grace of God that led the believer to put their faith in Christ will be sufficient to "carry them on in completion until the day of Christ Jesus" (Phil. 1:6).

OPPOSITION TO THE POSITION:

IF IT WERE TRUE that a regenerate believer was not able to lose their salvation, then why does Jesus Christ issue so many warnings about this very possibility becoming a reality? Jesus specifically instructed His disciples on the danger of falling away because he wanted to ensure they would not (Matthew 24:3–14). Additionally, the Apostle Paul speaks to the conditional nature of salvation in his letter to the Colossians (Colossians 1:21-23). Paul emphasized that just because a believer *thinks they are secure,* they nevertheless need to "be careful so that you don't fall!" (1 Corinthians 10:12) Why would Paul have issued such a warning if it were not a real possibility? Based on these verses from Scripture, we must concede that a truly regenerate person can fall away from the Faith and lose their salvation.

RESPONSE TO THE OPPOSITION:

ALLOW ME TO SHARE a modern-day example from my background in the U.S. Army to emphasize the eternal salvation that the believer can be assured of. When I arrived at Fort Sill, Oklahoma, for boot camp in the spring of 2004, my drill sergeants warned me "don't even think about going AWOL (absent without leave)—it's impossible." As the days and weeks of military training continued to march forward, I often reflected on this seemingly conflicted statement. Was it really impossible? An impenetrable wall did not surround the training area and barracks where new soldiers participated in Basic Combat Training. Certainly we could leave if we wanted to. However, the totality of what we were learning about the Army, the sense of fellowship with the other soldiers, the love for our nation, and the warnings about what could *theoretically happen* if we tried to leave (like a court martial!) compelled and motivated us to stay the course. And, most importantly, the drill instructors painted a beautiful picture in our mind of graduation day: the coveted and long-awaited day when we would graduate from boot camp and receive the honor, privilege, and joy of having passed the test and entered the esteemed ranks of the U.S. Army.

Fran, I use this example from my life to help you understand warnings in Scripture that seem to indicate that a believer can fall away from the Faith and lose their salvation. Take for example Hebrews 6:4, which suggests that for a believer who has fallen away, "it will be impossible to be brought back to repentance." In this sense, although *theoretically* it is possible for a believer to lose their Faith, it will not *effectually* happen because "no one can snatch them (the believer) out of my hand. My Father, who has given them to me (the regenerated believer) is greater than all; no one can snatch them out of my Father's hand" (John 10:28–29). Extreme cases of what appear to be a loss of salvation (as in the case of Judas) are in fact evidence that he was not regenerate in the first place. The good news is that when you accepted Jesus into your life as Lord and Savior, you were regenerated! There is a new heart dwelling within you—the very life of Christ—and you are in this new life just as much as this new life is in you (John 15:4). You can have full confidence in the words of our Lord: "I give you eternal life, and you shall never perish" (John 10:28a).

CHAPTER 18

WHAT ARE THE GIFTS OF THE HOLY SPIRIT?

Fran wants you to elaborate on the nature of the gifts of the Holy Spirit. Specifically, she asks you to speak to their nature, number, and character.

UNDERSTANDING THE POSITION:

THE BIBLE CLEARLY ESTABLISHES THAT the primary gift of the Holy Spirit is the Spirit Himself (1 Corinthians 2:12). At the moment of conversion, the same Spirit who came on Jesus at His baptism (Luke 3:21–22) and raised Him from the dead comes to dwell within the believer's new heart (Romans 6:10–11). This means that the most important work of the Spirit in the believer's life is at the moment we declare, "Jesus is Lord" (Matthew 16:17). The initial Spirit-empowered confession of faith subsequently empowers the believer to enter into a life of discipleship, ultimately becoming more like Jesus Christ Himself (1 John 2:6; 2 Corinthians 3:18).

The manifestations and gifts of the Spirit are not restricted to a particular number or type. Rather, believers are encouraged to seek an assortment of gifts that range from Spirit-animated natural abilities and talents to unique "eruptions of the Spirit" not previously known (1 Corinthians 12:7–9). No matter the number or type of gifts bestowed by the Holy Spirit, the purpose of the gifts always remains the same: to build and edify the Body of Christ (1 Corinthians 12:7). Rather than anticipating a unique "sign gift," such as speaking in tongues as evidence of second baptism, believers should have the confidence that the indwelling power of the Holy Spirit took place at conversion (John 14:17; 1 Corinthians 12:13; Titus 3:5) and is sufficient for salvation and a life of service within the Body of Christ.

SUPPORT FOR THE POSITION:

FRAN, AS WE DIVE into our treatment of the gifts of the Spirit, it is important to "begin at the beginning." In this sense, the life in the Spirit is what God intends for all Christians. At the moment of conversion, the Holy Spirit indwells believers, guiding them, leading them, sanctifying them, and empowering them for work in God's Kingdom (Romans 8:2–17). The notion that Christians are *in the Spirit*, and that the *Spirit dwells in them*, is such an important point to Paul that he reinforces it three times (Romans 8:9–11). In fact, it is the indwelling presence of the Holy Spirit in the heart of the believer that inspires Paul to write, "Everyone who is led by the Spirit of God are the children of God" (Romans 8:14).

Fran, as an illustration, imagine a parent who loves their child so much that they are compelled—out of love—to give their child a gift. The child, upon receiving the gift, is compelled to love the *giver of the gift* more than the gift itself. I believe this is an apt example of the exchange that takes place in the life of the Christian. Our Heavenly Father is eager to pour out into the lives of His children gifts. This means that on one hand, as children of God, we should eagerly anticipate His gifts. However, on the other hand (and arguably more important), we should seek greater intimacy with God—the *giver of the gift* rather than focusing solely on the gift itself.

In surveying the Apostle Paul's exposition on gifts of the Spirit (Romans 12:6–8; 1 Corinthians 12:4-11; Ephesians 4:11), some general conclusions can be reached. First and foremost, the gifts are bestowed on the Body of Christ and are therefore meant for the edification of the *entire Body,* rather than the enrichment (or boasting!) of an individual member of the Body (1 Corinthians 12:7). Second, the gifts are intended for use in cooperation with other believers. This means that not one person has all the gifts (1 Corinthians 12:28–30).

This is why Paul explains that each member of the Church is crucial for the Body of the Church to function properly. This logic leads Paul to explain that all the gifts of the Spirit are important (1 Corinthians 12:22–26) and that the Holy Spirit "distributes them just as He determines" (1 Corinthians 12:11).

Fran, I feel strongly that 1 Corinthians 12:13 is a key teaching verse that substantiates the fact that believers are baptized into the Body of Christ at the moment of conversion. Paul emphasizes the point that "one Spirit forms one body." This is an important qualification and is intended to be a source of encouragement and comfort in the believer's life. Paul seems to make the case that the same Spirit that raised Jesus from the dead comes to dwell within the believer at the moment of their conversion (Romans 6:10–11). Fran, I refer to this being a source of *encouragement* and *comfort* because without this assurance, a new Christian could be led to think there needs to be a dramatic experience with the Holy Spirit in order for their conversion to "be real." Needless to say, this uncertainty is unhealthy in the life of the Christian and leads to self-doubt and, even worse, fabricated testimonials about Spirit activity and encounters.

Fran, I think the important matter at hand is to heed the command of Scripture to "be filled with the Spirit" (Ephesians 5:18). Paul contrasts being "Spirit filled" with being "wine-filled." The former leads to glorifying God and the Body of Christ; the latter to debauchery and foolishness. Being "filled with the Spirit" implies the action is ongoing. However, rather than being led to think that this means that we effectually need "more of the Spirit," I think it means that we are to surrender more of our lives to Him. As Christians, we are called to give the Holy Spirit full control over every area of our life. After all, this in and of itself is the primary gift of the Holy Spirit—the Spirit's presence within us.

OPPOSITION TO THE POSITION:

CHRISTIANS SHOULD LOOK FORWARD to an experience of the Holy Spirit—and unique sign gifts of the Spirit—subsequent to their initial conversion. The primary evidence of the Second Baptism is speaking in tongues (Acts 2:1–4). The baptism in the Holy Spirit also empowers believers for greater acts of service within the Body of Christ. This being the case, the full range of Spirit-empowered gifts of healing, prophecy, tongues, and miraculous powers (1 Corinthians 12:7–11) are fully available for believers today and should be actively sought after (1 Corinthians 12:31a).

RESPONSE TO THE OPPOSITION:

FRAN, IT IS INTERESTING to note that very often proponents for a second baptism and "sign gifts" tend to focus on 1 Corinthians 12:31a, which states, "Now eagerly desire the greater gifts" while completely dismissing the continuing thought of Paul to "seek the most excellent way" (1 Corinthians 12:31b). And what was Paul's "most excellent way?" It was love! Paul emphatically explained that no matter how great the apparent "sign-gift" was in the believer's life, it amounted to nothing if the believer did not have love (1 Corinthians 13:1–3). This means that the real evidence of the Spirit at work in the believer's life is the *fruit of the Spirit itself*—"faith, hope and love. But the greatest of these is love" (1 Corinthians 13:13).

Scripture teaches that every Christian receives baptism in the Spirit at conversion (1 Corinthians 12:13). Speaking in tongues or any other type of "sign-gift" is not intended to be normal effectual work of the Spirit within the believer's life. Rather, Christ gives Spirit baptism when He welcomes individuals into God's family through faith and repentance (Acts 2:38). The basis of the Christian faith is that we are One Body—and the establishment of this Body is achieved through the "baptism by one Spirit" (1 Corinthians 12:13).

CHAPTER 19

WHAT IS THE BIBLICAL MODE OF BAPTISM?

Fran is very interested in the different views of baptism and the difference it makes within the life of the believer. She asks you to help her understand the implications of both the meaning of baptism and the specific mode in which the believer should participate.

STATEMENT OF THE POSITION:

THE BIBLE TEACHES THAT baptism is the beginning of the Christian life. This being the case, baptism by immersion into water is an outward symbol of the believer's inward change of heart—a physical demonstration of their faith in Jesus and "death to sin but resurrection to God in Christ Jesus" (Romans 6:11).[275] Baptism is also a sign of the believer's entry into the fellowship of the visible Body of Christ (Acts 2:41–42) and serves the purpose of distinguishing between those who believe in Christ and the rest of the world.

SUPPORT FOR THE POSITION:

FRAN, AS WE BEGIN our treatment of the mode of baptism, I think we need to start with the fact that the two specific sacraments that Jesus entrusted to His Church were the Lord's Supper (Matthew 26:26–28; 1 Corinthians 11:23–25) and baptism (Matthew 28:19). This being the case, baptism is a significant issue in the Christian life and must be properly understood and practiced. Due to the magnitude of what baptism symbolizes, the particular mode of baptism should complement and portray the Bible's description of the Christians first steps with our Lord.

Just as the establishment of the Lord's Supper goes back to Jesus Himself, it is important to note that when baptized by John, Jesus "came up out of the water" (Mark 1:10). The complete immersion of Jesus in this particular verse is unmistakable, and it seems to follow that His disciples should therefore follow His example. Other evidence for this position is abundant, including the fact that John specifically chose the location of Aenon to perform his baptisms

---

[275] The complete theology of "death to sin and resurrection into new life" is treated by the Apostle Paul in his letter to the Romans, chapter 6:1–11.

because "there was plenty of water" (John 3:23), and when Philip baptized the Ethiopian eunuch, *they both went down into the water, and then came up out of the water* (Acts 8:36–29—emphasis and interpretation mine).

In addition to the biblical examples of the mode of baptism, it is also significant that the Apostle Paul seems to suggest that the act of baptism is intended to symbolize a particular effect on the believer. In Romans 6:3–5, Paul connects the dots by explaining that the lowering into water symbolizes our lowering into the grave of sin and death (Romans 6:3). Following this logic, coming up out of the water symbolizes that "just as Christ was raised from the dead through the glory of the Father, we too may live a new life" (Romans 6:4). In other words, the mode of baptism by immersion into water (and the subsequent emersion from the water) is meant to symbolize "our union with Christ in a death like His, and a union with Christ in a resurrection like His" (Romans 6:5—my interpretation). In this sense, baptism by immersion into water best symbolizes the biblical picture of the believer's death to sin and resurrection with Jesus Christ.

OPPOSITION TO THE POSITION:

ALTHOUGH THE BIBLE CLEARLY portrays immersion as one of the ways that baptism is performed, it does not sufficiently address the complex theological meaning of what baptism is meant to symbolize. In addition to death and resurrection, baptism also portrays the pouring of the Holy Spirit into the new believer (Acts 2:3–4). In addition, when explaining the objective reality of the gift of the Holy Spirit, Peter quoted the Old Testament Prophet Joel (Acts 2:17–18) to emphasize the point that in baptism, the Holy Spirit is "poured into" the new believer. This being the case, in addition to immersion, it is appropriate for the mode of baptism to include pouring water onto the head of the new believer.

RESPONSE TO THE OPPOSITION:

FRAN, ALTHOUGH THE IMAGE of the Holy Spirit being "poured out" on God's people is an accurate symbol of the empowering effect of the Spirit, it is not the correct image for baptism, for it fails to account for the death and resurrection of the believer. Furthermore, although the words "pouring" and "sprinkling" are certainly part of the Old and New Covenant—these words are never specifically used in reference for baptism. Perhaps most importantly, when Jesus asked James and John, "Can you drink the cup I drink or be baptized with the baptism I am baptized with?," He almost certainly spoke metaphorically about the symbolic effect of baptism into death. This being the case, although other forms of baptism may be common practice in the Church, complete *immersion into water* and *emersion from water* best preserve the meaning of this defining moment in the Christian life: the believer's death to sin and resurrection into a new life in Jesus Christ (Romans 6:1–11).

CHAPTER 20

WHO GOES TO HELL?

Fran asks you to elaborate on the nature of hell, including who is there and what the punishment is like. Furthermore, she wants to know if people are kept in hell for eternity or if they are annihilated after a period of time.

UNDERSTANDING THE POSITION:

THE BIBLE TEACHES THAT HELL is the eternal separation of mankind from God (Matthew 7:23; 25:41; cf., 2 Thessalonians 1:9). The everlasting banishment from the presence of a loving God is so tormenting that "it would be better for him if he had not been born" (Mark 14:21). Humanity is unable to save themselves by any religious or self-righteous actions. Apart from a savior, we will eternally perish. This being the case, those who reject the Gospel of Jesus Christ and fail during their lifetime to worship God will eternally live apart from Him in hell (Matthew 25:46; Mark 9:48).

SUPPORT FOR THE POSITION:

FRAN, I WILL BE the first to admit that in discussions of hell, we are in "deep theological water." One of the ways that I have found success in conceptualizing hell is by illustrating the idea that God loves us so much, that He will let us choose which god we will serve in eternity. In other words, we can love the God of the Bible, and live in eternity with Him, or we can love a false god (an idol) and live in eternity apart from God. The choice is entirely up to us. In this sense, it's not so much that God "sends people to hell" but rather that people choose to go to hell—and remain there—entirely of their own free will.

Fran, let's look at three aspects of hell: who is there, the eternal nature of hell, and the experience of those who are there. One of the clearest biblical teachings on hell is found in Matthew 25:31–46. This particular teaching is portrayed within the context of a parable of sheep, goats, and a King (Jesus) on the final Day of Judgment. Those who know Jesus and have a saving relationship with Him will be given eternal life (Matthew 25:34), whereas those who do not know Jesus will be cast "into the eternal fire prepared for the devil and his angels" (Matthew 25:41).

This teaching on the contrast between eternal life and eternal death leads us to the next aspect of hell—namely, the eternal existence of those who are there. In other words, is hell eternal in duration, or in effect? Again, when we look to the teaching of Jesus, the answer becomes clear. In Matthew 25:46, Jesus describes hell as a place where the unregenerate go to "eternal punishment," whereas the redeemed go to "eternal life." Jesus reinforces the concept of eternal punishment in His description of hell as "eternal fire." Jesus also described what appears to be the conscious awareness of the torment that people experience in hell. For example, in Matthew 13:42, Jesus said that in hell, there will be "weeping and gnashing of teeth." Based on this description, it becomes clear that people in hell are conscious of the reality they have chosen for themselves. Furthermore, it is important to note that the description of the eternal punishment of the nonbelievers is deliberately contrasted with the eternal joy and life of the believers.

Even in the Old Testament this, concept was prevalent. For example, in Daniel 12:2, the author prophecies that there will be a resurrection of the dead, in which some will be given "eternal life" and others will be given "everlasting contempt." This particular Old Testament example, combined with the New Testament teaching, certainly begs the question: Why would the authors contrast everlasting shame (or death, torment, etc.) with everlasting life unless the punishment was as much an ongoing experience as the joy? Clearly, hell is eternal in nature for those who reject Jesus, just as the reward of eternal life with Jesus will be for those who believe.

This leads us to the third consideration of hell—what will it be like for the people who are there? The Bible describes hell is several different ways, including fire (Matthew 13:42), darkness (Matthew 25:30), exclusion from the presence of God (2 Thessalonians 1:9), restless (Revelation 14:11), and a "weeping and gnashing of teeth" (Matthew 13:42). Needless to say, all of these descriptions paint a very vivid picture of a place you do not want to be!

OPPOSITION TO THE POSITION:

ALTHOUGH THE BIBLE CLEARLY teaches that those who reject Christ will be punished eternally, it does not teach that the punishment will be *eternally endured*. Furthermore, how can we reconcile a loving God (1 John 4:8) with a God whose wrath keeps people in eternal misery? The Bible certainly acknowledges God's wrath against the wicked. However, His wrath is within space and time limitations and will not endure forever (Psalm 103:9). God is compassionate, and while rejection of Him will lead to hell, the torment will not be eternal in nature. Rather, God in His great mercy will annihilate people and "not harbor His anger forever" (Psalm 103:9).

RESPONSE TO THE OPPOSITION:

FRAN, I HAVE FOUND the story of the Rich Man and Lazarus to be a very fitting teaching on the nature of hell, who is there, and how long it is endured. In this parable, both the Rich Man and Lazarus die. The Rich Man finds himself in hell and, much to his surprise, looks up to heaven and sees Lazarus. The Rich Man's first concern (as it was while he was on earth) is only for himself. He cries out for Father Abraham to have pity on him and his immediate family (Luke 16:22–24). Reflecting on this teaching, we notice that the Rich Man, given every opportunity to cry out for salvation and forgiveness, instead asks for Lazarus to "dip the tip of his finger in water and cool his tongue" (Luke 16:24). In this sense, the Rich Man identifies Lazarus as the same "beggar covered with sores" (Luke 16:20–21) that he was while on earth. There has been no change of heart, nor will there be. This parable encapsulates the reality that unregenerate people, given every opportunity for salvation and the Light of the world, continue to choose darkness (John 3:19). This being the case, as noted by C. S. Lewis, the gates of hell are locked from the inside.

PART SIX

A BRIEF SUMMARY OF THE GOSPEL

SECTION SUMMARY:

IN THE CROSSFIT COMMUNITY, gym owners and individual athletes quickly discover the benefits of being able to summarize the methodology of the program for other people. In this sense, when new people venture into the gym and inquire about the program, veterans are able to quickly bring them up to speed on the fundamentals of CrossFit. Reasoning from this fact, Christian leaders can learn a great deal from the manner in which the Apostle Peter summarized the Gospel message and brought new converts of the Christian faith up to speed on the good news of Jesus Christ.

THIS IS GOOD NEWS!

WHEN MOSES WAS FACED with the seemingly impossible task of leading his people out of bondage and slavery, he asked God a question that so often reflects humanity's search for the promise of good news: "Who am I?" (Exodus 3:11). However, rather than answering the question, God directed Moses to a completely different and far more significant matter. The important question at hand was not *who Moses was* but rather *who God is and what God does* (Exodus 3:12-15). In this sense, Moses' question theologically represents mankind's futile attempts to find what we categorically define as "good news"—for apart from the gracious work of God it will remain altogether impossible to find.

The good news of the Gospel is that mankind's attempts no longer need to be in vain. Our savior has come. In the life, death and resurrection of Jesus Christ, the faithful believer can be reconciled with God (2 Corinthians 5:11-21; 1 Peter 2:24) and transformed into His image (2 Corinthians 3:18). The promise of the Gospel is that through the process of "putting on the new self" (Colossians 3:10) we will "gradually become brighter and more beautiful as God enters our lives and we become like Him" (2 Corinthians 3:18 MSG; cf. Acts 2:38-47).

A GOSPEL SUMMARY

IN ACTS 2, THE Apostle Peter succinctly and beautifully described a three-step movement that best illustrates the biblical Gospel message.[276] The first movement is the *revelation of what God did.* Peter declares that Jesus was "a man accredited by God to you by miracles, wonders and signs" (Acts 2:22). Apart from simply being another prophet or religious teacher, Jesus walked the earth in "the fullness of the deity in bodily form" (Colossians 2:9) and was "the radiance of God's glory and the exact representation of His being" (Hebrews 1:3).

---

[276] The "Three Step Spirit-Empowered Gospel" of Acts 2 was discovered in the outline of Chapter 1 of *Vintage Church* by Mark Driscoll and Gerry Breshears. In addition, the framework of the concept was elaborated on and further refined by Dr. Breshears in his lecture *What is the Gospel* for Western Seminary TH503.

Peter's declaration is echoed throughout the New Testament—Jesus was the God-Man to whom all religions point (John 14:6) and to whom all the prophets testified (Hebrews 1:1-3). Peter explains that according to God's plan and "with the help of wicked people" Jesus was put to death on the cross (Acts 2:23). However, far from being the end of the story, God raised Jesus from the dead in fulfillment of Old Testament prophecy (Acts 2:24-31; cf. Romans 8:11-13) and exalted Him to the right hand of the Father (Acts 2:32-33; cf. Romans 8:34). Finally, Peter addresses the "amazement and astonishment" of the people's response to the pouring of the Holy Spirit onto the faithful believers (Acts 2:12) by announcing that "Jesus received from the Father the promised Holy Spirit and has poured out what you now see and hear" (Acts 2:33).

The second movement of the Gospel involves *mankind's response to what God did*. Echoing the words of the Jewish converts in Scripture who were "cut to the heart" (Acts 2:37a), humanity cries out in brokenness, despair and acknowledgement of our need for a savior: "Brothers, what shall we do?" (Acts 2:37b). The result of the Spirit-empowered confession of sin is a fundamental change of heart about who God is. Far greater than a mere change of mind, the new believer's *change of heart* results in an *outward change of behavior* that springs from *an inward change of desires* (1 Samuel 16:7; Proverbs 4:23; Ezekiel. 36:26-27).[277] The radical change of heart results in receiving through faith the revealed message about Jesus Christ (Acts 2:41; 2 Corinthians 4:5-6). The objective outward demonstration of faith in Jesus is made visible by baptism and entry into a new community of faithful believers (Acts 2:41; cf. 1 Corinthians 12:12-14).

The final movement of the Gospel involves joyfully receiving *what God graciously gives*. Through the propitiatory death of Jesus, all who call on His name in faith receive forgiveness of sins (Acts 2:38; cf. Romans 10:13). The subsequent result is the gift of the Holy Spirit and the new life and heart of Christ (2 Corinthians 3:18; cf., Colossians 3:10). The regenerated Spirit-empowered heart is given for the purpose of living a new life as a Christian and participation in the body of Christ (Acts 2:41-47; cf. 1 Corinthians 12:12-27).

---

[277] Driscoll and Breshears, pg. 1 of Chapter 1 outline on *Vintage Faith*. This point was also emphatically made in James K.A. Smith's book *You Are What You Love* (Baker Publishing, Grand Rapids, MI. 2016) p. 65.

The Bible teaches that the "heart" often referred to the genuine self as distinguished from appearance, identification with the mind, and physical presence. The "heart-self" had its own nature, character and disposition, which affected the thoughts, words, and actions of the individual. Therefore, a believer whose "heart" is changed through the power of the Holy Spirit will never be the same again (Psalm 51:10; Ezekiel 36:26-27).[278]

---

[278] Walter A. Elwell and Barry J. Beitzel, "Wisdom, Wisdom Literature," *Baker Encyclopedia of the Bible* (Grand Rapids, MI: Baker Book House, 1998), p. 2149.

PART SEVEN

MODERN THEOLOGICAL TOPICS FACING
THE CHURCH AND THE GYM

SECTION SUMMARY:

THREE OF THE MAJOR topics of the Christian faith in the 21st Century deal with the work and person of the Holy Spirit, revelation of Holy Scripture, and the nature of humanity. This section will explore these topics through the lens of systematic theology in order to edify and build up the body of Christ. We must remember that the Church is not a corporation or business, but is rather a family, with Christ as our head. This being the case, just like any family, the Church can sometimes be a place that exhibits moments of both *unity* and *diversity* in surprising and unexpected ways. The theological exploration and treatment of the following topics are meant to provide you with a deeper understanding of the richness of the Christian faith and greater insight into modern topics facing the Church.

CHAPTER 21

WITNESSING THE GIFT

A THEOLOGY OF THE HOLY SPIRIT

INTRODUCTION

JESUS CHRIST'S LAST WORDS to His disciples were, "But you will receive power when the Holy Spirit has come upon you, and *you will be my witness* in Jerusalem and in all Judea and Samaria, and to the ends of the earth" (Acts 1:8-9 — my emphasis). Although in this context our Lord was specifically addressing the apostles, the Bible teaches that the promise of the Holy Spirit is freely available for every believer in Jesus Christ (Acts 2:38-39). All believers in Jesus receive the gift of the Holy Spirit at the moment of their conversion (Acts 2:38; Romans 5:5; Galatians 3:2). This means that when a believer confesses their sin and asks for God's forgiveness, they become a new person—not by their own deeds, works, or merit, but by the gracious work of God's Holy Spirit (Ephesians 2:9).[279] To use the terminology of our Lord, the believer is "born again" (John 3:3-7).

The Apostle Paul further elaborated on the supernatural "born again" new life of the Christian: "If anyone is in Christ, he is a new creation. The old has passed away; behold, the new has come (2 Corinthians 5:17). The moment the believer looks to Christ as Lord and Savior, the Holy Spirit comes to indwell their body, making it a "temple of the Holy Spirit" (1 Corinthians 6:19-20; cf., 2 Corinthians 6:16). According to Jesus, this transformational experience results in a *receipt of power* that enables the believer to *be a witness* of the Gospel message to the ends of the earth. This all boils down to one amazing promise, one astonishing mission, and one breathtaking responsibility for the individual believer and collective Body of Christ.

---

[279] Dr. Harold Sala. *Getting Acquainted with the Holy Spirit.* (Mandaluyong City, Manila. OMF Literature, INC., 2017), p. 58.

ARE OUR LORD'S EXPECTATIONS BEING MET?

I FIND THAT I must draw on a theological query from the great mind of author and pastor Francis Chan. Based on the inerrant *Word of God*, we have confidence that the *Spirit of God* dwells within every believer, which effectually makes every Christian a living and breathing *Temple of God's Holy Spirit* (1 Corinthians 3:16, 6:19). This being the case, then shouldn't there be a measurable and observable difference between the regenerated person who has the very Spirit of God within them, and another person who does not? [280] Although by conversion Christians can declare that they are *born again* and *dead to sin but alive in Christ* (Romans 6:3-8), we must caution ourselves against the possibility that these words have become nothing more than the parroted teaching of biblical doctrine. In other words, if someone outside the Body of Christ began to notice that there was no fundamental change or difference in the life of a converted person, then are believers truly *witnessing our faith* as our Lord commanded?

The late author and minister Martyn Lloyd-Jones once pointed out that there is a vast difference between being a *witness for Jesus* and an *advocate for Jesus*.[281] Whereas a great many people today are quite content to be an *advocate* of the Christian faith, only a few actively *witness* their spiritual gifts for the purpose of edifying the Body of Christ. Furthermore, many Churches seem to be more concerned with filling pews and developing new programs than in proclaiming the transformational power of a Spirit-filled life.[282] Reasoning from this fact, perhaps now is the time for renewed urgency in addressing the concern of A.W. Tozer: "The whole level of spirituality among us is low—the incentive to seek the higher plateaus in the things of the Spirit is all but gone."[283]

---

[280] This "theological question" was brought to my attention in Francis Chan's book *The Forgotten God – Reversing Our Tragic Neglect of the Holy Spirit.* (Colorado Springs, CO. David C. Cook. 2009), p. 32.

[281] Sala, p. 34. The Blue Letter Bible defines *witness* in the context of Acts 1:8 in the ethical sense as, "Those who after his example have proved the strength and genuineness of their faith in Christ by undergoing a violent death."

[282] Sala, p. 31.

[283] A.W. Tozer. Quoted in Francis Chan's book, *The Forgotten God – Reversing Our Tragic Neglect of the Holy Spirit.* (Colorado Springs, CO. David C. Cook. 2009), p. 27.

In his acclaimed book, *The Forgotten God,* Francis Chan argued that "there is a desperate need in the Church for the Holy Spirit of God to be given room to have His way." [284] Similar to the uneasiness felt by Tozer's observation of the generally low level of spirituality among Christians, Chan's sentiment that the Church is in desperate need of the Holy Spirit ought to compel the Body of Christ to question what's gone wrong. After all, according to the Apostle Paul, the Spirit of God dwells in believers (Romans 8:9), effectually making every individual follower of Christ a physical tabernacle of God's Spirit (1 Corinthians 3:16, 6:19-20). This means that the individual believer's body is the Spirit of God's temple—we are His dwelling place (John 14:23). Continuing this line of reasoning, Paul explained that "just as a body, though one, has many parts, but all its parts form one body, so it is with Christ" (1 Corinthians 12:12). In other words, if each individual believer is a temple, then the spiritual power of the collective Body of Christ should turn the world upside down. On the basis thereof, how are we to reconcile the declaration of the biblical testimony with the troubling observations of such influential ministers of God's Word as Chan and Tozer?

MAKING ROOM FOR THE SPIRIT

IN THE SPORT OF OLYMPIC weightlifting, few masters of the barbell have achieved the worldwide respect and admiration as that of Coach Mike Burgener.[285] In the CrossFit community, legend has it that when Coach Burgener walks into the gym, everyone in attendance on that particular day gain's five pounds on their former personal weightlifting records (a huge increase in strength considering that many weightlifting world records are set in increments of one-half pounds). Coach Burgener says nothing, offers no technical cues, nor demonstrates any particular hidden insights on the fundamental principles of the snatch or clean and jerk. How then do people account for the near instantaneous increase in strength?

---

[284] Chan, p. 27. Chan's book *Forgotten God* reached the *New York Times* bestseller list top 10 for 10 consecutive weeks.

[285] Mike Burgener's oldest son Casey broke the national record for the snatch at the 2004 Olympic Trials and won gold in the 2008 Pan American Championships.

Based on the testimony of hundreds of gym owners (each gym owner represents approximately 100 athletes), it can only be attributed to a combination of Mike's presence in the gym and his immediate proximity to each individual athlete.[286] Although seemingly impossible to quantify, ordinary people and world-class weightlifters alike increase in strength simply because they spend time in the presence of Coach Burgener. In all humility, Coach Burgener explains the phenomenon by saying that "people increase in strength because *they think then can.*" This account certainly begs the question—if people gain physical strength in the presence of a person who compels them to *think they can,* then how much more should believers manifest the miraculous gifts of the Spirit when God Himself dwells within them?

For our purposes of understanding the work of the Holy Spirit, this particular illustration has immense relevance. In fact, the spiritual principle involved is exactly what we read about in the book of Acts. In describing what happened when John and Peter went on trial before the Sanhedrin, Luke wrote, "When they saw the courage of Peter and John and realized that they were unschooled, ordinary men, they were astonished and they took note that these men had *been with Jesus* (Acts 4:13 — my emphasis). It was not about books, laws, regulations, or moral lessons (or in the weightlifting analogy, coaching cues, tips, or physical demonstrations). What set Peter and John apart was the fact that they had been with Jesus—*and they had stayed with Him* (John 1:37-39). And in the process, Jesus had completely transformed their lives.

In the Apostle John's beautiful account of our Lord's conversation with His first two disciples (John 1:35-42), we are witness to the Gospel-centered transformation that awaits those people who *stay with Jesus.* When our Lord asked the two men, "What do you want?" (John 1:38a), they immediately responded by asking a question of their own: "Rabbi, where are you staying?" (John 1:38b). How interesting to answer a question with a question—not to

---

[286] In addition to the sport of weightlifting, I have experienced similar testimonies from professional boxers who have trained under master-level trainers and coaches. Most recently, 6-time world champion Robert "The Ghost" Guerrero commented that his dad's presence ringside (his dad, Ruben Guerrero, is his longtime coach) has propelled him to victories that were otherwise seemingly impossible. My interviews with gym owners took place between the years of 2012 and 2014 during my world-wide travels teaching the CrossFit Goal Setting and Positive Self-talk course.

mention the seemingly mindless quality of the question. To ask where Jesus is staying? Couldn't these two former disciples of John the Baptist have come up with a more profound question? After all, here is the Lord of the universe asking, "What do you want? What are you looking for?" And they answer by asking, "Where are you staying?"

But I propose their instincts were in fact completely right. When Jesus was on the earth, His presence was limited to His physical and spatial locality. In this sense, in order for the first disciples to *stay with Jesus,* they needed to be physically in His presence. However, for the followers of Christ after His ascension to the Father, we now experience personal fellowship with Him through the Holy Spirit every moment of our life (Romans 8:9-11; Galatians 2:19-20; Titus 3:4-6). This means that Jesus Christ, as much as the Father, is the indwelling presence of God within every regenerated Christian believer— but only through the Spirit of God.[287] To this effect, Paul explained, "Anyone who does not have the Spirit of Christ, that person does not belong to him" (Romans 8:9) and believers are "dead to sin but alive to God" (Romans 6:11— MSG). Paul's logic would seem to suggest that when the Spirit of God dwells within the believer there should be a significant difference between that person and a non-Christian. But is this in fact the case in the life of the individual believer and the Body of Christ?

---

[287] M. Turner in T. Desmond Alexander's *The New Dictionary of Biblical Theology – Holy Spirit.* (Downers Grove, IL. Inter-Varsity Press, 2000), p. 550.

THE CENTER AND ITS CONTRAST[288]

THE BIBLE TEACHES THAT a life in the Spirit is what God desires for all Christians. At the moment of conversion, the Holy Spirit indwells believers, guiding them, sanctifying them, and empowering them for work in God's Kingdom (Romans 8:2-17). The notion that Christians are *in the Spirit*, and that the *Spirit dwells in them*, was such an important theological idea for the Apostle Paul that he reinforced it three times in his letter to the Romans (Romans 8:9-11), and succinctly culminated his argument with the resounding statement: "For those who are led by the Spirit of God are the children of God" (Romans 8:14).

The Apostle Paul's theology of the Holy Spirit has led Evangelical Christians around the world to share the doctrine that the Spirit is active in the lives of all believers.[289] A believer's first experience with the Spirit of God takes place within their heart the moment they put their faith in Christ. Emphasizing this very point, in his book, *The Small Catechism,* Martin Luther described the initial work of the Holy Spirit in his heart as essential to his conversion experience by saying, "I believe that I cannot by my own reason or strength believe in Jesus Christ, my Lord, or come to Him but the Holy Ghost has called me by the Gospel."[290] Echoing Luther's sentiment on the Holy Spirit, the great theologian J.I. Packer wrote, "Without the Spirit there would not be a Christian in the world."[291]

The Apostle Paul masterfully treats the issue of the believer's first experience with the Holy Spirit in 1 Corinthians 12:13: "For we were all baptized by one Spirit so as to form one body—whether Jews or Gentiles, slave or free—and we were all given one Spirit to drink." In this theologically packed verse, Paul makes four remarkable points: First, the baptism applies

---

[288] The idea for this particular section title and the accompanying organizational framework were brought to my attention in Gregory Boyd's book, *Across the Spectrum* (Grand Rapids, MI: Baker Academic, 2009).

[289] Timothy Tennent. *Theology in the context of World Christianity.* (Grand Rapids, MI: Zondervan, 2007), p. 166.

[290] Quoted in Mollie Ziegler Hemingway's piece "Faith Unbounded," *Christianity Today,* September 9, 2010, p. 74.

[291] J.I. Packer, *Knowing God.* (London: Hodder & Stoughton, 1984), p. 79.

to all believers; second, all believers are baptized by the same Spirit; third, believers are baptized into the Body of Christ; and fourth, the baptism and union with the Body of Christ take place *at the moment of conversion*. This means that when a new believer "confesses with their mouth that Jesus Christ is Lord, and believes in their heart that God raised Jesus from the dead" (Romans 10:9), they receive the indwelling power of the Holy Spirit (John 14:17), a new heart (Titus 3:5), and are incorporated into the Body of Christ (1 Corinthians 12:13).[292] Paul seems to suggest throughout his theological treatment on baptism that Christians become members of Christ's body by being baptized into it by the Spirit—and that this supernatural experience is either equivalent to conversion or simultaneous with it.[293]

This being the case, how do we account for cases in Acts where there was clearly a separation between conversion (or regeneration) and a subsequent baptism of the Spirit? The Pentecostals substantiate much of their doctrine based on the account in Acts 2, which records that on the day of Pentecost the Holy Spirit descended onto the Body of Christ in the form of "tongues of fire" and empowered those that received it for special service and bold witness (Acts 2:2-4). To account for what might otherwise be accepted as the norm, esteemed theologian Millard Erickson argues that Acts covers a transitional period in the life of the Church.[294] Although he acknowledges that in certain cases there was indeed a lapse of time between regeneration and the receipt of the Holy Spirit, these instances involved the last of the Old Testament believers who were regenerate because of the revelation they received and their faith in God.[295]

The issue of an immediate or post-conversion experience with the Spirit (in contrast with a more gradual *filling of the Spirit)* is significant and affects nearly every area of the Christian life. Accessing the biblical arguments on both sides of the equation leads us to a fundamental theological and doctrinal question: Should believers anticipate (and in this sense actively seek out and pray for) a subsequent filling of the Spirit beyond their initial conversion experience? Furthermore, to what degree would this unique and distinct second

---

[292] Dr. Gerry Breshears. Western Seminary TH503 outline on the Holy Spirit.

[293] Millard Erickson, *Christian Theology* (Grand Rapids, MI: baker Academic, 2013) p. 801.

[294] Erickson, p. 801.

[295] Erickson, p. 801.

encounter with the Spirit be objectively recognizable in the manifestation of miraculous spiritual gifts? And perhaps most important, to what extent should speaking in tongues be associated with the first evidence of a Second Baptism?

UNDERSTANDING PENTECOSTALISM

IN THE PENTECOSTAL TRADITION, many hold that a postconversion (or postregeneration) experience, often referred to as "the baptism in (or with) the Holy Spirit," will take place in the life of the believer.[296] Evidence of this unmistakable moment commonly manifests itself in the believer's life through a full range of gifts and miraculous manifestations of the Spirit that were evident during the era of the New Testament.[297] Pentecostal and Charismatic Christian theology teach that believers should look forward to an experience of the Holy Spirit—and unique sign-gifts of the Spirit—subsequent to their initial conversion.

The *Foundations of Pentecostal Theology* emphasizes, "The Baptism of the Holy Ghost is a definite experience, subsequent to salvation, whereby the Third Person of the Godhead comes upon the believer to anoint and energize him for special service."[298] This same body of doctrine holds that although "baptism with the Holy Ghost was given once and for all, as far as the Church in general is concerned" it does not necessarily mean that every believer is immediately *filled with the Spirit* upon conversion. [299] The Baptism in the Holy Spirit is meant to empower believers for greater acts of service within the Body of Christ. This being the case, the full range of Spirit-empowered gifts of healing, prophecy, tongues, and miraculous powers (1 Corinthians 12:7-11) are available for believers today and should be actively sought after (1 Corinthians 12:31a).

---

[296] Tennent. p. 166.

[297] Gregory Boyd. *Across the Spectrum.* (Grand Rapids, MI: Baker Publishing, 2009), p. 237.

[298] Dr. Gerry Breshears, "Holy Spirit" outline, Western Seminary TH503.

[299] Breshears.

THE GIFTS SHALL CEASE

A MORE CONSERVATIVE BAPTIST theology would point to the fact that very often proponents for a Second Baptism and "sign-gifts" tend to overly focus on 1 Corinthians 12:31a, which states, "Now eagerly desire the greater gifts" while completely dismissing the continuing thought of Paul to "seek the most excellent way" (1 Corinthians 12:31b). And what was Paul's "most excellent way?" It was love! Paul emphatically explained that no matter how great the apparent "sign-gift" was in the believer's life, it amounted to nothing if the believer did not have love (1 Corinthians 13:1-3). This means that the real evidence of the Spirit at work in the believer's life is the *fruit of the Spirit itself*—"faith, hope and love. But the greatest of these is love" (1 Corinthians 13:13). Baptists teach that every Christian receives the Spirit at conversion (1 Corinthians 12:13), and that speaking in tongues or any other objective "sign gift evidence" are not intended to be the normal effectual work of the Spirit within the believer's life. Rather, Christ gives the Spirit the moment He welcomes individuals into God's family through faith and repentance (Acts 2:38).

In addition to addressing the possibility that Paul taught that the gifts would cease, many theologians make a similar argument based on Hebrews 2:3-4, namely that the purpose of the "signs, wonders and various miracles" (Hebrews 2:4a) of the Holy Spirit was to authenticate the revelation of Jesus Christ. Given that the final revelation is now freely available in the completed canon of Scripture, the gifts have ceased. This line of reasoning seems to be supported by the Apostle John who explained that the purpose of our Lord's "signs in the presence of his disciples" was so that Christians would "believe that Jesus is the Messiah" (John 20:30-31). In other words, Cessationist theology would contend that the purpose of the miraculous gifts was to testify to the life and divinity of Christ in addition to our Lord's first apostles (Acts 2:34). This unique and historic purpose having once been fulfilled, the miraculous gifts become unnecessary and subsequently faded out of the Church.[300]

---

[300] Erickson, p. 800.

New Testament scholar William Barclay makes a compelling argument for Cessationist theology by suggesting that the miracles of the early Church were needed as a guarantee of the truth and power of the Gospel message. Furthermore, the apostles had uniquely benefited from personal contact with Jesus, empowering them for miraculous gifts and service in a way never to be repeated following their death. This, combined with a general atmosphere of expectancy of the Lord's imminent return, contributed to the supernatural presence of spiritual gifts.[301] As an afterthought, Barclay then proposes the question, "But have miracles in fact stopped?" A visit to any first-world emergency room would reveal doctors and surgeons doing *common* things that in apostolic times would have been seen as so *uncommon* they would be immediately regarded as a miracle. In this sense, for Christians, miracles are all around us when we have eyes to see them.

WRESTLING WITH THE EVIDENCE

WE NOW TURN OUR attention to addressing the implications and considerations raised by both sides of the dispute. However, before doing so I suggest that we set aside for a moment the particular issue of a distinct Second Baptism to wrestle with what appears to be the intimate cause and effect relationship between a subsequent encounter with the Holy Spirit and the evidence of the encounter made manifest through particular spiritual gifts. (As mentioned above, many hold that the initial evidence will be speaking in tongues). In other words, is one possible without the other? The potential danger in holding to a doctrine that teaches that objective and tangible evidence of a Second Baptism is to be expected is that a believer may be unintentionally compelled to focus on the gifts (the evidence) of the experience, rather than the actual encounter with the Holy Spirit Himself.

By way of an illustration, imagine a parent who loves their child so much they are compelled—out of love—to give their child a gift. The child, upon receiving the gift, is then compelled to love the *giver of the gift* more than the gift itself. I believe this is an apt example of the exchange that takes place in the

---

[301] William Barclay. *The Acts of the Apostles New Daily Study Bible.* (Louisville, KY: Westminster John Know Press, 2003), p. 36.

All this being said, it is equally important to heed the fact that Paul expected all Christians to "be filled with the Spirit" (Ephesians 5:18). Paul contrasts being "Spirit filled" with being "wine-filled." The former leads to glorifying God and the Body of Christ, the later to debauchery and foolishness. Being "filled with the Spirit" implies the action is on-going and continual. However, rather than being led to think this means that we effectually need "more of the Spirit," I think it means that we are to surrender more of our lives to Him. As Christians, we are called to give the Holy Spirit full control over every area of our life. After all, this in and of itself is the primary gift of the Holy Spirit—the Holy Spirit Himself.[304]

CESSATIONISM AND CONTINUATIONISM — THE HISTORY OF THE CHURCH

OVER THE YEARS THERE have been differing views on the active role of the Holy Spirit continuing to perform miracles such as divine healing, prophecy, and most notably, speaking in tongues. Generally speaking, four different views have been proposed to include *Cessationism, Functional Cessationism, Continuationism,* and *Word-Faith.* For our purposes, a brief overview of the first three positions (the *Word-Faith* movement is outside the scope of our discussion) is helpful in creating a framework for understanding the Church's historical positions on Second Baptism and spiritual gifts.

Continuationism holds that while Scripture is God's only trustworthy voice, He continues to speak to Churches and individuals through His Spirit. These unique revelations of His Word must be tested and weighed against the Bible. In addition, God continues to perform miracles (which may include speaking in tongues) and believers should pray for and expect these miracles to be a present reality within their life and the Body of Christ.[305] Continuationism holds that believers in Jesus Christ should expect (and look forward to) an experience of the Holy Spirit after their initial conversion. This distinct second blessing results in the manifestation of spiritual gifts in the believer's life.

---

[304] Dr. Gerry Breshears. *Spiritual Gifts Position Paper.* Grace Community Church, Gresham, OR.

[305] Breshears. Western Seminary TH503 outline on Holy Spirit.

life of the Christian. Our Heavenly Father is eager to pour out into the lives of His children a great many gifts (James 1:17). This means that on one hand, as children of God, we should eagerly anticipate and pray for His gifts. However, on the other hand (and arguably more important) we should seek greater intimacy with God—the *giver of the gift* rather than focusing solely on the gift itself. As Erickson so eloquently pointed out, "It is not a matter of getting more of the Holy Spirit—it is, rather, a matter of His possessing more of our lives."[302]

Returning then to the matter of spiritual gifts, we can glean a great deal of wisdom from a close study of the Apostle Paul's exposition on the matter. First and foremost, the gifts are bestowed on the Body of Christ and are therefore meant for the edification of the *entire Body* rather than the enrichment (or boasting!) of an individual member of the Body (1 Corinthians 12:7). Second, the gifts are intended for use in cooperation with other believers, meaning that not one person has all the gifts (1 Corinthians 12:28-30). This is why Paul explained that each member of the Church is crucial for the Body of the Church to function properly. This logic leads Paul to elaborate on the fact that all the gifts of the Spirit are important (1 Corinthians 12:22-26), and that the Holy Spirit "distributes them just as He determines" (1 Corinthians 12:11).

In 1 Corinthians 12:13, Paul emphasizes the point that "*One Spirit* forms one body."[303] Whether of the more conservative or the liberal theological camp, Paul's emphasis on the "one Spirit" holds remarkable implications in the believer's life. Paul makes the case that the same "*one Spirit*" that raised Jesus from the dead comes to dwell within the believer at the moment of their conversion (Romans 6:10-11). This particular verse should therefore be of resounding *encouragement* and *comfort* for all believers, because without this assurance, a new Christian could be led to think there needs to be a dramatic experience with the Holy Spirit in order for their conversion to "be real." Needless to say, this uncertainty is unhealthy in the life of the Christian and may lead to self-doubt, and even worse, fabricated testimonials about Spirit activity and encounters.

---

[302] Erickson, p. 802.

[303] My use of italics in this verse to emphasize the unity of God in the Spirit and to accentuate my argument made throughout the remainder of the paragraph.

In the Pentecostal tradition, this experience is commonly referred to as the "Baptism in the Spirit." According to this view, the primary objective evidence of the Holy Spirit baptism is speaking in tongues and empowerment for service in God's Kingdom.[306] Those who hold this view substantiate their position by noting that in Acts 2, the disciples "were filled with the Holy Spirit and began to speak in other tongues as the Spirit enabled them" (Acts 2:4). Because the disciples had been followers of Jesus for nearly three years, in addition to the fact that in John 20:22, "Jesus breathed on them (the disciples) and said, 'Receive the Holy Spirit," the logical conclusion is that there is a distinct Second Baptism. In other words, John 20:22 clearly establishes one baptism, whereas Acts 2:4 establishes another. The difference in Acts 2:4 (the Second Baptism) is that there is *objective evidence* of the Holy Spirit's work within the believer which is made manifest in *glossalilia*—speaking in unknown human languages.

Perhaps the strongest biblical evidence for Continuationism is the careful exegetical reading of 1 Corinthians 13:8-12. The Cessationist has historically connected the verse, "But when completeness comes, what is in part disappears" (1 Corinthians 13:10), to the close of the biblical canon, and concludes that miraculous gifts are no longer necessary or operational. In other words, the "completeness" in this particular verse is the complete canon of Scripture, which Paul foretold would result in the cessation of prophecy, tongues, and words of knowledge (1 Corinthians 13:8). However, a more through understanding of Paul's theology on spiritual gifts demonstrates that completeness is in fact the eternal state ushered in at the second coming of Christ. Furthermore, when Paul speaks in verse 12 of seeing "face to face," he most likely is referring to the eternal state, subsequent to the return of Christ.[307] Finally, it is vital to pay close attention to Paul's explicitly stated purpose for the gifts: namely, the edification of the Body of Christ (1 Corinthians 12:7). One would be hard-pressed to conclude that the Church is no longer in need of edification, and therefore beyond the need of Christians empowered by God's Spirit with unique gifts meant to build up and strengthen His Body.

---

[306] Tennent, p. 167.

[307] Sam Storms. *Practicing the Power.* (Grand Rapids, MI: Zondervan, 2017), p. 246.

The Functional Cessationist would hold that the purpose of the sign-gifts of speaking in tongues and miraculous healing most notably authenticated the Apostles (Acts 5:15, 19:12), yet there is no reason to believe that these gifts have ceased today (John 14:12-14; 1 Corinthians 12:31,14:1-18). Furthermore, Functional Cessationism holds that although the Bible is God's only trustworthy voice, believers should "let the Holy Spirit guide our lives" (Galatians 5:16) and leave room within the traditionally held Western Enlightenment worldview that tends to create a wall between the experiential framework of the senses and the supernatural framework of the biblical authors.[308] In other words, when guided by the Bible, believers have more to gain than lose in opening their mind to the idea that the same Holy Spirit who acted supernaturally in the lives of the Apostles and early Church is active and alive in similar ways today.

At the other end of the spectrum, many notable theologians believe in Cessationism and that the diffusion of miraculous gifts by the Holy Spirit was confined to the apostolic Church and subsequently passed away with it.[309] Because abuses and exaggerations of continuing miraculous experiences with the Holy Spirit are so rampant and abusive in the Church, it is better to rely solely on the revealed wisdom of the Bible.[310]

Although the Cessationist view contends that the miraculous gifts were reserved for the Apostles and served the purpose of establishing the Church, it is important to note that numerous non-apostolic men and women exercised these gifts including the 70 who were commissioned in Luke 10:9 and at least 108 of the 120 who were gathered in the upper room on the day of Pentecost. Furthermore, the Cessationist's appeal to Ephesians 2:20 that the gifts were for the first century period of time in which the Church was being built overlooks the fact that miraculous gifts (specifically the gift of prophecy) were not linked to the apostles and never functioned foundationally.[311]

Theologian Millard Erickson argues for what appears to be a Cessationist view and suggests that even if the Spirit were to actively dispense special

---

[308] Tennent, p. 178.

[309] B.B. Warfield in his book *Counterfeit Miracles* as identified in *Christian Theology*, p. 172.

[310] Dr. Gerry Breshears, "Holy Spirit" outline, Western Seminary TH503.

[311] Storms, p. 249.

gifts in the Church today, Christians "are not to set their lives to seeking them." Erickson points to Paul's teaching that the Spirit dispenses the gifts sovereignly, and that He alone will determine the recipients (1 Corinthians 12:11). This being the case, the Spirit may choose to give a believer a special gift regardless of their prayers or expectation of it. Erickson reiterates the fact that Paul's command to be "filled with the Spirit" (Ephesians 5:18) is a *present imperative*, which suggests an ongoing action and experience in the daily life of the believer.

A careful assessment of the totality of the positions (with a special emphasis on the points I feel were unfairly made by Erickson) compels me to lean toward a Continuationism theology. Although I certainly agree with Erickson's view of the sovereignty of the Spirit, it is supremely important to note that according to Paul, in the particular case of miraculous gifts, the Spirit can be quenched (1 Thessalonians 5:19-22). This is a remarkable thought considering that Paul is speaking about the sovereign Spirit of God who works all things together according to His will. Nevertheless, here Paul warns believers that God has granted Christians the ability to either "*restrict* or *release* what He does in the life of the local Church."[312] Furthermore, in 1 Corinthians 14:32, Paul explains, "The spirits of prophets are subject to prophets." This means that the Spirit is happy to align Himself with the believer's expectations for what is possible, and will "not act upon us or through us as if we were puppets." [313] This line of reasoning seems to contradict Erickson and suggests that believers have a responsibility to not just seek the Spirit—but so much of Him that we "fan the flame of the Spirit's fire" (2 Timothy 1:6).

Perhaps the most compelling reason to embrace the active pursuit of the Spirit is our Lord's teaching on the subject. In Luke 11:13, in the context of explaining the magnitude of God's grace, Jesus said, "If you then, who are evil, know how to give good gifts to your children, *how much more will the heavenly Father give the Holy Spirit to those who ask him*" (Luke 11:13 — my emphasis). In application within the believer's life, we have the confidence that God intimately knows our every need and is fully aware of the emptiness in our life. This means that on one hand God knows what we need even before we ask

---

[312] Storms, p. 180.
[313] Storms, p. 180.

for it, and on the other hand God wants us to ask (Matthew 7:7-11). Weighing all the evidence—with special attention given to our Lord's discourse—leads me to believe that God is far more willing to fill us with His Spirit than we are willing to ask.

EXERCISING OUR FAITH

I BELIEVE THAT ALL the gifts of the Spirit continue to be given by God to believers today, and are fully operative in the Body of Christ. These gifts may be immediately accompanied by the initial conversion experience; or similar to the way that a physical muscle grows stronger over time, the gifts may develop gradually throughout the believer's lifetime. This being said, I must emphasize the fact that I believe the Holy Spirit indwells believers at the moment of their conversion. The question we may very well consider at this point is what should be expected in the life of the believer *following their conversion*? The answer could not be any clearer—the Bible plainly teaches that following the initial conversion experience and the receipt of the Holy Spirit, the believer is called to a life of increasing sanctification and growing in Christlikeness (2 Thessalonians 2:13; Colossians 3:1,5). Fundamentally, I believe this means that although the Holy Spirit comes to indwell every person at conversion, there is an ongoing experience throughout the believer's new life in Christ of being continually *filled with the Spirit.*

By way of illustration, consider an athlete who enrolls into a CrossFit gym. The moment of conversion takes place during their initial entry and enrollment into the fitness studio. However, the real benefits to the athlete of the program are derived from the daily experience of applying the methodology of constantly varied, functional movement, at high intensity. Some athletes might enjoy rather sudden "breakthroughs" in advanced gymnastic movements or weightlifting skills, whereas others tend to need more time to see any evidence of growth. But in either case, the increase in strength (to borrow theological language—*filling the muscles*) is clearly subsequent to, and a secondary effect of, the initial entry into the gym.

Pressing this illustration into the context of the Church, the subsequent filling with the Spirit may be gradual or rather dramatic (1 Corinthians 12:7-11), and occurs as a result of living out the reality of being baptized by the Spirit.[314] This perpetual filling is not to be confused with a distinct second blessing of the Holy Spirit, but rather "an actualization of what we have already received at conversion."[315] This conclusion, however, brings us to face to face with very two very interesting and compelling questions: Should the believer actively pray for, seek out, and make room for the ongoing filling of the Spirit? And if so, what are the functional steps a believer should take in pursuit of an encounter with the Spirit? Returning for a moment to our CrossFit analogy, the athlete desirous of increasing in strength will take great measures to create the appropriate environment in their life to facilitate such growth. Should Christians model and adopt such athletic behavior into our spiritual life?

THE IMPLICATIONS OF THE EASTER INBREATHING

THE APOSTLE JOHN RECORDS a meeting that Jesus had with His disciples that is sometimes referred to as the "Easter Inbreathing." After appearing to His disciples in His resurrected body and showing them His hands and side, Jesus said, "'Peace be with you. As the Father has sent me, even so I am sending you.' And when He had said this, He breathed on them and said to them, 'Receive the Holy Spirit'" (John 20:21-22).[316] It is important to note that although Jesus gave the disciples the Holy Spirit on this particular day, He still commanded them to wait for a secondary experience that would take place when they would be "baptized with the Holy Spirit" (Acts 1:4-5). How can we reconcile what appears to be two distinct baptisms?

---

[314] Dr. Gerry Breshears, "Holy Spirit" outline, Western Seminary TH503.

[315] Breshears.

[316] In the context of our Lord's command to "Receive the Holy Spirit", in the *A Manual Grammar of the Greek New Testament,* H. E. Dana points out that Jesus used an aorist tense, the meaning of which is "right now!" In other words, the giving of the Holy Spirit took place immediately, and should not be confused with the idea that Jesus was speaking to a future event. H. E. Dana, *A Manual Grammar of the Greek New Testament* (New York, NY: Macmillan Publishers, 1957), p. 300.

I believe that the 11 disciples who were breathed on by Jesus are the archetype of Christians today who receive the Holy Spirit at conversion but remain idle (or even worse, powerless) to *witness their faith*. Although the 11 disciples initially received the Holy Spirit on the Easter Inbreathing, they were filled with the Spirit on the Day of Pentecost. It this sense, it was the second experience with the Holy Spirit that led to a "life-changing encounter that forever transformed them, turning ordinary men into firebrands for God, willing to face harsh criticism, beatings, and dying for the cause of Christ."[317] To recapitulate the series of events, when Jesus met with the disciples behind closed doors, breathed on them, and commanded them to receive the Holy Spirit, they received the Spirit of God in that very moment—representative of the experience believers have today when they first put their faith in Christ. However, when the 11 disciples were baptized by the Holy Spirit on the Day of Pentecost, they had a face-to-face encounter with the Holy Spirit that completely transformed their lives. This being the case, believers today have much to learn from those who *waited for the gift the Father promised.*

MINISTRY IMPLEMENTATION

JESUS MADE IT CLEAR to His disciples that there must be a "hunger and thirst for God" before that desire can be fulfilled. To this effect, the Apostle John elaborated on our Lord's teaching on the Holy Spirit by recording: "On the last day of the feast, the great day, Jesus stood up and cried out, 'If anyone thirsts, let him come to me and drink. Whoever believes in me, as the Scripture has said, out of his heart will flow rivers of living water'" (John 7:37-38). Christians alive today inhabit the world of the feast—the *great day* in which our Lord's Spirit will be poured out into those who believe (John 7:38-40). This means that believers must have an active and conscious desire for the Holy Spirit, while also praying that "the Spirit would have full control over the will, emotions, and reasoning faculties of the believer." [318]

---

[317] Sala, p. 108.

[318] Kenneth Wuest, "The Holy Spirit in Greek Exposition," *Bibliotheca Sacra, CXIIX.* Quoted in Dr Harold Sala's book, *Getting Acquainted with the Holy Spirit,* p. 119.

As a simple illustration from the CrossFit studio, in over 20 years of coaching athletes to achieve their first muscle-up, I have noticed a curious thing. Athletes who had a "hunger and thirst" for their first muscle-up (a very challenging gymnastic movement performed on the high-rings) achieved it in record time compared with people who thought it would never happen. In this sense, I propose there is an intimate connection between obedience, waiting on the Lord, and positive expectancy on the gift of the Holy Spirit. Acts 5:32 speaks of the Spirit "whom God has given to *those who obey Him.*"[319] This magnificent verse speaks to the great truth that believers can experience more of the Spirit, not based on anything that we do, but rather on the type of people that we are. Are we obedient? Do we have faith? Do we wait on our Lord?

Following our Lords command to *patiently wait* on the gift promised by the Father (Acts 1:4), Jesus's last words to His disciples were, "But you will receive power when the Holy Spirit has come upon you, and you will be my witness in Jerusalem and in all Judea and Samaria, and to the ends of the earth" (Acts 1:8-9). Whereas a great many people in the Church today are quite content to be an *advocate* of the Christian faith, it seems that very few are actively *witnessing* their faith to the extent that we read about in the New Testament. Therefore, let us note three characteristics of a true *Christian witness* and how they affect our pursuit of the spiritual gifts.

In a court of law, a witness testifies on their first-hand knowledge of an experience. In order for something to be admitted as actual evidence (as opposed to hearsay or mere speculation), the witness must be able to declare, "I *know* this to be true" rather than "I *think* this is true." Second, a real witness is not of words, but of deeds (James 2:14-26). Peter and John astonished the Sanhedrin because of their courage (Acts 4:13). In other words, it was *who they were that was significant*, which led the inquisitors to conclude: "These men had been with Jesus" (Acts 4:13b). New Testament scholar William Barclay relates a story in which journalist Sir Henry Morton Stanley, having spent time with evangelist David Livingstone in central Africa, said: "If I had been with him any longer, I would have been compelled to be a Christian—and he never spoke to me about it at all." And perhaps most importantly, the Greek word for

---

[319] My use of italics in this verse to emphasize obedience to the Lord resulted in the gift of the Holy Spirit.

witness and the word for *martyr* is the same (*martus*). To be a witness means to be loyal to the faith—no matter the cost.[320]

The world that Christians inhabit today moves at an extremely fast pace. In a fiber-optic Internet cable, the speed at which a data packet can travel is nearly 200,000 kilometers per second, (or 124,300 miles per second).[321] Considering the circumference of the Earth is about 40,000 kilometers, this is *mind-boggling fast*. Caught up in the speed of the world around us, is it possible that a believer's expectation for an immediate life-changing encounter with the Holy Spirit at the moment of conversion—or at a time subsequent to conversion—has been unfairly swayed by common culture? In the context of the CrossFit studio, the most discouraging reality athletes must face is the fact that fitness goals often take a very long time to achieve. In many cases, I have discovered that unless athletes are able to experience near immediate evidence of progress, it can be difficult for them to sustain the necessary momentum to eventually achieve—and perhaps even surpass—what they think is possible. In this sense, what is the capacity for a believer today to wait an indefinite period of time for either a distinct second encounter, or a more gradual filling, of the Holy Spirit? And is the principle and expectation of waiting even biblical?

Moving our illustrations of waiting from the CrossFit studio to the Body of Christ, believers must hold within their mind two seemingly conflicting ideas. On one hand, it is important to note that in the New Testament, the coming of the Spirit is the fulfillment of the promise of Jesus: "And remember, I am with you always, to the end of the age" (Matthew 28:20). This means that at the moment of conversion, Jesus is with us through His Spirit, and in this sense there is no waiting at all. On the other hand, in Acts 1:4, the apostles are specifically commanded to *wait for the coming of the Spirit*. How are we to reconcile what appears to be a "now—then" reality?

---

[320] The three qualities of a "Christian Witness" were brought to my attention William Barclay's *The Acts of the Apostles Daily Study Bible*. (Louisville, KY: Westminster John Knox Press, 2017), p. 13.

[321] NetworkingGuides.com

I believe that Christians would gain more power and confidence to witness their faith if they followed the example of the apostles and learned to wait for the Lord. In other words, Christians today (in particular Christian athletes within the CrossFit culture) need to develop *skillfulness in stillness*. Amid a world of hurry-up and get things done, we must cultivate space in our heart to slow down and receive. Given that everything about the sport of CrossFit revolves around the principle of *doing more work in less time*, the prophet Isaiah's words are more applicable today than ever before: "Those who wait for the Lord shall renew their strength" (Isaiah 40:31).

In his book *Baptism and Fullness*, author John Stott relates, "The baptism was a unique initiatory experience; the fullness was intended to be the continuing, the permanent result, the norm. As an initiatory event the baptism is not repeatable and cannot be lost, but the fullness can be repeated and in any case needs to be maintained."[322] When I first started in CrossFit in December 2001, the program's founder told me that I should look forward to 20 years of favorable athletic adaptation and steady physical development. Reflecting on the past 20 years of CrossFit training, my increasingly high stack of fitness journals is evidence of the resounding truth of the founder's statement. I can't help but conclude that the relationship between my subjective thoughts and expectations about my progress, and the actual objective measurement of my progress, were intimately connected. In other words, I have a strong sense that my physical progress and growth in the program are directly attributed to my expectations about the possibility for such growth in the first place. Succinctly stated, the thought preceded (and arguably produced) the outcome.

Against this background, it is interesting to note the role of faith in receiving a subsequent encounter with the Holy Spirit following conversion. I find that I must differentiate between different types of faith in order to make this point. All believers exercise the first type of faith, which I refer to as *converting faith*— this faith takes place at the moment of our conversion, and is present in every born-again believer. The second type of faith is a *continuing faith*, which is that daily confidence that God is with us, and that He will never leave or forsake us (Deuteronomy 31:6). In biblical-historical context, Abraham demonstrated

---

[322] John Stott, *Baptism and Fullness* (Downers Grove, IL: InterVarsity Press, 1964), p. 62.

converting faith when he "obeyed when God called him to leave home and go to another land" (Hebrews 11:8a), and *continuing faith* when he pressed forward each day "without knowing where he was going" (Hebrews 11:8b).

In addition to *converting* and *continuing faith,* I also believe there is a third type of faith that author and pastor Sam Storms has defined as *charismatic faith,* which is a "sudden, supernatural surge of confident assurance that God is going to do something right now, right here."[323] To this effect, it is interesting to note that when Jesus returned to His hometown of Nazareth, He was only able to accomplish a few miracles there because of the people's lack of faith (or perhaps *charismatic faith?*—Matthew 13:54-58). On the other hand, in instances of Jesus healing people, it was commonly accompanied by the fact that they had faith in Him (Luke 7:50, 8:48, 18:42). Given the relationship between faith and healing, it would seem that faith in God's ability to enable a distinct encounter with Him might very well be largely in the hands (or head) of the believer.

It is also important to remember that Paul wrote, "The spirits of prophets are subject to prophets" (1 Corinthians 14:32). Paul's point is that the Holy Spirit does not move through believers as if we were mindless sedentary beings. Rather, the "sovereign Spirit happily subjects Himself to our decisions."[324] In other words, believers who hold in their theological framework the idea that a distinct experience with the Holy Spirit is possible are far more likely to have their expectations and prayers met than someone who believes it's just not going to happen.

Legendary Drug Enforcement Administration (DEA) supervisory Special Agent and Firearms Instructor John Browning told my investigative group, "It's better to have a back-up gun and not need it, then need a back-up gun, and not have one." In the perilous moment that a Law Enforcement Officer finds himself in need of a back-up gun, it means that something has gone horribly amiss, and lives are on the line. Pressing the street-savvy wisdom of Agent Browning into a theological construct, we may very well conclude that it's far better to believe that a powerful encounter with the Holy Spirit is possible after conversion and

---

[323] Storms, p. 53. The distinctions between, "Three Types of Faith" were brought to my attention by Storm's section on "The Role of Faith" in his masterful book, *Practicing the Power.*

[324] Storms, p. 180.

not experience it during our lifetime—than to discover in the afterlife that while on earth the Holy Spirit was desirous of uniquely empowering us to edify the Body of Christ—yet sadly we never thought to ask.

HOLD ON A MINUTE—WHAT ABOUT SPEAKING IN TONGUES?

IN SOME PENTECOSTAL AND charismatic denominations, a theology gradually developed that taught absent the spiritual gift of speaking in tongues, a believer has not been baptized in the Holy Spirit. This doctrine is based primarily on the fact that speaking in tongues was often accompanied by the outpouring of the Holy Spirit (Acts 2:4, 10:46, 19:6). From this reasoning, one could easily conclude that the outpouring of the Spirit and speaking in tongues should constitute a normal and anticipated experience for everyone. However, this conclusion tragically overlooks the fact that this would mean that anyone who does not speak in tongues is not Spirit-filled—a concept that is clearly not in alignment with the biblical teaching of baptism (1 Corinthians 12:27-31). Furthermore, this position would put a great number of renowned men of God in the category of "not Spirit-filled" including Billy Graham and Charles Spurgeon.[325]

When Paul addressed the matter of speaking in tongues, he asked the question, "Do all speak in tongues?" (1 Corinthians 12:30). As renowned New Testament scholar Harold Sala has pointed out in his book, *Getting Acquainted with the Holy Spirit,* in the Greek language a question can be asked in such a way that the speaker makes it clear that either a "Yes" or a "No" is expected. In the case of the question asked by Paul, the expected answer is "No!"[326] I must reiterate at this point that I do not mean to imply that tongues have ceased, or that a believer and should not actively pray for or exercise this particular gift. Rather, I humbly suggest that the Body of Christ must be careful not to overemphasize the gift of tongues or require it as demonstrable proof of a Spirit-filled life. God knows His children better than we know ourselves, and when we invite Him to be Lord over our life, our encounter with Him will be as completely unique as the individual believer himself.

---

[325] Sala, p. 133.
[326] Sala, p. 134.

CHAPTER 22
A GLIMMER OF LIGHT

A THEOLOGY OF REVELATION

ESTABLISHING OUR FOUNDATION

REVELATION IS THE DISCLOSURE by God of truths about Himself that people could not arrive at independent of His divine initiative. By God's sovereign decision and enabling, His revelation to humanity is accomplished by both general (Psalm 19:1-3; Romans 1:19-20) and special revelation. The means of special revelation were accomplished by God's manifestation of Himself through historical events (Deuteronomy 26: 5-9; Acts 13:16-41), His divine speech (2 Timothy 3:16-17; 2 Peter 1:20-21), and most importantly through the incarnation of His Word in the person and deity of Jesus Christ (Colossians 1:15-19; Hebrews 1:2-3).

General revelation is God's communication and display of Himself to all persons at all times and places through nature (Psalm 19:1-3), history (Acts 17:26), and mankind (Genesis 1:26-28; Romans 2:11-16).[327] At the most rudimentary level, Jesus taught that evidence of God could be identified through observance of the natural order of agriculture (Matthew 6:28-30). Even the seemingly obvious fact that God had chosen to preserve mankind by providing rain, crops of food for bodily nourishment, and emotional wellbeing (Acts 14:17) points to evidence of His presence within both creation and history (Acts 14:15-18). Although these modes of revelation are clear and leave people without excuse (Romans 1:20), the sinful nature of mankind distorts our thinking, hardens our heart (Romans 1:21, 3:23; 1 John 1:8), and corrupts the truth about God in exchange for a lie (Romans 1:25).

Special revelation differs from general revelation in the sense that God communicates essential qualities of His being that could not be discerned through human reasoning or understanding (1 Corinthians 2:14). God's special revelation has manifested itself through historical events (Job 12:23), divinely inspired speech subsequently recorded in the written Word of God (2 Peter 1:20-21), and the incarnation of the Word in the person and deity of Jesus Christ (John 1:1; 18). Special revelation supremely and uniquely announces God's intention to reconcile mankind onto Himself (John 3:16) by grace through faith in Jesus Christ (Ephesians 2:8). In the life of Christ, mankind is no longer limited to knowing *about God,* but may now *know God* by entering into a personal, saving, and loving relationship with Him (John 17:3).

[327] Erickson, Millard. *Christian Theology* (Grand Rapids, MI: Baker Academic, 2013), p. 122.

The Christian Church holds that the 66 books of the Bible are the *theopneustos* Word of God (2 Timothy 3:16) written by man through the power of the Holy Spirit (2 Peter 1:21) who shaped the thoughts and directed the subsequent written and recorded words of the human authors (1 Corinthians 2:13). The original biblical autographs contain the powerful (Genesis 18:14; 1 Corinthians 2:4-5), authoritative (2 Timothy 3:16-17), clear (Deuteronomy 30:11-14; Romans 10:6-8), sufficient (1 Corinthians 2:9-10), inerrant, (Matthew 19:4-5), and inspired (Acts 1:16; 2 Samuel 23:2) Word of God.

Additionally, the Church has traditionally held that the 66 books of the Bible are the *complete and final canonical revelation* of God to mankind (1 Thessalonians 2:13). Although God chose to speak through human authors at many times and in various ways (Hebrews 1:1), the most complete revelation of His triune nature and program of redemption was made visible through Jesus Christ (John 20:31; Hebrews 1:2-4; Colossians 3:4-7). The canonical books of the Bible have been given authority by Christ himself (Matthew 28:19-20) and are the believer's supreme rule of both doctrine (John 10:35) and behavioral practice (2 Timothy 3:16-17; Titus 1:6-9).

In the Holy Scriptures, the believer encounters the living Word of God and comes to understand it not only says things, but also does things (Psalm 33:6). The interpreter of the biblical text, through the indwelling power of the Holy Spirit, experiences spiritual realities with Spirit-taught words (1 Corinthians 2:10-16) that fundamentally change their entire life (Romans 15:4).

THE BEGINNING OF TIME

SINCE THE BEGINNING OF CREATION at the hand of God (Genesis 1:1; John 1:1-3), revelation about God's nature and Being have been made manifest throughout the universe (Psalm 19:1-3).[328] Through God's sovereign decision and enabling, the gift of His self-disclosure has been accomplished by a variety of means that *can be universally discerned* by all human beings. On one hand, the doctrine of general revelation would suggest that even the seemingly obvious fact that God had chosen to preserve humanity by providing

[328] Yarbrough, R. W. "Revelation" in *The New Dictionary of Biblical Theology* (Downers Grove, IL: InterVarsity Press, 2008), p. 732.

rain, crops of food for bodily nourishment, and emotional wellbeing (Acts 14:17), points to evidence of His presence within both creation and history (Acts 14:15-18).[329] General revelation is self-evident, universally clear, and leaves people without excuse (Romans 1:20).

On the other hand, special revelation is unique in the sense that God has also chosen to communicate essential qualities of His being that *could not have been discerned* through human reasoning or understanding (1 Corinthians 2:14). God's special revelation has manifested itself through historical events (Job 12:23), divinely inspired speech subsequently recorded in the sixty-six canonical books of the Holy Bible (2 Peter 1:20-21; 2 Timothy 3:16), and the incarnation of Word of God in the person and deity of Jesus Christ (John. 1:1; 18). Of particular significance for the investigative purposes of this biblical theology, special revelation treats the historical communications and manifestations of God as now uniquely and exclusively available through the consultation of certain sacred texts.[330]

The special revelation contained within the sixty-six books of the Bible supremely and uniquely announces God's intention to reconcile mankind onto Himself (John. 3:16) by grace through faith in Jesus Christ (Ephesians. 2:8). In other words, all Scripture is a unified story that ultimately leads to Jesus (Luke 24:27-45).[331] In the life of Christ, humanity is no longer limited to knowing *about God,* but may now *know God* by entering into a personal, saving, and loving relationship with Him (John. 17:3). In this sense, Jesus is the complete and perfect fulfillment of every conceivable means of God's revelatory self-disclosing communications and manifestations ever made within creation (John 14:6).

---

[329] Erickson, Millard. *Christian Theology* (Grand Rapids, MI: Baker Academic, 2013), p. 125.

[330] Erickson, p. 122.

[331] The founders of the Bible Project beautifully articulate this position in their doctrinal intention: "To help people see the Bible as a unified story that leads to Jesus."

INTO THE GREAT UNKNOWN

IS IT POSSIBLE THAT A GLIMMER OF LIGHT—a faint ray of God's glory or a shadowy representation of His Being[332]—could be present within the sacred texts of other world religions? Similar to the uniqueness of a human fingerprint whose impression is retained on everything it touches, is God's "fingerprint" within His creation (Psalm 8:3), however dusty or distorted, still faintly visible on the pages of sacred texts outside the Judeo-Christian faith? Within the hearts and minds of the great thinkers and mystics of world religions outside of God's covenant people (Deuteronomy 14:2), might it be the case that the residue of His eternal nature and Divine essence (Ecclesiastes 3:11) was recorded as a forerunner to the arrival of the Gospel of Jesus Christ?

What are the implications for sharing the Gospel if the sacred texts of all the world's religions recorded *before the birth of Christ* retained varying degrees of the "hidden manna" (Revelation 2:17) that Jesus Himself spoke of?[333] Additionally, if *after the birth of Christ* God had continued to clandestinely encode varying degrees of His nature within such texts as the Koran, then much like Nicodemus who timidly sought the Lord in the safety of a dark night, the connective tissue of all spiritual seekers is adequately primed for the arrival of the good news that Jesus ushers in (John 3:1-15).[334] In other words, all the world religions now eagerly await the dawn of a new day and the testimony of the heavenly things our Lord promised that all nations would receive. In the fullness of the Gospel, all of God's children can now receive the baptism of the Father, the Son and the Holy Spirit, and the surrendering to the Lordship of Jesus Christ that the first disciples set out to achieve (Matthew 28:19-20).

---

[332] This sentence is an intentional contrast to Jesus Christ's "*full radiance* of God's glory" and "*exact representation* of God's being" described by the author of Hebrews (reference Hebrews 1:1-3).

[333] I make a distinction that the glimmer of light within the sacred texts of world religions are specific and unique to the historical era before the birth of Christ. Jesus is the fulfillment and final Word of God (John 1:1-3; Hebrews 1:1-3).

[334] Needless to say, there seems to be a stronger argument that Divine revelation is the sacred texts of world religions *before* rather than *after* the birth of Christ. Although we can intuitively sense that varying degrees of revelation in such sacred texts as the Vedas served as a cultural "Old Testament" and forerunner for the Gospel, once the "Word had become flesh," the necessity for continued revelation outside the Gospel would not seem prudent. Additionally, any revelation that contradicted the Gospel would, according to the Apostle Paul, "be under God's curse" (Galatians 1:8).

PREPARING THE HEARTS AND MINDS

MUCH LIKE A SPECIAL OPERATIONS TEAM who deploys in advance of the main element for the purpose of preparing the hearts and minds of the ingenious people, if even a dimly prophetic Word of God was revealed to other world religions for the purpose of preparing them for the arrival of the Gospel, then Christian evangelists have much cause to rejoice (Matthew 28:19-20).

The great Christian theologian C.S. Lewis expressed belief that general revelation of God throughout humanity is evidenced within our conscious choice between right and wrong, and the long history of all world religions that try (and fail) to obey it.[335] Even the "queer stories scattered all through the heathen religions" ultimately and miraculously find their meaning, fulfillment, and explanation in the person of Jesus Christ.[336] Perhaps the mystery of this marvelous Truth about God is best expressed in the words of the Apostle Paul who wrote that God is "over all and through all and in all" (Ephesians 4:6), and proclaimed, "In Him we live and move and have our being" (Acts 17:28).

Throughout the ages, the great prophets, sages, mystics, and gurus of world religions outside of the Judeo-Christian faith have attempted through the constraints of human language to express the inexpressible mystery and Oneness of God (The Bhagavad Gita 4:6; The Tao Te Ching 25:1; The Surangama Sutra[337]). The collective voices of these *rishis* (literally "seers") of ancient India synthesized their understanding of the Divine in a fashion later described as Perennial Philosophy.[338] The universality of mankind's quest for Divine understanding and relationship was consolidated into three truths: (1) There is an infinite and changeless reality that lies behind the world of change; (2) This same reality resides within human consciousness; (3) The purpose of life is to discover this changeless reality: In other words, to realize God while still here on earth.[339]

---

[335] Lewis, C. S. *Mere Christianity* (New York: Collier Books, 1952), p. 39.

[336] Lewis, p. 40.

[337] The Buddha is recorded to have said, "One intrinsic Unity enfolds all manifestations." The Surangama Sutra: Identified in the book by Richard Hooper, *Jesus, Buddha, Krishna and Lau Tzu: The Parallel Sayings* (Charlottesville, VA: Hampton Road Publishing, 2007), p. 57.

[338] Easwaran, Eknath. *The Bhagavad Gita* (Tomales, CA: Nilgiri Press, 2007), p. 17.

[339] Easwaren p. 17.

In this sense, the Indian sacred texts including the Upanishads, the Bhagavad Gita, and the Dhammapada were prophetic announcements of a future experience of the Kingdom of God on earth.[340] The dim light of the *rishis* inspired voices were in many respects anticipating a time when a complete, accurate, and fully embodied representation of the Divine would be manifested for the entire world to see.

The Indian Christian Bishop A.J. Appasamy argued in his book, *Temple Bells,* that Indian Christians should become acquainted with the sacred texts of Hinduism.[341] Similarly, those evangelists intent on introducing Christ within the context of Indian thought must become acquainted with the "storehouse of terms, images, and metaphors" that resonates with the Indian mind.[342] Much of Appasamy's theology rests on his conviction that Jesus "came to fulfill, not to destroy" (cf. Matthew 5:17). Given the magnitude of Hindu spiritual thought that is foundational to Indian culture, Appasamy believed that approaching Christianity through the "impulses, instincts, questions, longings, and aspirations" within his nation's sacred texts was the key to revealing that Christ is the fulfillment to the deepest longings of the Hindu heart.[343]

In the canonical texts of the New Testament, the author of Hebrews summarized the universality of this phenomenon when he wrote, "In the past God spoke to us through the prophets at many times and in various ways" (Hebrews 1:1). Much like the testimony of John the Baptist in explaining the purpose of his authorized bearing of revelation, a liberal position would hold that the purpose of God's prophetic voice throughout the Old Testament, in addition to the sacred texts of other world religions, was "to make straight the way for the Lord" (John 1:23).[344]

---

[340] Easwaran describes the Upanishads as the oldest of the three and functioning much like a roadmap to understanding consciousness. The Dhammapada has traditionally been attributed to sayings of the Buddha. The Bhagavad Gita is considered by scholars both a "map and guidebook" to spirituality. The oldest Hindu scriptures are the Rig Veda, written in a prototype of the Sanskrit language approximately 1500 B.C., and are foundational to the other sacred texts.

[341] Tennent, p. 55.

[342] Tennent, p. 55.

[343] Tennent, p. 55.

[344] This view is held by modern spiritual teacher Eckhart Tolle, who has sought to find the similarities between Buddhism, Hinduism, Sufi mysticism, Judaism, and Christianity.

The conservative position within the Christian faith would hold that the spoken Word of God has indeed come to human beings at many times and in various ways (Hebrews 1:1). However, God's Divine Word is specifically reserved to the canonical books of the Holy Bible. The Word of God recorded in the pages of the 66 canonical books of the Bible are the expression of God's will to humankind, and they supremely define what we are to believe and how we are to live.[345] Additionally, Scripture itself draws no distinction between the authority and Divine origin of God's oral or written revelation (2 Timothy 3:16; 2 Peter 1:19-21).[346] In this sense, the 66 books of the Bible are the complete and final Word of God to mankind (1 Thess. 2:13). This view holds that the prophets who heard God speak are themselves restricted to the canonical books of the Bible itself. Most supremely, the Bible has been given authority by Christ Himself (Matt. 28:19-20) and is the Christians' ultimate rule of both doctrine (John. 10:35) and behavioral practice (2 Timothy 3:16-17; Titus 1:6-9).

At the other end of the spectrum, certain Indian Christian theologians hold that the sacred texts of their religious history are *their equivalent of the Old Testament*.[347] These theologians look to New Testament passages such as the account of Jesus on the road to Emmaus and his explanation that "all the Scriptures concern himself" (Luke 24:27), and subsequently apply this to Jesus's presence in India today. In their view, "Jesus walks alongside Indian Christians and explains to them how the Indian scriptures point to and bear witness in him."[348] These same theologians note the similarity of the Divine words of Jesus Christ with parallel statements of the Buddha and the spiritual wisdom of Krishna portrayed in The Bhagavad Gita, and then reverse engineer them to a single source, mainly the same One True God. This perspective certainly has merit, and seems to suggest that the commonality and continuity

---

[345] Erickson, p. 211.

[346] John Frame. *The Doctrine of the Christian Life* (Phillipsburg, NJ: P&R Publishing, 2008), p. 141.

[347] Tennent, Timothy. *Theology in the Context of World Christianity,* (Grand Rapids, MI: Zondervan, 2007), p. 53.

[348] Tennent, p. 54.

between Jesus's teaching and the teaching of other world religious leaders before Christ's incarnate ministry on earth were a component of God's general revelation to all humanity.[349]

ENLISTING SUPPORT

OBEDIENT OF THE COMMISSION to "make disciples of *all the nations*" (Matthew 28:19 – my use of italics), and aware that the Gospel of Jesus Christ must be shared with a sensitivity to the diverse spiritual backgrounds of world religions, I support a position that there may indeed be a *glimmer of light* within the sacred texts outside the Judeo-Christian faith. Perhaps the most intriguing and greatest support for this position, in addition to the integration, interconnectedness, and single-Source of all written revelation about God, comes from the mouth of God Himself (Colossians 2:9). In the company of His apostles, Jesus revealed that everything ever recorded in the Scriptures was ultimately about Him and fulfilled in His life (Luke 24:27, 44).

In this sense, all the sacred texts of the world's religions recorded *before the birth of Christ* retain a *glimmer of light* that shines forth most brilliantly and perfectly in the Divine Light of Jesus Christ (John 1:4-5, 9). In other words, although the sacred texts of world religions may contain revelation about God, the most complete and final revelation is made manifest in Jesus Christ. This position therefore gives final authority to the inspired 66 canonical books of the Holy Bible (2 Timothy 3:16, 2 Peter 1:21).[350] If the words of the great Christian mystic and theologian A.W. Tozer ring true, then the prophetic voices of centuries long ago served the purpose of preparing humanity to *think rightly* about God. Therefore, to achieve the final and supremely right thought about God, one must have an

---

[349] As researched by Richard Hooper in his book, *Jesus, Buddha, Krishna & Lao Tzu* (Charlottesville, VA: Hampton Roads, 2007), this was a view held by the Catholic monk and mystic Thomas Merton. Much of Merton's life was spent finding the similarities between Western and Eastern monasticism and mysticism. In his final work, *The Asian Journal,* Merton expounded on the importance of the sacred Hindu text, The Bhagavad Gita.

[350] This view is held by Bishop Robert Barron as discussed in his book, *To Light a Fire on the Earth* (New York: Image Books, 2017), and his Podcast *Word On Fire,* "Following The Star."

encounter with the person of Jesus Christ (John 14:9) as specifically revealed within the Holy Bible.[351]

Although the sacred texts of ancient world religions may contain a glimmer of light, or in the words of Emil Brunner, "Be God's voice, but scarcely recognizable,"[352] there remains an important distinction between the Judeo-Christian view of a personal and loving God who searches for us (Luke 15:1-32), as opposed to a human seeker in search of God. In this sense, the spiritual seeker of the ancient world religions is finally found by God Himself in the revelation of Jesus Christ. In many respects, the Magi depicted in the Gospel of Matthew (Matthew 2:1-12) symbolically represent the embodiment of spiritual seekers in search of God from ancient to modern times.

The Gospel of Matthew describes the Magi as "wise men from the East." These wise men are likely a combination of a modern-day astrologer and astronomer. They were part of a stargazing culture that sought to discern the will and nature of God by studying the planets and stars.[353] These wise men represent the spiritual traditions of the human race from ancient to modern times including the Hindu, Buddhist, and Sufi religions. The Magi are the universal embodiment of the spiritual seeker who desires a greater understanding of the nature of God (Reference Acts 8:31). The Magi in the Gospel of Matthew and the Ethiopian eunuch in the book of Acts are spiritual seekers in pursuit of Divine explanation and direction. However, they do not know precisely where to go or what to think until they meet representatives of God's covenant people who tell them on the basis of special revelation the Gospel of Jesus Christ (Matthew 2:5-6; Acts 8:31-35).

If the dim light of revelation within the sacred texts of the world religions is akin to the star the Magi followed, then evangelists of all Christian denominations have reason to celebrate. Like the mysterious gravitational pull of nature that migrating birds use to navigate across vast oceans, all spiritual seekers are drawn toward the "true light that has come into the world" (1:9).

---

[351] A. W. Tozer wrote, "What comes into our mind when we think about God is the most important thing about us." *The Knowledge of the Holy* (New York: HarperOne, 1961), p. 1.

[352] Erickson, p. 160.

[353] The illustration of the Maji and the relationship to the modern-day astrologer was identified in Bishop Robert Barron's Podcast *Word On Fire,* episode titled "Following The Star."

Although the Magi were able to follow the star in the general direction of Christ (Matthew 2:2b), they ultimately inquired and were dependent on the experts of the Torah to tell them precisely where Jesus was to be born (Matthew 2:2a; 5-6, cf. Micah 5:2,4).

The prophet Isaiah foresaw that "Nations will come to your light, and kings to the brightness of your dawn, all assemble and come to you; your sons come from afar. All from Sheba will come, bearing gold and incense, and proclaiming the praise of the LORD" (Isaiah 60:33-4, 6). The great prophetic voices of Israel seemed to sense that something of extraordinary importance was afoot. The spiritual privilege that Israel had long enjoyed was never intended for Israel alone. Rather, Israel's glory was intended to benefit the entire world. This biblical position would seem to suggest that whatever the other nations were looking for would *ultimately* and *only* be found in Israel. In other words, what the spiritual seekers of other nations were pursuing inchoately and without full understanding, Israel had found and was worshiping explicitly.

Although still a mystery shrouded in a fog of revelation, the world religions *outside the covenant people of Israel* were in fact hungry and thirsty *for the God of Israel*. All of their accomplishments and spiritual achievements were in some sense an echo of anticipation for what God would accomplish through Israel. If Isaiah was correct in his prophecy, then the "distant sons from afar" represent all the world's religious, philosophical, artistic, literate, and scientific achievements. The world's deeply encoded desire for eternal light would in fact be discovered in the light already shining on Israel.

THE LIGHT OF THE WORLD

THE CLAIM OF THE CHRISTIAN FAITH is that Jesus is not just another great spiritual teacher, guru, philosopher, radical political figure. Rather, Jesus is the incarnate "Word became flesh" (John 1:14). This means that the Divine mind, the intelligibility through which all things are both created and sustained, was made manifest in the life and person of Jesus. If on one hand Christians affirm this magnificent truth, then on the other we must concede that any attempt to find the good, the true, the beautiful, the transcendent, and the eternal must ultimately lead to and be fulfilled in Christ. Thus, the light shining on Israel is meant to be a light for the entire world to see.

The contrast between the disclosure of Christ's birth to the shepherds and the Magi is meant to represent the contrast between the simple and sophisticated. In this sense, the Magi symbolically portray the cultural, intellectual, scientific, philosophical, and spiritual longings of the human heart. The Magi's studying of the night sky is evocative of the world's collective searching for the good, true, and beautiful. In their attempt to discover a meaningful arrangement of the stars, the Magi are instead brought face to face with the Maker of the stars Himself. Through Divine inspiration, the prophet Isaiah intuitively knew that all spiritual seekers would be drawn toward the light that would illuminate the entire world.

The spiritual seeker depicted in the saga of The Bhagavad Gita is the warrior Arjuna. In the company of his teacher Krishna and through their dialogue together, the path to knowing God is made clear. The attraction to spiritual seekers across the ages has been the promise of following the "spiritual roadmap" of the Gita, and like Arjuna, arriving at the feet of God. However, within the context of the Bible, following the Gita or any other spiritual text will at best only point you in a very vague and general direction of the Divine. Much like the Magi who arrived in a land they did not recognize, specific revelation uniquely given to God's covenant people will always be required before proceeding further. However, in welcoming the fullness of revelation recorded within God's Word by the Divinely inspired authors of the Bible (2 Timothy 3:16), the Magi and all spiritual seekers can finally come to worship at the feet of Jesus (Matthew 2:11).

In the context of this specific example, the Magi did indeed find what they were looking for. However, they would not have found it without the fullness of God's Word as revealed to His covenant people. And in a more general sense, all spiritual seekers who "follow the star" and dim light of revelation within their historical sacred texts may ultimately arrive at the gates of the New Jerusalem (Revelation 3:12, 21:2). However, in order for the seeker to know God in the fullness of His revelation, then like the Magi of centuries long ago, they too must bow down and worship at the feet of Jesus (John 14:6; 2 Peter 2:4).

Jesus Christ is the "fullness of the Deity in bodily form" (Colossians 2:9) and is the "exact representation of God's being" (Hebrews 1:3a). The complete and final revelation of God is "His Word become flesh" (John 1:14) that can only be discovered through the *specific sacred texts* of the Judeo-Christian faith contained in the 66 canonical books of the Bible. In this sense, it is Israel and God's chosen people who announce the coming of Christ and gather together all the spiritual seekers of the human race.

Therefore, the sacred texts of the world religions may indeed contain great wisdom and inspire the "loving, joyful abandon to God" so common within Hindu devotion.[354] This position and view also gives credence to the rich heritage of Indian spirituality and potentially creates greater opportunity for meaningful dialogue across cultural boundaries. However, all the spiritual seeking outside of the Bible will remain largely incomplete unless it draws the archetypal Magi to the God of Israel revealed in the person of Jesus Christ.

ALTERNATIVE POSITIONS AND A UNIFIED SOURCE OF WISDOM

ONE OBJECTION TO OUR PROPOSED position contends that because of the similarity of the teachings of Jesus, the Buddha, and Lau Tzu, the source of their collective wisdom must be from the same God. Therefore, independent of whom the spiritual seeker is choosing to follow or study, the locality of the revelation will ultimately be the same. This position calls into question how two different teachers (in this particular case, Jesus and the Buddha) who lived during different eras, in countries widely separated, and whose religions were quite different, make almost identical statements about spirituality and the meaning of life.[355]

This position looks to the specific words of the great religions and seeks to reduce meaning to statements of universal truth. Because of the unlikelihood these spiritual teachers were influenced by each other, a conclusion is reached that the source of their wisdom was beyond human intellect or understanding. The authors were in touch with the Divine source of all wisdom, and their subsequent recording of these great spiritual insights serve as a means of revelation to humanity.

[354] Tennent, p. 54

[355] Hooper, p. 11.

The problem with this position is the authors do not take into consideration that the God of the Bible is more than a mere source of wisdom. In other words, there is no acknowledgement of the degree of revelation that has taken place. For this reason, I contend that although revelation may in fact be present in the sacred texts of other world religions, it is only a *glimmer of light*. The God of the Bible is supremely revealed as relational within Himself, and in His capacity and desire to be a loving Father to His creation (Matthew 6:9-13). The God of the Bible is much more than a mere source of wisdom: He is a personal, individual being, capable of feeling, choosing, and having a reciprocal relationship with other personal and social beings.[356] The spiritual seeker's view of God reduces Him to something to be used to solve problems or meet personal needs. However, the biblical view of God reveals that He is first and foremost relational, and that the only means of establishing relationship between God and mankind is through Jesus Christ Himself (1 Timothy 2:5-6).

Another interesting objection to our view asserts the lack of revelation in the sacred texts of other world religions is their inability to prepare the reader to meet the Triune God of the Bible. The Islamic monotheistic view of God leaves no room for biblical themes such as the Trinity, the incarnation of God in Jesus Christ, and the suffering and death of Jesus as an atoning sacrifice for the sins of the world.[357] In the context of the Hindu religion, although particular gods such as Visnu or Shiva may be known for certain deeds or attributes, many scholars believe all the gods may simply be different names for the One Divine Reality.[358] In this sense, the wide arrangement of Hindu gods could potentially still be reduced to One Being, thus posing a complicated monotheistic paradigm quite apart from the Judeo-Christian faith. This would seem to be a hindrance to sharing the Christian faith and evidence of the lack of revelation within the eastern spiritual texts.

However, the Vedic understanding of consciousness and self-realization may in fact provide an evangelistic context for sharing the doctrine of the Trinity. In yogic philosophy, one particular position holds that when the Supreme Being was made aware of himself, it was akin to the *beholder* becoming aware

---

[356] Erickson, p. 240.

[357] Tennent, p. 37.

[358] Tennent, p. 25.

of the *beheld*. This view further holds that the flow of *awareness* between the *beholder* and the *beheld* is fundamental to understanding the essence of the threefold nature of the Supreme Being.

In this sense, a bridge is formed between two vastly different worlds of religious thought, and a foundation is established for sharing the full biblical revelation of the Trinity established in the relationship between the Father, His begotten Son, and the Holy Spirit.[359]

TAKING IT TO THE STREET

THE IMPLICATIONS FOR ACKNOWLEDGING a *glimmer of light* within the sacred texts of other world religions is immense and of particular importance for evangelistic purposes. Similar to the approach that the apostle Paul took when he acknowledged that the people of Athens were deeply religious (Acts 17:22), we should make every effort to recognize the rich spiritual heritage of ancient world religions and their respective sacred texts. However, like Paul so wonderfully exemplified, we must then capitalize on every opportunity to share the God they do not yet know (Acts 17:23).

If the "queer stories scattered all through the heathen religions about a god who dies and comes to life again"[360] are the narrative of God's fingerprint within human consciousness (Psalm 8:3), then the advanced element in clandestine preparation for the fullness of God's revelation has long been underway. We must remember that Jesus is not restricted or locked into the tightly bound covers of a book; Jesus Christ is the "true light that gives light to every man" (John 1:9).[361] Evangelists should be sensitive to the possibility that the dim flicker of light within the sacred texts of other world religions is there in anticipation of being completely embraced and brought into the fullness of revelation in the brilliant True Light of Jesus Christ.

---

[359] This insight into Vedic philosophy was brought to my attention in an interview with Raja John Bright on November 23, 2019 in Santa Cruz, CA. Bright is a Vedic subject matter expert, teacher of The Bhagavad Gita, and former personal student of the renowned Eastern spiritual teacher Maharishi Mahesh Yogi.

[360] Lewis, p. 39.

[361] Tennant, p. 69.

Students of theology and missionaries whose hearts are set on sharing the Gospel must strive to understand that Jesus Christ does not arrive as a stranger in any culture.[362] However shrouded in darkness a particular sacred text of a world religion might be, there could still remain a small window of God's grace to prepare them for the day they will receive the "radiance of God's glory in the person of Jesus Christ" (Hebrews 1:3a). Much akin to the spiritual seekers described in the Gospel of Matthew, the rising star of God's True Light (John 1:9) has come into the world and is drawing all the nations toward Him.

---

[362] Tennent, p. 69.

CHAPTER 23

SPITTLE AND MUD

A THEOLOGY OF HUMANITY

INTRODUCTION

"LET US MAKE MANKIND IN OUR IMAGE, IN OUR LIKENESS" (Genesis 1:26a). With these words, the Bible history of mankind begins. The Word of God reveals both the origin of the human race ("Let us make man") in addition to the eternal purpose to which our race is destined ("In our image, in our likeness"). In the beginning of time, God proposed to make a godlike being, an image bearer that would reflect His image and likeness, and would become a *visible manifestation* of the *invisible One* who brought him to life.[363]

In order for humanity to truly know and image our *essential nature,* we must look to Jesus Christ—Himself the *essential example* of both deity and humanity (Matthew 5:48; Hebrews 1:1-3, 4:15).[364] Only from this vantage point can we ever hope to *become like Him* (1 John 3:2; 2 Corinthians 3:18). Because Jesus is the "image of the invisible God" (Colossians 1:15) and the "exact representation of God's nature" (Hebrews 1:3), mankind must arrive at the realization that the image of God *(Imago Dei)* is best exemplified in Jesus's life and teaching.[365] However, far more is needed to image God than to remain satisfied with parroting the teachings of Jesus Christ or modeling His behavior or individualized actions. To actualize the essence of God's image within mankind an entirely new paradigm must be created—the *old man* must pass away in order for the new man to come to life (Romans 6:6; Ephesians 4:22-24).

---

[363] The concept of mankind being an *image bearer of God* and a *visible manifestation of the invisible One* was brought to my attention by Michael Heiser in his masterful book, *The Unseen Realm* (Bellingham, WA: Lexham Press, 2015), p. 59, and the chapter *Preaching Christ our Example* in Andrew Murray's book *The Essential Works of Andrew Murray.*

[364] Murray, Andrew. *The Essential Works of Andrew Murray* (Uhrichsville, OH: Barbour, 1962), p. 1380.

[365] Marc Cortez makes the outstanding argument in his book, *Resourcing Theological Anthropology,* that "the *Imago Dei* has been constricted to such an extent that only one person actually qualifies (Jesus Christ). Cortez, Mark. *Resourcing Theological Anthropology.* (Grand Rapids, MI: Zondervan, 2017), p. 114.

The disciples were the first to discover that mankind must learn to define humanity by examining the human nature of Jesus, for Jesus alone most fully embodies what humanity was meant to be (Hebrews 5:8-9).[366] Yet the disciples and great biblical saints who worshiped Jesus as Lord and God did far more than just contemplate His human nature. Rather, the disciples *rubbed Jesus into their eyes* (John 9:6), they *plugged Him into their ears* (Mark 7:33), they *submerged themselves in Him* (John 9:7), they *attached themselves to Him* (John 15:1-5), and they *ate His flesh and drank His blood* (John 6:56). In other words, the believer's *submersion into God* and *consumption of God* meant that God Himself would take up residence within the psychosomatic unity of their being. The change of manhood would be so drastic that friends and family would beg the question: "Is this the same man?" (John 9:8-9).

A STARTLING PROPOSITION

WE THUS ARRIVE AT THE CORNERSTONE of a complex theological position—much akin to a battle line drawn in the sand—that Jesus Christ is mankind's essential source for knowledge about God (John 1:18) and knowledge about ourselves (1 John 4:2).[367] This means that the only way for mankind to fulfill our creation mandate of imaging God will be through the supernatural experience of God Himself taking up residence within us. Until Jesus transforms us from the "inside out," humanity will remain weak, broken, and sinful—a mere skeleton of the image we were meant to be.[368] In this sense, God became man for the purpose of turning mankind into a new type of humanity—a change so drastic we transform from being a creature of God into being children of God.[369] When Jesus breathes into humanity *His breath of life* (Genesis 2:7; John 20:22; cf. Acts 1:8), we awaken in spiritual brotherhood to the man who cries out, "I once was blind, but now I see" (John 9:25).

---

[366] Alexander, T. Desmond. *The New Dictionary of Biblical Theology* (Downers Grove, IL: InterVarsity, 2000), p. 566.

[367] The great theologian Andrew Murray wrote: "Jesus came to show to us at once the image of God and our own image." *The Essential Works of Andrew Murray* (Uhrichsville, OH: Barbour, 1962), p. 1380.

[368] C. S. Lewis wrote that "God became man to turn creatures into sons: not simply to produce better men of the old kind but to produce a new kind of man." *Mere Christianity*, p. 167.

[369] Lewis, p. 175.

SUPPORTING THE POSITION

THE WORLD'S GREATEST CHRISTIAN MINDS have long wrestled with the meaning of mankind's ability to image God (Genesis 1:26). Traditionally there have been three ways of conceptualizing and describing what the image of God *(Imago Dei)* would entail for humanity. These views are referred to as *substantive, relational,* and *functional.* We will briefly examine each of these more commonly held ways of understanding the image of God before proceeding into a somewhat more challenging theological position.

The *substantive view* holds that human beings have a unique and definite characteristic or quality within their makeup, and this same characteristic represents the *Imago Dei.* At one end of the spectrum this would suggest that the image of God is an aspect of humanity's physicality or bodily makeup, while at the other end of the spectrum the image would be more related to a spiritual quality in human nature, mainly reason.[370] Many theologians argued that after the fall in Genesis 9:6, only a relic of the image of God remained in humanity. Furthermore, the locus of the image (although broken) remained as a resident quality within all humans whether or not they choose to recognize God's existence.[371]

The second view is *relational* and focuses more on a quality of mankind that is within our human nature. In this sense, the focus shifts from something substantial about imaging God and turns the attention to the manner in which humanity is intended to experience God within the context of a relationship.[372] Only by studying the Word of God can we realize what humanity was originally created and intended to be—and God Himself in the person of Jesus Christ is the most perfect expression of that revelation (Colossians 1:15). The relational view means that rather than imaging God in a structural manner, the *Imago Dei* is more a matter of one's relationship to God as made possible through faith in Christ (John 14:6).

---

[370] Erickson, p. 460.
[371] Erickson, p. 463.
[372] Erickson, p. 464.

The final view treats the *Imago Dei* as something *functional* and holds that the image consists in something that humanity measurably, tangibly, and constructively does. In this sense, humans image God in an objective way. The biblical support is taken from an association between mankind being made in the image of God (Genesis 1:26a) and the subsequent functional command to "rule over the fish of the sea ...." (Genesis 1:26b). The implication of Genesis 1:26 is that mankind's ability to participate in rule and dominion is itself the image of God.[373]

We now turn our attention to a somewhat more challenging treatment of conceptualizing the *Imago Dei*. This view is referred to as *divine presence* and suggests that the *Imago Dei* is a *status* conferred by God onto all humans. In other words, God created human persons to be the physical means by which He would display and manifest His divine presence in the world, but God is not necessarily restricted to making His presence known only through humans.[374] This unique and privileged status includes the responsibility of representing (or being an image bearer of) God. The attributes that God gives humanity are the *means to imaging*, but not the image status itself. In this sense, God's original intent was to equip His imagers with both the will (relational) and ability (functional) to carry out His decrees and to "extend Eden over all the earth."[375] Thus, there is indeed an innate quality *within the substantive makeup* of human beings that enables us to image God. In addition, because humans are the primary means by which God manifests His presence on Earth, the *Imago Dei* is intimately linked to the indwelling presence of the Holy Spirit.[376]

---

[373] Erickson, p. 466.

[374] Cortez, Marc. *Resourcing Theological Anthropology* (Grand Rapids, MI: Zondervan, 2017), p. 109.

[375] Heiser, Michael. *The Unseen Realm* (Bellingham, WA: Lexham Press, 2015), p. 59.

[376] Cortez, p. 112.

JESUS CHRIST – THE TRUE IMAGE OF GOD

AS IMAGE BEARERS OF GOD, the human race is uniquely situated to learn something about God as we simultaneously learn something about ourselves. However, history has demonstrated that along the path of humanity's quest for greater understanding of our inherent nature, we routinely set off in the wrong direction and with a broken compass—we are comparable to a flock of hopelessly lost sheep (Luke 15:3-7, 19:10). The reason for mankind's perpetual wandering is due to our focus on the *existential* and traditionally held empirical conceptions of *who we think we are* rather than the *essential nature* of humanity as perfectly revealed in the person of Jesus Christ.[377] Apart from divine revelation, the journey of self-discovery will succumb to seeking answers through the severely limited inductive investigation of ourselves and other human beings (Romans 1:22).[378]

Humanity has long suffered from the ill-fated consequences of imposing upon ourselves *who we think we are* rather than *who we were made to be.*[379] The theological implications of this position are staggering, for none of us is humanity as God intended it to be, or as it first came from His hand (Romans 3:23).[380] By way of illustration, inductive reasoning is akin to a *painting* telling the *painter* the vision for his picture, or a *machine* attempting to explain its inherent functioning mechanism to the *inventor of the machine itself.*[381] In a word, this means that eternity may very well lie in the heart of mankind (Ecclesiastes 3:11), yet apart from divine revelation we will remain woefully unable to realize it.

---

[377] Similar to Millard Erickson, I use the terms *essential* and *existential* humanity to differentiate between humanity from the perspective of God's original and intended creation (essential) and humanity's attempt to study and understand itself apart from God (existential).

[378] Erickson, Millard. *Christian Theology* (Grand Rapids, MI: Baker Academic, 2013), p. 671.

[379] This observation seems to be consistent with all the major world religions. The Indian sage Ramana Maharshi explained human suffering in the context of "forgetting who we are," and the Bible likewise contains accounts of people not realizing (or forgetting) who they were destined to become (Es. 4:1-17).

[380] Erickson, p. 671.

[381] The great Christian mystic and theologian C. S. Lewis used a similar illustration when describing *the cost of discipleship* in his book, *Mere Christianity.*

The Bible is full of rich examples of the consequences of inductive reasoning into the limited view of humanity, the skewed sense of our essential nature and the negligent conception of our divinely created image. As a case study, when the disciples took Jesus into their boat *just as he was* (Mark 4:36), they imposed upon Jesus the restricted framework of their individual and collectively held ideas about *who they thought Jesus was* (Mark 4:35-41).[382] However, when Jesus calmed the storm and saved their lives (Mark 4:37-38), the disciples begin to sense there remained a great deal still to learn about *who Jesus actually was* (Mark 4:41). The tension in this particular biblical account is that the person the disciples *thought Jesus was*, and the Person whom they would *discover Jesus to be*, were altogether different.[383] In other words, the disciples' preconceived and limited understanding of humanity was extended onto the very person who had come to model for them what humanity was intended to be (1 Corinthians 1:11).[384]

The marvelous account of Jesus calming the storm also demonstrates that even one critical moment of Holy Spirit illumination can reveal what we could never discover through the tools of individualistic learning or inductive reasoning (1 Corinthians 2:16). While in the boat, asleep with His disciples, Christ suggests that place in mankind where to varying degrees we remain unknowingly rooted in the goodness of the divine image in which we were first created (Genesis 1:31).[385] However, once awakened, the sleeping Christ rebukes the winds and calms the waves (Mark 4:39), thus supremely revealing that humanity's greatest source of identity and strength will only be found within Him. Finally, the story teaches that although mankind cries out for

---

[382] I argue here that the disciples use of the word "teacher" in addressing Jesus, and further the inquiry amongst themselves, "Who is this?" is evidence they had not yet arrived at the realization that Jesus was the "fullness of deity in bodily form" (Col. 2:19).

[383] The words of the great Christian mystic A. W. Tozer are most fitting to mention here: "The thoughts that come into your mind when you think about God are the most important thoughts about you." Tozer, A. W. *The Knowledge of the Holy*. (New York: Harper One, 1961), p. 1.

[384] Rakestraw, Robert. *Becoming like God: An Evangelical Doctrine of Theosis*. Journal of the Evangelical Theological Society 40.2 (1997).

[385] *By varying degrees and unknowingly rooted*, I suggest that although the invisible qualities of God have been plainly visible within creation since the beginning of time (Ro. 1:20), woefully large populations of mankind remain ignorant of His glory. At the other end of the spectrum, even many Christians alive today may not fully realize the extent to which we are called to conform ourselves to the image of Jesus Christ (Ro. 8:29).

understanding, there can be no understanding apart from divine revelation, and divine revelation will never be possible apart from accepting Jesus Christ as the God-Man that He said He was.[386]

Finally, the account of Jesus calming the storm is just one of several instances of New Testament authors emphatically teaching that the true *Imago Dei* is constricted to one person—Jesus Christ.[387] The Apostle Paul and the author of Hebrews make the case that *Jesus alone* is the "exact representation of God" (Hebrews 1:3) and the only "image of the invisible God" (Colossians 1:15). However, although Jesus is indeed the one true *Imago Dei*, these same authors proclaim the good news that mankind can be "transformed into his image" (2 Corinthians 3:18) through the process of "putting on the new self" (Colossians 3:10) so that our lives "gradually become brighter and more beautiful as God enters our lives and we become like Him" (2 Corinthians 3:18 MSG). This means that although Jesus Christ is history's only example of the *Imago Dei* present in all its fullness (Colossians 2:9), through union with Christ, humanity can participate in the *Imago Dei* and experience the *fullness of what we were meant to be* (2 Corinthians 3:18; Romans 8:29).[388]

The great theologian C.S. Lewis wrote, "The Son of God became a man to enable men to become sons of God."[389] This means that until the study of mankind uniquely and supremely points to the perfect example set by Jesus Christ (Hebrews 2:14-17), we will fail to actualize the awesome image that God intended humanity to be (Psalm 8:4-6). Because God directly created the human race according to His image and likeness (Genesis 1:26-27; 2:7; 1 Corinthians 11:7; James 3:9), only God is able to reveal to mankind the image that He wants us to emulate. In other words, God is the Creator and we are His *creation*.

---

[386] The distinction of "taking Jesus as who He says He is" is of crucial significance. As I will argue throughout the *support section*, absent knowing Jesus as Lord and Savior in both the fullness of his deity and humanity, mankind will never be able to fully experience the *Imago Dei*.

[387] Cortez, p. 114.

[388] Cortez makes a similar argument in his chapter on *Divine Presence*. Cortez, pp. 114–115.

[389] Lewis, C. S. *Mere Christianity* (New York, NY: Collier Books, 1952), p. 139.

The incredible privilege of imaging and representing God is a status conferred upon mankind by God. By obvious implication of this realization, every human life is precious and sacred because we are the creatures that God put on Earth to represent Him.[390] Much like a soldier who wants to become like his commanding officer (2 Timothy 2:4), mankind must ultimately conform to our Creator in order to become fully alive in the image we were created to be (1 Corinthians 1:11).

WHO AM I?

WHEN MOSES WAS FACED WITH THE seemingly impossible task of leading his people out of bondage and slavery, he asked God a question that so often reflects humanity's inquiries into our nature: "Who am I?" (Exodus 3:11). However, rather than answering the question, God directed Moses to a completely different and far more significant matter. The important question at hand was not *who Moses was* but rather *who God is* (Exodus 3:12-15). In this sense, Moses represents mankind's misdirected quest for meaning and identity. We cry out in vain, "Who am I?" rather than asking God, "Who are you?" Moses speaks for the entire human race in his impaired and broken vestige of what essential humanity was meant to be.

In addition, Moses reflects the futility and impossibility of imaging God apart from God Himself modeling for us *what the image should be like*. In other words, biblical history revealed and demonstrated that God would need to show His creation what the image was meant to be. This means that Jesus's humanity was something quite different than the humanity of sinful human beings. As the supreme and perfect image bearer of God, "Jesus was not merely as human as we are; he was in fact *more human than we are*."[391]

In the context of human development, the implications of Jesus's divinity and humanity result in two staggering conclusions. First is the discovery that although the human race was made in the image of God (Genesis 1:26), apart from Jesus, our ability to know God and fully image our Creator will remain altogether

---

[390] Heiser, Michael. *The Unseen Realm* (Bellingham, WA: Lexham Press, 2015), p. 59.
[391] Erickson, p. 671. My use of italics.

impossible (John 14:6). Second is the promising realization that in Christ, mankind is ultimately transformed into *the likeness of Christ Himself*—the only perfect imager of God the world has ever known (Romans 8:29; 1 John 3:2).

OBJECTIONS AND OPPOSING IDEAS

IN MANY RESPECTS THIS THEOLOGICAL POSITION has brought us into very deep and challenging waters. Without too far a stretch of one's imagination it becomes quite easy to foresee the stark opposition to such claims that apart from Jesus, "Humanity is not human." This notion would suggest that although there remains one human race, there are varying degrees of ideal humanness, and that until one is able to truly image God through the indwelling presence of Christ, that same individual remains less than human.[392] We must therefore treat these difficulties by examining other historical world religions and modern approaches to the *Imago Dei*, in addition to carefully investigating the specific manner in which the human development movement outside the Christian faith bears witness to Jesus Christ.[393]

---

[392] I am not specifically treating the status of infants or those without the mental capacity to make the conscious decision to receive Jesus Christ as their Lord and Savior. In summary, I take the position of Erickson in reflecting upon the fact our Lord did not regard children as under condemnation. Given that the mental acuity of adults with severe mental disorder is akin to a child, I extend the same grace to them, with hopeful expectation they will inherit the Kingdom of God (Mt. 18:3, ⸱9:14). Erickson, p. 581.

[393] I focus my world religion investigation on primarily the Hindu and Yogic traditions of ancient India in addition to the modern crosspollination of Yogic texts commonly studied in a traditional Western Yoga school. The Self-help and Human Development movement subject matter experts I refer to include the prominent scholars Dr. Wayne Dyer, Dr. Deepak Chopra, and Dr. Michael Hawkins. Collectively, these scholars acknowledge the humanness of Jesus but not the fullness of his deity as proclaimed by the Christian faith (Heb. 1:1-3; Col. 2:9).

The modern self-help and human development movement teaches that throughout the course of history there have been certain individuals who have been channels of great power—the spiritual principles they taught during their relatively brief existence within human history managed to influence the lives of millions of people over long periods of time.[394] These figures often loom larger than life and include such household names as the Buddha, Lord Krishna, Mahatma Gandhi, Mother Theresa, and Jesus Christ.[395]

Yet even the enormous power that was realized through the life of Bill W., the co-founder of Alcoholic Anonymous, could arguably be included in the list of great spiritual accomplishments. Bill. W.'s work and dedication to treating alcoholics has positively touched the lives of countless people, and *Life Magazine* lists him as one of the 100 greatest Americans who have ever lived. Bill W. has even been credited with being the originator of the entire self-help, self-mastery, and self-improvement movement.[396] From this perspective, many modern spiritual teachers and human development experts make the argument that although Jesus Christ is a great human to emulate (or image), and a man that possessed an extraordinarily high level of spiritual awareness (he was enlightened), he would nevertheless be included alongside other ancient and modern masters of metaphysics and Universal Truth teaching (he was a Guru).[397]

---

[394] Hawkins, David R. *Power vs. Force* (New York, NY: Hay House, 2002), p. 180.

[395] The significant point here is that rather than being *elevated in his deity* Jesus is seen only in the realm of his humanity. Although Jesus "spoke on his own authority" (Mt. 7:29) he is relegated into the company of those who speak on the authority of others.

[396] Hawkins, p. 186.

[397] Hawkins argues in *Power vs. Force* that the *teachings* of Jesus Christ, despite his short three-year period of ministry, managed to transform much of Western society, and that man's encounters with these *teachings* have remained at the center of Western history for the last 2,000 years. Yet Hawkins makes this observation independent of the biblical revelation of Jesus Christ, and thus sidesteps the implications of *who Jesus Christ is*. As a case in point, Hawkins lists the spiritual accomplishments of Bill W., the co-founder of AA, alongside the spiritual accomplishments of God Himself in the person of Jesus Christ.

A THIRD JESUS

ANOTHER OBJECTION TO THE CHRISTIAN CONCEPT of the *Imago Dei* is what modern spiritual guru Deepak Chopra has labeled the *Third Jesus Movement*. Rather than addressing the humanity or deity of Jesus, a third model of His life and teaching is presented. The essence of the position is that if you were to meet Jesus in the world today as He was in "real life," there would be a gap between your level of consciousness and His. Closing the gap in consciousness is not a matter of performing more *outward acts of spiritual or religious devotion*. To emulate Jesus and achieve His level of God-consciousness, a disciple must turn their attention inward through the practice of expanding one's awareness through meditation.

In this sense, whereas traditional Christianity sees Jesus Christ as the only means to reach the Father (John 14:6), the *Third Jesus Movement* reduces the path of God-consciousness to a matter of increasingly expanding one's level of meditative awareness.[398] Rather than knowing God *through Jesus*, one could foreseeable come to know God by *acting like Jesus*.

Deepak Chopra is the modern mouthpiece of India's great lineage of spiritual teachers who taught that God-consciousness was possible through meditative practices designed to "saturate the brain with a divine presence."[399] An illustration common in traditional Yogic philosophy is that of a diamond and a lump of coal. Although God's light shines equally on all His children, due to delusive ignorance and a false belief in separateness, not all of God's children receive and reflect His light alike. The association then becomes clear: Sunlight falls on both a lump of coal and a diamond, but only the diamond is able to absorb and reflect the light in brilliant beauty. Although the carbon in the coal has within it the ability to become a diamond, its sense of isolation from the light prevents the necessary transformation. The spiritual principle involved is that in order to receive and reflect God's light, you must come to realize that God is already at work within you, and this is achieved though the practice of meditation.[400]

---

[398] Chopra, Deepak. *The Third Jesus* (New York, NY: Three Rivers Press, 2008), p. 44–45.
[399] Iyengar, B. K. S. *Light on Life* (New York, NY: Rodale Press, 2005), p. 79.
[400] Gates, Rolf. 200-hour Yoga Teacher Training Course, Santa Cruz, CA, student guide to Yogic philosophy and Asana.

Enlightenment and God-consciousness is thus a matter of experiencing "that which we heal in ourselves we heal in the world, and that which we heal in the world, we heal in ourselves."[401]

The final objection resides within the historical realm of emerging Christian theology and serves the purpose of consolidating much of society's misperceptions of mankind's ability to image God apart from Jesus Christ. The traditionally held construct of *kenoticism* taught that Jesus Christ—the Second Person of the Trinity—laid aside His divine qualities for human qualities instead. In other words, the incarnation itself consisted of an exchange of His distinctly divine nature for human characteristics.[402]

This view of an exchange of divine for human attributes runs parallel to much of historical Yogic philosophy in addition to more modern *Third Jesus Movements*. In this sense, the idea of a successive yet reductionist appeal to God becoming man, then man being "absorbed back into God," is akin to the modern Yogic notion that humans are similar to "drops of water," and that through meditation a spiritual devotee can be absorbed back into the "Ocean of God."[403]

REBUTTAL TO OBJECTIONS

THESE OBJECTIONS COLLECTIVELY RESULT IN a pileup of misinformation and minimization of the world's independent, supreme authority on both God and mankind. For it is exactly Jesus Christ's *deity* that allows Him to perfectly represent *essential humanity*. In other words, it takes the Creator to explain the nature of that which is created. There was a two-fold work that Jesus accomplished in His lifetime. On one hand, Jesus had to reveal in His life the likeness and image of God, so that mankind might finally understand what a life in that likeness and image was.[404] Yet Jesus did more than provide humanity

---

[401] Gates.

[402] Erickson, p. 668.

[403] Erickson succinctly describes *kenoticism* as the idea that "with respect to certain attributes Jesus is God, then he is a human, then God again" (Erickson, p. 668). This description influenced my use of the *successive yet reductionist* illustration of God becoming man (successive) then returning to His divine nature (reductionist – i.e., returning to God). The Yogic concept of "drops of water absorbed into the ocean" was a predominant illustration taught by B. K. S. Iyengar.

[404] Murray, p. 1380.

with the exact representation of God—Jesus also provided humanity with an image of the ideal human being (Hebrews 1:1-3, 5:8-9; 1 Corinthians 11:1).

And herein we crash into our society's predominant roadblock to understanding *who Jesus Christ is* and *what He came to do*. For if Jesus Christ is lumped into the long lineage of other spiritual masters, gurus, and self-help experts, then the point will have been entirely (and perhaps conveniently) missed. In this sense, the danger is not so much in *denying or rejecting* Jesus. Rather, it is accepting Jesus on terms that are in contradiction to those that He established during His ministry on Earth. Thus, the Christian evangelist today must realize that the great majority of objections to the idea that Jesus is mankind's best source for knowledge about God (John 1:18) and mankind (1 John 4:2) is not in direct opposition to the biblical claim itself.

Rather, it is sidestepping the issue altogether by assembling a hodgepodge of spiritual teachers—a little of this and a bit of that—and creating onto oneself a false image of a godlike teacher. In other words, the danger is in accepting the *teaching of Jesus* absent the *teacher Himself*. This is all to say that the question of our Lord—"Who do you say I am?"—continues to reverberate through the ages in a rhetorical and haunting tone (Matthew 16:13-15).

TAKING IT TO THE STREET

DR. DAVID HAWKINS' WORK IN THE FIELD of applied kinesiology now serves the purpose of providing modern scientific context for our transition of *Imago Dei* from theory to application. Kinesiological experiments have convincingly proven that there is a significant and decidedly different bodily response to all manner of *original* and *forged creation*.[405] In one particular experiment, subjects tested strong when looking at an original painting and weak when looking at a mechanical (forged) reproduction. Even the most precisely computer-generated reproduction of an original piece of art resulted in the test subject immediately going weak. Perhaps even more intriguing was that this testing outcome was consistent regardless of pictorial content—an original painting of a disturbing object would make the test subject go stronger than a forged copy of a pleasant one.[406]

By way of juxtaposing modern scientific knowledge across the revelation of biblical history, let us consider the implications of Hawkins' remarkable discovery in the context of David and Goliath. When David requested permission from King Saul to fight against Goliath, it was granted on the condition that David "dresses up" in Saul's armor (1 Samuel 17:38). David momentarily consented, donning the armor, but then exclaimed, "I cannot go in these.... I am not used to them" (1 Samuel 17:39).

Reverse engineering this moment in time through the lens of modern kinesiology leads us to a most startling realization. The donning of the armor was akin to forgery—the attempt to alter human identity by making a change from the "outside in" rather than the "inside out."[407] With the armor in place, David went weak. When the armor was removed, David became strong. Although

---

[405] Hawkins, p. 190. The testing procedure includes a test subject and tester. The tester will press down on the test subject's outstretched arm to determine strength or weakness. Positive stimuli result in the arm going "strong" while negative stimuli result in the arm going "weak." A "strong arm" is firm against resistance while a "weak arm" will immediately fall even with the slightest amount of applied pressure.

[406] Hawkins, p. 190.

[407] Incidentally, this breakthrough in kinesiology also gives incredible credence to the Lord telling Samuel, "Although people look at the outward appearance, the LORD looks at the heart" (1Sa. 16:7).

seemingly counterintuitive to the precepts of modern warfare, a hidden spiritual key is discovered. Any meaningful change in a human being's essential nature will only result from a fundamental reconstruction within their *inner man*.[408]

And herein we discover the hinge-point to the profoundness of understanding *Imago Dei* in the context of human development. No amount of "armor" will result in a change in the nature and constitution of mankind grand enough to substantiate the true image or likeness of God. In this sense—and indeed this contention may navigate us into uncharted waters—even the isolated adoption of Christ's teachings *absent Christ Himself* would not be sufficient to image God (John 2:23-25; Matthew 12:34).

The Bible teaches that steadfast adherence to religious customs and traditions were not what our Lord required of His followers (John 3:1-7). Rather, Jesus was much like a force field in which His disciples would be drawn into—a Body in which their very cells and molecules would reside within. Jesus knew that the change in mankind required to conform to the true *Imago Dei* was so great that Jesus Himself would need to take up residence within the believer (Luke 19:5). Whitewashed tombs were not what God was desirous of; a complete death of the *old man* (Romans 1:18-3:20) and resurrection of the *new man* would be needed (Romans 3:21-26).

From this perspective a most starling conclusion is reached. In anticipation of our Lord's arrival, mankind remains blind from birth (John 9:1). In this sense, how can a blinded humanity hope to image God apart from the indwelling presence of God Himself? Lest we fool ourselves, blindness only begins to portray the fallen state of mankind; not only are we blind, but neither can we hear or speak (Mark 7:31-37). The independent hope and exclusive only way for such a depraved being to image a perfect God is for the divine presence of God Himself to live within us.[409]

Although a seemingly radical proposition, the basic premise of this concept was at the heart of our Lord's teaching (John 7:37; 15:1-8). Being the very embodiment of the power by which God makes and sustains the world, Jesus

---

[408] Needless to say, the implications of modern kinesiology for the Apostle Paul's claim that "we are God's handiwork" is astounding (Eph. 2:10). When mankind looks at the true image of who we are in Jesus Christ, we become strong. When mankind distorts the image we "forge our attempt" and become weak.

[409] This idea was shaped in my mind through the work of Michael Heiser in his book *The Unseen Realm*, pp. 58–60.

promised that when *grafted onto Him* a new life would begin (John 15:5). Flipping the illustration upside down implies that apart from Jesus we have *no life*. On the positive application of the lesson, professing the Lordship of Jesus and receiving the Holy Spirit leads to *new life*. The Spirit of God within the believer is akin to sunlight that illuminates the air on a bright day. Take away the sun, and you take away the light. To press the metaphor even further—God within us is like the air we breathe. Take away the oxygen, and we are no longer alive.[410]

Lest we remain blind from birth, we now turn our attention to the manner in which Jesus healed those who called on His name in preparation of the miraculous new life that awaits His indwelling presence. Jesus healed the blind man with a combination of *spittle* and *mud*. The spittle represents the divinity of Jesus— the mud His humanity. The merging of the two, when *rubbed into the blind man's eyes,* became the first step in the awesome transformation from blindness to sight. The final step, however, is even richer in spiritual significance. Jesus required that the man go and "wash in the Pool of Siloam" (John 9:7). The word "Siloam" means "sent" and provides immediate correlation to the very purpose of Jesus's life—the God-Man who was "sent" to save mankind (Jn. 3:16). With our Lord's humanity and divinity now assimilated into the blind man's eyes, the final moment of transition into a new life of *Imago Dei* took place when the man submerged himself into Jesus—the One sent from God to enable humanity to faithfully image God Himself.

---

[410] The sermon Podcast by Bishop Robert Barron on June 4, 2017, helped me frame and conceptualize the ideas and illustrations in this paragraph.

PART EIGHT

THEORY TO APPLICATION

---

12 BIBLE LESSONS FOR CHURCH INSIDE THE GYM

SECTION SUMMARY:

THE BEST PART OF understanding theology and Holy Scripture are sharing the magnificent lessons of the Bible in ways that people can relate to. In other words, it is the combination of theology and exposition (also referred to as homiletics or preaching) that changes people's lives. This being the case, CrossFit gym owners are in a unique position to share the Gospel with a demographic of people who are predisposed for physical, mental, and spiritual growth. In short order, the whiteboard can be transformed into a pulpit, and rubber mats, medicine balls, and plyometric boxes into pews from which athletes can hear the Word of God. As a starting point for Christian leaders intent on bringing the *Gospel into the gym,* the following section contains twelve Bible lessons that can theoretically cover one year (assuming meeting once a month for a year) of Church attendance within a respective gym.

LESSON ONE

TURNING WATER INTO WINE

LESSON ONE
TURNING WATER INTO WINE

MY BROTHERS AND MY SISTERS, may the grace of our Lord Jesus Christ, the love of God, and the fellowship of the Holy Spirit, be with you (2 Corinthians 13:14). I want to study with you today the topic of *Turning Water into Wine*. Let's begin our journey together in an environment that many of you are very familiar with: the CrossFit culture. In the sport of gymnastics, an athlete on the high rings is awarded points based on three factors: risk, originality, and virtuosity. Of these three attributes, the most coveted and illusive is virtuosity—*the ability to do the common uncommonly well.*

These days, I'm more and more impressed and amazed by the greater implications of virtuosity, especially considering that the majority of the things that I do are fairly common to begin with. Let me explain, for I suspect that we are more alike than we are different in this regard.

All through the day, I breathe. Breathing is common. In fact, through the miracle of human creation, God enabled the life-sustaining function of breathing to happen beneath our consciousness and perceptive awareness. It's hardwired into our bodies' automatic nervous system. However, even though it happens automatically—and in this sense it's very common—I can bring my awareness to the next breath that I take, and I can take it with an intention of virtuosity. In other words, I can breathe—which is common—uncommonly well.

How about thinking? Have you noticed that you tend to think a lot—or is it just me? Research has demonstrated that the average person has about 60,000 thoughts a day. What's even more interesting (and concerning) is that of these thousands of thoughts, nearly 80 percent are negative, and 95 percent are the same repetitive thoughts as the day before. This leads me to believe that just like breathing, thinking is also among a long list of "common" shared human experiences.

However, just like I can overcome the mundane and common function of breathing, I can direct my awareness to the next thought in my mind, and I can think that particular thought with the intention of virtuosity. In this sense, I can think—which is common—uncommonly well.

Without a far stretch of the imagination, the implications for how much of our life is common is staggering. Unless we are exceedingly careful, our life can become victim to being lived out in a common, routine, average, and predictable way. However, when we remember that we are made in the image of God Himself, then every cell in our body should cry out: VIRTUOSITY!—a hunger and thirst for the uncommon life! Because if there is one thing we very quickly learn about our God, it is that He is uncommon! And as image bearers of God, our life should be uncommon as well.

THE BASICS—WHY WE STUDY THE BIBLE

MY BROTHERS AND MY SISTERS, I propose that we approach our study of God's Word—which for some of us may very well be a common activity—with the spirit of virtuosity. How is this possible?

I propose that there are three steps we can take together to accomplish this goal:

1) Mastery of the Basics: Why the Bible?
2) Knowing the Gospel Message
3) Understanding the Purpose of Jesus Christ's Signs and Miracles

The first reason that we study the Bible is that we believe it is the Word of God. However, we need to be able to conceptualize what this effectually means in our life—and understand it with a level of maturity that empowers us to share our faith with others. This was the expectation of Jesus Himself who encouraged (and commanded) believers to go into the world and to "teach others to obey the commands I have given you" (reference Matthew 28:19–20). So again, why the Bible?

Let's open the Bible to see what it has to say about itself. In his letter to Timothy, the Apostle Paul wrote, "All Scripture is God *theopneustos*" (2 Timothy 3:16a).

The word choice that Paul settled on to describe and explain the inherent power of the Scripture was a word that he essentially made up! The Greek word *theopneustos* is composed of two other Greek words: *Theo,* which means God or Supreme Being—and *pneó,* which means either wind, spirit, or breath. When we combine these two thoughts into one word, we have the essence of "God Breathed" or "Inspired by God."

However, God did not actually write the words of Scripture. The verse we just read was written by the Apostle Paul, a human being just like you and me. To get a sense of how a human being can write the Word of God, let's turn to the Apostle Peter, who explained it like this: "No Scripture came about by the prophet's own interpretation of things. For prophecy [or Scripture] never had its origin in the human will [or intellect] but the prophet [or author] though human, spoke from God as they were carried along by the Holy Spirit" (2 Peter 2:20–21—my interpretation within brackets).

So here we have it. God's Spirit—the eternal Third Person of the Trinity— "carried the author along" by empowering them for the purpose of recording God's thoughts onto paper—becoming what we now have the opportunity to study in the form of God's Word.

This means that the Word of God is alive! It's a supernatural book full of power—transformational, life changing, and life-giving power. In theology, we refer to God's Word as *special revelation.* This means that unless and until we *open the Bible,* we will remain unaware of *revelation* about God that, at the most fundamental level, we need to know. You see, my friends, by implication and definition, *revelation* means that a person other than the observer needs to take the initiative. In this sense, revelation is God making Himself known to us. And we need to know God!

By way of illustration, when I was in the Drug Enforcement Agency (DEA), I had our nation's highest level of security clearance. I had a need to know matters of national security. It's the same for you, my brothers and sisters—and for everyone under the Sun. The revelation in the Bible is something that we *need to know* because we need to know God! And most supremely, the Bible reveals to us the nature, image, and exact representation of God in the person of Jesus Christ (Hebrews 1:1–3; Colossians 1:15–19, 2:9).

Jesus Himself said, "I am the way, the truth, and the life. No one comes to the Father except through me" (John 14:6). If we reverse engineer what our Lord said, then until we read the Bible, we will never have an opportunity to receive the revelation of the Gospel message, and we will never know God.

Continuing the thought of Paul, once we know where the Bible *comes from,* we next need to understand *what the Bible does.* Yes—you heard me correctly—the Bible actually does something! How is this possible? Well, the Bible is not your normal book. The same Power that wrote the Book is alive in the Words the book contains. When we receive the Gospel message, supernatural things begin to happen in our life. Look closely at what Paul was describing: "All Scripture is God-breathed and is useful for teaching, rebuking, correcting, and training in righteousness" (2 Timothy 3:16). Let's take an exegetical approach and unpack what Paul meant:

1) Teaching = God shows me the path;
2) Rebuking = God shows me where I got off the path;
3) Correcting = God shows me how I can get back on the path; and
4) Training = God shows me how I can stay on the path.

Now that we know what the Bible is, and what the Bible does, we need to turn our attention to the One unifying message that the One original Author wants you to know. And in this sense, the Author wants you to Know His Word, and His Word is His Son. This is why the Apostle John wrote that "In the beginning was the Word, and the Word was with God, and the Word was God.... And the Word became flesh" (John 1:1, 14). This means that "the Word is a Person!"

In the spirit of virtuosity—doing the common uncommonly well—let's turn our attention to the heartbeat of the Bible, the Gospel message of Jesus Christ.

UNDERSTANDING THE GOSPEL

IN ACTS 2, THE APOSTLE PETER succinctly and beautifully described a three-step movement that best illustrates the biblical Gospel message. The first movement is the revelation of what God did. Peter declares that Jesus was "a man accredited by God to you by miracles, wonders and signs" (Acts 2:22). Apart from simply being another prophet or religious teacher, Jesus walked the earth in "the fullness of the deity in bodily form" (Colossians 2:9) and was "the radiance of God's glory and the exact representation of His being" (Hebrews 1:3).

Peter's declaration is echoed throughout the New Testament—Jesus was the God-Man to whom all religions point (John. 14:6) and to whom all the prophets testified (Hebrews 1:1–3). Peter explains that according to God's plan and "with the help of wicked people," Jesus was put to death on the cross (Acts 2:23). However, far from being the end of the story, God raised Jesus from the dead in fulfillment of Old Testament prophecy (Acts 2:24–31; cf. Romans 8:11–13) and exalted Him to the right hand of the Father (Acts 2:32–33; cf. Romans 8:34). Finally, Peter addresses the "amazement and astonishment" of the people's response to the pouring of the Holy Spirit onto the faithful believers (Acts 2:12) by announcing that "Jesus received from the Father the promised Holy Spirit and has poured out what you now see and hear" (Acts 2:33).

The second movement of the Gospel involves mankind's response to what God did. Echoing the words of the Jewish converts in Scripture who were "cut to the heart" (Acts 2:37a), humanity cries out in brokenness, despair, and acknowledgment of our need for a savior: "Brothers, what shall we do?" (Acts 2:37b). The result of the Spirit-empowered confession of sin is a fundamental change of heart about who God is. Far greater than a mere change of mind, the new believer's change of heart results in an outward change of behavior that springs from an inward change of desires (1 Samuel 16:7; Proverbs 4:23; Ezekiel 36:26–27). The radical change of heart results in receiving through faith the revealed message about Jesus Christ (Acts 2:41; 2 Corinthians 4:5–6). The objective outward demonstration of faith in Jesus is made visible by baptism and entry into a new community of faithful believers (Acts 2:41; cf. 1 Corinthians 12:12–14).

The final movement of the Gospel involves joyfully receiving what God graciously gives. Through the propitiatory death of Jesus, all who call on His name in faith receive forgiveness of sins (Acts 2:38; cf. Romans 10:13). The subsequent result is the gift of the Holy Spirit and the new life and heart of Christ (2 Corinthians 3:18; cf., Colossians 3:10). The regenerated Spirit-empowered heart is given for the purpose of living a new life as a Christian and participation in the body of Christ (Acts 2:41–47; cf. 1 Corinthians 12:12–27). The Bible teaches that the "heart" often referred to the genuine self as distinguished from appearance, identification with the mind, and physical presence. The "heart-self" had its own nature, character and disposition, which affected the thoughts, words, and actions of the individual. Therefore, a believer whose "heart" is changed through the power of the Holy Spirit will never be the same again (Psalm 51:10; Ezekiel 36:26–27).

The good news of the Gospel is that the savior of mankind has come. In the life, death, and resurrection of Jesus Christ, the faithful believer can be reconciled with God (2 Corinthians 5:11–21; 1 Peter 2:24) and transformed into His image (2 Corinthians 3:18). The promise of the Gospel is that through the process of "putting on the new self" (Colossians 3:10) we will "gradually become brighter and more beautiful as God enters our lives and we become like Him" (2 Corinthians 3:18 MSG; cf. Acts 2:38–47).

WATER INTO WINE

THE APOSTLE JOHN WROTE THAT the purpose of Jesus Christ's signs, wonders, and miracles was "so that you may believe that Jesus is the Messiah, the Son of God, and that by believing you may have life in His name" (John 20:30–31). This is the hermeneutic by which we should interpret every sign, demonstration, and miracle of Jesus. In some way, shape, or form, everything that Jesus said and did was recorded by the Author (upper case "A") so that we could know Him, believe in Him, and have a relationship with Him.

That being the case, let's direct our attention to the wedding feast and Jesus Christ's first miracle. What was Jesus up to? I mean, after all, what we have at first glance is Jesus helping people enjoy their wedding celebration by increasing the amount of wine they can drink. And reflecting on my wilder years on the UC Santa Cruz water polo team, I know firsthand what happens when there is "an increase in wine" at a party. People get drunk! So—again— what was Jesus up to?

The Apostle John was a brilliant theologian. Everything that he wrote in his Gospel and letters contains a rich mosaic of meaning. In the Old Testament, the Prophet Isaiah described the union of God and His people in the context of a wedding celebration. In the 62nd chapter of his prophecy, we find the words, "Indeed, the LORD will delight in you and make your land His spouse. As a young man marries a virgin, your builder will marry you" (Isaiah 62:4). Think for a moment about the magnitude of these words—the One who made the universe—described by Isaiah as "the great builder"—will marry His people. This means that God wants you to participate in His life—and God is eternal. God wants you to participate not just in a human and temporal life on earth, but also in a miraculous way, a divine and eternal life with Him in Heaven.

It's also important that we see the unique biblical view of God presented by Isaiah and all the prophetic voices of Scripture—that God is not some distant deist who winds up the universe and lets it go. The God of the Bible is no "big bang" or blind force, or unified field of consciousness, or cosmic energy. Rather, the God of the Bible is a person who speaks, and acts, and makes an astonishing declaration that He wants to marry His people.

Remember, my brothers and sisters, that Jesus is not just one more prophet in a long lineage of prophets. He is not a spiritual guru or a great teacher. Jesus consistently speaks and acts in the very person of God, and therefore we should not be that surprised that this motif of marriage and wedding comes up in His ministry—in particular, the start of His ministry as recorded by John. In other words, Jesus is in His very person the marriage of divinity and humanity. He's the wedding of Heaven and Earth.

On the other hand, sin is the great divorce—the great chasm of division between God and man. And with the arrival of Jesus, we see the reversal of the pain and anguish of the separation—we are able to see and participate in the reconciliation, the reunion, and the marriage of Heaven and Earth.

Now, what do we see as the narrative unfolds? Jesus's mother is the first to speak in John's telling of the story, and what she says is very direct and to the point. She says, "They have no more wine" (John 2:3).

Remember once again, my friends, that we are reading from the Gospel of John, so we are compelled to approach everything that we read on a number of different levels. On the surface level, Mary is indeed commenting on a social disaster. Running out of wine at a wedding celebration would be embarrassing for the new couple. So on one hand, Mary is asking Jesus to do something very practical. But if that's all she is doing, then we might feel a bit let down, or even worse, to be led to believe that the purpose for a relationship with Jesus is mainly for practical, everyday purposes. In modern speech, it's asking Jesus to do a beer run. So there must be more!

And, of course, there is much, much more. Wine in the Bible is a symbol of exuberance and the intoxication of the divine life. When God is with us, and His Spirit is residing within us, we are lifted up, made joyful, full of life, transfigured, and our minds and our hearts refreshed and renewed. So from this perspective, when Mary says, "they have no more wine," her words are of profound significance. She's speaking at the symbolic and spiritual level about a great lack at the heart of the entire human race. Perhaps some of you today who are reading these words are experiencing the spiritual pain of "having no more wine." In other words, maybe you've run out of the divine life. To a varying degree, the entire human race is experiencing the results of sin, which as depicted in the vivid imagery of our Gospel story, is the result of the great divorce and having "no more wine."

Now, when we see Mary's words within this theological framework, then we can get a sense of the purpose of Jesus's question, "Woman, why do you involve me?" (John 2:4). The implied answer is that Mary is involving Jesus, because the lack of wine has everything to do with Him. In addition, in John's archetypal positioning of Mary, we now understand the greater implications of who Mary becomes in the story. Mary is Eve, the mother of the living—she is the archetypal woman of the Old Testament. As Eve was the mother of the fallen humanity, Mary will become the mother of the renewed humanity.

I think that Mary's next and last line in the Bible is one of the most overlooked and profound verses in the totality of Scripture: "Do whatever He tells you" (John 2:5). On one level, Mary instructs the stewards to do whatever Jesus tells them. However, as we read the story more symbolically, Mary speaks for all the great voices of the Bible—Abraham, Isaac, Jacob, David, Moses, Isaiah, Jeremiah, and Daniel. Mary speaks for the prophets of the Bible who, in more or fewer words, proclaimed, "Do whatever God tells you and you will find life." Think about the implications of Mary's words in your own life as you read the story! Mary is your symbolic, spiritual mother, who says about her Son, our Lord Jesus Christ, "do whatever He tells you."

What Jesus does next is so crucial for us to see and understand. Jesus instructs the servants to fill six stone water jars that were used for ceremonial washing with water. Now, this might seem like a trivial detail. However, by now, we should be anticipating that there is something more afoot—something very important just underneath the surface. And indeed, my friends, there is.

The jars are evocative of the entire tradition of Jewish religion, tradition, and ritual. In other words, the jars and the "ceremonial washing" are representative of the ways that the Israelites tried to make themselves acceptable to God. Now, on one hand, it's important to see that Jesus is not discounting this. However, what's intriguing is that Jesus now elevates and transfigures it. Jesus wants humans to bring Him all of their power and resources, because Jesus wants to transform, and magnify, and multiply everything we bring Him, precisely so that Jesus can take what we give Him and use it to expand His Kingdom. And when the servants do what Jesus asks, what happens? There are 180 gallons of wine—representative of the essence of the divine life—the wine that never runs out.

As we reach the end of our Gospel story and first Bible lesson, let's pause for a moment and reflect on the purpose of John's Gospel. Everything that John wrote—and remember that everything John wrote was God-breathed—was written so that you would believe that Jesus is the Messiah, the Son of God, and that by believing you would have life in His name.

This being the case, what does the author of this Gospel message have for us today? My brothers and sisters, I propose that God wants you to understand that when you "confess with your mouth that Jesus is Lord, and believe in your heart that God raised Jesus from the dead" (Romans 10:9), you get hooked up to the divine life. In the spirit of today's message, you are married to God, and in this sense your life never runs out. When we join ourselves by grace, through faith in Jesus, the celebration of our new life begins.

YES and AMEN.

LESSON TWO

DEVELOPING SPIRITUAL VISION

LESSON TWO
DEVELOPING SPIRITUAL VISION

THE WORD OF GOD:

As Jesus went along, he saw a man blind from birth. His disciples asked him, "Rabbi, who sinned, this man or his parents, that he was born blind?"

"Neither this man nor his parents sinned," said Jesus, "but this happened so that the works of God might be displayed in him. As long as it is day, we must do the works of him who sent me. Night is coming, when no one can work. While I am in the world, I am the light of the world."

After saying this, Jesus spit on the ground, made some mud with the saliva, and put it on the man's eyes. "Go" he told him, "wash in the Pool of Siloam (this word means "Sent").

So the man went and washed, and came home seeing.

His neighbors and those who had formerly seen him begging asked, "Isn't this the same man who used to sit and beg?" Some claimed that he was, while others said, "No, it only looks like him."

But the man himself insisted, "I am the man." The formerly blind man continued to explain; "The man they call Jesus made some mud and put it on my eyes." Then some of the Pharisees turned to the blind man and said, "What have you to say about him?"

The man replied, "He is a prophet." Then a second time the Pharisees summoned the man who had been blind. "Give glory to God by telling the truth."

The man replied, "If this man were not from God, he could do nothing."

Later in the day Jesus found the man and said, "Do you believe in the Son of Man?"

"Who is he, sir?" the man asked. "Tell me so that I may believe in him."

Jesus said, "You have seen him; in fact, he is the one speaking with you."

Then the man said, "Lord, I believe," and he worshiped him.

(John 9:1–7, 8–9, 16–17, 24–33, 35–38).

MY BROTHERS AND MY SISTERS, may the grace of our Lord Jesus Christ, the love of God, and the fellowship of the Holy Spirit, be with you (2 Corinthians 13:14). I want to study with you today the awesome topic of *Developing Spiritual Vision.*

According to the Gospel of Matthew, the very first word that our Lord spoke at the inception of His public ministry was *"metanoeō."* In context, Jesus said, *"metanoeō* for the Kingdom of Heaven has come near" (Matthew 4:17). The Greek word *metanoeō* means: "To change your mind *for the better."* In this sense, Jesus said, "Change your mind for the better, because I am here." My friends, I am so encouraged by this verse! I believe this verse contains a fundamental principle of the Christian faith that can completely transform your life. Speaking about Himself, Jesus explained that in order to have a relationship with Him, your thoughts about Him would need to change—and they would specifically *need to change for the better.*

In the spirit of radically changing the way we think about God, let's turn our attention to today's magnificent Gospel reading from the Gospel according to John.

In our Bible study today, we come face-to-face with a historical account of Jesus healing a man born blind. The Apostle John explained that all of Jesus's miracles were recorded so that "you may believe that Jesus is the Messiah, the Son of God, and that by believing you may have life in his name" (John 20:31). In this sense, the story of the healing of the man born blind serves the purpose of authenticating the life, ministry, and divinity of Jesus. However, what are the implications of this ancient story for you right here, and right now? In other words, what effect is this story meant to have on your life today? How is an ancient story about a man born blind meant to impact and change you—especially if you can already see?

Let's discover the deeper meaning of this miraculous healing by taking the story one step at a time.

The Bible says, "As Jesus went along, he saw a man blind from birth" (John 9:1). I propose that this is a significant detail in the story because Jesus takes the initiative in healing the blind man. Furthermore, John clues us in to the fact that the blindness has afflicted the man from the moment of his birth. We draw from our Lord's observation of the blind man two conclusions:

On one hand, Jesus can see and relate to our suffering. Jesus loves us and wants us to be well. However, it also means something so much more. We are also dealing here with an archetypal story of coming to spiritual vision. Perhaps even more important than healing us physically, Jesus wants to heal us spiritually.

Jesus came into the world to redeem and heal all of humanity—not merely this one isolated individual some 2,000 years ago. In other words, in this particular story, we are all meant to identify with the man born blind. You are the blind man in this story, and Jesus longs to restore your sight. The Bible teaches that we have all been born blind through original sin. This means that humanity suffers from a compromised will and an obscured mind. Simply put, although the eyes in your head might be working just fine, due to the sinful nature of your heart, you still do not see things right, and in this sense you remain blind. Sin blinds us and we are unable to clearly see the deepest truth and reality of the way things are meant to be.

Lest you think I am being cynical or overly negative about the sinful state of human nature, consider the words of the Apostle Paul, who wrote; "Everyone has sinned and we all fall short of the glorious standard of God" (Romans 3:23). And the worst problem of all is that this spiritual blindness and sin have been part of our human nature from the very beginning. We are all born spiritually blind and we don't even know it.

When Jesus observed the suffering blind man, He said, "While I am in the world, I am the light of the world" (John 9:5). This is an astonishing announcement of the divinity of Jesus Christ. As I've said many times in sermons and lectures, Jesus is not just another spiritual teacher, or guru, or even a prophet. Jesus is so much more than this, and in this magnificent self-description, we discover that Jesus is the light by which we see the true nature of God. Jesus is the light that provides you with vision. Jesus is the light by which you safely walk. Jesus teaches you how to see, how to move, and how to act—and this is all conditioned upon Jesus's ability to illuminate the world. My friends, this also implies that without Jesus in your life, you are living in the dark.

Let's turn our attention for a moment to our Gospel author—the Apostle John. In studying the Scriptures, this is an extremely important exegetical detail. By understanding the mind of the original author, we can gain a better understanding of the inspired thoughts within the author's mind at the moment their words were recorded.

What we know for certain about John is that he had an affinity for the Old Testament, in particular, the account of God creating the world. This claim is based on the fact that in the Gospel of John, there is very often a correlation between the life of Jesus and the creation of the universe that we read about in Genesis. For example, John's Gospel begins with the words, "In the beginning" (John 1:1), and this is the same sentence found at the commencement of the entire Bible. John in this sense depicts Jesus as the creative Word of God. And in Genesis, what is the first thing that God creates? According to Genesis, Chapter 1, verse 3, God first created light: "God said, 'Let there be light,' and there was light" (Genesis 1:3). And now we see that the same God who created light in the beginning of the world manifests Himself as the Light of the World in the Person of Jesus Christ.

Throughout the Bible, this is why light is associated with God and the things of God. So in this sense, our Gospel story today is about re-creation, new beginnings, making things new and right, and starting over. The link to creation is then intensified by the next detail we come across. The Gospel story continues and reveals that, "Jesus spat on the ground, made some mud with saliva, and put it on the man's eyes" (John 9:6). This is clearly another connection to Genesis. In Genesis, we read that God fashioned the first human beings from the clay of the earth and then breathed His breath of life into them (Genesis 2:7). In this sense, what we have in the healing of the man born blind is a recapitulation of the creation of the very first human being. John describes for us how the Son of God—the Word became flesh—is going to restore the spiritual life of the man born blind.

This beautiful detail is one of the ways that this story immediately impacts your life today. Jesus is going to restore and complete His creation. This is what Jesus does in your life. He restores and completes you. Now think about this for a moment: If Jesus completes you, this must mean that without Jesus you are incomplete, and in the context of today's Gospel story, without Jesus you are blind.

Friends, let me share with you one of my favorite details about this healing. Notice that Jesus is bringing healing to the man from out of His own substance—which John illustrates as the "spittle" or "saliva" of Jesus. In the beginning, God created *ex nilio*—the Latin theological expression for "out of nothing." Creation was achieved through the Word of God, and the Word came forth out of God's own substance. And now Jesus Christ, as the "word became flesh," does the same thing. The spittle of Jesus comes from His own inner life and mixes with the earth. The inner substance of Jesus is then rubbed into the blind man's eyes. In this sense, healing is a result of an immersion into Jesus and His creative power.

What happens next is another wonderful detail in the story. Jesus then tells the man to wash in the pool of Siloam (John 9:7). In the event we overlook or miss the significance of this moment in the healing process, John goes so far as to tell us that the "Pool of Siloam" means, "Sent." Why do you think that John mentions this detail? When we see the "big picture" of John's Gospel, we notice that Jesus continually refers to Himself as the one who has been sent by the Father. In fact, one of the most well-known Bible verses speaks to this very point: "For God so loved the world that *He sent His one and only son*" (John 3:16—my emphasis). Therefore, the Pool of "Sent" is also a symbol of Jesus. The man born blind is now washed in the pool of Christ—a clear indication and reference to baptism. Theologically, baptism is a complete immersion into the life of Christ (reference Romans 6:1–11). This is when the sight is restored: "So the man went and washed, and came home seeing" (John 9:7).

It would be easy to think that the story has reached its pinnacle moment—the man who was born blind can now see. However, what we in fact discover is that the story is just getting started. John wants us to see (no pun intended) that this physical healing is an invitation to spiritual healing. In other words, there is a connection between what is happing physically and what is happening spiritually—and it is the spiritual healing that has the greatest impact on us.

Let's begin by noticing the effect that the healing had upon the friends and family of the blind man—in addition to the formerly blind man himself. When the blind man's friends and neighbors ask: "Isn't this the same man who used to sit and beg?" (John 9:8) there were mixed answers. Some people said, "Yes," while others said "No." What's astonishing is the answer the formally blind man gives when people ask, "Is this the same guy?" With great simplicity the man says, "I am the man" (John 9:9). Now, the English translation here misses a very crucial detail. The man's response in the Greek is *Ego Eimi,* which literally translated into English means "I am" or "I am the one." Once again, when we see this detail within the "big picture" of John's Gospel, the implications are staggering.

The "I Am" phrase is used up and down throughout John's Gospel by Jesus to describe Himself: For example, Jesus says, "I am the bread of life" (John 6:35)—"I am the good shepherd" (John 10:11)—"I am the vine" (John 15:5). And most significantly, just moments before the healing of the blind man took place, Jesus said, "Before Abraham was, I am!" (John 8:58). We notice that once again John is bringing the reader back to the Old Testament.

The "I Am" statements of Jesus—and of the blind man—echo the Old Testament book of Exodus when Moses asked God for His name, and God replied, "I AM WHO I AM" (Exodus 3:14). For our purposes, this means that in addition to his physical healing, the blind man is also experiencing spiritual healing. Having been immersed into the life of Christ, the blind man gains his physical and spiritual vision and is able to see. Through his restored sight, the man is now able to identify with the very life of Jesus. In other words, in addition to having new physical vision, the man has a new spiritual life (reference Romans 6:1–11).

As we progress through the remainder of the story, we are witness to deepening and expanding stages of spiritual vision. This is why the story is relevant for us today. We catch a glimpse of the path of discipleship. We are privy to what happens to our vision and our life as we follow Jesus.

When asked by family and friends the question, "How were your eyes opened" (John 9:10), the man's first response is: "The man they call Jesus made some mud and put it on my eyes" (John 9:11). As we unpack this seemingly insignificant verse, we discover there is so much here. Notice the man initially puts his answer into the realm of what other people profess about Jesus. He says, "The man *they call Jesus.*" This is remarkable, because Jesus demands an answer directly from us, not based on what other people think. For example, in the Gospel of Matthew, Jesus first asks his disciples what *other people say* about Him. After their answer is given, Jesus intensifies the question by asking, "But who do you say I am?" (Matthew 16:15)

This means that Jesus wants a personal relationship with you. Jesus wants each of you to be able to speak from experience about who He is. As we will study throughout this book, this is why faith in Jesus is more than simply following the teaching of Jesus. It's one thing to know about Jesus—it's another thing altogether to actually *know Jesus.*

To this very point, notice what happens next. The Pharisees are mad because Jesus healed on the Sabbath, and they question the blind man about the incident. Remember that the man's first response to the question about Jesus was, "The man they call Jesus." However, here we see something significantly different. When the Pharisees press him with the inquiry, "What have you to say about Him?" The man replies, "He is a prophet" (John 9:17).

Do you notice what's happening here? It started with, "this man Jesus" but then the man's spiritual vision begins to deepen. Now, the answer is more profound and more in alignment with a personal relationship: "This man is a prophet." When the Pharisees argue further the man says, "If this man were not from God He would not be able to do anything" (John 9:33). This answer portrays an even deeper and more profound level of vision. First Jesus was "a man," then "a prophet," and now "Jesus is from God." Having found his physical vision, the man is coming to deeper and deeper levels of spiritual vision.

Now we approach the true pinnacle and climax of the story. Rather than being asked by other people about Jesus, Jesus Himself asks the man: "Do you believe in the son of Man?" to which the formerly blind man says, "Who is he that I may believe in him?" Jesus replies by saying, "You have seen him; in fact he is the one speaking with you now" (John 9:36–37).

This is the moment of the man's complete spiritual–vision restoration. The underlying invitation behind Jesus's question is this: "Are you ready to accept the One?" In other words, Jesus asks, "Are you ready to accept the One who is more than a mere man, more than a mere prophet, more than someone who is from God? Are you ready to accept the One who is God?"

The blind man's response captures the heart of discipleship: "I do believe" the man says, and then he worshipped Jesus. And that's the whole point of the story. Yes, this is an ancient story about physical healing. But at a deeper level, this is a story about *metanoeō—about changing our mind for the better* and coming to see spiritually who Jesus is.

And how do we know that we are seeing Jesus correctly? Much like the formerly blind man, we know that we see clearly when we worship Jesus as Lord and God.

YES and AMEN.

LESSON THREE

A FAITH THAT WORKS

LESSON THREE
A FAITH THAT WORKS

Our first reading takes place just moments before the epic battle of David and Goliath. Due to the fact that David was not enlisted in the Army of Israel, he needed the permission of King Saul to face Goliath in single combat. Let's drop into the scene together to get a better sense of exactly what happened on that historic day.

THE WORD OF GOD:

Saul replied, "You are not able to go out against this Philistine and fight him; you are only a young man, and he has been a warrior from his youth."

But David said to Saul, "Your servant has been keeping his father's sheep. When a lion or bear came and carried off a sheep from the flock, I went after it, struck it and rescued the sheep from its mouth. When it turned on me, I seized it by its hair, struck it and killed it. Your servant has killed both the lion and the bear; this uncircumcised Philistine will be like one of them, because he has defied the armies of the living God."

Saul said to David, "Go, and the LORD be with you."

Then Saul dressed David in his own tunic. He put a coat of armor on him and a bronze helmet on his head. David fastened on his sword over the tunic and tried walking around, because he was not used to them.

"I cannot go in these," David said to Saul, "because I have not tested them." So he took them off.

(1 Samuel 17:33–39)

Our second reading is from the Apostle Paul's letter to the Churches in Rome:

"The night is nearly over; the day is almost here. So let us put aside the deeds of darkness and put on the armor of light … Clothe yourselves with the Lord Jesus Christ, and do not think about how to gratify the desires of your flesh." (Romans 13:12, 14)

MY BROTHERS AND MY SISTERS, may the grace of our Lord Jesus Christ, the love of God, and the fellowship of the Holy Spirit, be with you (2 Corinthians 13:14). I want to study with you today the topic of *A Faith That Works*.

The more time I spend studying the Old Testament, the more I see that it is full of pictures and images that achieve their greatest portrait of truth in the New Testament. In this sense, although the Old Testament contains biblical history, it also provides a framework for many great theological principles that are more fully developed in the New Testament and life of Jesus Christ. Although the story of David and Goliath may be very familiar to you, in this study, I hope to educate and inspire you to fully understand the magnitude of the spiritual significance that this epic battle contains. Speaking from my own experience in both reading and teaching the story of David and Goliath, we often settle for a very superficial understanding of the story rather then investing in the greater realization that God wants us to achieve. If we think the story is simply a childhood fable about overcoming your giants, then we still have a lot to learn.

Reflect back on the former interpretations of the story of David and Goliath that you have heard about, read about in a book, or seen on TV. If your experiences were anything like mine, you were likely told to "be like David" in an assortment of different ways. Be brave. Believe in yourself. Have confidence in your abilities. Make the most of what you already have. And the most biblically inaccurate interpretation of all: have faith in yourself.

Reaching these conclusions from the text manages to completely miss the point of the story. They instill in us a false sense of hope and tend to focus our attention on the size of our faith, rather than the size of our God. In other words, if we base our chances of victory over Goliath on anything other than God, then it's only a matter of time before our faith falls apart. Allow me to painfully state what should now be obvious: a lot of faith in the wrong thing is a recipe for disaster. However, even faith *the size of a mustard seed*—which is really small—in the right thing (or should we say right Person) is enough to move mountains. That's because it is not the size of our faith that matters. *It's the Size of the One we put our faith in that ultimately makes the difference.*

Here is the main point that I want to make in today's study: if you want to have "A Faith That Works," then you need to take the emphasis off the faith itself and instead focus on the One True God who makes your faith work.

HISTORICAL CONTEXT

THERE ARE TWO OVERLOOKED details of the story that I must bring to your attention. The first is an ancient artifact of biblical era warfare that was referred to as decisive single combat. It was common practice for large armies in the era of King David to select representatives to enter into combat against each other—in these cases, the winner of the match would determine the outcome of the forthcoming battle. This is why in 1 Samuel 17:8–9, Goliath says, "Choose a man to come and fight me. If he is able to fight and kill me, we will become your subjects; but if I overcome him and kill him, you will become our subjects and serve us."

In other words, Goliath was prepared to be the representative of the Philistines, and he wanted the Israelites to select their own representative. The terms of the fight were straightforward: If Goliath won, then the Israelite nation would surrender and serve the people of Philistine. On the other hand, if the representative of the Israelite army won, then the Philistine nation would surrender and serve Israel. This meant that the two opponents that faced each other in one decisive battle would determine the outcome for the lives of the thousands of people that each of them represented. That's a lot of pressure, if you ask me!

There is one other matter of historical significance—the specific location where the battle was taking place. The battle lines had been drawn up in a territory that was already owned and occupied by the nation of Israel—and it was in this place that rightfully belonged to the people of God that Goliath was breathing out defiance and insult.

Although the ancient concept of single decisive combat and the historical locality of the battle may seem like small background details, they are in fact absolutely crucial to understanding key themes that run throughout the entire Bible:

1) As believers in Jesus Christ, the battle has already been won;
2) As believers in Jesus Christ, we live in enemy occupied territory.

In order to have a faith that works, we need to learn how to clearly navigate the battlefield in front of us. This means that we must read the story of David and Goliath both *literally* and *symbolically* in order to apply the spiritual lessons of this great moment in history into our life.

Let's begin with the obvious. Symbolically, who do you think Goliath is in the story? The Scriptures reveal that when Goliath stepped into sight, "All the men of Israel fled from him and were so afraid" (1 Samuel 17:24). Although the people of Israel were in a special covenant relationship with God, the story teaches us that they were held captive in the bondage of fear before Goliath and all that he stood for. This means quite simply that Goliath represents Satan. We know this because biblically speaking, Satan aims to stand against the people of God.

This realization leads us to another startling discovery and a fundamental fact of the Bible. The issue is not about the forces of evil arrayed against the forces of good—rather it is about the devil against God. This means that on the battlefield that fateful day all those thousands of years ago, a decisive battle did in fact take place. What happens to the prince of the powers of darkness—represented by Goliath—happens to all who follow him. And what happens to our Lord—represented by David—happens to all who follow Him.

You see, my brothers and sisters, in this Old Testament story, David represents the New Testament picture of Jesus Christ. However, there is more! On one hand, David is a picture of Jesus Christ who overcame the universal Goliath of sin and death. On the other hand, David is a picture of every child of God who is being made One with Christ through faith and obedience to Him. The Bible teaches that Christ is the Head of His Body. This means that because Jesus achieved victory over the sin and death of Goliath, than through faith in Jesus, so have you.

Through Christ, every battle you ever face during you life has already been won. Are you starting to see the implications of what it means to have "A Faith That Works?" No matter how big the Goliath of your fears may appear to be, the battle is not yours to begin with. In fact, just seconds before David approached Goliath, he said: "The battle belongs to the LORD" (1 Samuel 17:47). This is crucial to understand, remember, and apply in your life. When you catch yourself in a moment of fear, anxiety, uncertainty, or self-doubt, it should be a "red-light warning" that you have put your faith in the wrong thing.

I remember that when I was going through U.S. Army Basic Combat Training, my senior drill instructor said to me, "Everyone wants to be in the Army on a bright, sunny day." Following a dramatic pause he said, "But there aren't any sunny days in the Army!" In my walk with God, I've found that it's the same thing. It's easy to have faith when everything is going well and it's a bright, sunny day outside. However, what happens when your world falls apart and there is hurricane beating down your door? *That's when the size of your faith really doesn't make much difference. What matters is the size of your God.*

I'd like to share with you a few other key details from the story of David and Goliath that direct our attention to Jesus Christ. We have already discovered that David was not in the army. This certainly begs the question—what was David doing on the battlefield? We find our answer in 1 Samuel 17:17. David's father Jesse told David, "Take this roasted grain and loaves of bread to the battlefield for your brothers."

I am immediately awestruck by two incredible New Testament insights into what this means: First, the Scripture teaches us that Jesus Christ Himself is the "bread of life" (John 6:35). The bread that Jesse gave David was to be given to his brothers who were fighting in the battle. Symbolically then, the Old Testament bread that David brought to his brothers becomes the New Testament bread of life that sustains believers in Jesus Christ during every battle we ever face. Second, the Apostle John wrote: "The Father sent the Son to be the Savior of the world" (1 John 4:14). In the same way that David was sent by his father to be the "savior of the day"—Jesus Christ was sent by His Father to be our savior right here, and right now.

OUR IDENTITY IN CHRIST

AS WE APPROACH THE END OF our lesson, I want to bring your attention to one final metaphor from the Old Testament account of David and Goliath. You will recall that King Saul tried to dress David up in his suit of armor. And what was David's response? Although he momentarily donned the armor of Saul, David quickly realized he could not fight in it. The armor did not fit. Specifically, David said, "I have not tested this." This is a significant detail. David was not about to put his faith in a coat of armor that he had not tested. David's faith rested in God alone.

On the other hand, Saul was convinced that his armor would protect David. Remember, it was after Saul had said to David, "Go, and the LORD be with you" that he dressed up David in his armor. This meant that Saul had the formula—but he lacked the faith.

I really want you to get this point. It's absolutely crucial.

Saul believed in God, that was not the issue. The issue was that despite *believing in God,* Saul still put his faith in his armor. Like most things in the Old Testament, the armor in this case represents more than just a bronze helmet or breastplate. The bronze armor that Saul had put his faith in is distinctly different than the "breastplate of righteousness" that the Apostle Paul speaks about in the New Testament (Ephesians 6:14). Saul's bronze armor symbolizes all our idolatrous attempts to put our faith in something other than God Himself. The bronze armor is our bank account, our jobs, our homes, our health, our fitness, our network of friends, our social status, and our ego. The bronze armor is anything and everything other than God.

So on one hand, we see that David took off the armor that he did not identify with. But that begs the question: Where was David's identity? Clearly, it was in God.

My brothers and sisters—I put this question before you: What does this ancient story have to do with you today?

Before you answer the question, I want to introduce you to another character on the battlefield that day that you might not know about. His name was Jonathan. He was Saul's son—next in line to the throne—and he was a witness to everything that happened during the battle of David and Goliath, and everything leading up to it. Following David's victory, the Bible says, "Jonathan made a covenant with David because he loved him as himself. Jonathan took off the robe he was wearing and gave it to David, along with his tunic, and even his sword, his bow, and his belt" (1 Samuel 18:1–4).

The King James version of this text says, "Jonathan loved David as his own soul." In other words, Jonathan had knit and bound his soul together with David's. Jonathan saw something in David that he wanted in his own life. The fact that Jonathan gave David everything that identified his royal succession to the throne is extremely significant. Jonathan was giving away all of the carnal weapons and associations with Saul in order to cast himself in faith upon David. Jonathan no longer wanted to be identified with his old self. He wanted a new identity.

CONCLUSION

WHAT HAPPENED TO DAVID ON the battlefield that fateful day happened to David's people. David's victory was their victory. The people of Israel who were assembled on the battlefield didn't even need to lift a finger. David did all the work for them. If King David is an Old Testament picture of King Jesus, what does this ancient story mean for believers today? It means that what happened to the King of Kings at the cross in His death, burial, resurrection, and ascension is something that happens to all those who put their faith in Jesus.

In Paul's letter to the Churches in Rome, this is what he referred to when he wrote that believers should "clothe yourself with the Lord Jesus Christ" (Romans 13:14). The believer's identity is now in Jesus Christ—this means the deliberate, conscious Lordship of Jesus over all our desires, motives, and deeds.

Rather than reading the story of David and Goliath and walking away thinking, "I want to be like David," we should in fact pray that through God's grace we could be like Jonathan. Becoming like Jonathan means that we love the Lord Jesus with all our soul, our entire mind, and every bit of our strength. In the spirit of Jonathan, we love Jesus so much that "our soul is knit to His." We love Jesus so much that we lie down at his feet in worship, and we surrender before him every idolatrous item of faith that is in opposition to Him. Just like Jonathan surrendered his tunic and his robe—representing the artifacts of his ego—we must likewise surrender every aspect of our life to God. When we come to God in faith through Jesus Christ, God will give us new life and new power that we could never achieve on our own. In other words, we win the battle, not according to anything that we do, but according to the victory that Jesus has already won.

YES and AMEN.

LESSON FOUR

STAYING WITH THE LORD

LESSON FOUR
STAYING WITH THE LORD

Our Gospel reading for today's Bible study is from the Gospel according to John.

THE WORD OF GOD:

The next day, John was there again with two of his disciples. When he saw Jesus passing by, he said, "Look, the Lamb of God!" When the two disciples heard him say this, they followed Jesus. Turning around, Jesus saw them following and asked, "What do you want?" They said, "Rabbi" (which means "Teacher"), where are you staying?" "Come," he replied, "and you will see."

So they went and saw where he was staying and spent that day with him. It was about four in the afternoon. Andrew, Simon Peter's brother, was one of the two who heard what John had said and who had followed Jesus.

The first thing Andrew did was find his brother Simon and tell him, "We have found the Messiah" (that is, the Christ). And he brought him to Jesus.

(John 1:35–42)

MY BROTHERS AND MY SISTERS, may the grace of our Lord Jesus Christ, the love of God, and the fellowship of the Holy Spirit, be with you (2 Corinthians 13:14). I want to study with you today the magnificent topic of *Staying with the Lord.*

If you recall from our second Bible lesson, the very first word that our Lord spoke at the inception of His public ministry was "*metanoeō.*" In context, Jesus said, "*Metanoeō* for the Kingdom of Heaven has come near" (Matthew 4:17). The Greek word *metanoeō* means "to change your mind *for the better.*" In this sense, Jesus said, "Change your mind for the better, because I am here." My friends, I am so encouraged by this verse! I believe this verse contains a fundamental principle of the Christian faith that can completely transform your life.

Speaking about Himself, Jesus explained that in order to have a relationship with Him, your thoughts about Him would need to change—and they would specifically *need to change for the better.*

The great theologian and author A.W. Tozer wrote: "The thoughts that come into your mind when you think about God are the most important thing about you." You see, my friends—the thoughts in your mind about God do not change God. The thoughts in your mind about God change you, and they change you for the better or worse, and in direct proportion, to your better or worse thoughts about God. Therefore, of first priority in today's study is adopting two ideas about God that can fundamentally change the way you think about Him as well as the way you think about yourself.

The first thought (or idea) about God that I want you to adopt is this: God knows you better than you know yourself. The second thought about God that I have for you is that He wants you to *stay with Him.*

Let's take these big ideas (or thoughts) one at a time. First things first—the idea that God knows you better than you know yourself. In order to understand what this big idea means, we need to go back in time: 2,000 years back in time!

In biblical-era Palestine, ox yokes were made of wood. In application, a farmer brought his ox to a carpenter to begin the process of measurement taking and a careful study of the animal's disposition, characteristics, strengths, and unique tendencies. The yoke was then meticulously constructed so that it would fit well and not hurt the neck of the animal. In other words, each yoke was handmade with love and a great deal of care so that it would perfectly fit and support the ox.

During a Bible study with my dear friend and pastoral-mentor Chaplain Richard Johnson, he shared with me an ancient legend that Jesus, Himself a carpenter, fabricated the finest ox yokes in all of Galilee, and that men from all over the country came to Him to buy the best yokes that human hands could make (refer to the William Barclay NT Bible commentary on Matthew, Chapter 11).

Similar to our business practices today, shops had signs above their door in biblical times. In Messianic–Rabbinic verbal tradition, it is said that the sign above the door of our Lord's carpenter shop in Nazareth read: "My yokes fit well." Although this ancient story is not from Scripture, we should certainly take note that Jesus often referred to Himself as a yoke. For example, in the

Gospel of Matthew, Jesus said to his disciples, "Take my yoke upon you and learn from me, for I am gentle and humble in heart, and you will find rest for your souls, for my yoke is easy, and my burden is light" (Matthew 11:29–30).

In my daily walk with Jesus, I have happily discovered that He tailor makes for me a "yoke" of exactly what I need at the exact time I need it. In other words, it's as if Jesus whispers in my heart: "Let me tailor make for you what you need to go through life." How can Jesus possibly "tailor make for me what I need?" Well, of course He can! God created me—He knit me together in my mother's womb; He knows the sound of my voice; He's counted every hair on my head—which is all to say that He knows me better than I know myself. My brothers and sisters—it is the same for you. God knows you. God loves you. God sees you and He knows the sound of your voice. And God wants to have a relationship with you, which leads us to our next big idea. You see, my friends, the first big idea is about God loving you. The second big idea deals entirely with your response to God's gracious love.

The second big idea about God that I want to share with you is that He wants you to *stay with Him.* To understand the significance of what this means in your life, let's turn our attention to our Gospel reading, and the awesome exchange between Jesus and His disciples.

To begin, we must understand and appreciate the brilliant mind of our Gospel author, the Apostle John. A literary master, John wrote his Gospel and epistles in such a way that he designed sacred word-pictures that are meant to reflect and portray our relationship with God. The scene that we read in our Gospel took place in the vicinity of the Jordan River, where John the Baptist was baptizing. John is standing with two of his disciples and observes Jesus walk by (John 1:36). Without hesitation, he tells his followers, "Behold the lamb of God" (John 1:36).

My friends, let's not kid ourselves about what John the Baptist said. There is something terrifying in this description. John is telling his disciples that Jesus is the one who will be sacrificed for the sins of the world. The "lamb of God" is not a gentle and meek image. In fact, it's quite the contrary. As the lambs were brought into the temple to be slaughtered for the sins of the people, Jesus would be put to death for the sins of the world.

So who were these two disciples with John? For our purposes tonight, these two figures become immediately important. These two disciples are a symbolic, spiritual, and archetypal reflection of you. So who are they? The two men with John were youthful people—maybe 18 or 19 years old—and a fine example of the spiritual seekers of their time. They were young people filled with spiritual enthusiasm and passion for meaning, purpose, and mission in life. This is what had brought them to John the Baptist in the first place. Now do you understand why you are meant to identity with these two disciples? These two young people are trying to figure life out—just like you are! These disciples are a reflection and image of you trying to figure it all out and find the secret to life. And so, when their great mentor says, "There is the lamb of God," they drop everything and go after Him. Keep in mind that these two young people were Jews, so they knew exactly what John meant by Jesus being the "Lamb of God." But nevertheless, they followed after Him.

This is such a beautiful detail of the spiritual life. We need to have the courage to follow Jesus even when it does not make perfect sense. Even when we don't know exactly where we are going, we still need to follow after Him. Even when what He says goes against the grain of what we want to do—we still need to listen, follow, and obey.

The Bible speaks a great deal about the human quest for God. And we see it here, in the way these two young people run and follow after Jesus. However, the Bible is not primarily about our quest for God. *It's about God's quest for us.* And we are able to see it here in John's Gospel picture. The two young men initially come running after the Lord. However, notice what happens next. Jesus turns on them and asks them a question (John 1:37–38).

In the traditional discipleship path of other world religions, it is the devotees who ask the guru questions about life. But here, we see something entirely different. We see God asking the question. And what a question it is! Jesus asks, "What do you want?" (John 1:38). Let that sink in for a few moments. Allow this to be a point of meditation for the remainder of your life. And even right now, in this very moment that you read these words—allow this profound question to sink deeply into your heart. Imagine that our Lord is right in front of you, and He turns and asks you, "What do you want? What are you seeking?"

What would you say in that moment? That is why this question is so important! What would you say? It's interesting that very often in life, we do have a sense of what we want. However, after you get what you want, have you noticed that you want something else, or more of what you already received? Or perhaps you no longer want what you had toiled so long and hard to get! In the context of profession, material wealth, relationship, and education—we know the answer to these questions.

But the Lord brings the question from the head to the heart. And because it's a question of the heart, it's unlikely that you would respond to Jesus by saying "Lord, I want more money, more pleasure, more success." Something in your heart would give you a gentle nudge and say, "This is definitely not the right answer." We know at a place deep within us that these things do not give us the joy we are looking for. That being the case, would you ask for contentment, peace, joy, meaning, mission, or purpose in life? After all, these desires seem to be more "spiritual" and in alignment with the path of discipleship.

Well, perhaps. After all, these are certainly legitimate answers. But listen to how the disciples respond. It's a great question from Jesus, and it's going to be a great question from the disciples! The disciples answer the Lord's question with a question of their own: "Rabbi, where are you staying?" (John 1:38).

How interesting to answer a question with a question—not to mention the seemingly childlike quality of the question. To ask where Jesus is staying? Couldn't these two guys come up with a better question? Here is the Lord of the universe asking, "What do you want? What are you looking for?" And they ask, "Where are you staying?"

But I propose their instincts were in fact completely right. Just a few moments before this scene took place, we read one of the most important verses in the entire Bible: "The Word became flesh and dwelt among us" (John 1:14). What does this mean? The "Word," or *Logos* in Greek, speaks to the creative power and mind of God. And here is the main point that John makes about the Word of God. God's Word—His nature, power, and mind—became flesh. This means that God's Word does not remain something abstract and distant, something you have to go off and search for or read about. "God's Word became flesh and *dwelt among us*." God's Word became a person whom we can see, and touch, and talk to. In fact, this is exactly what the Apostle John explained about Jesus in his first epistle: "We offer you the word of life. The word that our eyes have seen, that we have looked upon, that our hands have touched" (1 John 1).

There is the entire story of the Bible in a single verse—the entire message of the Christian faith in one line of Scripture. The word became flesh, a person, whom we can have a relationship with. And that is why the instinct of the disciples in this scene is so good. They know the answer to the deepest longings and desires of their heart are to stay with Jesus. In other words, what they are searching for is not going to be found in a book, or spiritual laws, or new sets of ideas. Nor was it going to be found by walking a particular religious path. It was to be found in the person of Jesus Christ—and by staying in fellowship with Him.

This detail of the story reminds me of the first time I met Londale Theus. I was a brand new deputy sheriff in Santa Cruz County. In the roll-call room, I noticed a flyer advertising a "Knife Defense Course for Law Enforcement" offered by the Santa Clara County Sheriff's Office. The course topic sounded intriguing, and the following week I drove to a small martial arts dojo near Hayward to experience the training firsthand. Within just moments of meeting the course instructor, Londale Theus, I knew that I had found a man I wanted to follow. Londale was the first American law enforcement officer to become a certified Krav Maga Black Belt with the prestigious Krav Maga Association of America. He had served as a sergeant on the Santa Monica Police Department SWAT Team and had a commanding presence that I had never seen before (and have not since). So what did I do following the course? I followed Londale! For the next eight years, I spent as much time with him as possible. In other words, I did everything I could to *stay with him.* This means that the lessons of the dojo were secondary to the lessons of life that Londale was imparting to me.

This remains a key feature of discipleship and in our relationship with Jesus. In fact, this is exactly what we read about in the Book of Acts. In describing what happened when John and Peter went on trial before the Sanhedrin, Luke wrote that, "When they saw the courage of Peter and John and realized that they were unschooled, ordinary men, they were astonished and they took note that these men had *been with Jesus* (Acts 4:13—my emphasis). It was not about books, or about laws, or commands, or lessons. What set John and Peter apart was the fact that they had been with Jesus. *They had stayed with Him.* And Jesus had completely transformed their life.

Here is another great detail from our Gospel reading. John tells us that is was 4PM. Nothing is incidental in John. Just like every brushstroke of a master painter is important, every detail that John writes is significant. We hear that Jesus died at 3PM (Mark 15:33). Therefore, spiritually, the 4PM time designates and speaks to what comes after the Cross. It designates the time of the resurrection. This means that these two disciples who come and stay with Jesus at 4PM are evocative of all of us who want to stay with the Lord. Why is this the case? Because Jesus Himself said, "Very truly I tell you, it is good for you that I am going away. Unless I go away, the Advocate will not come to you; but if I go, I will send Him to you" (John 16:7). In other words, when Jesus was on the earth, His presence was limited to His physical locality. In order for the disciples to *stay with Jesus,* they needed to be physically in His presence. However, for the followers of Christ after His ascension to the Father, we now experience personal fellowship with Him, through the Holy Spirit, every moment of our life.

So how do you stay with Jesus and experience the fellowship of the Holy Spirit? Daily prayer. Meditation. Fellowship with other believers in the Body of Christ. Reading from the Word of God. Attending Church, ministry gatherings, and Bible studies, just like you are doing right now. These are all ways of staying with the Lord and welcoming the Spirit of God into our life.

It is at this point in our Gospel story that we discover the name of one of the disciples. Andrew is the brother of Simon (Peter). The first thing that Andrew does upon leaving the presence of Jesus is to tell his brother about the person he had met. "We found the Messiah!" (John 1:40–41). Notice the enthusiasm and passion for evangelism! And it wasn't that Andrew simply told his brother about Jesus. He did more than that. The Bible says that Andrew *brought his brother* to Jesus. I am so inspired by Andrew's heart for evangelism.

When you see a great movie, you want to tell people about it. When I found Krav Maga and CrossFit, I wanted to share them with everyone. In fact, they are what inspired me to open my CrossFit and Krav Maga studio in Santa Cruz! It seems to be built into our psyche—when we find something beautiful that we love, we want to share our good fortune with others. And that's what happened here. Once the disciples stayed with Jesus, they wanted to share what they had found with their family and friends.

And notice the person whom Andrew brought to Jesus. It was none other than Peter, the "rock" that Jesus would build His Church upon. It was Peter, who would be the chief of the Apostles. It was Peter, the apostle who would become the focal point of the Church. It was Peter, who would walk on water! And without Andrew and his heart for evangelism, then Peter would have never come to Christ.

This is our call to action. We all know someone like Peter. Each one of you knows someone whom you should bring to Christ. Do you think that Andrew could have imagined the power and magnitude of what his introduction to Jesus would result in for Peter? This leads me to believe that we never know the long-term effects that our Gospel-centered words of encouragement and love will have in the lives of other people. And lest you think that you are not gifted enough to preach the Gospel, take comfort in these words of Saint Francis of Assisi: "Preach the Gospel at all times. When necessary, use words." In application within your life, this means that just like Peter and John, people should look at you and think: "This person has been with Jesus."

And so here we have it, my brothers and sisters. God loves you. In fact, He loves you so much that He asks you, "What do you want?"

And how you answer this question might just change your life.

YES and AMEN.

LESSON FIVE

SITTING AT THE FEET
OF JESUS CHRIST

LESSON FIVE
SITTING AT THE FEET OF JESUS CHRIST

THE WORD OF GOD:

As Jesus and His disciples were on their way, He came to a village where a woman named Martha opened her home to Him. She had a sister called Mary, who sat at the Lord's feet listening to what He said. But Martha was distracted by all the preparations that had to be made. She came to Him and asked, "Lord, don't you care that my sister has left me to do all the work by myself? Tell her to help me!"

"Martha, Martha," the Lord answered, "you are worried and upset about many things, but few things are needed—or indeed only one. Mary has chosen what is better, and it will not be taken away from her."

(Luke 10:38–41)

MY BROTHERS AND MY SISTERS, I come bearing the *euangelion* of the Bible—the Gospel of Jesus Christ. The Greek word *euangelion* means "good tidings" or "good news." The promise of the Gospel is that when Jesus Christ enters your life, your life will gradually become brighter and more beautiful as God transform you into the image of His son and you become more like Him (2 Corinthians 3:18—my interpretation).

This means that when you put your faith in Jesus, God begins the process of changing you from the inside out. In some cases, the transformation is immediate—in other cases, the process is more gradual. However, one thing is always certain: when the Spirit of God Himself dwells within you (1 Corinthians 6:19), your world is turned upside down. You begin to realize that you have new priorities. New values. New mission. New purpose. New desires. New heart. New life. The people who have known you for years are going to be astonished.

In our Bible study today, we will be seeking the answer to two critical questions that have resounding implications for our daily walk with Jesus. The first question deals with affirming the deity of Jesus Christ. Once we understand *who Jesus Christ is*, we are then prepared to ask our second question—How we can become more like Him? The answers to these profound questions have an astonishing impact on your life.

THE DEITY OF CHRIST

THE MOST CRUCIAL TOPIC IN CHRISTIAN discussion today is the deity of Jesus Christ. In theological studies, the doctrine of Christ's deity is referred to as Christology, and it sits at the very heart of the Christian faith. What sets a disciple of Jesus apart from a disciple of Lord Buddha, Lord Krishna, Lao Tzu, or any other spiritual teacher from the various world religions, is the believer's grace-empowered profession of faith that God walked the earth in human flesh in the person of Jesus Christ (John 1:1, 14; Colossians 1:15–19, 2:9; Hebrews 1:1–3).

You really need to hear this astonishing biblical claim in the fullness of what it means: Jesus was not just some extraordinary person—not even the most extraordinary person who has ever lived. Although I would certainly not argue against the fact that Jesus was indeed the greatest and most extraordinary human being the world has ever known, I contend that we cannot stop with the greatness of Jesus Christ's *humanity*. Rather, we must turn our attention to Jesus Christ's *deity*. The Christian faith rests on Jesus actually being God in human flesh (Colossians 2:9).

There are several reasons why this is important—for the purposes of our study today, I will focus on what I feel are the two most significant. The first is that Jesus allows mankind to have real knowledge of a transcendent God. Jesus said, "Anyone who has seen me has seen the Father" (John 14:9). Whereas in the past, there were many prophets who spoke the Word of God, in the person of Jesus, we now have God Himself speaking (Hebrews 1:1–3). This is why the Apostle John wrote: "In the beginning was the Word, and the Word was with God, and the Word was God … and the Word became flesh" (John 1:1, 14). This is crucial for us to understand. What instills Jesus Christ's words, teaching, and demonstrations with such power, significance, and authority over our life? It's the fact that Jesus is God! The author of Hebrews explained it like this: "Going through a long line of prophets, God has been addressing our ancestors in different ways for centuries. Recently, God spoke to us directly through His Son" (Hebrews 1:1–2 MSG).

Here is a practical way to strengthen your understanding of this verse: there was a time in human history when prophets told mankind *information about God*. However, in the incarnation, humanity now has the awesome opportunity not just to be told *about God*—now we can actually *know God*. Even more astonishing is the fact that believers are indwelt by the Spirit of God Himself (Romans 6:10–11). Listen to these words from the Apostle John to really drive home the power of what this all means: "That which was from the beginning, which we have heard, which we have seen with our own eyes, which we have looked at and our hands have touched—this we proclaim concerning the Word of Life" (1 John 1:1). Notice the descriptive words that John used: John *heard Jesus*—*saw Him* with his own eyes—*touched Jesus* with his own hands. That is remarkable because it means that for John, it was not theoretical *head knowledge about God*. John had actually experienced a relationship with God Himself.

Now, what do John's words, written two thousand years ago, have to do with you today? We needn't guess, because John plainly tells us: "So that you can experience it right along with us" (1 John 1:3). Notice John's use of the word *experience*. John wants you to have the same *experience of God* that he did! Not read about. Not talk about. Not be told about. John makes the radical claim that believer's can actually *experience* Jesus—and therefore God—in a real, tangible, and life-changing way.

The second reason Jesus Christ's deity is significant is that it compels us to *worship Him*. Jesus is not just another great spiritual teacher in a long lineage of spiritual teachers. He is not a guru. He is not a self-help master or someone who we can have a casual Sunday-school day of communion with. Because Jesus is in the *same sense* and to the *same degree* as God Himself—then Jesus equally deserves the praise, adoration, obedience, and worship that we give to God. This means that although we have many love relationships in our life, we need to love Jesus supremely, uniquely, and in a way that is unlike any other relationship we have ever known. As our Gospel story will help us understand, we need to relate to Jesus in such a way that He is the *one thing necessary*.

EXPERIENCING GOD

OUR STUDY THUS FAR HAS resulted in substantiating the biblical witness to the deity of Jesus Christ. In theological terms, the biblical witness of Jesus Christ is referred to as *special revelation*—in other words, revelation is God's own self-disclosure of truth about Himself that we would not be able to discern through any other means. Through His Word contained within the pages of the Bible, God showcases (or "represents," according to Hebrews 1:3) His nature uniquely and supremely in the person of Jesus Christ.

As important and significant as biblical revelation is, it is equally important to understand that it is only one side of the coin. This is due to the fact that revelation has the potential to result in *information* absent any *transformation*. In addition to learning about what God does, we must also pay attention to *what we do in response to what God reveals*. Borrowing from the incredible insight of C. S. Lewis: "It is Christ Himself, not the Bible, who is the true Word of God. The Bible, read in the right spirit … will bring us to Him."

This being the case, the question becomes: What is our response? How do we respond to the deity of Jesus? To answer the question, we turn to the words of Jesus Christ Himself: "Love the Lord your God with all your heart, and with all your soul, and with all your mind" (Matthew 22:37). With the great commandment of Jesus Christ as the basis for how we respond to God, let's revisit our Gospel story to help us understand how we take the *information* we have in our mind about Jesus and *move it into our heart*.

MARTHA AND MARY

OVER THE AGES, THERE HAVE been three main interpretations of the account of Jesus at the home of Martha and Mary. The first centered on the active lifestyle demonstrated by Martha, in contrast to the contemplative lifestyle demonstrated by Mary. The second interpretation focused on the priority of the spiritual life witnessed by Mary, as opposed to the distractions of the world that consumed Martha. It's interesting to note that the popular secular and business principle of focusing on *The One Thing* indirectly borrows from this interpretation of the Gospel story.

Finally, many scholars have emphasized an interpretation of the story that focused on Christ's concern for the needs of outcasts and less fortunate members of society. During biblical times, it was common for men to gather around the feet of a rabbi to receive instruction. This was the traditional locality for men, whereas women would be relegated to such tasks as preparing food and tending to other housekeeping matters. Needless to say, Mary seated at the feet of Jesus, in the company of a room full of men, ran against the socially normative practices of the time.

Although I find these three different interpretations of the story compelling, very recently, the Holy Spirit opened my eyes to yet a fourth way of understanding the Gospel account. In light of the theme of our study, *I propose that Mary and Martha could symbolically be seen as the same person experiencing two different states of consciousness.* In this sense, we are reading an ancient story about our current state of being—this makes the story immediately relevant to our daily life. Therefore, the tension between Martha's concern for the *many things* and Mary's concern for *the one thing that matters most* represent the struggle that takes place within our mind as we attempt to discern the priority of the different thoughts that consume our attention.

In other words, what we could call the fourth model of interpretation builds on the historical understanding of the duality between the active and contemplative lifestyle. The traditional view and interpretation of the early Church Fathers was their focus on the superiority of the contemplative life—in the story of Martha and Mary, this is represented in the tension between action and contemplation. Although Martha (representing action) asks Jesus to tell Mary (representing contemplation) to help her, Jesus does not allow it. Mary and Martha are sisters with distinct gifts, and they are meant to live together in harmony. Nevertheless, Jesus seems to suggest that Mary, representing contemplation, has greater access to the presence of what matters most— God Himself in the person of Jesus Christ. This is why Jesus says, "Mary has chosen what is better, and it will not be taken from her" (Luke 10:42).

Something very similar happens in the Gospel of John and the account of the resurrection of Lazarus (John 11:1–45). In this story, Martha and Mary (the sisters of Lazarus) represent two different levels of spiritual understanding— what we will define as *head knowledge* and *heart knowledge*.

Martha represents *head knowledge*—however, she may not fully understand all that she is saying or even thinking. Despite the fact that her brother Lazarus has been dead four days, she declares: "Lord, if you had been here, my brother would not have died. But even now I know that God will give you whatever you ask of Him" (John 11:22).

Martha clearly has great intellectual understanding about what Jesus is theoretically capable of. She thinks that if Jesus had arrived earlier, her brother would not have died. In her mind, she also thinks that Jesus has the ear of God, and that even now there might be something that Jesus can do, although it is not specified what that might be. In this sense, her mental posture is one of activity—she grasps the doctrine, but misses the person. This means that although our mind might be filled with ideas about God, our hearts could still remain far from Him. Martha soon leaves the scene, returns home, and tells her sister Mary, "The Teacher is here, and He is asking for you" (John 11:28).

Even the title that Martha uses in referring to Jesus—a teacher—seems to suggest her overemphasis on intellect, and less on heart. Martha now hands over the conversation to Mary and, in doing so, it is important to take notice that the transition happens in secret. This means that the shift in consciousness is not immediately available for others to see, because it occurs in the hidden depths of the believer, symbolized by Mary's posture at the feet of Jesus in the Gospel of Luke. In addition, it is important to see that Jesus calls for Mary. Whenever Jesus calls someone, it is for the purpose of participating in the fullness of His life. Although Martha went out to meet Jesus on her own— perhaps suggesting on her own terms—Mary is called by name, the way a good shepherd calls his sheep. Mary responds to Jesus according to the terms that He has established.

This means that in Mary, the believer is witness to something that we are called to model as we respond to who Jesus Christ says He is. In alignment with our interpretative key of Mary and Martha symbolically representing the same person in two different states of consciousness, we see the great chasm of difference between knowledge of the head and the wisdom of the heart. The Scripture tells us: "When Mary reached the place where Jesus was and saw Him, she fell at His feet and said, 'Lord, if you had been here, my brother would not have died'" (John 11:32).

Does this verse sound familiar? It should! That's the exact same thing that Martha said only moments earlier. However, notice the change of posture—physical, spiritual, and mental. Mary is at the Lord's feet, with the same posture we see her adopt in the Gospel story of Luke. Her confession of faith is not just a matter of reciting doctrinal truth about Jesus. Rather, Mary's faith in Jesus has moved from her head into her heart. The intimacy of Mary and Jesus in the scene is witnessed in their mutual weeping over the death of Lazarus—a key detail that was missing in the interaction with Martha.

AT THE FEET OF JESUS

RETURNING TO THE STORY OF Jesus at the home of Martha and Mary, we now have a most powerful means by which we can enter into the presence of Jesus and worship Him as Lord and God. As we seek to model the behavior of Mary and sit at the feet of Jesus, we must understand that we are not choosing between two different characters—and thus two different lifestyles—the active and the contemplative. Rather, we are distinguishing between two different states of our own consciousness. On one hand, the Gospel story reveals the importance of physically removing ourselves from those things that "worry and upset us." On the other hand, the story also reveals how easy it can be to relocate our physical body to one place, while our thinking is left behind—painfully consumed with what worries and upsets us.

How do we embrace both the physical and mental posture of Mary and learn to "sit at the feet of Jesus, listening to what He says" (Luke 10:39)? I propose that sitting at the feet of Jesus means that we enter into His presence, and this is achieved through the practice of meditative prayer. However, we must distinguish between prayer as the activity of an already busy mind, and rather see it in the context of a disciplined and regenerated heart.

For many people, prayer means nothing more than the mental activity of speaking to God. We use the same "voice in our head" that we use at every other moment throughout the day. Even if we "speak to God" through the recital of memorized verses of Scripture, the tendency of our consciousness is to use the same faculty of our mind that we use to recite any other information that we have committed to memory.

But notice in the Gospel story that Mary is not talking—she is listening. In addition, the physical posture of her body—seated at the feet of the Lord—implies a posture of rest, submission, and worship. In this sense, it is both a physical, mental, and spiritual posture.

Prayer of the heart is distinctly different than prayer of the mind, and for our purposes, will be referred to as biblical meditation. In humility, I offer this definition: *Biblical meditation is sitting in the presence of God with our mind in our heart.* To borrow from the imagery of the account of Jesus at the home of Mary and Martha—it is that point of our being where there are no divisions or distractions—we are no longer worried or upset about the many things—we have come to rest in the presence of the One who matters most. Mary teaches us that the presence of God dwells in our heart, and it is here that the great encounter with our Lord can take place. It is here that *heart speaks to heart*—it was this encounter of two hearts becoming one that resulted in such profound intimacy that Mary and Jesus wept together.

It is imperative that we understand the way the word "heart" is used in its full biblical meaning. In the Bible, the heart is the seat of human will: thus, the heart is the central and unifying organ of our personal life. Our heart is the place where God dwells and is therefore the ideal place of prayer. To pray with our heart means that we direct our consciousness to God from the center of our innermost being.

THE PRAYER OF THE HEART

WE NOW TURN OUR ATTENTION to the means by which we can pray with our heart. In other words, we discern the biblical path to meditation. There is a general framework to meditation that should be understood more as characteristics rather than hard and fast rules:

1) The prayer of the heart is nurtured by short, simple prayers;
2) The prayer of the heart is repetitive; and
3) The prayer of the heart carries no judgment or expectation.

In my meditative prayer life and walk with our Lord, I have found great comfort in the fact that it was one simple phrase on the tax collector's lips that was enough to win the mercy of God (Luke 18:9–14); it was one faithful and humble request of a thief on a cross that resulted in eternal life (Luke 23:42–43); and it was Mary's tears at the feet of Jesus that captured and moved His heart.

Following a slow and deep breath through the nostrils, the silent repetition of the ancient prayer—"Lord Jesus Christ, Son of God, have mercy on me"—can help you descend with your mind into your heart.[411] If it is more agreeable to you, a word or short verse from Scripture repeated silently with your eyes closed can achieve the same affect. In both instances, the prayer of the heart can help you concentrate and create an inner stillness and thus listen to the voice of God. On the contrary, if you sit still, close your eyes, and try to force your mind to be silent, it often results in the opposite effect—you find yourself bombarded by thoughts and ideas, and in the context of our Gospel story, you become consumed by many things that "worry and upset you." However, when you use a simple phrase such as "Lord Jesus Christ, Son of God, have mercy on me" or other verse from Scripture, it is easier to let the many distractions of life pass by without being misled, ensnared, or consumed by them. The simple and repetitive prayer of the heart can slowly empty out your crowded interior life and create a quiet space where you can dwell with God.[412]

The prayer of the heart contains one additional principle—it should take place without judgment, and without expectation. In other words, when you close your eyes and begin to repeat your prayer, do so in the spirit of Mary at the feet of Jesus. No agenda. No plans. No anticipated feelings or outcome. No expectations. And if you should notice that you are thinking a thought other than your prayer, notice that thought without judgment. Simply recognize the departure from your prayer—and then quietly and gently return to the prayer itself.

---

[411] The *Prayer of the Heart* was first brought to my attention in the masterful book *Into the Silent Land* by Martin Laird and by subsequent spiritual discipleship with Father Kevin Joyce.

[412] Henri Nouwen, *The Way of the Heart* (New York, NY: Ballantine Books, 1981), p. 74.

The beauty of the prayer of the heart (what we now refer to as biblical meditation) is that if you are faithful to the prayer and practice at regular times each morning, the prayer will open your awareness to God's active presence throughout the remainder of your day. For example, when you sit quietly with your eyes closed in the morning and repeat, "The Lord is my shepherd" (Psalm 31:1a), the Scripture takes up residence within your heart and remains embedded there throughout the day. Even while you navigate the hustle and bustle of your day, the prayer continues to maintain a steady pulsation within your heart and keeps you attuned to God's active presence in your life. In this sense, through the power of the Holy Spirit, the prayer continues to "pray itself" within you even while you fully participate in the demands of your daily life.[413]

There is one final characteristic of the prayer that serves as both a blessing for your life and the lives of all the people who God has entrusted to you. When you take your prayer, and move from your mind into your heart, you bring with you into the presence of God all the other mental preoccupations that were of concern to you before you started praying. Those concerns or thoughts in your mind that are offensive to God's Holy nature are purified from your consciousness (Psalm 51:10; 139:23–24). On the other hand, when you descend from your mind into your heart with loving thoughts of other people, then all those who have "been on your mind" are also led into the healing presence of God.

The prayer of the heart is how your individual prayer life can enrich your walk with the Lord and enable you to become more like Him. Furthermore, the prayer of the heart can be a ministry and blessing to your family, your friends, your loved ones—and the entire world. In other words, the prayer of the heart is one way that you can "Love the Lord with all your heart, with all your soul, and with all your mind—and love others as yourself" (Matthew 22:37–39).

YES and AMEN.

---

[413] I am indebted to Henri M. Nouwen and his book *The Way of the Heart* for helping me frame and conceptualize this section on *praying with the heart*.

LESSON SIX

GETTING CLOSE TO THE FIRE

LESSON SIX
GETTING CLOSE TO THE FIRE

THE WORD OF GOD:

When it was almost time for the Jewish Passover, Jesus went up to Jerusalem. In the temple courts he found men selling cattle, sheep and doves, and others sitting at tables exchanging money. So he made a whip out of cords, and drove all from the temple area, both sheep and cattle; he scattered the coins of the moneychangers and overturned their tables. To those who sold doves he said, "Get these out of here! Stop turning my Father's house into a market." His disciples remembered that it was written, "Zeal for your house will consume me."

(John 2:13–17)

When they saw the courage of Peter and John and realized they were unschooled, ordinary men, they were astonished and they took note that these men had been with Jesus.

(Acts 4:13)

That which was from the beginning, which we have heard, which we have seen with our own eyes, which we have looked at and our hands have touched—this we proclaim concerning the Word of Life.

(1 John 1:1)

MY BROTHERS AND MY SISTERS, may the grace of our Lord Jesus Christ, the love of God, and the fellowship of the Holy Spirit, be with you (2 Corinthians 13:14). I want to study with you today the topic of *Getting Close to the Fire*. Whenever we open the Word of God, we do so with the intention of "increasing in wisdom, stature and favor with God and Mankind" (Luke 2:52). To this extent, we study the *words* of Scripture. As important and valuable as this pursuit is, we need to continually remind ourselves of the miraculous truth that these words proclaim: "The Word became flesh" (John 1:14). This means that *until* and *unless* our study of Scripture leads us into the fire of a personal, loving, and saving relationship with the Word—God Himself in the Person of Jesus Christ—then the words we read in the Bible could just as easily be the words we read on our social media feed.

Before we move into an exegetical survey of our Gospel readings, I'd like to begin with two complementary illustrations—one true story from my life, and the other imaginary—to help provide context for our study. The purpose of framing our Bible study in this fashion is to really drill down and understand the difference between reading from the Word of God—and having a relationship with the Word of God Himself.

AN ILLUSTRATION FROM MY LIFE

WHEN I WAS SERVING AS a special agent in the DEA, I attended a 30-day assessment and selection course to test for a position on the Forward Advisory Support Team (FAST)—the federal government's equivalent of a domestic SWAT team. The course was held in Quantico, Virginia, during the winter of 2010. My previous assignment was on a Border Enforcement Security Taskforce on the southwest border of Calexico and Mexicali. Needless to say, I was far more accustomed and acclimated to the desert heat than the frigid East coast winters.

Part of the training, assessment, and selection included survival training in which candidates were taught how to make a field-expedient fire. In the classroom, I gained "head knowledge" about the dangers of hypothermia and the steps to mitigate the harmful effects of prolonged ice and snow exposure. Twenty-four hours later, all the head knowledge about fires, warmth, and gradually reheating the body did me absolutely no good—I didn't need theory, I needed application!

During a land navigation exercise, I'd slipped while climbing on a branch over a freezing-cold, fast-moving river and had fallen in—completely submerging myself. I had only a few minutes to reheat my body's core temperature or I was going to be in serious trouble. What I needed was a fire—not just "head knowledge" about the benefits of a fire in the context of a hypothermic episode. I needed the real thing! Thankfully, I was able to make the fire; draw near to it; and gradually reheat my body, my gear, and my uniform.

Put yourself in my situation. Imagine you are freezing cold and have a book in your hand that describes all different types of fires: small fires, big fires, fireplace fires, bonfires, woodland fires, commercial fires, beach fires, gas-stove fires—the list goes on and on. If you're minutes away from freezing to death, will the words in the book describing the varying degrees of heat produced by the different types of fires suffice to save your life? Or do you want to actually experience the heat that the words in the book are describing?

Very well, then. Now imagine that you are freezing cold and off in the distance see a well-lit fire. You are close enough to see the fire—perhaps even hear the sound of the crackling wood—but you are still too far away for the heat of the fire to effectually provide you with any warmth. What do you do? Well it's common sense—you draw near to the fire. And because you are so cold, you want to do more than simply draw near or walk by. You want to sit down and warm yourself by the fire.

THE DESERT FATHER TRADITION

NOW LET'S PRESS THIS ILLUSTRATION into a beautiful story from the Desert Father tradition. I was introduced to the Desert Fathers in my first year of seminary studies at Western Theological Seminary. The Fathers were ascetic monks who lived in the Egyptian desert during the 4th and 5th centuries. When Church persecution ended, these monks had escaped into the desert as a way of following Jesus and escaping the temptation of conformity to the world. The Fathers found inspiration in St. Paul's exhortation: "Do not model yourselves on the behavior of the world around you, but let your behavior change, modeled by your new mind. This is the only way to discover the will of God and know what is good, what it is that God wants, and what is the perfect thing to do" (Romans 12:2—New Jerusalem Bible).

And now, our story from the desert.

THREE YOUNG MEN USED TO GO and visit blessed Father Anthony every year. Two of the young men would discuss their thoughts and the salvation of their souls with him, but the third always remained silent and did not ask him anything. After a long time, Father Anthony said to him: "You often come here to see me, but you never ask me anything," to which the young man replied, "It is enough to see you, Father."

PAUSE FOR A MOMENT and reflect on your daily routine. If your days are anything like mine, then you are a very busy person. We have meetings to attend, many visits to make, many people to see. Even if our social life were temporarily put on hold during the recent shelter in place—the life of our *social media* kept plugging away, perhaps at an even more rapid pace than before. Our calendars are filled with appointments, our days and weeks filled with engagements, our years filled with plans and projects. We are pulled in so many different directions, with so many seemingly conflicting priorities, that we tend to be at the mercy of social compulsions—which ultimately results in very compulsive behavior.

I think *compulsive* is really the best term here. I know it's a harsh and accusatory term when we apply it to ourselves—but sometimes we need a wake-up call in order to produce radical change in our life. *Compulsion* points to mankind's ongoing and increasing need for affirmation. We ask ourselves, "Who am I?" And our answer is, "I'm the one who is liked, praised, admired, loved, disliked, hated, despised." Whatever your profession or role in society, what tends to matter is the way that you are perceived by others. If being busy is perceived by others as being a good thing—then you need to be busy. If having money is perceived by others as a good thing—then you must earn more money, and cling to the money you already have. If knowing lots of people is perceived by others as a good thing—then you will have to make more contacts. In other words, the compulsion manifests itself in the lurking fear of failing and the steady urge to prevent this failure by accumulating more of the same—more work, more money, more friends.

Compulsive thinking and behavior are the result of the two main enemies of the spiritual life: anger and greed. These destructive tendencies of our ego prevent us from obtaining loving relationship with ourselves, with each other, and—most importantly—with God. Reflecting on our first Gospel story, anger and greed are evocative of the livestock drivers and money marketers who take up residence within the sacred Temple Courts.

And here we must momentarily pause to prayerfully contemplate the words of the Apostle John: "The light shines in the darkness, and the darkness has not overcome it" (John 1:5). John, of course, in his use of the word "light" is referring to Jesus Christ. When we feel surrounded by darkness—the sinister feelings of anger, pride, greed, anxiety, fear, jealously, insecurity—no amount of theoretical head knowledge or self-help guru gibberish is going to work. We need to draw near to the Light—the Fire—the Word become flesh—Jesus Christ.

Within this framework and context, let's review and examine our second and third Gospel readings:

SECOND GOSPEL READING

When they saw the courage of Peter and John and realized they were unschooled, ordinary men, they were astonished and they took note that these men had been with Jesus.

(Acts 4:13)

THIRD GOSPEL READING

That which was from the beginning, which we have heard, which we have seen with our own eyes, which we have looked at and our hands have touched—this we proclaim concerning the Word of Life.

(1 John 1:1)

WHAT WAS IT ABOUT PETER and John that had the Pharisees shaking in their sandals? There was something about these two guys that was both *astonishing* and *captivating*. They couldn't take their eyes off of them. These were a couple of nobodies: no formal education, no wealth, no social contacts, no Instagram followers, and no Facebook account. So what was it about Peter and John that astonished the Pharisees? It was the fact that they had *been with Jesus*. Rather than reading about the fire, or observing the fire from a distance, Peter and John had been at the fire's side for three years. In this sense, they had set themselves on fire!

The Pharisees were astonished because they were beholding two guys who had been set on fire by God Himself. The fruit of the Spirit—love, joy, peace, forbearance, kindness, goodness, faithfulness, gentleness, and self-control (Galatians 5:22–23)—these gifts of the Spirit are not manifested by *reading about them in a book*. They happen as a result of the Spirit of God Himself taking up residence within you. The fire burns inside of you, and the heat of your life blesses others. In other words, your life is a ministry. People see Christ in you. The Message translation of the Bible describes it like this: "We are transfigured much like the Messiah, our lives gradually becoming brighter and more beautiful as God enters our lives and we become like him" (2 Corinthians 3:18 MSG).

The Apostle John describes something similar in his first Epistle (our third Gospel reading). Notice how John describes his relationship with Jesus—seeing Jesus, hearing His voice, touching His hands. It was not about doctrine, theology, laws, regulations, or rituals. It was about cultivating a relationship with Jesus. And how was the relationship cultivated, fostered, developed, and maintained? By spending time with Jesus.

My brothers and sisters, I propose that what we need *now more than ever* is to spend time—in silence and in solitude—with Jesus. To use the beautifully descriptive mandate of the Bible: "You need to sit alone in silence, for the LORD has put it upon your heart" (Lamentations 3:28). No agenda. No plans. No wordy prayers. No music. No journal. No headspace app. Just you and Jesus sitting still before God's mighty throne of grace. This is how we pick up His heat—how we warm ourselves—how we restore and refresh ourselves and recalibrate our mind and our heart. And what should we expect to happen when we spend time with Jesus? Speaking from experience—sometimes when Jesus comes into our life, he comes with a whip! He overturns what we think is important, and He reestablishes order.

JESUS AT THE TEMPLE COURTS

THE APOSTLE JOHN'S STORY OF Jesus clearing the temple is a wonderful testimony of how people who are spiritually asleep, blind, deaf, and mute (not to mention dead) do not actually look that way *on the outside.* However, no matter how grandiose our outward appearance may appear to be, it always pales in comparison to the inward disposition of our heart (1 Samuel 16:7). At the temple courts, for all intents and purposes, the people appeared to be engaged, energetic, and even keenly entrepreneurial—strategically positioned within the temple itself; the cattle yard and money market meant that those who came to *pray* first had to *pay.* Jesus's sharp rebuke, "Stop turning my Father's house into a market!" (John 2:16), seems to suggest His general dissatisfaction with the human tendency to desecrate what God makes Holy and sets apart for His purposes.

When Jesus enters the temple, His purpose is to reestablish order. To turn the temple back into the place it was meant to be—a place of worship. Now keep that image in your mind for a moment—Jesus entering the temple, driving out everything that is impure, reestablishing order, putting first things first—keep this in mind as you consider the remarkable words of the Apostle Paul: "Don't you know that your body is a temple of the Holy Spirit?" (1 Corinthians 6:19). What Paul was explaining to the Churches in Corinth was that the true dwelling place of God was no longer in the temple in Jerusalem. Now the temple is in the very bodies of the followers of Jesus. Did you hear that? As a disciple of Jesus, your body is the place where God dwells.

Jesus described it like this: "Whoever has my commands (my Words) and keeps them (lives by my Word) is the one who loves me. The one who loves me will be loved by my Father, and I too will love them and will manifest myself to them. Anyone who loves me will obey my teaching (my Words). My Father will love them, and we will come to them and make our home in them" (John 14:21–23—my interpretation within the parentheses).

I think these words of Jesus are what led Paul to explain to the Churches in Rome that believers should "Make their body a living sacrifice" (Romans 12:1). The backdrop of Paul's remarkable statement must be understood in the context of Old Testament sacrificial rituals of temple purification. The purpose of the sacrifice was that humans were signaling their desire to be one with God—the sacrifices were meant to accomplish the unity of Divinity and humanity. And now Paul exhorts the Churches in Rome that disciples of Jesus need to purify themselves! Why? Because as believers in Jesus Christ, our body is now the place where the unity of Divinity and humanity are meant to come together.

Now that we are warmed up, let's make this real. When we bring the "body-temple" insight of Paul alongside the image of Jesus clearing out the Temple Court together—we have ourselves a radical hermeneutic by which we can understand our Gospel story. If your body is meant to be a temple where God is praised, that means that every aspect of your life needs to be turned over to the Lord—everything needs to be dedicated to Him—everything needs to be a sweet offering—a sacrifice onto the Lord. Your mind. Your will. Your heart. Your body. Your business. Your friendships. Your exercise. Your entertainment. Everything in you is meant to be a living sacrifice of praise onto the Lord.

PRACTICAL APPLICATION

MY BROTHERS AND MY SISTERS—what would happen if you allowed Jesus with that whip of cords to enter into the temple of your body— what would happen? That's the purpose of the story! It's not something intriguing that Jesus did long ago. It's something He wants to do right now. Today. Maybe even in this very moment! I'll be the first to admit that it takes immense humility and courage—but as disciples of Jesus, we need to let Jesus loose in our life. We need to allow Him to knock some things over.

Did you notice the mess He made in the temple that stirred everybody up? That's going to be very similar to the mess He makes in us when we allow Him into our life to cleanse, purify, and reestablish order. This means that whatever in you that is not utterly dedicated to God needs to be transformed—turned over—and given to Him. The great theologian Abraham Kuyper put it like this: "There is not one square inch in the whole domain of our human existence over which Christ, who is Sovereign over all, does not cry out: 'Mine!'"

In the spirit of our illustration—sometimes it gets hot by the fire! But the heat is good for us. It purifies us. The implications for one of the most frequently referenced Proverbs in the warrior tradition are immense: "As iron sharpens iron, so one person sharpens another" (Proverbs 27:17). The heat and fire of the furnace is the context for the hammering and forging process the Author speaks to in this verse. Who is this Person who wants to come into our life to sharpen us? God Himself, in the person of Jesus Christ.

So now we have it, my friends. We need to spend time every day with Jesus. But how do we know we are in His presence, and that His presence is with us? Well, coming back to our Gospel story—we should expect that some pieces of our life are going to get turned upside down! Suddenly you notice that you have new priorities. New values. New mission. New purpose. New heart. New life. The very people who have known you for years are going to be astonished.

YES and AMEN.

LESSON SEVEN

SALT AND LIGHT

LESSON SEVEN
SALT AND LIGHT

Our Gospel reading for today's lesson is from the Gospel according to Matthew.

THE WORD OF GOD:

Jesus said, "You are the salt of the earth. But if the salt loses its saltiness, how can it be made salty again? It is no longer good for anything, except to be thrown out and trampled underfoot. You are the light of the world. A city built on a hill cannot be hidden. Neither do people light a lamp and put it under a bowl. Instead they put it on its stand, and it gives light to everyone in the house. In the same way, let your light shine before others, that they may see your good deeds and glorify your Father in heaven."

(Matthew 5:13–16)

MY BROTHERS AND MY SISTERS, may the grace of our Lord Jesus Christ, the love of God, and the fellowship of the Holy Spirit, be with you (2 Corinthians 13:14). I want to study with you today the topic of *Salt and Light*. My goal in today's study is to provide you with inspiration and education on the concept of your *personal identity*. Now, you might be thinking to yourself—*I already know who I am*. Reasoning from this fact, take a few moments to reflect on *who you think you are*. How do you describe yourself—to yourself? Here are a few prompt's to help you get started:

What are your greatest attributes?

What are your strengths as a person?

What are the character traits you are most proud of?

Now that you're all warmed up, consider this question—how much of your daily thinking do you allocate to thinking about the thoughts you have about yourself? Where do these thoughts come from? Are they even true? To what do they owe their source? Are they serving your greater good or are they a downward spiral of self-destruction? And most importantly, is the person who you *think you are* consistent with the person who *God says you are*?

Lest we remain under the assumption that positive self-talk and self-affirming personal descriptions are a function of modern psychology, we need to remember that the very first set of complementary questions ever asked of mankind—in other words, the first question that appears in the Bible—had to do with human identity and *who we think we are.* In the creation account of Genesis, God asked Adam the question: "Where are you?" (Genesis 3:9). The complementary set of parallel questions, "Where are you?" (Genesis 3:9), and "Who told you that you were naked?" (Genesis 3:11), speak to the physical and metaphysical nature of human identity. Our "location" treats humanity's physical posture in our relationship to God, whereas our "nakedness" speaks to our guilt and total depravity.

Now reflect back on those character traits and self-descriptive attributes that you came up with a few moments ago. Perhaps you described yourself as strong, handsome, and well spoken. Or, maybe you thought that you were weak, ugly, and tongue-tied. But in either case, the theological question that you should really be asking yourself is this: "Who told you that you were strong, handsome, well spoken, weak, ugly, or tongue-tied?" In this sense, the basis for the question that God asked Adam is now the basis for the question that God asks you: "Who told you that you are who you think you are?"

You see, my friends, as our Creator, God has exclusively reserved for Himself the right to elaborate, define, describe, and detail the person who you are. God does not want anyone else—including you—to tell you who you are. God wants to do it Himself.

Why would this be the case? Well, in the context of the question that God asked Adam, the answer becomes immediately clear. You see, my friends, Adam did not know that he was naked until someone else told him that he was naked. Now, you might be asking yourself, "what's the big deal with nakedness" The biblical and theological idea of nakedness represents shame—and shame was not an idea organic or original to Adam's mind. Rather, someone else (Satan) impregnated the idea of shame into Adam's mind.

So again, let's return to this question of your identity. Who do you think you are? How convinced are you that the person who you think you are is the person who you really are? Let's take this a step further: How certain are you that the person who you think you are is the same person who God says that you are? Now that's the million-dollar question!

Before we go any further, I want to be clear on something: I certainly have no intention of speaking against positive self-talk. I actually think it's very important. In fact, for years, I traveled around the world teaching the CrossFit Goal Setting and Positive Self-Talk Course. I instructed thousands of people on the benefits of developing a positive mental attitude and maintaining a healthy sense of personal identity. However, here is something I realized in all those years of teaching: no matter how grandiose someone's sense of self-worth was—I have never met anyone who described himself or herself as *salt, light,* or *a city set on a hill.*

A NEW SENSE OF SELF

IN OUR GOSPEL READING FOR today's lesson, Jesus compares His disciples to three things—*salt, light,* and a *city set on a hill.*

As we begin a close exegetical reading of Mathew 5:13–16, notice that all three of the descriptive characteristics that Jesus speaks to—*salt, light,* and *a city set on a hill*—do not exist for themselves. Rather, all three exist for something or someone else.

Salt. I feel very confident in writing that you did not describe yourself as being *salt.* Am I right? However, if Jesus is describing you as *salt,* then there must be something about salt that is absolutely essential for you to understand and relate to. Therefore, let's start with salt and the historical context of this now common and readily available household-cooking item.

In Jesus's time, salt was used to season and preserve meat. Keep in mind this was 2,000 years ago—eons before the idea of electricity or a refrigerator had even been conceived of. In the times that we now live, we can simply put our steak and chicken into the refrigerator to keep them from going bad. However, in biblical times, meat had to be cured in order to preserve it and prevent it from spoiling. And the curing agent that was relied upon to this effect was salt.

Although the predominant purpose of salt during biblical times was to preserve food—in this sense to maintain the *fertility of food*—it was also used for the exact opposite effect: to render the earth *infertile.* For example, when a conquering nation wanted to utterly eliminate an enemy city, they would tear down its walls, burn all of its buildings to the ground, and then, in a final and decisive act of total destruction, salt the earth. The process of salting the earth would ensure that nothing would ever grow there again. So salt in this sense serves two purposes: salt can preserve, and salt can destroy.

Notice in both instances that salt was not used itself. In other words, salt is not valuable itself—rather salt is valuable in *what it does* and *how it affects* other things.

By the same token, light is not for itself. Rather, light allows us to see things by it. Light ensures that we are walking on the right path and not getting lost in the dark. Light illuminates things upon which it shines. Most importantly, light is a quality and descriptive characteristic that the Bible uses for Jesus Christ. For example, the Apostle John speaks to the fact that Jesus Christ is the "light of all mankind" and the "light that shines in the darkness." John described Jesus as the "true light that gives light to everyone else" (Reference John 1:4–9) and the author of Hebrews described Jesus as the "radiance (sunlight) of God's glory" (Hebrews 1:1–3).

Remember that Jesus—as the very embodiment and perfect example of everything that light should be—did not come into the world for Himself (reference John 3:16). The purpose of Jesus Christ's light was to benefit others. In this sense, we can now understand that in the context of *salt* and *light,* in both instances, Jesus is implying that they are qualities and attributes about *who you are* that are meant to *benefit other people.*

With *salt* and *light* out of the way, let's turn our attention to a *city set on a hill.* At first reading, we are faced with the strange idea that somehow and someway we are meant to relate to ourselves as a city: but not just any city. Specifically, Jesus tells us that we are a *city set on a hill.* What did Jesus mean by this? Much like describing yourself as *salt* (very unlikely) or *light* (well, perhaps), it is unlikely that you have ever described yourself as a *city set on a hill.*

However, think back to the beginning of our study. The thoughts that you believe about yourself are only valuable to the degree that they are in alignment with what God says about you. And God plain as day tells you that you are a *city set on a hill!* In fact, this is exactly how Jesus both sees you and describes you. So in this sense, just like *salt* and *light,* we have a hermeneutical clue: there must be something about a *city set on a hill* that benefits other people. And indeed there is!

In ancient times, a *city on a hill* was a point of navigation. Travelers walking across a vast and open desert-land would make their way through the wilderness by navigating according to a *city set on a hill*. In other words, a *city set on a hill* was like a compass. And because this particular city was set on a hill, it could be seen far off in the distance. In another navigational context, a *city set on a hill* might be compared to a lighthouse used by maritime captains to safely travel across the vast and open ocean. Furthermore, a *city set on a hill* would be a refuge for travelers and a safe place for them to take shelter, seek restoration, and find refreshment from endless days in the desert.

SELF-SERVING OR BLESSING OTHERS

THINK BACK ONCE AGAIN TO the way that you described yourself at the beginning of our study. It's interesting to note that when we describe ourselves—our attributes, qualities, and unique gifts—we tend to focus on the qualities that benefit us. However, the way that Jesus sees you and describes you has more to do with your relations to the world around you rather than with your relations to yourself. Remember, Jesus describes you as *salt, light,* and *a city set on a hill.* In this sense, what matters most to God is that you matter most to other people.

In the same way that Jesus brought light into the world, through His Spirit within you, you can bring His light into the world with everything that you say and do. In the same way that Jesus enhances, sustains, and saves your life—as salt, you are called to enhance, sustain, and share the good news of the One who came to save the world. In the same way that Jesus is the "city on a hill that all nations flood to" (reference Isaiah 2:1–3) you are called to be a city by which other people can see what is good, and just, and right. In other words, all of the unique and special gifts that God gave you—including the fact that you are *salt, light*, and a *city set on a hill*, are not meant for yourself. They are meant for others.

MISSION AND PURPOSE IN LIFE

THIS ALSO MEANS THAT YOU find mission, purpose, and fulfillment in your life to the degree that you bring God's love to others. As followers of Jesus, you are meant to be *salt*. Being *salt* effectively means that you preserve and enhance what is best in society around you. On the other hand, you are *salt* in the sense that you undermine and confront what is evil, unjust, dysfunctional, and sinful in the surrounding culture.

This might be a radical notion for some of you. Have you ever thought of your life in the way that God describes you? Have you ever considered your mission and purpose in life as being *salt,* or *light* or a *city set on a hill*? Well, according to God's Word—to preserve, highlight, season, illuminate, set apart, and position on high all that is best in God's Kingdom is exactly what you are called to do. By implication, this also means that whether it is through prayer, lawful social action, or service in the warrior professions, as *salt* you are also called to confront the injustices and evils of the world.

God also describes you as *light*. This means that you are *light* to the degree that people around you are able to see what is worth seeing. You help illuminate the right path for other people. You shine light into darkness. You bring hope and brightness into people's lives.

God is calling you to be a beautiful, just, holy person—*a light*—and by the integrity and brightness of your light, you can shed light around you. You illuminate what is beautiful and, by the same token, help people see what is unhealthy, sinful, and out of alignment with the will of God.

In other words, by the very integrity of your life, you will highlight what is good in society—and contrast it with what is dysfunctional. The clear implication of being *salt, light,* and a *city set on a hill,* is that you make the world a much better place! You help people see what is good. You illuminate the right path. People can navigate their life based on the example you set. People look at your life and think, "Oh, that's what we are meant to be. That is what God wants."

In the event you have not thought of yourself along these lines, I want you to read this once again. I want this Truth of God's Word to move from your head right down into your heart.

Through the Power of God's Holy Spirit...
You are the city by which people can navigate their lives.
You are the light by which people can clearly see.
You are the salt that adds seasoning, flavor, and joy to life!
My brothers and my sisters—to this I say:
YES and AMEN.

LESSON EIGHT

THE WORK OF LOVE

LESSON EIGHT
THE WORK OF LOVE

THE WORD OF GOD:

Jesus said, "For the kingdom of heaven is like a landowner who went out early in the morning to hire workers for his vineyard. He agreed to pay them a denarius for the day and sent them into his vineyard.

"About nine in the morning he went out and saw others standing in the marketplace doing nothing. He told them, 'You also go and work in my vineyard, and I will pay you whatever is right.' So they went.

"He went out again about noon and about three in the afternoon and did the same thing. About five in the afternoon he went out and found still others standing around. He asked them, 'Why have you been standing here all day long doing nothing?'

"'Because no one has hired us,' they answered.

"He said to them, 'You also go and work in my vineyard.'"
(Matthew 20:1–7)

MY BROTHERS AND MY SISTERS, may the grace of our Lord Jesus Christ, the love of God, and the fellowship of the Holy Spirit, be with you (2 Corinthians 13:14). I want to study with you today the topic of *The Work of Love*. Humanity has much to learn about the divine origins of our creation. After having been seemingly lost for several days, Jesus's parents found the young boy inside the temple. Deeply distressed, Mary said to Him, "Son, why have you treated us like this? Your father and I have been anxiously searching for you" (Luke 2:48). Gazing into His parents eyes, Jesus replied "Didn't you know I had to be in my Father's house?" (Luke 2:49). Has anything changed for mankind today? We are akin to Joseph and Mary as we anxiously search for the One Person who provides meaning in our life and the proper context for a relationship with each other. And all the while the essence of Jesus's words reverberates through the Universe: we must learn to see the "Father's house" as a reflection of the locality within human nature where God Himself longs to dwell.

SOCIAL STATUS AND POSTURE

THERE SEEMS TO BE A DRIVE within human nature to strive for social status. Theologically speaking, posturing with extravagant outward religious acts of prayer, almsgiving, and fasting are practiced because people "want to be seen" (Matthew 6:1–18). Mankind's outer emphasis on social esteem (How many likes? Are my followers increasing? Did that post get a comment?) prevents us from attending to the spiritual vitality of the sacred interior space of the heart. The pollution and contamination of our temple-body prevents contact with our "Father who sees in secret." Vigorous effort for notoriety in the social order of things—*often expressed in the social media of things*—tends to blunt spiritual maturity and proper discernment between *the many things* and *the One thing that matters most* (Luke 10:41–42).

Recent events in the United States are harsh evidence of what happens when social preoccupation takes a particularly dark turn in an effort to either maintain or disrupt economic and civil arrangements. The Bible has much to say on these matters. In fact, the Gospel often presents the people on top of the social ladder as obsessed with their position and willing to do anything to keep it: Gentile leaders are sharply rebuked because they "lord their position" over others instead of leading by example and helping those in need (Matthew 20:25; 1 Peter 5:3); the rich man who wears fine apparel and feasts on gourmet food easily ignores the nearly naked and starving beggar at his gate (Luke 16:19–31); astute leaders put heavy burdens on others without lifting a finger to actually help them (Matthew 23:4); and as the tension of our Gospel story will reveal, men can plan to stone only one party in a two-act crime in order to trap a prophet (John 8:3–6).

The Bible reveals that when people become overly consumed with rules, laws, and regulations that govern the relationship between human beings, it becomes woefully easy to completely dismiss the spiritual dimension of life. Quite simply, idolizing the law takes time and energy. Most importantly, when law becomes god, mankind becomes derailed, distracted, and ignorant to the Maker of the Moral Law Himself.

THE MORAL LAW

THEREAPPEARS TO BE A unifying feature of moral life. An abiding hunger and thirst for something more—for an eternal reality that transcends the fleeting beauty of the world. There is *something within our nature* that points us toward *something beyond our nature*. The Bible puts it like this: "God put eternity in our hearts" (Ecclesiastes 3:11). It is a desire for something more—but a "more" that is distinctly apart from anything that we can satisfy by our own efforts. This desire was certainly being expressed in the life of the rich man as he ran toward Jesus. The Bible tells us that he is rich—this means that he had accomplished many great things of the world—yet he still hungered for something more.

"What good thing must I do to inherit eternal life?" (Matthew 19:16).

We see here the fundamental expression of Mosaic faith—the association between doing something and achieving something in return. Although an ancient religious tradition, it nevertheless begs the question: Has anything changed for us today? We are hardwired for eternity—to seek something more—but at the same time humanity seems to have a self-imposed governor within our mind that equates a *particular amount work* with a *particular amount of reward*. At the socioeconomic level, this is played out in the principle of a fair hourly wage—working an hour to receive in return an hour's worth of wages. However, this is a function of the limitations of mankind's mind—not of God's Kingdom. In fact, Jesus turns this worldly principle completely upside down in the parable of the *Workers in the Vineyard* (Matthew 20:1–16).

THE PARABLE OF THE VINEYARD

WE BEGIN BY NOTING THAT SEVERAL workers were hired at different times of the day—all of them on the agreement of receiving a denarius (the usual daily wage of a day laborer) for a full day's work. The landowner went out early in the morning—likely before sunrise—then again at 9AM, 12PM, 3PM, and 5PM, each time enjoining workers to come and work in his vineyard.

At the end of the day, the landowner told the foreman to call the workers and pay them for their wages, beginning with the last ones hired and going on to the first (Matthew 20:8). The workers who were hired at 5PM came and received a denarius, and the same amount was paid to the workers hired at 3PM, 12PM, and 9AM.

Well, friends, what do you think the workers who were hired before sunrise—the first laborers to be employed by the foreman—expected to be paid? After all, they were hired first, which means they worked the longest. Economically speaking, they worked more hours then the workers hired at 9AM, 12PM, 3PM, and most certainly the workers hired at 5PM—thus it would seem to follow in their reasoning that because they had the privilege and honor of working the entire day, they were entitled to (and should expect) a *greater reward* for the *greater amount of time, effort, toil, and work* they had expended.

The Scripture teaches that this was indeed their expectation: when those who were hired first came to the foreman to be paid, they *expected* to receive more. But each of them also received a denarius. When they received it, they *began to grumble* against the landowner. "These who were hired last only *worked for one hour*, yet you made them equal to us who have borne the burden of *working all day* in the heat of the sun" (Matthew 20:12—my emphasis).

It follows from this parable that mankind is hardwired to expect to be either rewarded or punished for what we do or fail to do. But can you see how this mindset and predisposition is antagonistic to the Grace of God? God always gives us what we do not deserve, what we cannot even begin to work for, and what we cannot achieve on our own. This is the Gospel message of Grace. Paul says it best: "For it is by grace you have been saved, through faith—and this is not from yourselves, it is the gift of God—not by works, so that no one can boast" (Ephesians 2:8–9).

THE RICH MAN

IN OUR GOSPEL READING TODAY we are privy to a front row seat in the arena of the tension between work—effort, toil, labor, "good deeds"—and the Grace of Jesus Christ. So what happens? How does Jesus answer the question of the rich man when he asks, "What do I need to do?"

First, we must notice and admire the fact that the rich man comes to Jesus—in fact he runs—to God Himself—to find the answer to the burning question in his heart: *How do I find what matters most?* He is seeking the good that can only come from Jesus—the only person in whom any sense of Ultimate Good can be found. Notice therefore the posture in which this places the rich man. The rich man is in the passive rather than the active. He is ready to listen to what God says. And what does God say?

Jesus responds, "If you want to inherit life, keep the commandments" (Matthew 20:17). What our hearts need to see in this verse is the relationship and interplay between *Jesus Himself* and the *commands to which Jesus speaks*. Where else in the Scripture does Jesus speak on the principle of obedience to the Commands of God? This question lands us squarely within our theology of Christology. As fully God and fully man (Hebrews 1:1–3; Colossians 2:9), Jesus points to Himself as the One to whom we are called to obey. For example:

1) "If you love me, obey my commands" (John 14:15).
2) "Anyone who loves me will obey my teaching" (John 14:23).
3) "Anyone who does not love me will not obey my teaching" (John 14:24).
4) "If you keep my commands, you will remain in my love" (John 15:10).
5) "You are my friends if you do what I command" (John 15:14).

What we discover is that according to Jesus, the teaching and Teacher are inseparable. We love, obey, follow, listen to, and surrender to a Person—God Himself—not a collection of crafty philosophical or spiritual doctrines. This is why at the reinstatement of Peter, Jesus asked him three times "Do you love me?" (John 21:15–19). Never once did Jesus ask Peter, "Do you love my teaching? Do you love my lessons?" No. Jesus wanted a loving relationship with Peter. Jesus knew that everything else would flow perfectly from that.

Jesus tells the rich man to follow the commandments. However, it is interesting to note that the commandments that Jesus speaks to are from what is historically referred to as "the Second Tablet." Jesus enumerates and puts in first position those commandments that have a negative form—"You *shall not* murder, you *shall not* commit adultery, you *shall not* steal, you *shall not* give false testimony" (Matthew 19:18).

This means that if you want to live in friendship with God—if you want fellowship and entry into the life of discipleship with Jesus Christ—then it seems to follow that there are certain things you have to remove from your life. In other words, if there are things in your life that are egregious to God—then you have to cut them out. So in this sense it's interesting to note that the "work" of the commandments that Jesus points to depicts what we are *not to do rather than what we are to do.* Expressed another way, this remarkable verse teaches us that *sometimes in the spiritual life what we refrain from doing is equal if not more important to what we effectually* (or *actually; in fact) do.*

AN EXAMPLE FROM THE GYM

LET'S PRESS THIS INTO a context that many of you are familiar with. Imagine that you are a CrossFit gym owner who greets an enthusiastic potential new client at the threshold of the doors to your studio. This person asks you in a matter-of-fact fashion, "What must I do to enroll in your gym?" You happen to notice that the person is holding a Coca-Cola in one hand and a cigarette in the other, their eyes are bloodshot, and they reek of alcohol. Now, speaking for myself as a gym owner, before I entered into a dialogue about what the person would do once they joined the gym, I would first address what they needed to do before they joined the gym! I would say, "Listen friend, you need to stop smoking—stop drinking excessive amounts of alcohol—and stop drinking cans of sugar water."

It's the same thing when I counsel young people who show an interest in military and law enforcement careers. There are certain lifestyle choices that may need to be cut out of that person's life that could otherwise jeopardize the application process for unique positions of service within our community.

Returning to our Gospel, we notice what the rich man said in response to Jesus. The rich man told Jesus that he had kept the commands—in other words, he had already removed those acts from his life that at the most fundamental level would prohibit discipleship and real intimacy with God.

What was the response of Jesus to such a bold claim? Jesus looked at him with love (Mark 10:21). This is such a great detail that we cannot afford to miss it. The Scriptures teach us that God is love—not simply that God loves—but that *GOD IS LOVE* (1 John 4:8). And with the Love of God Himself, Jesus looks at the young man. This means that because God is love, a life with God is a life of total love—self-forgetting love—a love that starts with God, then radiates out into the lives of everyone whom our individual life comes into contact with.

Theologically, this is what it means to "sell everything you have." It's a call into radical love. It's an "all in" attitude. In our CrossFit analogy, it's no longer that we have a potential client coming to the threshold of the gym with a cigarette in hand—it's that same person who after a year of dedicated training now tells the coach—"OK, I've been at this for 365 days! Everything that was once a toxic and pollutant in my life has been removed—I'm ready for the big leagues! I want to go to the CrossFit Games!" Notice how the conversation changes at this point, doesn't it? It's no longer a matter of what NOT to do for this athlete—now it becomes altogether about WHAT YOU DO IN FACT DO!

And what, according to Jesus, do you do?

"If you want to be perfect, sell your possessions and give to the poor, and you will have treasure in heaven. Then come, follow me" (Matthew 19:21).

You throw it all away! And what do you throw away? Those possessions that make us who we think we are—and at the spiritual level—the greatest possessions we have are right between our ears—our thoughts. This is why the great theologian A. W. Tozer said, "The thoughts that come into your mind when you think about God are the most important thing about you." The Gospel compels us to change the way that we think about God, about ourselves, and about each other.

So let's focus the rest of our study together on what Jesus calls us to do in the *positive application* of the commandments.

We are privy to our Lord's teaching on the greatest commandment—this comes in Matthew, Chapter 22. When Jesus was asked what the greatest commandment was, He replied in a straightforward manner—to the point and with the authority of God Himself—by reciting the Shema.

The Shema is a prayer derived from a passage in the sixth chapter of the book of Deuteronomy. I'll write in here in Hebrew, which is probably the way Jesus would have said it: *"Sh'ma Yisrael Adonai Eloheinu Adonai Ehad."* It means, "Hear, oh, Israel, the LORD our God, the LORD is one." It follows from this fundamental belief a moral imperative and anticipated response on our part—and the only appropriate response is found in the words of Jesus Christ Himself: "Therefore, you shall love the Lord your God with all your heart, with all your soul, and with all your strength" (Matthew 22:37).

So what does the prayer mean? Notice the first word, *Shema.* "Hear." We are above all a people called upon to hear the *voice of God's Word*—and to have a personal, loving, and saving relationship with Jesus Christ—the Word and the Voice of God become flesh (John 1:14). This means that we don't set our own agenda. We don't determine our own path. We don't write our own story. We are akin to the rich man who asks Jesus, "What do I do?"

This biblical truth works against the grain of everything our American way of life teaches us from a very young age: freedom, self-determination, YES you can! Pick yourself up by your own bootstraps; even beyond our American way of life, the tendency of mankind to believe that we have to "work" for our "earnings" is an economic framework within our mind that spills over into our spiritual life. At the most fundamental level, this is the theological equivalent of mankind's attempt to create our own gods—the god of my own effort. The Bible teaches that anything can become a god—I mean, if the people of Israel once worshipped a golden calf, then clearly we can worship anything—including the god of our own ego. Mankind seems bent on the mantra of "I will write *my own* story on *my own* terms"—but as Christians, we must realize this is antagonistic to the Shema and the Commandment of Jesus.

The prayer of the Shema places us in the passive voice. We are spoken to by a power outside of ourselves. We stand in the shadow of the rich man before Jesus, eagerly awaiting our Lord's response.

In the negative sense, this means that God is not some vague force, some generic spiritual energy, some presence in the deep background of our life. Most importantly, this means that God is not something you can tap into whenever you happen to feel like it. In the positive sense, this means that God is as present to us as the air that we breathe. The Bible teaches that the presence of God Himself dwells within us, and, by His grace, we gradually become brighter and more beautiful as we become more like His Son, Jesus Christ (2 Corinthians 3:18).

OUR RESPONSE TO THE SHEMA

NOW, WHAT ARE THE BEHAVIORAL implications of the Shema—in other words, what is your response to the prayer as the one who hears the Word of God?

At the most fundamental level, the prayer teaches that we must love our LORD with the entirety of our being. God must be in some very real sense, the *only One* that we love: the one that we love above all things, with our whole heart, our whole soul, and all our strength.

Let's take these specifications one by one, just as Jesus taught.

The Shema says we must love God with our whole heart. In the Bible, the heart means the seat of our desires. In other words, we must love God with the totality of our emotions and our desires. God must be our one thing—the center of our gravity—the one thing in our life around which everything else in our life revolves.

How is this even possible? It's possible since God is the source, and the ground, and the goal of all things. As you've read in previous studies, Jesus Christ is not one prophet in a long lineage of prophets; He is not a spiritual guru; He is not another great moral teacher. This is entirely the wrong way to think about Christ.

Rather, the Bible teaches that Jesus is the fullness of the deity in bodily flesh (Colossians 2:9) and the exact representation of God's being (Hebrews 1:3). The Bible says that all things were made through Christ. For example, the Apostle John wrote that "Through Christ all things were made; without him nothing was made that has been made" (John 1:3). This means that God is the creative source of all that is: the Scriptures teach us that God is under all, in all, and through all (Ephesians 4:6). In the words of the Apostle Paul, "In God we live, and breathe, and have our being" (Acts 17:18).

For our purposes, this holds that if we desire things other than God Himself, we can still desire those things in a God-loving way—because we can desire God in, through, and under them.

A FEW RELATABLE EXAMPLES

YOU DESIRE TO GO TO THE CrossFit gym to work out. Good! There is nothing wrong with that. That's a good desire. But, in light of the Shema, you now see the beauty and complexity of CrossFit as strengthening your mind and focusing your will. You now see the combined power and grace of the functional movements demanded by the sport of CrossFit as reflective of the Power and Grace of God's being. In other words, your workout becomes worship.

Another example:

Are you a public safety officer or military operator who desires a profession of protection and service? That's also a good desire! However, in light of the Shema, you now see that there is no authority except what God has established (Romans 13:1). You realize that God has entrusted you to be a servant for good, and that as your profession may require others to submit to your authority, *you yourself* are submitted in mind, body, and spirit to *God Himself.*

Here's another example we can all relate to:

Do you desire a delicious dinner in the company of your loved ones? Good! Nothing wrong with that desire, either. But in light of the Shema, you now appreciate the food as something that strengthens you for God's service. In this sense, you can love God and chiefly desire God, even as you desire worldly things.

NOW LET'S MAKE THIS REAL

DO YOU LONG FOR JUSTICE IN our nation? Do you desire political righteousness and the accountability of those in power? Good! But we must see these pursuits and act on them as Jesus Christ Himself commanded. We must see justice and accountability as demands of God that ultimately lead back to the worship and praise of God Himself.

In addition to loving God with our heart, Jesus also commands that we love God with all our strength and our will. In the Bible, the strength and will of mankind always depict and call for the sacrifice of all that we have. In this sense, it is never our strength or our willpower that gets the job done—it is the strength of God, working in and through us. We are His instruments.

THE TOTALITY OF THE SHEMA

LET'S REVISIT THE GREATEST COMMANDMENT of Jesus Christ:

Jesus replied, "Love the Lord your God with all your heart and with all your soul and with all your mind. This is the first and greatest commandment. And the second is like it: Love your neighbor as yourself" (Matthew 22:37–40).

The trajectory of the Shema leads us into the terrain of what our country most needs. Loving God compels—even demands—that we love each other. Everything in our life hinges on these two commands. Apart from obedience to these commands, nothing in our life—nothing within our circle of influence—can be right. Let's turn the coin over for the positive application: when you love God and others, then all the pieces (or as Jesus explained, all the extremities) of your life will fall perfectly into place.

The Bible teaches that through faith in Jesus Christ, we all become children of God. The tendency of our minds and the eyes in our head is to see patterns of complex differences. We systematically categorize things that we see as separate from other things that we see. However, we can learn to create new categories in our life. The question is *how we achieve this.*

The indwelling presence of Christ gives us a new mind, a new heart, even new eyes—Jesus gives us new ways of creating categories in our life. However, rather than categories that have historically *separated us*, Jesus provides a radical new category that *unites us*. In Jesus Christ, we are all One (Galatians 3:28). We are brothers and sisters. As one body of faithful believers we are told to Shema—to hear the voice of God—and to respond to it by loving God, and loving each other.

We return now to the beginning of our study—the rich man—who is every one of us in the Bible study today—asking Jesus Christ, "What must I do?"

Feel in your heart the Love of God looking upon you, and loving you just the way you are. What the Gospel teaches us is that rather than *doing something with an expectation of receiving something in return,* it's about *receiving something we do not deserve and cannot earn.*

Read this to yourself one more time, because this is the heart of the Gospel message: The Gospel teaches us that rather than *doing something with an expectation of receiving something in return,* it's about *receiving something we do not deserve and cannot earn.*

This is Grace, my brother and sisters, and it all begins with "confessing with your mouth that Jesus is Lord, and believing in your heart that God raised Him from the dead" (Romans 10:9).

YES and AMEN.

LESSON NINE

ON THE BATTLEFIELD OF LIFE

An Exposition of Paul's Prayer

for the Ephesians

LESSON NINE
ON THE BATTLEFIELD OF LIFE
An Exposition of Paul's Prayer for the Ephesians

Our Gospel reading today is from the Apostle Paul's letter to God's holy people in Ephesus (Paul's letter to the Ephesians).

THE WORD OF GOD:

I keep asking that the God of our Lord Jesus Christ, the glorious Father, may give you the Spirit of wisdom and revelation, so that you may know Him better. I pray that the eyes of your heart may be enlightened in order that you may know the hope to which He has called you, the riches of His glorious inheritance in His holy people, and His incomparably great power for us who believe.
(Ephesians 1:17–19)

MY BROTHERS AND MY SISTERS, may the grace of our Lord Jesus Christ, the love of God, and the fellowship of the Holy Spirit, be with you (2 Corinthians 13:14). I want to study with you today the topic of *The Battlefield of Life.* Early in my military career, a longtime mentor of mine pulled me aside and said, "Greg, good leaders are able to reveal things to subordinates that they could otherwise never see on their own." His words resonated deep within my soul, and I was held captive by the idea that something obvious to me could be seemingly invisible to someone else. The implications on the battlefield were immense: unless I opened the eyes of my soldiers and helped them see potential dangers within their midst, catastrophic injury would surely be their end. However, once the danger was revealed to them, their "battlefield knowledge" increased, and they would be more likely to navigate risk independent of my supervision. And perhaps even more encouraging, with their newfound wisdom, the subordinate soldier would be in a position to help reveal to their peers what they would never see on their own.

In many respects and to varying degrees, we are all soldiers on the battlefield of life. Twists, turns, peaks, and valleys are part of the terrain we need to successfully navigate in order to reach our final destination.

However, in addition to dangerous valleys, there are also magnificent mountaintops that our soul longs to summit. Yet, unless revealed to us by a trusted source of wisdom and knowledge much greater than ourselves, the tendency is to rely on our independent understanding, which often leads to a closed loop of crisscrossing back and forth across the dark valleys of life.

I recall learning the fundamentals of land navigation during U.S. Army Basic Officer Leadership Training in the hills of North Dakota. During daylight hours, the task was fairly simple. Given a compass and map, I navigated across open terrain to specific points or "plots" that my instructor had assigned me. However, in the pitch-black night, unable to see the tips of my fingers with my arm outstretched, the task became altogether impossible. On one particular night, and very characteristic of North Dakota summers, there was a great lightning storm. Although startling and a bit nerve-racking, I soon discovered the lightning was a blessing in disguise. When it struck, it was much like a flare bursting in the night. The terrain all around me was instantly illuminated. For a few seconds, the imprint of my surroundings made an impression on my mind. I could essentially "see in the dark." Although brief, those momentary intervals of revelation of my surroundings were enough to allow me to successfully complete the navigation course.

THE POWER OF VISION

IN THE BOOK OF PROVERBS, it says, "Where there is no vision, the people perish" (Proverbs 29:18). In order to navigate the battlefield of life, we need to clearly identify the obstacles before us. However, as my mentor counseled me years ago, we also need a trusted source to reveal to us what we could otherwise not see on our own. The idea of "not being able to see on our own" is elaborated on in the Bible with these words: "Be not wise in thy own eyes" (Proverbs 3:7). In other words, if we rely on our own understanding, knowledge, and worldly acquired wisdom, we will not be able to see clearly.

The potential pitfall and shortcoming of limited understanding and "battlefield blindness" was certainly at the heart of the Apostle Paul in his letter to the Ephesians. In Ephesians 1:17, we read, "I pray that the God of our Lord Jesus Christ, the Father of glory, might give you spiritual wisdom and revelation in the knowledge of Him." In other words, Paul's prayer was that

God would grant us a specific type of spiritual wisdom we could otherwise never arrive at on our own.

We may interpret through verse 17 that Paul was specifically describing a type of wisdom that could only be achieved through the power and working of the Holy Spirit. Paul specifically prayed that the Ephesians would experience a supernatural endowment of wisdom that would be achieved through God's revelation of Himself. Paul's contention, therefore, was to ensure the believer understood that worldly wisdom, gained through the intellect of humanity, would never be enough to truly know the "surpassing greatness" of God. Paul's use of the term "revelation" referred to God's own self-disclosure, which would be experienced supernaturally by the believer.

In the New Testament Epistle of James, the author made clear the distinction between wisdom of the world and wisdom revealed by God. James describes worldly wisdom as "earthly, unspiritual and demonic" (James 3:15–16). In the context of navigating the battlefield of life, the result of following and "seeing" through the eyes of our own wisdom is like a landmine waiting to be stepped upon. A torrential explosion of "envy, selfish ambition, disorder and evil" (James 3:15–16) is dangerously underfoot. The Apostle Paul foresaw the treacherous terrain that the Ephesians, in addition to future believers, would need to safely transverse, and through his prayer, Paul's hope was that God would reveal Himself to us. Through this supernatural revelation, our wisdom and knowledge would be increased to heavenly proportion, which is distinctly different and abundantly more important than worldly wisdom.

James articulated this difference in verse 3:17: "Wisdom that comes from heaven is first of all pure; then peace-loving, considerate, submissive, full of mercy and good fruit, impartial and sincere." With this newfound perspective of "Heavenly wisdom" held in mind, we turn once again to the beauty and magnitude of the opening line of Paul's prayer. With gratitude in our heart, we discover that Paul prayed that you and I would have a direct experience of the power and glory of God. Like a flash of lightning in the middle of a dark night, Paul's prayer was such that we would experience an imprint of God on our minds and hearts, and that through this divine revelation, our spiritual wisdom would be increased.

THE EYES OF THE HEART

THE SECOND COMPONENT OF PAUL'S prayer for the Ephesians was equally inspiring and complemented the revelation of God invoked in verse 17. Paul prayed, "Since the eyes of your heart have been enlightened, that you would know what is the hope of His calling, what are the riches of the glory of His inheritance in the saints." By focusing on Paul's use of the word "heart" in this verse, and through an understanding of the bodily function of the heart, we can truly appreciate the magnitude of Paul's prayer.

Because you were made in the image of God, you have an ordained birthright and divine capacity to know and *experience* the presence of God. Before going any further, let us turn our attention to the words of Jesus, who said, "This is eternal life, *that they may know you*, the one true God, and Jesus Christ, whom you have sent" (John 17:3). Oftentimes when reading the Bible and the words of Jesus, it is equally important to note what Jesus said in addition to what *Jesus did not say.* Therefore, take special consideration that Jesus's prayer was for you and me to *know God.* He did not say, "Know *about* God." In other words, Jesus's prayer and hope was that you and I would have a direct experience and firsthand knowledge of God. And now, through the words of Paul in Ephesians verse 1:17, we arrive at the understanding that this knowledge of God will not be possible through our own understanding or human intellect. Knowing God is a supernatural experience, which is the direct result of God revealing Himself to us.

In the context of any personal relationship, this makes total and complete sense. No matter how hard we might try, in order to really know someone, they ultimately need to reveal their mind and soul to us. This specific type of "revelation," understood through verse 18 of Paul's prayer, was experienced within the "eyes of our heart" that were enlightened through the revelation of God. In the same manner in which our mind has thinking, reasoning, and intellectual capacities, Paul understood that our heart shared these capacities on an even deeper and more spiritually significant level. In fact, according to Paul, the mind may have even blunted the true spiritual wisdom of the heart.

In his letter to the Corinthians, Paul wrote, "Their minds are made dull because a veil covers their hearts" (2 Corinthians 3:14–15). We can interpret through Ephesians 1:17–18 that Paul's prayer for the believer was to "see" that if truth, wisdom, and knowledge about God were to be faithfully grasped, then the heart must be enlightened. Furthermore, as the heart is a central and life-sustaining organ of the body, it is responsible for circulating both blood and oxygen throughout the entire cellular system. Thus, when Paul prays for the "eyes of our heart to be enlightened," he is praying that in addition to knowing *about* God at the intellectual level of our mind, that through the circulation of God's love throughout every cell of our body, we would be "enlightened" to truly *know God* by the revelation of His presence. Finally, it is important to note that in the Bible, the word "heart" often referred to the genuine self, as distinguished from appearance, identification with the mind, and physical presence.[414] And this "heart self" had its own nature, character, and disposition, which ultimately affected the thoughts, words, and actions of the believer.[415] Therefore, a believer whose "heart" was illuminated by the revelation of God would radically change the entire makeup of their life and would never be the same again.

Because of the tendency of our human intellect to attach through the senses to material objects and "desires of the flesh" (Galatians 5:17), Paul's prayer centered on *spiritual* acquisition. For example, we observed that in verse 17, Paul's hope was that we would acquire *spiritual wisdom* in the knowledge of God. Through the revelation of God in our lives, the eyes of our heart would be enlightened, allowing us to faithfully see what truly mattered most. Therefore, as we continue to journey though the totality of Paul's prayer, we observe the "riches" that Paul desires that we both see and inherit are meant to be enjoyed spiritually and not worldly.

We take note that verse 18 concludes with Paul's use of the word *inheritance*. This word is of immense importance and is best understood through the context of the Old Testament. Time and time again, we note that God referred to His creation as His own inheritance. In Deuteronomy, we read that God took His creation, "As the people of His inheritance" (Deuteronomy 4:20) and that God's people were "His own inheritance, redeemed by His great

---

[414] Walter Elwell and Barry J. Beitzel, "Wisdom, Wisdom Literature," in *Baker Encyclopedia of the Bible* (Grand Rapids, MI: Baker Book House, 1988), p. 2149.

[415] *Baker Encyclopedia of the Bible*, p. 2149.

power" (Deuteronomy 9:26). As sons and daughters of God, our relationship with Him is similar to that of Father and child. The intimacy of this relationship is absolutely vital for us to comprehend, and was at the heart of Jesus's ministry. In the first two words of the "Lord's Prayer," Jesus explained the nature of our relationship with God by the declaration, "Our Father" (Matthew 6:9). In this manner, Jesus invoked our understanding of the divine connection to our "Father of glory." Jesus embraced and perfectly articulated the magnitude of this relationship and his divine right to the inheritance of his Father when he declared, "All I have is yours, and all you have is mine" (John 17:10).

Paul's prayer as expressed in verse 18 is therefore twofold. First, his hope is that we would embrace our relationship with God as that of Father and child. Second, through the context of this Fatherly relationship and through spiritual revelation, Paul prayed that we would embrace our true inheritance as sons and daughters of God. It is exceedingly important to take note of Paul's use of the word *glory*, which is evident in verses 17 and 18. In verse 17, God was declared to be the "Father of glory." Throughout the Old Testament, the glory of God was oftentimes so bright and of such overwhelming power that it was shrouded in a cloud (Exodus 16:10). In verse 18, we discover that the brilliance and intensity of God's glory is to be shared with us as a component of our inheritance as children of God.

THE SURPASSING GREATNESS OF GOD

IN VERSE NINETEEN OF PAUL'S prayer, we take special note of the connection between the "surpassing greatness" and power of God, in direct proportion toward those who believe in Him, and "what is the surpassing greatness of His power toward us who believe, in accordance with the working of the strength of His might." As described by Paul, it was according to one's level of belief, which was furthermore achieved only through God's revelation of Himself, that a believer could fully experience the "strength of His might." Paul's use of the phrase "surpassing greatness," when understood within the context of navigating the battlefield of life, is worthy of our thankfulness and delight. *Surpassing* can best be understood as "superior," or ranking higher than any other type of power, regardless of how immense our intellect may attempt to convince us it is. The magnificent, supreme, and nearly incomprehensible power of God's greatness is directed with love toward those who believe in Him. Through God's own revelation of Himself, we may thus be faithfully "inherited" into His enduring love and embrace.

CONCLUDING THOUGHTS

NAVIGATING THE BATTLEFIELD OF LIFE can be a treacherous task, full of unsuspecting danger. However, this same battlefield, when faithfully illuminated, can become a place of beauty and spiritual splendor. In order for the terrain around us to become visible, a transformation will need to take place within both our mind and our heart. The biblical word "grace" was described to me once as the "effect of God giving us what we do not deserve," and "mercy" taking place when "God *does not give us* what we do deserve." Paul's prayer invokes this very measure of grace in his hope that you and I would experience the revelation of God, and through this supernatural opening and enlightenment of the "eyes of our heart," we would fully embrace our right to an inheritance of epic proportion.

YES and AMEN.

LESSON TEN

A PAULINE THEOLOGY ON SPIRITUALITY

LESSON TEN
A PAULINE THEOLOGY ON SPIRITUALITY

THE WORD OF GOD:

Don't you know that you yourselves are God's temple and that God's Spirit dwells in your midst?

The body is not meant for sexual immorality but for the Lord, and the Lord for the body. By his power God raised the Lord from the dead, and he will raise us also. Do you not know that your bodies are members of Christ himself?

Do you not know that your bodies are temples of the Holy Spirit, who is in you, whom you have received from God?

(1 Corinthians 3:16, 6:13-15, 19)

MY BROTHERS AND MY SISTERS, may the grace of our Lord Jesus Christ, the love of God, and the fellowship of the Holy Spirit, be with you (2 Corinthians 13:14). I want to study with you today the awesome topic of *Developing A Pauline Theology on Spirituality.* Understanding the biblical model of spirituality is extremely important in a world in which nearly everyone claims to be "spiritual." It is imperative that we consider what the original biblical authors meant when they preached on matters of spirituality and the essence of the human experience.

CONTEXT AND HISTORICAL BACKGROUND

UNDERSTANDING THE CULTURAL and philosophic background of the city of Corinth in the time of Paul is fundamental to grasping Paul's theology of spirituality. Paul's letters to the Churches in Corinth (1 and 2 Corinthians) were significantly influenced by an array of existing problematic conditions within the Church and an abundance of cultural secular practices and ideologies that were in stark contrast to the Gospel message. By first outlining the sociological characteristics of Corinth, in addition to the religious and philosophical practices of the region, the study of 1 and 2 Corinthians comes alive with actionable principles of decision-making on issues that still challenge God's people today.

The city of Corinth was a great commercial center strategically situated on the isthmus that linked the Peloponnesus with mainland Greece. Mariners frequenting the two ports of Corinth, Cenchreae on the Aegean Sea to the east, and Lechaeum on the Adriatic Sea to the west moved their ships on rollers across the narrow isthmus on a stone-paved road. This narrow passageway served as a central artery into Corinth, and contributed to the overt heartbeat of the city that became known for its wealth, indulgence, and sexual immorality.[416]

Paul faced an uphill struggle against a city populace overly concerned with reputation and social status, self-promotion to gain recognition over others, ambition to succeed at all costs, and an interest in Greek philosophy and wisdom over the Christian message.[417] To make matters even more challenging, Paul's message proved to be against the current of a city with an established international reputation for trade, vice, and promiscuity.[418]

Against the backdrop of Paul's teaching on the sacredness of the human body (1 Corinthians 3:16; 6:19) was the fact that Corinth was plagued by immoral sexual behavior including the worship of the goddess Aphrodite that resulted in prostitution in the name of religion (1 Corinthians 6:9-20).[419] The awareness in Paul's mind of the immense challenges he faced in Corinth were evident in the self-admitted "fear and trembling" (1 Corinthians 2:3) he experienced in his missionary work within the city. So difficult and complex were the issues that Paul faced in Corinth that the Lord appeared to him in a vision and said, "Do not be afraid; keep on speaking, do not be silent. For I am with you, and no one is going to attack and harm you, because I have many people in this city" (Acts 18:9-10).

In addition to understanding the cultural and philosophic background of Corinth, it is important to appreciate Paul's general strategic approach to ministry in the context of his arrival at Corinth in the first place. Paul seemed to sense

---

[416] Laney, Dr. Carl. "First Corinthians" in *Essential Bible Background*. p. 191. The first century geographer Strabo recorded that there were 1,000 temple prostitutes who served in the temple of Aphrodite within the city of Corinth.

[417] A. C. Thiselton. "1 Corinthians" in *The New Dictionary of Biblical Theology*. p. 297.

[418] Tuck, Dr. Gary. "First Corinthians" in *The Arguments of the Books of the New Testament*. p. 96.

[419] In addition to the accepted practice of prostitution in the name of religion, Paul wrote in 1 Corinthians 5:1-2 of a "sexual immorality of a kind even the pagans do not tolerate: A man is sleeping with his father's wife."

that the key to rapidly spreading the Gospel message was establishing Churches in major cities whose trade and commerce increased the likelihood that a large demographic of people would take it back to their villages and start smaller Churches by proclaiming the "word of the Lord" (Acts 19:9-10).[420] Having made little headway on his missionary journey in Athens (Acts 17:13-15), Paul set his sights on the next largest city, Corinth (Acts 18:1).

THE BODY AND THE SPIRIT IN PAULINE THEOLOGY

PERHAPS IT WAS THE severity of the challenges facing Christians living in the city of Corinth, combined with the contrast between their proclaimed faith in Jesus as Messiah (1 Corinthians 2-3; 18) and the simultaneous retention of worldly lifestyle choices, that prompted Paul to ask on two occasions, "Don't you know that you yourselves are God's temple and that God's Spirit dwells in your midst?" (1 Corinthians 3:16; 6:19).[421] Paul illustrates that when the Corinthians received Jesus as their King (1 Corinthians 1:23), a transformation was initiated that advanced the believer into a state of "righteousness, holiness and redemption" (1 Corinthians 1:30). For Paul, this state of holiness was even more precious than purity, and therefore necessitated that the Corinthians' abstain from practices that would defile their body (2 Corinthians 7:1).

Paul stresses that purification, cleansing the body, and ceasing practices that defile the temple of God within the believer was essential to being filled with the character and holiness of Jesus (2 Corinthians 7:1). The life and Spirit of Christ within the believer resulted in their "sanctification in Christ" and transformation "into his holy people" (1 Corinthians 1:2). Paul was certainly aware of the implications for the holiness of the tabernacle in the Old Testament, and seemed to draw a correlation between the holiness of the tabernacle when filled with God's

---

[420] Longman, Temper III and David E. Garland. *The Expositors Bible Commentary on Galatians*, p. 242.

[421] This insight was developed in my mind by Dr. Tuck's class notes on Corinthians. As pointed out by Dr. Tuck, although the Corinthians professed with their mouths faith in Christ, their actions remained world-bound and not Spirit-focused: They were concerned with matters of the world (2 Corinthians 4:16-18); they were walking by faith and not by sight (2 Corinthians 5:7); and they were living as people who "were still worldly" (1 Corinthians 3:1).

presence (Exodus 29:43, 45) and the holiness of the believer when indwelled by the Spirit of God.

By asking a series of five rhetorical and increasingly pointed questions (2 Corinthians 6:14-16), Paul confronts the Corinthians with the ultimate inquiry: "What agreement is there between the temple of God and idols?" (2 Corinthians 6:16). This series of questions illustrates and expounds upon Paul's observation of a divergent gap between the Corinthians' reception of the Gospel message (1 Corinthians 1:18) and their insistence on remaining "people who are worldly" (1 Corinthians 3:1-3). For Paul, belief in Christ constitutes a resurrection into a new life (1 Corinthians 5:7), the evidence of which would be a shedding of worldly tendencies and desires (1 Corinthians 3:18; 6:12-20).

Returning to Old Testament reference and correlation, Paul then seems to answer his own questions by explaining that as God's people (2 Corinthians 6:16b), the Corinthians are to separate themselves from "unclean things" and to abstain from practices that would lead to defilement (2 Corinthians 6:17). The body, according to Paul, is daily wasting away (2 Corinthians 4:16), and therefore, to appease the physical desires of a perishable body is antagonistic to, and a distraction from, the Christian message.

However, rather than losing hope or being overly concerned with the "outward body," Paul encourages the Corinthians to see that "the inward body is being renewed day by day" (2 Corinthians 4:16). Paul encourages the Corinthians to turn their attention to the unseen spiritual reality of the indwelling presence of God, and to focus "not on what is seen, but on what is unseen, since what is seen is temporary, but what is unseen is eternal" (2 Corinthians 4:18).

UNITY AND DIVISION IN PAULINE THEOLOGY

A GREAT MAJORITY of the issues that Paul addresses in his letters to the Corinthians can be traced back to the pervasive values of the surrounding culture.[422] The Corinthians' interest in self-promotion to gain recognition over others, ambition to succeed at all costs, and the influence of the Hellenistic culture tended to focus their minds on matters of materialism and "worldly

---

[422] Dr. Gary Tuck, "Corinthians" outline, BT503, Western Seminary

pursuits" (1 Corinthians 3:1-3).[423] Naturally, these concerns served as a means of division within the Church and fostered a general sense of jealousy and quarreling (1 Corinthians 3:3). Paul encouraged the Corinthians to understand that the purpose of the Gospel message was to create one "Church of God" (1 Corinthians 1:1) and one "body of Christ" (1 Corinthians 6:17; 10:17; 11:29; 12:12-16, 27), where a sense of unity, love, and cohesiveness would prevail.

Paul addressed the issue of disunity by declaring the Corinthians were "acting like mere humans" (1 Corinthians 3:3). For Paul, to have received the Gospel message (1 Corinthians 1:18) yet to continue to live in a state of "jealousy and quarreling" was simply not compatible and overt evidence of spiritual immaturity (1 Corinthians 3:2-4).[424] Utilizing a brilliant illustration of the individual and corporate body of Christ, Paul demonstrates that if Christians really are the "temple of the living God" (1 Corinthians 3:16, 6:19; 2 Corinthians 6:16), then both individually and collectively they are unified in Christ (2 Corinthians 6:15).

In an interesting metaphor of competitive athletic training and competition, Paul paints a word picture for the Corinthians against the canvas backdrop of the biennial Isthmian Games. Paul points out that when runners participate in a race, only one will achieve the victory, which on face value would seem to create division and a sense of strife between believers (1 Corinthians 9:24). However, Paul then shifts his tactic by illustrating the unity the athletes experienced during the strict training regime that preceded the race (1 Corinthians 9:25). Creating contrast between the temporal and the eternal, and the individual and the collective, Paul emphasized that "everyone who competes in the games goes into strict training" for the purpose of "winning a crown that will not last" (1 Corinthians 9:25a). In the context of Paul's metaphor, the race that Christians compete in is not an individual race where only one person wins and where the prize is temporal. Rather, Christians "go into strict training together" in preparation to collectively run a race while supporting each other in pursuit of a "crown that will last forever" (1 Corinthians 9:25b).

---

[423] A. C. Thiselton. "1 Corinthians" in *The New Dictionary of Biblical Theology*. p. 297.
[424] Tuck.

Paul argues that the Corinthians, as believers in Jesus Christ, have a duty to turn from every source of defilement and thereby "perfect their holiness out of reverence for God" (2 Corinthians 7:1). According to Paul, living for Christ (2 Corinthians 5:15) meant an equal combination of separation from outward evil (2 Corinthians 6:17) and a loving fellowship with other believers. Therefore, the more important issue that Paul addressed was not the isolated problem of being "mere human" (1 Corinthians 3:3), but rather the fact that the outer "flesh" was sin-cursed and fundamentally rebellious against God. Conversely, the inward redeemed spirit is the very Spirit of Christ within the believer, which is fundamentally obedient to God.[425]

One of Paul's key arguments that further illustrates the antagonistic nature of the "flesh" in opposition to the indwelling Spirit of Christ within the believer can be found in 2 Corinthians 4:3-6. Here Paul distinguishes between the effects of idolatry to the "god of this age" and true obedience and faithfulness to Jesus Christ as Lord. Those serving the "flesh" are spiritually blinded by the sin-cursed nature of first creation (2 Corinthians 4:4). However, those indwelt by the power of the Spirit of God receive "the light of the knowledge of God's glory displayed in the face of Christ" (2 Corinthians 4:6).

CONCLUDING THOUGHTS

UNDERSTANDING THE CULTURAL and philosophic background of Corinth in the time of Paul is fundamental to grasping his theology of spirituality. Paul's letters to the Churches in Corinth were significantly influenced by an array of existing problematic conditions within the Church and an abundance of cultural differences, secular practices, and ideologies that were in stark contrast to the Gospel message. Against the backdrop of sexual immorality, disunity, and the behavior of "mere men" (1 Corinthians 3:3), Paul argues that the redeemed believer and follower of Christ should reflect a transformation of values and lifestyle choices that is evident within every area of their life.

---

[425] Tuck.

LESSON ELEVEN

THE STONES OF OUR FAITH

LESSON ELEVEN
THE STONES OF OUR FAITH

THE WORD OF GOD:

Then David took his staff in his hand, chose five smooth stones from the stream, and put them in the pouch of his shepherd's bag and, with his sling in his hand, approached the Philistine.

(1 Samuel 17:40)

MY BROTHERS AND MY SISTERS, may the grace of our Lord Jesus Christ, the love of God, and the fellowship of the Holy Spirit, be with you (2 Corinthians 13:14). I want to study with you today the awesome topic of *The Stones of Our Faith*. It never ceases to amaze me how often I return to the epic story of David and Goliath. It seems that each time I do, I discover something "new and wonderful" in God's Word (reference Psalm 119:18). Let's revisit this familiar story with a sense of adventure and joyful expectancy of the transformational power of Holy Scripture.

....

A YOUNG MAN LOOKED DOWN into a stream of clear water at the very bottom of a valley. Above him on the hilltop stood two opposing armies. At the highest point on the landscape, having already captured the coveted terrain feature of the high ground, loomed a fearsome giant, covered head to toe in bronze armor, holding a sword nearly the length of a grown man's body.

If this young man had taken the time to study the reflection of his image in the stream, he would have seen a handsome face, slightly sunburned from long hours of being outdoors in the sun. Described by a friend as "strong, handsome, courageous, and well spoken" (1 Samuel 16:8), this young man was respected as being a hard worker and loyal to his craft.

However, this young man had not come to the stream to look at his face in the water. He had come to look for stones. Five smooth stones, to be exact. You see, this young man was looking for a particularly smooth, flat stone that would sit perfectly in the leather strap of his shepherd's sling. He had already used the sling to great effect, having killed a lion and a bear that once threatened his flock. However, his target today would walk on two feet, instead of four, and was tormenting not sheep but rather the army of Israel, and had been for forty days, and forty nights. This young man had come to fight a giant. Perhaps you have heard his name before—I am speaking of none other than David, the mighty man after God's own heart.

Goliath blatantly strutted in the distance, a formidable foe. In fact, not a single man had dared to step forward to face him in combat. King Saul, the appointed king of the army of Israel, was for all intents and purposes responsible for engaging the enemy. However, even the king remained hidden away within the refuge of his tent. If Goliath had looked and seen David, alone there by the creek, he would surely have laughed at the prospect of any outcome other than the small man's death by the hand of his sword. Goliath was a big man. Scripture says he stood 9 feet, 9 inches tall, and carried 160 pounds of armor. And, to make matters worse, Goliath relentlessly provoked the army with the words, "This day I defy the ranks of Israel, give me a man and let us fight each other" (1 Samuel 17:8). But nobody showed up. In fact, those on the battlefield had turned and run the other direction.

That is, everyone but David. Which begs the question: What was David doing on the battlefield? After all, he was not enlisted in the army. He'd never been trained in military maneuvers, and although he had fought and killed predatory animals, he had never faced a giant. The Scripture reveals that David had been sent by his father to bring bread to his brothers. You see, David's brothers were in the army, and David had come to bring them the fellowship of a family meal.

HOW TO GO UP IN LIFE

THE FIRST POINT I WANT to emphasize in this lesson is the supremacy of God's grace. God's grace is everywhere you look in the Scriptures—you just need to have the spiritual key to unlock and discover what might have otherwise remained buried in the sands of an ancient battlefield. Did you know that Jesus said that all the Scriptures were about Himself? In explaining the purpose of studying the Scriptures to a group of His disciples, Jesus said, "the Scriptures testify about me" (John 5:39). On another occasion, He said, "everything must be fulfilled that is written about me that is written in the book of Moses, the Prophets and the Psalms" (Luke 24:44). This means that in some way, shape, or form, our task whenever we study the Bible is to look for Jesus. This also means that as we recall the familiar story of David and Goliath, we must discipline ourselves to see it not with the eyes in our head, but rather the eyes in our heart.

Grace is described in the Bible as underserved. Freely given. A gift from a loving God. The Apostle Paul provides a litmus test for grace—there is nothing you can do to earn it, and you can't claim any responsibility for having received it. In other words, you can't brag about grace. And we see it here on the battlefield. David, as a symbol of a loving father's grace, brings his brothers a meal. And not just any meal—bread, to be exact. When we remember in the New Testament that Jesus referred to Himself as the bread of life, immediately the connection is made. David's brothers were marked for death that fateful day, as was everyone else in King Saul's army. This means that Goliath represents the enemy of sin and death, and when David came onto the scene, he took the place of his brother and fought the battle for them. There needed to be what is referred to in the military as a "change of command." David was that change, and he brought with him not only lunch, but also life. This is exactly what Jesus does in your life, my friends.

As we study the Scriptures and imagine this particular scene, it's interesting to access the terrain features of the ancient battlefield. In the days of close combat, when the tip of a spear and the edge of a sword settled battles, the opponent who secured the high ground had a decisive advantage. And the high ground was precisely the terrain that Goliath had claimed. This means that the enemy had the highest terrain, whereas David had seemingly retreated to the lowest. You see, the stream that David went to in search of five smooth stones was, geographically speaking, the lowest place you could go.

This leads us to the second point of today's study: If you want to go up in life, you first need to go down. James, the half-brother of Jesus, wrote, "humble yourself before the Lord, and he will lift you up" (James 4:10). The temptation we all have whenever we face a giant—whether it is the giant of a job loss, a career change, the breakup of a relationship, or the anxiety caused by the effects of a disease—is to access the giant according to our own strength. We ask ourselves, "How am I going to face this giant?" That, my friend, is entirely the wrong question to ask. It's not the size of the giant that matters, it's the size of our God. Well, you might ask yourself, "There certainly must be something that I need to do. What is my responsibility in the battle? What is my share of the work?" To answer this, we need only look to the words of Jesus, who said, "The work of God is this: to believe in the one he has sent" (John 6:29).

Now, I know that's challenging to do! Part of us always feels like we need to do something, and it's always a double-edged sword. Either I'm not capable of doing what I think needs to be done, or I do something that only complicates the problem and makes matters worse. Did you know that in the context of our story, David's own brothers did not believe in the one whom their father had sent? In fact, they ridiculed David and said that he had no part in the battle. Even James, Jesus Christ's own brother, didn't believe that Jesus was sent from the Father until James saw Jesus after the resurrection. Then he humbled himself, and, from that day forward, referred to himself as "a servant of God and of the Lord Jesus Christ" (James 1:1). The Bible declares that God wants to fight your battles for you, and that you only need to be still. In this stillness, there is humbleness and faithfulness in the goodness of God.

The third and final point I want to emphasize is the importance of establishing the foundation of your faith. To help set the proper context for the importance of what I want to share with you, imagine this scenario: an active shooter has just walked onto an elementary school campus. Immediately, a 911 call goes out, and a fraction of a second later, the dispatch center alerts a police officer on patrol less than a block away. However, rather than immediately responding to the school, the officer drives in the other direction! They head to a local sporting goods store to purchase ammunition for their firearm. Although they were on active criminal patrol and were wearing their uniform, complete with a duty belt, handgun, and even extra magazines, they did not have a single round of ammunition anywhere on their person. Well, clearly, this just doesn't make sense. And in the context of our biblical story, it doesn't make any sense that David would arrive on the battlefield carrying his sling (the equivalent of a firearm) with his shepherd's pouch (the equivalent of a magazine pouch) without a single stone (the equivalent of a round of ammunition).

Therefore, when David retreated down the valley to the stream to gather five smooth stones, the stones appear to represent more than just physical objects. I think God wants us to see something more important. I propose that David already had plenty of ammunition stored in his pouch. What David wanted and needed on that fateful day is the same thing that you and I need today: a moment of reprieve from the intensity of the battle. David needed a moment of silence, and solitude, and peace in the presence of God in order to remind himself of all the ways that God had blessed his life. And this is exactly the same thing we need—in the intensity, complexity, uncertainty, and difficulty of our days, we need to humble ourselves before God and remind ourselves of his goodness. Here is the key to understanding this ancient story: *before David faced his giant, he needed to face his God.* And before you face your giants, you first need to face your God.

FIVE SMOOTH STONES

I PROPOSE THAT SYMBOLICALLY, each of the five stones represents one of the foundations to our faith. A wonderful spiritual exercise is to reflect on the "stones of your faith." Based on what we know about David, I'll share with you five compelling stones to store in your shepherd's pouch. To make these stones easy to remember, they all begin with the letter "P."

1) The stone of prayer (Go down before you go up!)
2) The stone of persistence (David was prepared for multiple opponents!)
3) The stone of priority (Only David talked about God!)
4) The stone of positive expectancy (David talked about victory!)
5) The stone of physical training (David was strong!)

Let's begin with the stone of prayer. In the context of CrossFit, if you want to lift a barbell *upward,* you need to apply force *downward.* Although it seems counterintuitive, the fact remains that the degree of force you can apply downward against the earth has a direct effect on the amount of power you are able to generate upward on the barbell. This being the case, why would we think it would be anything different in the spiritual ordering of things?

David knew that the key to overcoming the challenges that he faced in life was through prayer and intimate fellowship with God.

David also knew that sometimes it took more than one prayer to defeat a giant. In this sense, the second stone speaks to the importance of persistence in your prayer life. Furthermore, whether you like it or not, everything in your life has been achieved (either intentionally or unintentionally) through the power of persistence. In any given moment of your life, you have an opportunity to take an inventory of everything that you are grateful for and then to identify the variable that you had persistently practiced in order to bring your goals to fruition. On the other hand, if there are things in your life that you do not want to carry with you into the next season, you can identity the associated variable and stop doing it!

The third stone addresses the principle of "putting first things first." Whereas everyone else on the battlefield was focused on the giant, David was focused on God. In fact, it's all that David could talk about! In 1 Samuel 17 (the chapter in the Bible that records David and Goliath), it is incredible to see that David spoke about God on nine different occasions, compared to the two mentions that David made of Goliath. And based on the stone of positive expectancy, it is no wonder that when David did speak about Goliath, it was in the context of defeating him in battle! As one of my mentors used to constantly remind me, "You need to make God your first priority, and not your last resort."

The fourth stone serves to remind us of the awesome power of our expectations. By a mysterious law of creation, we tend to move in the direction of the thoughts and expectations we have for ourselves, for each other, and for God. It's interesting to note that in the context of David and Goliath, whereas everyone else on the battlefield was *expecting defeat,* David was *expecting victory* (reference 1 Samuel 17:24–26). David was so certain that he would defeat Goliath that he was already thinking about the reward "for the man who kills this Philistine and removes this disgrace from Israel" (1 Samuel 17:25–26). Reasoning from this fact, it is exceedingly important for you to remain positive in both your speaking and thinking. An outstanding Bible verse that reiterates this is Proverbs 4:23: "Above all else guard your heart, for everything you do flows from it." If you recall from Lesson 5, in the Bible, the heart is the seat of human will; thus, the heart is the central and unifying organ of our personal life. When our deepest and innermost thoughts (our heart) are absolutely convinced of the goodness of God, then a sense of positive expectancy about every season of life is the natural result.

The fifth and final stone reminds us of the importance of physical training and proper care of our body. Your body is the temple of the Holy Spirit and the instrument by which God can work in and through your life. The incarnation means that God took upon Himself a human body to live in and work through. In Paul's Letter to the Romans, he wrote, "present your bodies to God" (Romans 12:1). In historical context, this was an astonishing thing to say! To the Greeks, what mattered was the spirit; the body was only a prison house, something to be despised and even ashamed of. However, in Paul's theology of the human body, he taught that a Christian's body was just as important to God as was their soul, mind, and spirit. This means that we can serve God through the totality of our human makeup. Reasoning from this fact, a strong physical body can be an instrument in the service of God's Kingdom. In other words, your daily workout can be worship!

CONCLUDING THOUGHTS

IN CONCLUDING THIS LESSON, I would be amiss if I did not mention David's complete reliance on the strength of God. Everyone on the battlefield that fateful day looked at Goliath and observed an *impossible situation*. However, David looked at God and believed that God could make the *impossible entirely possible*. This means that as long as you go through life thinking that everything depends on your own effort, you are bound to be a pessimist and will tend to gravitate toward a negative outlook on every challenge you face. On the other hand, when you realize that it is never about your own effort—but rather it is always God's grace and power that matter, then you become an optimist. Like David, you embrace a faith that proclaims, "With God on my side, all things are possible."

And to this I say,

YES and AMEN.

LESSON TWELVE

THE SUPREMACY OF GOD'S GRACE

LESSON TWELVE
THE SUPREMACY OF GOD'S GRACE

THE WORD OF GOD:

The next day, John was there again with two of his disciples. When he saw Jesus passing by, he said, "Look, the Lamb of God!"

When the two disciples heard him say this, they followed Jesus. Turning around, Jesus saw them following him and asked, "What do you want?"

They said "Rabbi" (which means "Teacher"), "where are you staying?"

"Come," Jesus replied, "and you will see."

(John 1:35–39)

MY BROTHERS AND MY SISTERS, may the grace of our Lord Jesus Christ, the love of God, and the fellowship of the Holy Spirit be with you (2 Corinthians 13:14). I want to study with you today the awesome topic of *The Supremacy of God's Grace*. This being the twelfth and final lesson of this section, I thought it would be fitting to embrace the principle of *virtuosity* in our Gospel reading by "reviewing the basics." Although we studied John 1:35–41 in Lesson Four, I feel that we need to revisit the astonishing revelation of God's grace contained within these few verses (specifically 1:35–39). I am so encouraged by the incredible touch of God's grace found within this short passage of Scripture. Although it is only four verses, I promise that we shall soon discover a deep reservoir of spiritual wisdom, revelation, and knowledge that will fill your heart with joy. In the words of the great biblical scholar William Barclay, "Never was a passage of scripture fuller of more important revealing touches than this."

Let's begin by noticing the prominent figure of John the Baptist. Characteristic of John was his humbleness before the Lord and his desire to point people beyond himself. Have you noticed how easy it is to point people to yourself? We seem to be hardwired to desire attention, accolade, acclaim, and the acknowledgment of others. However, John teaches us that there is another way of abiding in the world, and that is to take the attention off ourselves and put it onto God. This was the pattern of all the great saints of the Bible. In one way or another, Abraham, Daniel, Moses, and David—all those who were called friends of the Lord—had the uncanny ability and meekness of heart to freely recognize their own shortcomings. However, in their weakness was their strength, for God Almighty was able to freely work through the conduit of His children.

Perhaps one reason that we are fearful of turning attention away from ourselves is that we are jealous of others and—maybe at a level so deep it only influences the subconscious mind—we are jealous of God. The root of all sin is idolatry, which is turning something other than God into God. Very often, the god we worship is the god of our own pride, acclaim, popularity, and social status. This is one reason that I love and admire John the Baptist. He must have known very well that to speak to his disciples about Jesus the way that he did was to invite them to leave him and transfer their loyalty to this new and greater teacher. Yet he still did it. There was not a single ounce of jealousy in John. He had come to lead other people to Christ, not to himself. There is no harder task than to freely surrender to second place; nevertheless, as soon as Jesus emerged on the scene, John never had any other thought than to send people to Him.

This being the case, did you notice to whom John sent his disciples? "The Lamb of God" meant only one thing—this story would not end well for the disciples. Jewish people were all too familiar with the implications of the sacrificial lamb—it was put to death as atonement for the sins of the people. This means that when we follow Jesus, we must be prepared to take up our cross and to follow Him even when the road becomes rough. I recall one of my Army instructors chiding me and saying, "Everyone wants to be in the Army on a bright sunny day!" The funny thing is, in twelve years of military service, I recall only a handful of sunny (let alone bright) days. Rather, they were filled with stormy weather and were in uncomfortable environments and conditions that I would have rather done without.

Surely the disciples knew what they were in for. Reasoning from this fact, although they had left John to follow Jesus, perhaps they were a bit timid and followed from a respectful and uncertain distance. Maybe they were shy. We could even imagine that they were afraid. In the traditional spiritual path of other world religions, it is the devotees who follow after their guru. In this sense, the text for a moment seems to suggest that a similar series of events is now taking place in the lives of the two disciples. But then Jesus did something that is both radical and entirely characteristic of God. He turned and spoke to them. That is to say, Jesus met them halfway. He made things easier for them. He opened the door so that they might come in. He invited them into His life.

FOLLOWING AFTER JESUS

THIS IS WHAT JESUS DOES when He comes into your life. He opens your eyes and enables you to see things that you never saw before. He turns you from darkness to light. Before people enter into a relationship with Jesus, they are essentially walking in the wrong direction, immersed in a life of sin. It's interesting that the Aramaic word for sin that Jesus used, *Kata*, was an ancient archery term that meant three things: to miss the target, to fall short of the target, or to shoot the arrow in the entirely wrong direction. In either event, when Jesus comes into your life, He forgives your sins. Your past is forgiven and, for the future, your life is re-created and purified—what we refer to in theology as increasingly sanctified and comforted to His image.

We also see in Jesus's actions a symbol of the divine initiative of God's grace. It is always God who takes the first step. The moment that our thoughts go to God, and our heart reaches out to Him, God comes to meet us far more than just halfway. God will never leave a man or woman to search and search after Him. Rather, God goes out to meet you wherever you are. The great theologian and early Church Father Augustine said, "We could not even have begun to seek God unless He had already found us." This means that when we go to God, we do not go in vain. Nor are we dependent on the work of our hands, the intellect of our mind, or the capacity of our heart to enjoy fellowship with Him. Rather, by grace through faith, God enters our life and transforms us into the image of His Son.

Jesus began by asking these two men the most fundamental question in life: "What do you want?" In Greek, the word that Jesus used was *Zeter*, which means "to seek after or to strive for." In other words, Jesus asked, "What are you seeking?" It's interesting to note that in other world religions, it was the common practice of the devotee to ask the guru a question. However, here we see something entirely different, yet at the same time so beautifully characteristic of God. After all, in the creation account of Genesis, God asked Adam (Hebrew for "mankind") two illuminating questions: "Where are you?" (Genesis 13:9) and "Who told you that?" (Genesis 13:11). Consider how this "trifecta" of questions impacts your life today. The question "Where are you?" speaks to your physical nature and everything that makes up the material existence of your daily life. The question "Who told you that?" speaks to your innermost thoughts—the way that you think about yourself, about other people, and, most importantly, about God. A. W. Tozer said, "The thoughts that come into your mind about God are the most important thoughts about you." And finally, "What do you want? What are you searching for? What are you seeking, and striving after?"

It would be well with us if every now and again we were to ask ourselves all three of these profound questions. However, for our purposes within this lesson, let's contemplate for a moment the implications of the question that Jesus asked His disciples, "What are you looking for? What is your aim and goal? What do you really want to get out of life?"

Perhaps some of you are searching for security. You would like a position in life that is safe and provides enough money to meet the needs of life, plus a little left over for material comforts. This is not a wrong aim, but it is a low aim and an inadequate thing in which to direct all of your life energy. As our world has painfully witnessed, there is no safe security in the changing tides of life. In the final analysis, we leave everything behind and take nothing with us. This is akin to our arrow falling short of the target.

So, perhaps we aim higher. Maybe you are searching for a career, or purpose, meaning, and mission in life. If this motive is in service of others, then indeed the arrow may very well now be on target but still miss the mark—you've not yet hit the bull's-eye.

What, then, are we searching for? What is the right answer? Perhaps when it is all boiled down, we are all searching for the same thing. In this sense, we are truly brothers and sisters, of the same family. Could it be that we are all searching for some kind of peace? Are we all searching for something to enable us to be at peace with ourselves, with each other, and, most importantly, with

God? I propose that in our heart of hearts, this is what we all want, and this is why, to a greater or lesser degree, we all want (and desperately need) God.

So what did the disciples of John say to Jesus? What was it they were searching for? It is interesting that according to our Gospel author, the Apostle John, the two disciples address Jesus as "Rabbi," a Hebrew word that literally means "My great one." However, John was not writing to a Jewish audience, but rather to a Greek audience, so John inserts the Greek word *Didaskalos,* which means "Teacher." In both the Hebrew and Greek, what was implied by the way they responded to Jesus was that they did not only want to speak with Him on the open road, in passing, as a happenstance meeting that would result in the exchange of only a few words.

Rather, they wanted to stay with Jesus, and talk out their problems of life, and open their hearts to their troubles. What they really wanted was to be with Jesus, and the only way they could foreseeably be with Him was to know where He was staying. For our purposes, this means that the man or woman who would be a disciple of Jesus can never be satisfied with a passing word. In other words, in the deep recesses of our heart, we want to meet Jesus, not as an acquaintance in passing, but as a friend within His own house. What a different concept this is than what we are so accustomed to. Rather than inviting Jesus into my life—and my home—which is akin to declaring that He must enter my life according to my specifications, my needs, and my conditions—rather, I humbly step into His house. I leave my life behind to take up my new life in Christ.

Jesus's answer was, "Come and see!" The Jewish Rabbis had a way of using that phrase in their teaching. They would say, "Do you want to know the answer to this question? Do you want to know the solution to this problem? Come and see, and we will think about it together. Come and see, and we will do life together, and I will be with you every step of the way." When Jesus said, "Come and see!" he was inviting them, not only to come and talk, but to come and experience the life that only He could provide.

CONCLUDING THOUGHTS

IN CONCLUDING THIS LESSON, let's focus on one final and often overlooked detail of the story. Did you notice the stringent conditions under which the disciples were invited to follow Jesus? Did you happen to see the long list of things they needed to do? All the religious steps they had to take? Of course not—there weren't any! This is what I refer to as the "Supremacy of God's Grace." In other words, God's grace is everywhere you look. It is the key to unlocking the message of the Gospel. The gift of God's grace is freely given, through faith in Jesus Christ. The Apostle Paul said it best: "It is by grace that we have been saved, through faith. And this faith is not of yourselves, it is a gift from God. It is not by works, so that no one can boast" (Ephesians 2:8–9—my translation).

And to this I believe that we can all lift our voices and proclaim:

YES and AMEN

PART NINE
DOCRTINE OF THE GYM

SECTION SUMMARY:

IN THE SAME WAY THAT a CrossFit gym owner benefits from a clearly stated mission statement, biblical leaders must strongly consider establishing doctrinal statements that distinctly define their position on matters of the Christian faith. The following doctrinal statements lean toward the Conservative Baptist position and were shaped by my theological studies at Western Seminary. Unlike the theological treatment of a subject that enjoins arguments on both sides of an issue, a doctrinal statement should be concisely stated and substantiated by two or three key verses from Scripture.

THE DOCTRINE OF REVELATION
GENERAL – SPECIAL – AND HOLY SCRIPTURE

INTRODUCTION

REVELATION IS THE DISCLOSURE by God of truths about Himself that people could not arrive at independent of His divine initiative. By God's sovereign decision and enabling, His revelation to humanity is accomplished by both general (Ps. 19:1-3; Ro. 1:19-20) and special revelation. The means of special revelation were accomplished by God's manifestation of Himself through historical events (Deut. 26: 5-9; Acts 13:16-41), His divine speech (2 Tim. 3:16-17; 2 Pet. 1:20-21), and most importantly through the incarnation of His Word in the person and deity of Jesus Christ (Col. 1:15-19; Heb. 1:2-3).

GENERAL REVELATION

GENERAL REVELATION IS GOD'S communication and display of Himself to all persons at all times and places through nature (Ps. 19:1-3), history (Acts 17:26), and mankind (Gen. 1:26-28; Ro. 2:11-16).[426] At the most rudimentary level, Jesus taught that evidence of God could be identified through observance of the natural order of agriculture (Mt. 6:28-30). Even the seemingly obvious fact that God had chosen to preserve mankind by providing rain, crops of food for bodily nourishment, and emotional wellbeing (Acts 14:17) points to evidence of His presence within both creation and history (Acts 14:15-18). Although these modes of revelation are clear and leave people without excuse (Ro. 1:20), the sinful nature of mankind distorts our thinking, hardens our heart (Ro. 1:21, 3:23; 1 Jn. 1:8), and corrupts the truth about God in exchange for a lie (Ro. 1:25).

---

[426] Millard Erickson, *Christian Theology* (Baker Academic, Grand Rapids, MI. 2013), p. 122.

SPECIAL REVELATION

SPECIAL REVELATION DIFFERS FROM general revelation in the sense that God communicates essential qualities of His being that could not be discerned through human reasoning or understanding (1 Cor. 2:14). God's special revelation has manifested itself through historical events (Job 12:23), divinely inspired speech subsequently recorded in the written Word of God (2 Pet. 1:20-21), and the incarnation of the Word in the person and deity of Jesus Christ (Jn. 1:1; 18). Special revelation supremely and uniquely announces God's intention to reconcile mankind onto Himself (Jn. 3:16) by grace through faith in Jesus Christ (Eph. 2:8). In the life of Christ, mankind is no longer limited to knowing *about God,* but may now *know God* by entering into a personal, saving, and loving relationship with Him (Jn. 17:3).

HOLY SCRIPTURE

THE BIBLE TEACHES THAT the sixty-six books of its inspired contents are the *theopneustos* Word of God (2 Tim. 3:16) written by man through the power of the Holy Spirit (2 Pet. 1:21) who shaped the thoughts and directed the subsequent written and recorded words of the human authors (1 Cor. 2:13). The original biblical autographs contain the powerful (Gen. 18:14; 1 Cor. 2:4-5), authoritative (2 Tim. 3:16-17), clear (Deut. 30:11-14; Ro. 10:6-8), sufficient (1 Cor. 2:9-10), inerrant, (Mt. 19:4-5), and inspired (Acts 1:16; 2 Sam. 23:2) Word of God.

The sixty-six books of the Bible are the complete and final canonical revelation of God to mankind (1 Thess. 2:13). Although God chose to speak through human authors at many times and in various ways (Heb. 1:1), the most complete revelation of His triune nature and program of redemption was made visible through Jesus Christ (Jn. 20:31; Heb. 1:2-4; Col. 3:4-7). The canonical books of the Bible have been given authority by Christ himself (Mt. 28:19-20) and are the believer's supreme rule of both doctrine (Jn. 10:35) and behavioral practice (2 Tim. 3:16-17; Tit. 1:6-9).

In the Holy Scriptures, the believer encounters the living Word of God and comes to understand it not only says things, but also does things (Ps. 33:6). The interpreter of the biblical text, through the indwelling power of the Holy Spirit, experiences spiritual realities with Spirit-taught words (1 Cor. 2:10-16) that fundamentally change their entire life (Ro. 15:4).

THE DOCTRINE OF GOD

THE NATURE OF GOD

THE BIBLE DECLARES THAT there is only One true (Deut. 6:4; 1 Cor. 8:4-6) and living God (1 Thess. 1:9) who reigns eternally (Pss. 90:2; Deut. 32:40; 1 Tim. 1:17) and infinitely (1 Ki. 8:27; Pss. 113:4-6) within His creation (Gen. 1:1; Isa. 66:1-2; Jn. 1:3). God is exalted over His creation (Isa. 55:8-9; Pss. 113:5-6) while simultaneously present and involved in the world as the sustainer of all things (Job 27:3; Jer. 23:24; Acts 17:27-28). God personally describes Himself as compassionate, gracious, slow to anger, and abounding in love and faithfulness (Ex. 34:6). God graciously rewards those who diligently seek after Him (Heb. 11:6). However, this same God will not tolerate injustice (Neh. 9:32-33; Pss. 58:11), hates all sin (Pss. 5:5-6; Ro. 1:18), and will not leave the guilty unpunished (Ex. 34:7; Ro. 6:23).

The objective, intrinsic, and unchanging (Pss. 102: 26-27; Mal. 3:6) qualities and attributes of God are made known through both general (Ps. 19:1-3; Ro. 1:19-20) and special revelation (Deut. 26:5-9; 2 Tim. 3:16-17; Heb. 1:2-3).[427] God is perfect in His wisdom (Ro. 16:27), power (Job 37:23), holiness (Ex. 15:11; Pss. 99:3), righteousness (Jer. 9:24), goodness (Ex. 34:6), love (1 Jn. 4:82; Cor. 13:11) and truth (Jn. 14:6). God is the Supreme Being (Deut. 10:17).[428] He is the One whom I confess is Lord (Mt. 16:16), and the only One I desire to please with both love and obedience (Jn. 14:15).

The Bible teaches that in the unity and equality of the Godhead, the Father, the Son and the Holy Spirit are revealed as three Persons who are One in substance, power, and eternity (Mt. 3:16-17; 28-29; 2 Cor. 23-14).[429] The Father is neither begotten nor made (Pss. 100:3). The Son is not made, but is rather eternally begotten of the Father (Jn. 1:14, 18; Heb. 1:2-3).[430]

---

[427] Millard Erickson, *Christian Theology* (Baker Academic, Grand Rapids, MI. 2013), p. 236.

[428] Erickson, p. 271.

[429] Adopted from the Westminster Confession of Faith: *Of God, and the Holy Trinity* and Erickson, pg. 309.

[430] C.S. Lewis wrote, "Christ is begotten, not created. To beget is to become the father of, to create is to make. And the difference is this: When you beget, you beget something of the same kind as yourself." C.S. Lewis, *Mere Christianity* (Collier Books, New York, NY. 1943), pg. 123.

The Son is the exact and perfect image of the Father (Heb. 1:2-3; Col. 1:15, 17, 2:9), and is the only means by which one can come to know God (Jn. 14:6; Ro. 7:25). Jesus Christ is the head of the Church, and the final judge of both believers and unbelievers (2 Cor. 5:10; Rev. 20:15; Ro. 14:11). The Holy Spirit is the equal third Person of the Trinity (Gen. 1:2; Jn. 3:5-7), who eternally proceeds from the Father and Son (Acts 5:3-4; Jn. 16:8-11; Mk. 3:29; Jn. 15:26; Gal. 4:6).[431]

---

[431] Bishop Robert Barron said that, "God is a play between a lover, the Father, a beloved, the Son, and he love that they share, the Holy Spirit." – Bishop Barron, Sermon on "God's Marvelous Choice." May 1, 2018. From the *Word On Fire* sermon series.

THE DOCTRINE OF THE WORK GOD

GOD IS SUPREMELY ENTHRONED above His creation (Isa. 37:16, 40:22; Pss. 102:12-22), yet He is also intimately at work within it (Pss. 139:13-14; Heb. 3:4; Ro. 3:20). God created the entire universe and everything in it independent of preexisting materials (Gen. 1:1; Jn. 1:1-3; Heb. 11:3).[432] Without compulsion or necessity, God chose to create of His free will (Gen. 1:1; Jn. 1:1-3). God is the Supreme reality, and everything that exists within His creation is ultimately for His purpose and glory (Pss. 19:1; Col. 1:16).

God is the author and sustainer of history (Neh. 9:6; Pss. 139:16; Job 14:5; Col. 1:17) and He continually maintains, directs, and works out everything to its proper end (Pss. 33:11; Prov. 16:4, 19:21; Job 38:4). Nothing can interrupt, deter, or thwart the purposes and plans of God (Jer. 10:23-24). God's redemptive work (Gal. 3:8, 4:4-5), His gracious and sovereign choice of people-groups and nations (Ro. 9-11), and the selection of individuals even before birth (Gal. 1:15) are all part of the tapestry of His divine and perfect plans (1 Cor. 12:18, 15:18).[433]

The will and purposes of God's eternal plan are accomplished without mitigating human responsibility or approving of sin (Pss. 5:4, 139:16; 2 Tim. 1:10, Js. 1:13-14). Rather than spontaneously directing events as they occur within the human understanding of finite time, history unfolds according to God's plan, from all eternity, from before the beginning of creation (Ro. 9:20-23; Eph. 1:11-12).[434] By His grace and love, God saves from sin all who come to Him in faith through Jesus Christ (Eph. 2:8-9; Heb. 7:25).

---

[432] Erickson, pg. 340.

[433] Erickson, pg. 322.

[434] Erickson, pg. 323.

THE DOCTRINE OF THE PERSON OF CHRIST

THE HOLY SCRIPTURE TEACHES that Jesus Christ is the image of the invisible God and the exact representation of His being (Heb. 1:1-3; Col. 1:15), which is to proclaim by faith that Jesus is Himself God (Jn. 20:28). Jesus is the *Word became flesh*—the incarnation of the eternal Second Person of the Trinity (Jn. 1:14a). Being Himself equal with the Father in eternity (Jn. 1:1-3), Jesus possesses all the divine attributes of God, and is Himself deserving of our love, praise, worship, and obedience (Jn. 14:15; Rev. 5:12-14).

Although *fully God*, Jesus took upon Himself the nature of mankind, and with the exception of sin, lived a *fully human* life (Jn. 1:14b; 1Pe. 2:22). Jesus was conceived through the power of the Holy Spirit and was born of the Virgin Mary (Isa. 7:14; Mt. 1:23; Lk. 1:26-35). During His lifetime on Earth, Jesus freely accepted the psychosomatic characteristics of humanity in both mind and body (Php. 2:7-8) while simultaneously maintaining all the fullness of His deity and divine attributes (Php. 2:6; Col. 2:9). As the God-Man, the perfect unity of Christ's humanity and deity were inseparably joined together in one person without division or confusion of the two natures (Mt. 16:16; Jn. 5:23; 1Ti. 3:16).[435]

Although tempted (Mt. 4:1-11; Mk. 1:12-13; Lk. 4:1-13), Jesus lived an exemplary life without sin in perfect obedience to the will of His Father (Heb. 4:15, 5:8-9; 1Co. 5:21). Jesus endured the most painful of human sufferings (Mt. 26:37-38; 27:27-50; Lk. 22:44), was crucified (Mk. 15:24, 37), died, and was buried (Mt. 27:60; Php. 2:8). On the third day, through the power of the Holy Spirit, God raised Jesus from the dead (1Co. 15:3-4; Lk. 24:39; Jn. 20:25-27). Jesus ascended into Heaven in the resurrected body in which He had appeared to His disciples (Lk. 24:50-51) and is now seated at the right hand of His Father (1Pe. 3:22). At the end of times, Jesus will come again personally and visibly to judge mankind and establish His Kingdom on Earth (Ac. 1:11, 10:42; Jn. 5:28-29; Rev. 11:15).

---

[435] Adapted from the Westminster Confession of Faith, Chapter 8.

THE DOCTRINE OF THE WORK OF CHRIST

THE BIBLE TEACHES THAT according to God's eternal purposes and will (1Pe. 1:19-20), He did ordain His only begotten Son (Jn. 3:16) to be the mediator between God and mankind (1Ti. 2:5). In this capacity, the eternal Second Person of the Trinity, our Lord Jesus Christ, faithfully fulfilled the offices of Prophet (Acts 3:20, 22), Priest (Heb. 5:5-6) and King (Lk. 1:33).[436] Jesus is the Head of His Church (Eph. 5:23), the Heir of all things (Heb. 1:2), and will come again in glory to judge both the living and the dead (Mt. 25:31; Acts 17:31, 2 Ti. 4:1). I believe that before the foundation of the world God chose mankind in Christ (Eph. 1:14) so that in time humanity would be called, redeemed, justified, sanctified, and glorified (1Ti. 2:6; 1Co. 1:30; Ro. 8:30). In Christ, mankind is reconciled to God and is capable of appearing blameless before Him (2Co. 5:18-19).

The Bible teaches that Jesus Christ's obedience to His Father and death on the cross is the perfect sacrifice for the sin of mankind (Isa. 53:4-5; Ro. 5:19; Heb. 9:6-15). Christ's substitutionary work on the cross pleased God and achieved a once-for-all atonement for the sins of the human race (Lev. 4:35; Heb. 9:12).[437] The blood of Christ sanctifies the believer (Heb. 13:11-12) and completely satisfies the divine justice of God (Gal. 4:4-5). Christ's victory over death achieved not only humanities reconciliation with God but also an everlasting life in His Kingdom (Col. 1:20; 2Co. 5:18; Jn. 3:16). Impossible to earn and without merit (Eph. 2:8-9) the free gift of God's grace through faith in Christ Jesus justifies the believer and presents us righteous before God (Ro. 1:17, 3:22, 5:1-2; 2Co. 5:21).

---

[436] Adapted from the Westminster Confession of Faith, Chapter 8.

[437] Millard Erickson, *Christian Theology* (Baker Academic, Grand Rapids, MI.) 2013, p. 741.

THE DOCTRINE OF HUMANITY AND SIN

INTRODUCTION

THE DOCTRINE OF HUMANITY is foundational to understanding the nature of God and the totality of His creation. Being made in the image and likeness of God (Gen. 1:26-27), mankind is perfectly situated to learn something about God as we simultaneously learn something about ourselves. However, until the study of mankind uniquely and supremely points to the perfect example set by Jesus Christ (Heb. 2:14-17), we will fail to grasp the magnitude of the chasm between our sinful fallen state and the awesome image that God intended humanity to be (Ps. 8:4-6).

HUMANITY

THE HUMAN RACE WAS directly and immediately created by God according to His image and likeness (Gen. 1:26-27; 2:7; 1 Cor. 11:7; Jas. 3:9). Through a supernatural and seamless integration of both "dust and breath" (Gen. 2:7a), the first man became a living being (Gen. 2:7b). The Bible presents the human person in a state of conditional unity: a perfect yoking of their physical and spiritual essence and a divinely appointed cohabitation of their subjective and objective psychosomatic elements.[438]

Humanity was created free of sin with a rational nature, intelligence, self-determination, free will, and moral responsibility to God (Gen. 2:15-25; Jas. 3:9).[439] Although created alongside the animal kingdom (Gen. 1:24-26), humans are uniquely capable of having a conscious and personal relationship with God (Jn. 6:40, 15:5; 1 Jn. 3:1). God endowed humanity with an immortal soul (Gen. 2:7; Eccl. 12:7, 3:11; Lk. 22:43) and His law is written on our hearts (Ro. 2:14-15). Mankind's image and likeness to God is a special characteristic of the entire human race, uniquely distinguishing mankind from other creatures and making our salvation of supreme importance to God (Jn. 3:16).

---

[438] Erickson, p. 493.

[439] Erickson, p. 493.

Originating from one human pair (Gen. 1:27-28, 2:21-24), the entire human race thus shares a unified sacred value bestowed upon us by God (Gen. 1:31). Adam served as both the *first* and *universal* human through whom all forthcoming humans would likewise share in the image and likeness of God (Gen. 1:26; Col. 3:10; Eph. 4:24). The image of God in mankind is not relegated to something that humanity uniquely *has* or *does* (1 Sam. 16:7).[440] Rather, the image and likeness of God is a status conferred upon us by God Himself, and entails a combination of *ability* and *responsibility* for representing God on earth.[441] It is by the grace-given virtue of our creation and existence that a human being is intrinsically bestowed with the privilege of being an image bearer of God (Mt. 5:48).[442]

SIN

ALTHOUGH GOD CREATED HUMANITY without sin, our first parents were seduced by the temptation of evil and freely disobeyed the will and Word of God (Gen. 2:15-17, 3:1-19; 2 Cor. 11:3). By willful disobedience to God, the first created pair of humans fell from their original state of communion and fellowship with God and became dead in their sin (Gen. 2:17; Eph. 2:1-3).[443] Being the root and original inception of all mankind, the sinful nature and guilt of our first parents has been subsequently and perpetually transferred to every generation and has corrupted the entire human race (Ps. 51:5; Acts 17:26; Eph. 2:3, Ro. 3:13-18, 5:12, 15-19).

The penalty for our sin is both physical and spiritual death (Gen. 2:16-17; Ro. 6:23). Sin is spread throughout the entire human race and completely infects the totality of each person's individual being (Ro. 3:13-18, 3:23). Sin negatively affects human life from beginning to end (Gen. 8:21; Tit. 1:15) and leaves mankind utterly helpless in any attempt to recover or save himself (Jn. 3:36; Ro. 6:23; 1 Cor. 2:14; 1 Jn. 1:8). Apart from the perfect example of Jesus Christ, mankind is unable to understand or image what God originally intended

---

[440] Erickson, p. 470.

[441] Michael Heiser, *The Unseen Realm* (Lexham Press, Bellingham Press, WA. 2015), p. 58.

[442] Heiser, p. 58.

[443] Adopted from the Westminster Confession of Faith, Chapter 6, *The Fall of Man*.

for His creation (1 Col. 15; 2 Cor. 4:4; Heb. 1:3; Ro. 5:12-17). Furthermore, due to the corrupted nature of the human race and our inability to inherently correct our course of thinking and behavior (Prov. 20:9; Eccl. 7:20; Mt. 15:19; Ro. 7:14, 17-18), salvation of mankind is made solely possible by God's grace through faith in Jesus Christ (Jn. 3:16; 2 Cor. 3:18; Ro. 5:15) and is not the basis of human merit or works (Eph. 2:8-9).

THE DOCTRINE OF THE HOLY SPIRIT

THE PERSON OF THE HOLY SPIRIT

THE HOLY SPIRIT IS the eternal and coequal Third Person of the Trinity who proceeds from the Father and the Son (Jn. 3:16-17, 15:26; 1Jn. 5:7; Gal. 4:6). The Person of the Holy Spirit was active in the beginning and continuation of creation (Gen. 1:2, 26; Ps. 104:30; Job 26:13), the inspiration of Scripture (2Ti. 3:16; 2Pe. 1:20-21), and the continuing work of salvation (Jn. 3:5-7; 2Thes. 2:13; Tit. 3:5).

The Person of the Holy Spirit is eternal, coequal, and consubstantial with God the Father and God the Son (Mt. 28:19; Acts 5:3-4). The Holy Spirit's attributes of personhood and deity include His will (Acts 16:6; Ro. 8:26; 1Co. 12:11), eternality (Heb. 9:14), personality, intellect, and emotion (Acts 5:3-4, 15:28; Eph. 4:30; 1Co. 2:10-13), omnipresence (Ps. 139:7-10), omniscience (Isa. 40:13-14; Jn. 14:26; 1Co. 2:10-11), omnipotence (Lk. 1:35; Ro. 15:13, 19) and truthfulness (Jn. 16:13).[444] In all His divine attributes, the Person of the Holy Spirit resides in perfect equality with the Father and the Son (Jer. 31:31-33; 1Co. 12:4-6; Heb. 10:15-17).

---

[444] Adapted from *The Masters Seminary* doctrine statement on *God the Holy Spirit*.

THE WORK OF THE HOLY SPIRIT

THE HOLY SPIRIT the eternal and coequal Third Person of the Trinity who proceeds from the Father and the Son (Jn. 3:16-17, 15:26; 1Jn. 5:7; Gal. 4:6). The Holy Spirit was active in the beginning of creation (Gen. 1:2, 26) and throughout its completion (Ps. 104:30; Job 26:13). In the Old Testament, the Holy Spirit played a special role in giving prophecy (2Ki. 2:15; Ezk. 2:2, 8:3) and writing Scripture (2Ti. 3:16; 2Pt. 1:20-21). The Holy Spirit enabled unique skills for various tasks (Exod. 31:3-5; Hag. 1:14) in addition to establishing justice, righteousness, peace, (Isa. 11:16-20) and devotion (Isa. 11:2-5, 44:3-5).

From the moment of our Lord's conception (Mt. 1:18, 20) the Holy Spirit was active in the life and ministry of Jesus Christ (Mt. 3:16). In the present age, the work of the Holy Spirit began at Pentecost when He came from the Father as promised by Jesus (Jn. 14:16-17; Acts 2:1-41). Throughout the lives of the Apostles, the Holy Spirit was active in the establishment of the Body of Christ, which is His Church (1Co. 12:13).

The Holy Spirit convicts the world of sin, righteousness, and judgment (Jn. 16:7-11). At conversion and regeneration, the Holy Spirit indwells the believer and baptizes them into the Body of Christ (Acts 1:5, 1Co. 12:13). The Holy Spirit sanctifies, comforts, instructs, transforms, and empowers believers for service, and seals them until the coming of Jesus Christ (Acts 9:31; 2Co. 3:18; Ro. 8:29; Eph. 1:13-14; 1Pe. 1:2).

The Holy Spirit gives gifts to believers for the purpose of edifying the Church, glorifying Christ, redeeming the lost, and encouraging one another (Acts 1:8; Jn. 16:13-14; 1Co. 12:4-11; 1Thes. 5:11; 1Pe. 4:10-11). Although the sign-gifts of speaking in tongues and miraculous healing most notably authenticated the Apostles (Acts 5:15, 19:12), there is no reason to believe that these gifts have ceased today (Jn. 14:12-14; 1Co. 12:31,14:1-18).

THE DOCTRINE OF THE CHURCH

THE UNIVERSAL CHURCH

THE BIBLE TEACHES THAT EVERYONE who puts their faith in Jesus Christ is immediately joined by the power of the Holy Spirit into one Spiritual Body—the Church, which is the bride of Christ (1Co. 12:12-13; 2Co. 11:2; Col. 1:18). The Church was formed on the Day of Pentecost (Acts 2:1-21), and will continue until the return of Christ in His glory (1Co. 15:51-52). The Church is an invisible and spiritual organism that consists of all born-again believers throughout the ages who are gathered into Christ's Body (Eph. 1:10; Col. 1:18; Heb. 11:1-40). The Church is distinct from Israel and remained a hidden mystery until this present age (Eph. 3:1-12).

Jesus Christ is the head, cornerstone, and builder of His Church (Isa. 28:16; Mat. 16:18; 1Co. 11:3; Col. 1:18). As a representation of Christ on earth the purpose of the Church is to glorify God and continue Christ's ministry in the world (Ephesians 4:13-16).[445] Through the power of the Holy Spirit, this is primarily accomplished by preaching of the Word (2Ti. 2:2), keeping the sacraments (Lk. 22:19-20; Acts 2:28-42), and by advancing the Gospel to all the ends of the world (Mat. 28:19).

THE LOCAL CHURCH

THE ESTABLISHMENT OF THE Local Church is meant to serve as a visible representation of the invisible-spiritual Body of Christ (Acts 14:23, 27; 20:17, 28; 1Co. 12:12-27). Believers in Christ are to join together in local assemblies to encourage and build one another up (1Th. 5:11; Heb. 10:25). Under the headship of Christ (1Co. 11:3), localized authority resides within the assembly of regenerated Spirit-led believers (Acts 6:3-5, 15:2-3; 1Pe. 2:9-10). Each congregation is free from any external control and may enjoy the right of self-government (Titus 1:5).

The two specific biblically designated offices in the Church are male-elders and deacons, an office open to both men and women (Titus 1:6; 1Ti.

---

[445] Millard Erickson. *Christian Theology* (Baker Academic, Grand Rapids, MI: 2013), p. 970.

2:8-15). Elders (also called pastors, bishops, and overseers—Acts 20:17, 28; Titus 1:5-9) are men who shepherd the Local Church, exercise oversight, teach the Word, and equip believers for ministry and works of service (Eph. 4:11-12; 1Pe. 5:2). The position of elder and deacon are selected by the local congregation, and must meet the biblical qualifications of the office (1Ti. 3:1-13; Titus 1:5-9).

Two sacraments have been entrusted to the Local Church: Baptism and the Lord's Supper (Mat. 28:19; Acts 2:38-42; 1Co. 11:23-25). The sacraments serve as visible symbols of God's grace (Ro. 4:11), and to distinguish those who belong to Christ and the rest of the world.[446] Baptism by immersion into water is an outward symbol of the believer's inward change of heart—a physical demonstration of their faith in Jesus and "death to sin but resurrection to God in Christ Jesus" (Ro. 6:11).[447] Baptism is also a sign of the believer's entry into the fellowship of the visible Body of Christ (Acts 2:41-42). Whereas baptism is an initiatory rite, the Lord's Supper is a continuing sacrament of the Local Church.[448] The elements of bread and wine function as a symbolic commemoration and proclamation of Christ's redemptive work on the cross and future triumphant return (1Co. 11:23-26). Therefore, the Lord's Supper is restricted to Christians and should be done with an attitude of self-examination (Co. 11:28).

---

[446] Adapted from the Westminster Confession of Faith: "Of the Sacraments."

[447] The complete theology of "death to sin and resurrection into new life" is treated by the Apostle Paul in his letter to the Romans, chapter 6:1-11.

[448] Erickson, p. 1034.

THE DOCTRINE OF LAST THINGS

INDIVIDUAL ESCHATOLOGY

THE BIBLE TEACHES THAT at death, the bodies of mankind will return to dust (Ge. 3:19; Acts 13:36), whereas their souls, which have an immortal subsistence, will remain in conscious existence and return to God (Ecc. 12:7).[449] The souls of believers will pass immediately into the presence of Christ (Lk. 23:43) to remain in joyful fellowship with Him while awaiting the full redemption of their bodies (2Co. 5:1, 6). The souls of unbelievers will be in misery and torment as punishment for their sin while they await the final judgment (Lk. 16:23-24; Jude 6). At the end of time, those found alive will not die but will be changed (1Th. 4:17; 1Co. 15:51-52). At this time all the dead shall be raised and reunited with their souls (Job 1:26; Acts 24:15), the righteous onto imperishable and glorified bodies (Ro. 8:10-11; Rev. 20:6); the unrighteous onto disgrace and eternal damnation (Jn. 5:28-29).

GENERAL ESCHATOLOGY

THE BIBLE TEACHES THE personal, glorious, bodily return of our Lord Jesus Christ (Acts 1:11; Rev. 19:11-16). Preceding our Lord's return, the world will endure an approximate 7-year period of great tribulation in which the righteous judgment of God will be poured out upon the unbelieving world (Da. 9:24-27; Jer. 30:7). Although God's elect will be present during the tribulation period (Jn. 17:15; Acts 14:22; 1Th. 3:3), they will be divinely protected from His wrath (Mat. 24:21-22; Jn. 16:33; Rev. 9:4). Following the tribulation, Christ will physically return in glory with His saints to resurrect His own and to establish a millennial reign over all the nations of the earth (Acts 1:11; Rev. 19:11-16, 20:1-8). The millennium will include a period of great peace and justice (Isa. 11:1-16) at which time God's righteous will reign with Him on earth, overthrow the Antichrist and False Prophet, and imprison Satan (Da. 7:17-27; Rev. 20:1-7).

---

[449] Adapted from the Westminster Confession of Faith, Chapter XXXII

At the end of Christ's millennial reign, Satan will be released from prison in a futile attempt to deceive the nations at which time his army will be forever destroyed (Rev. 20:8, 10-15). At the final judgment of the Great White Throne, our Lord Jesus Christ, who is the Judge of all men (Jn. 5:22), will resurrect the wicked and cast them into an eternal existence of conscious punishment and separation from God (Mat. 25:41; Jn. 5:28-29; Rev. 20:10-15). God will then create a new heaven and new earth where His people will live in peace and enter an eternal state of glory with the One to whom all glory belongs (2Pe. 3:10-13; Rev. 21:1-4; 22:5).

CONCLUSION

CONCLUDING THOUGHTS

THE THOUGHTS IN YOUR MIND about God are the most important thing about you.[450] In other words, if you think incorrectly about God, it is not God who changes. You change for the better or worse and in direct proportion to your better or worse thoughts about God.

Being a *good soldier* and *fighting well, finishing the race, and keeping the faith* are all unequivocally dependent upon your ability to first think rightly about God (2 Timothy 2:3, 4:7). For the purposes of concluding this book, I encourage you to embrace three foundational ideas about God:

1) God is entirely devoted to your spiritual advancement.[451]

2) When you trust God to lead you, He will trust you to lead others.[452]

3) God is good.[453]

Having faith in the idea that God is good, devoted to your advancement, and desirous of enabling you to lead yourself and others, is tantamount to your success, fulfillment, and happiness. Your entire outlook on life will be instantly changed when your heart knows that God, although exalted in power and majesty, loves you and is eager to be your friend, and that He only wants what is best for you.

When the great theologian and biblical scholar Karl Barth was asked to summarize the extensive volumes of his work, he smiled and said, "Jesus loves me, this I know, because the Bible tells me so." Simple in doctrine yet profound in meaning, I can think of no better way to conclude our time together than this:

Jesus loves us, this we know, because the Bible tells us so.

YES and AMEN.

---

[450] The great Christian mystic A.W. Tozer said, "What comes into our mind when we think about God is the most important thing about us."

[451] Jeremiah 29:11 promises that the plans God has for you are meant to prosper you, to give you hope in your endeavors and a bright future.

[452] 2 Samuel 3:1 explains that King David's faith in God and obedience to Him enabled David to become stronger and more capable of leading others both in peacetime and in war.

[453] James 1:17 states that every good and perfect gift comes from God, and in Mark 10:18 Jesus Christ said that only God is good.

WORKS CITED

WORKS CITED

Alexander, Desmond and Rosner, Brian. *The New Dictionary of Biblical Theology* (Downers Grove, IL: InterVarsity Press, 2000).

Barclay, William. *The Acts of the Apostles Daily Study Bible.* Louisville, KY: Westminster John Knox Press, 2017.

Barron, Robert. *To Light a Fire on the Earth* (New York, NY: Image Books, 2017).

Boyd, Gregory and Eddy Paul. *Across the Spectrum.* Grand Rapids, MI: Baker Publishing, 2009.

Carson, D. A. and Douglas Moo. "Colossians." In *An Introduction to the New Testament* (Grand Rapids, MI: Zondervan, 2006), pp. 516–531.

Chan, Francis. *The Forgotten God – Reversing Our Tragic Neglect of the Holy Spirit.* Colorado Springs, CO: David C. Cook. 2009.

Ciampa, R. E. "Galatians." In *The New Dictionary of Biblical Theology*. Edited by Alexander, Desmond and Rosner, Brian (Downers Grove, IL: InterVarsity Press, 2000), pp. 311–315.

Dana, H.E. *A Manual Grammar of the Greek New Testament.* New York, NY: Macmillan Publishers, 1957.

Donfried, K. P. "Romans." In *The New Dictionary of Biblical Theology*. Edited by Alexander, Desmond and Brian Rosner, (Downers Grove, IL: InterVarsity Press, 2000), pp. 291–296.

Easwaran, Eknath. *The Bhagavad Gita* (Tomales, CA: Nilgiri Press, 2007).

Erickson, Millard. *Christian Theology* (Grand Rapids, MI: Baker Academic, 2013).

France, R. T. "Hebrews." In *The Expositor's Bible Commentary.* Edited by Longman, Tremper III and David E. Garland (Grand Rapids, MI: Zondervan, 2008), pp. 19– 195.

Hawthorne, Gerald F., Ralph P. Martin, and Daniel G. Reid (Downers Grove, IL: InterVarsity Press, 1993), pp. 147–153.

Hooper, Richard. *Jesus, Buddha, Krishna & Lao Tzu: The Parallel Sayings* (Charlottesville, VA: Hampton Roads, 2007).

Johnson, Alan. "Revelation." In *The Expositor's Bible Commentary.* Edited by Longman, Tremper and Garland, David E. (Grand Rapids, MI: Zondervan, 2008), pp. 573– 789.

Laney, Carl. "Colossians." In *Essential Bible Background* (CreateSpace, 2016), pp. 210–213.

Laney, Carl. "Hebrews." In *Essential Bible Background* (CreateSpace, 2016), pp. 237–240.

Laney, Carl. "1 and 2 Corinthians." In *Essential Bible Background* (Create Space, 2016), pp. 189–198.

Lane, W. L. "Hebrews." In The *Dictionary of the Later New Testament and Its Developments.* Edited by Martin, Ralph P. and Davids, Peter H. (Downers Grove, IL: InterVarsity Press, 1997), pp. 443–458.

Lewis, C. S. *Mere Christianity* (New York, NY: Collier Books, 1952).

Mackie, Timothy. "Galatians." In *Read Scripture: Illustrated Summaries of Biblical Books* (Portland, OR: The Bible Project, 2017), p. 110.
Mackie, Timothy. "Hebrews." In *Read Scripture: Illustrated Summaries of*

Biblical Books (Portland, OR: The Bible Project, 2018), p. 130–131.

O'Brien, P. T. "Colossians." In *The Dictionary of Paul and His Letters.* Edited by Packer, J.I. *Knowing God.* London: Hodder & Stoughton, 1984.

Rapa, Robert. "Galatians." In *The Expositor's Bible Commentary.* Edited by Longman, Tremper III and David E. Garland, (Grand Rapids, MI: Zondervan, 2008), pp. 549–640.

Sala, Harold. *Getting Acquainted with the Holy Spirit.* Mandaluyong City, Manila. OMF Literature, INC., 2017.

Storms, Sam. *Practicing the Power.* Grand Rapids, MI: Zondervan, 2017.

Stott, John. *Baptism and Fullness.* Downers Grove, IL: InterVarsity Press, 1964.

Still, Todd. "Colossians." In *The Expositor's Bible Commentary.* Edited by Longman, Tremper and Garland, David E. (Grand Rapids, MI: Zondervan, 2008), pp. 265– 360.

Tennent, Timothy. *Theology in the Context of World Christianity* (Grand Rapids, MI: Zondervan, 2007).

Thiselton, A. C. "1 Corinthians." In *The New Dictionary of Biblical Theology.* Edited by Alexander T. Desmond Alexander and Brian S. Rosner. (Downers Grove, IL: InterVarsity Press, 2000), pp. 297–306.

Tozer, A. W. *The Knowledge of the Holy* (New York, NY: Harper One, 1961).

Tuck, Gary. "Revelation." In *The Arguments of the Books of the New Testament* (Western Seminary San Jose, 2016), pp. 197–209.

Tuck, Gary. *Revelation Book (A Readers Guide to the Book of Revelation),* (Western Seminary San Jose, 2019), pp. 1–81.

Tuck, Gary. "Colossians." In *The Arguments of the Books of the New Testament* (Western Seminary San Jose, 2016), pp. 133–137.

Tuck, Gary. "Hebrews." In *The Arguments of the Books of the New Testament* (Western Seminary San Jose, 2016), pp. 159–169.

Tuck, Gary. "Galatians." In *The Arguments of the Books of the New Testament,* pp. 112–119.

Tuck, Gary. "First Corinthians." In *The Arguments of the Books of the New Testament,* pp. 95–104.

Tuck, Gary. "Romans." In *The Arguments of the Books of the New Testament,* pp. 83–94.

Tennent, Timothy. *Theology in the Context of World Christianity.* Grand Rapids, MI: Zondervan, 2007.

Turner, M. in Desmond, T. Alexander. *The New Dictionary of Biblical Theology – Holy Spirit.* Downers Grove, IL. Inter-Varsity Press, 2000. Verbrugge, Verlyn. "1 Corinthians." In *The Expositor's Bible Commentary.* Edited by Longman, Tremper III and David E. Garland. (Grand Rapids, MI: Zondervan, 2008), pp. 241–414.

Warfield, B.B. in his book *Counterfeit Miracles* as identified in *Christian Theology.*

Ziegler, Mollie. "Faith Unbounded" in *Christianity Today,* September 9, 2010

SUBJECT INDEX

SUBJECT INDEX

ALSO FROM BESTSELLING
AUTHOR GREG AMUNDSON

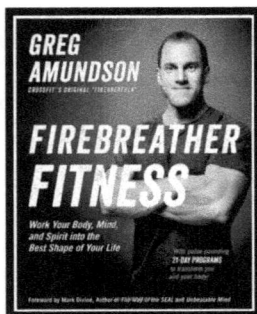

Greg Amundson's effective guides to functional fitness, nutrition, goal-setting, pain tolerance, honing purpose and focus, and exerting control over your mental state are designed to help meet any challenge. Packed with practical advice, vetted training methods, and Amundson's guided workout programs, *Firebreather Fitness* is a must-have resource for athletes, coaches, law enforcement and military professionals, and anyone interested in pursuing the high-performance life. Includes a foreword from *New York Times* bestselling author Mark Divine.

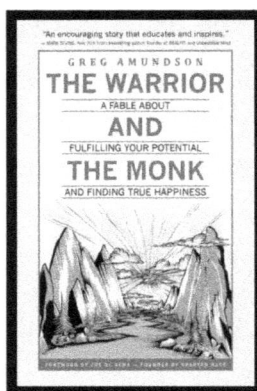

The *Warrior and The Monk* tells the extraordinary story of a young warrior who seeks the counsel of a wise monk on the universal quest to find true happiness. This is Greg Amundson's #1 Amazon multi-category bestselling book.

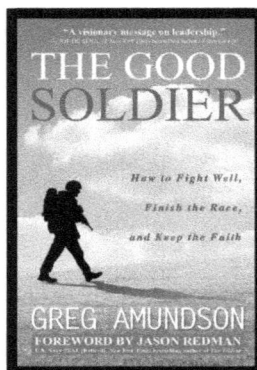

From #1 bestselling author Greg Amundson comes the nations first biblical theology on leadership through the perspective of the warrior archetype. Greg's book *The Good Soldier* opens the Bible in a fresh and relevant new way, and provides actionable steps that you can take to fight well, finish the race, and keep the faith. This is the leadership book that is redefining what it means to be a leader and a modern day warrior.

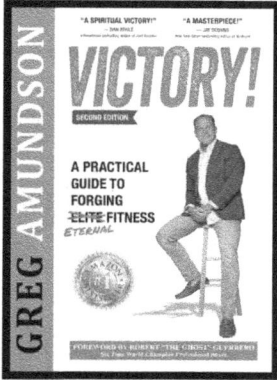

Greg Amundson's book *VICTORY* offers people of all faiths powerful strategies and practical guidelines for bringing health, happiness, fitness, and purpose into their lives and the lives of others. Renowned for his ability to merge fitness and faith, Greg offers a proven methodology for establishing life-affirming beliefs, understanding Divine wisdom, tapping into the power of prayer, integrating physical fitness with spiritual practice, and optimizing the power of mental and physical nutrition.

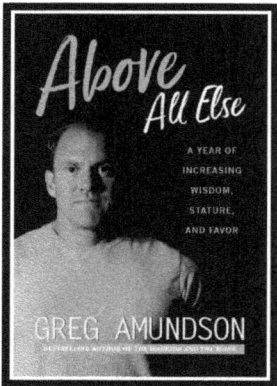

In a unique and groundbreaking new voice, Greg Amundson merges biblical truth with modern day lessons on leadership, positive psychology, and the warrior spirit. Each day of the year, you will be scripturally guided through the key principles and teachings from the Bible, resulting in a more intimate relationship with God and greater understanding of His Word. Greg's message will help you internalize disciplined practices and ways of thinking that are central to developing your full potential, and achieving your greatest dreams and goals. Greg's integration of the Mind, Body, and Spirit offers a unique perspective to keep you thriving in all aspects of your life.

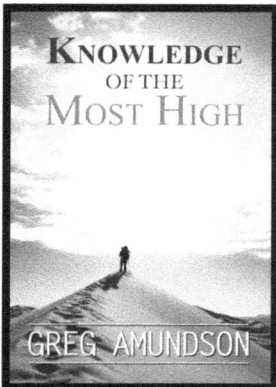

Following a three year masters degree program at Western Seminary, Greg Amundson provides the reader with an exposition of systematic theology and increased knowledge of God.

ABOUT THE AUTHOR

An alumnus of the University of California at Santa Cruz (BA Legal Theory) and Western Seminary (MA Ministry and Leadership), Greg Amundson has spent nearly twenty years in warrior professions to include assignments as a Special Weapons and Tactics Team Operator (SWAT) and Sniper in Santa Cruz County, a Captain in the United States Army, a Special Agent with the Drug Enforcement Administration (DEA) on the Southwest Border and an Agent on the highly effective Border Enforcement Security Taskforce (BEST) Team.

In addition to his extensive government work, Greg is recognized as a thought leader in the field of integrated wellness practices, and is a prolific author and speaker whose message has positively influenced the lives of thousands of spiritual seekers. A former owner of the nation's first CrossFit gym, Greg has traveled around the world teaching functional fitness and self-mastery principles for over nineteen years.

Greg is a Krav Maga Black Belt and honor graduate of the Los Angeles Police Department Handgun Instructor School (HITS). Greg currently serves as a Reserve Peace Officer and Law Enforcement Chaplain in Santa Cruz. Greg is a four-time #1 Amazon bestselling author, and the founder of Eagle Rise Publishing, a Christian focused publishing platform that has produced numerous bestselling books. Connect with Greg at www.GregoryAmundson.com.

KEYNOTES AND SEMINARS

Greg Amundson is one of North America's most electric, encouraging, and motivating professional speakers. Greg has logged more than 10,000 hours of dynamic public speaking on topics including leadership, intrinsic motivation, holistic wellness practices, functional fitness, warrior spirit, and God's Love. Greg speaks around the Country to Law Enforcement Departments on integrating disciplined warrior practices to foster increased Officer Safety while simultaneously generating stronger community relationships. A plank owner of the highly regarded Eagle Rise Speakers Bureau, Greg is renowned for his ability to transcend boundaries and speak to the heart of Spirituality. His use of captivating storytelling results in a profound and transformational learning experience.

To book Greg Amundson at your next conference or in-house event please visit www.GregoryAmundson.com.

EAGLE RISE PUBLISHING

EAGLE RISE PUBLISHING

Eagle Rise Publishing is a Christian book publisher dedicated to advancing the Kingdom of God by empowering authors to share their unique voice with the world. We offer full service "pen to publish" opportunities for aspiring authors, in addition to mentorship, powerful networking and relationship building, interior and cover design, manuscript editing and book polishing. We have published over seven #1 bestselling books, and your book can be next!

Visit www.EagleRisePublishing.com to learn more and get involved.

PODCAST

The Greg Amundson Show on iTunes is a weekly Podcast where Greg will educate and inspire you to live with passion, purpose, and a greater understanding of God's Word. Greg's use of storytelling to illuminate life changing principles and concepts is world renowned, and will become a cherished addition to spiritual seekers from all faith backgrounds.

BECOME A PATRON

If you have been blessed by the work of Greg Amundson and Eagle Rise Publishing, then there are several ways you can join our team of generous benefactors and supporters. One of the best ways to help is to post a review of this book on Amazon and share it with a friend. Reviews on Amazon and endorsements of the book on your social media platforms help new readers to find the book. You can also become a financial benefactor of Eagle Rise Publishing and help support the next generation of authors as they share their voice with the world.

Visit www.Patreon.com/GregAmundson to learn more and get involved.